T.A. Crerar
A Political Life

T.A. Crerar was a part of Canadian public life from 1917 to 1966, serving under prime ministers Borden, King, St Laurent, and Pearson. The only politician to serve in two wartime cabinets, Crerar participated in some of the major political events in Canada of this century, from the conscription crisis and formation of Union Government in World War I to the conscription crisis and Canada's disgraceful failure to aid Jewish refugees from the Nazis in World War II. J.E. Rea provides insight into Crerar's role as a minister and senator and uses this insider's perspective to explore the Canadian political scene.

Born in June 1876, Crerar's Scots inheritance and rural Manitoba upbringing gave him a life-long commitment to the liberal values of independence, self-reliance, thrift, and co-operation. He became the founding president of United Grain Growers in 1917 and was Borden's Minister of Agriculture during World War I. When the federal government refused to lower protective tariffs after the war, Crerar left the Cabinet in protest and became the leader of the newly formed Progressive Party, bringing an end to the two-party political system in Canada and leading to the first minority government in 1921. Crerar resigned the leadership of the Progressive Party in 1922 and later joined King's Cabinet, serving as a member of what may have been the strongest Cabinet in Canadian history. In 1945 Crerar was appointed to the Senate, where he held a prominent position until his retirement in 1966.

J.E. REA is professor of history, University of Manitoba.

T.A. Crerar

A Political Life

J.E. REA

McGill-Queen's University Press
Montreal & Kingston · London · Buffalo

© McGill-Queen's University Press 1997
ISBN 0-7735-1629-8

Legal deposit fourth quarter 1997
Bibliothèque nationale du Québec

Printed in Canada on acid-free paper

This book has been published with the help of
a grant from the Humanities and Social Sciences
Federation of Canada, using funds provided by the
Social Sciences and Humanities Research Council
of Canada. Publication has also been assisted by a
grant from the United Grain Growers.

McGill-Queen's University Press acknowledges the
support received for its publishing program from the
Canada Council's Block Grants program.

Canadian Cataloguing in Publication Data

Rea, J.E. (James Edgar), 1931–
    T.A. Crerar : a political life
    Includes bibliographical references and index.
    ISBN 0-7735-1629-8
    1. Crerar, T.A. 1876–1975. 2. Politicians – Canada –
    Biography. 3. Canada – Politics and government –
    20th century. I. Title.
    FC621.C74R43 1997   971.06'092   C97-900362-8
    F1034.3.C74R43 1997

Typeset in Palatino 10/12
by Caractéra inc., Quebec City

Contents

Preface / vii

Illustrations / ix–xviii, 9, 45, 95, 165, 233

Introduction / 3

PART ONE   A LIBERAL IN THE GRAIN
TRADE, 1876–1917

1 Grain and Cooperation, 1876–1915 / 11

2 Political Apprentice, 1909–17 / 27

3 Turning-Point, Summer 1917 / 35

PART TWO   UPHEAVAL IN OTTAWA,
1917–22

4 Minister of Wheat, 1917–19 / 47

5 Leading the Progressives, 1919–21 / 64

6 A Divided House, 1921–22 / 80

PART THREE   WORKING FROM
WINNIPEG, 1922–34

7 Wheat Pools and the Home Bank,
1922–25 / 97

8 Rethinking Canada, 1923–24 / 110

9 Progressive Absorption, 1925–29 / 125

10 Rethinking Liberalism, 1929–34 / 142

vi   Contents

PART FOUR   MINISTRY OF TALENTS,
1935–45

11 Mines, Wheat, and Keynes, 1935–39 / 167

12 Men and War, Federalism and Wheat,
1939–42 / 194

13 War and Reconstruction, 1942–45 / 214

PART FIVE   THE SENATE AND AFTER,
1945–75

14 Guarding the Treasury, 1945–57 / 235

15 The Last Gladstonian Liberal,
1957–66 / 249

16 Retirement and Reflection, 1966–75 / 262

Notes / 269

A Note on Sources / 297

Index / 301

Preface

As a teacher of Western Canadian history, I could not avoid Tom Crerar. He dominated the early grain trade, he led its most important political protest, he represented the region in the dominion cabinet for years – including during both world wars – and he graced the Senate of Canada for the last twenty years of his public life.

Tom Crerar was born in June 1876, retired from the Senate in May 1966, and died in April 1975. For sixty years, "T.A.," as he was widely known, played a prominent role in the agrarian and political life of Canada. From his Scots inheritance and his rural Manitoba upbringing, Crerar derived his life-long commitment to the sturdy liberal values of independence, self-reliance, thrift, and voluntary association. Individuals, freely associated in cooperative action, could look after themselves much better than any government could. In Crerar's view, to surrender one's independence in return for security would, in the long run, jeopardize both.

Early in the twentieth century prairie grain growers turned to cooperative action to defend themselves from what they considered the predatory assaults of the banks, railways, and manufacturers. With the dominion government in the hands of "the big interests," they felt that they must marshall their strength through the cooperative movement to ensure economic success. An early result was the farmer-owned Grain Growers' Grain Company, their own marketing agency, created to compete with the private grain dealers. It became the United Grain Growers in 1917 and has continued a strong, successful company until the present. Crerar was president from 1907 until he resigned in 1929. During the Great War, the grain business was taken over by the government of Canada, and Crerar entered the Union government of Sir Robert Borden as representative of the grain growers.

ed reduce production costs by lowering the

ame leader of the Progressive party, the political

viii Preface

After the war, Crerar resigned from the cabinet when the national government declined to reduce production costs by lowering the tariff, and he became leader of the Progressive party, the political vehicle of the organized farmers. Its entry into the dominion campaign of 1921 meant the end of two-party politics in Canada and resulted in the nation's first minority government. But the Progressives failed in their primary purpose – to lower the tariff. At the end of 1922 Crerar went back to United Grain Growers. He was never really far from politics, however, though he was closely engaged in protecting the fortunes of the company during the emergence of the pooling movement on the prairies.

In 1929 Crerar entered William Lyon Mackenzie King's cabinet, just in time to share the Liberal defeat in the election of 1930. The party returned to office in 1935, and Crerar spent the next ten years as a member of what may have been the most able cabinet in Canadian history. As minister of mines and resources, he (with his colleagues) played a part in many of the critical developments of the time – expansion of the mining industry and the opening of the north, the revolution in government financing with the advent of deficit budgeting, Canada's disgrace in failing Jewish refugees fleeing the Nazis, the Second World War and the conscription crisis, and the coming of the welfare state.

In 1945 Tom Crerar went to the Senate, and for the next twenty years he warned of the dangers of public debt, of bureaucratic power, and of the growing culture of dependence ushered in by the expansion of social programs. However out of sympathy with modern society, he never stopped extolling what he cherished as the enduring values of the country. Crerar deserves a book. I hope he would be pleased.

The obligations incurred in a project such as this are manifold. Archivists across the country were willing and friendly allies; but I must particularly thank George Henderson of the Archives of Queen's University at Kingston, who made the most arduous of my research tasks so pleasant and stimulating. The John Wesley Dafoe Foundation of Winnipeg provided timely financial aid, for which I am grateful. So also did the Social Sciences and Humanities Research Council, through its Aid to Publication Programme.

John Parry copy-edited the manuscript. His enthusiasm, skill, and fine judgment would delight any author. We worked with Joan McGilvray, coordinating editor at McGill-Queen's University Press, whose cheerful efficiency made passage through the hoops much easier. Philip Cercone, director of the press, has an old friend's affection and gratitude. My final thanks must go to Eleanor Stardom, wife, friend, companion, and colleague. This book is dedicated to her.

CANADIAN COUNCIL OF AGRICULTURE. FEB 1ST 1917. WINNIPEG, MAN.

Meeting of the Canadian Council of Agriculture. Crerar is standing, centre rear. Courtesy Archives and Special Collections, Dafoe Library, University of Manitoba

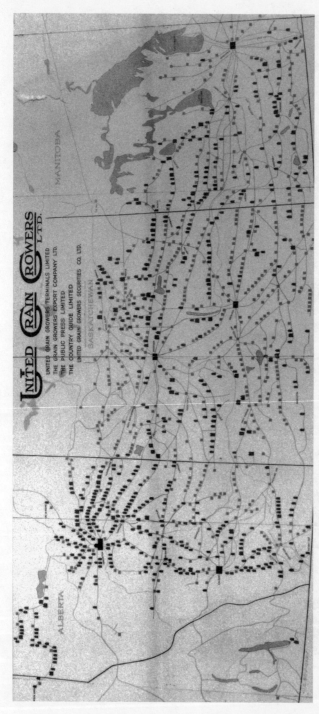

Map of United Grain Growers' line and terminal elevators, 1923. Courtesy Archives and Special Collections, Dafoe Library, University of Manitoba

Crerar in the summer of 1939, leaving for a tour of mining properties in the far north. Courtesy Archives and Special Collections, Dafoe Library, University of Manitoba

Crerar and Montreal barrister J.M. Isaacs on Tudor Street, London, November 1939. Note the gas mask. Copyright Associated Press, Winnipeg Tribune Collection, University of Manitoba

Crerar with an unidentified sergeant of the Canadian Scottish Regiment, London 1939. Copyright Associated Press, Winnipeg Tribune Collection, University of Manitoba

Jessie and T.A. Crerar promoting Manitoba foods, c. 1941. Courtesy
Archives and Special Collections, Dafoe Library, University of Manitoba

Crerar and C.D. Howe at Green Gables golf course early in the war.
Copyright Canadian National Railway, Winnipeg Tribune Collection,
University of Manitoba

Jessie and T.A. Crerar aboard the *Empress of Canada* en route to Liverpool
in 1952 to visit their daughter, Dorothy. Copyright Canadian Pacific
Railway, Winnipeg Tribune Collection, University of Manitoba

Crerar holding forth at a Saskatchewan picnic in August 1955. Jimmy Gardiner is to his right, and Tommy Douglas, to his left. Copyright Gordon Hilyard, Regina, Winnipeg Tribune Collection, University of Manitoba

A Break in the Clouds

On the occasion of Crerar's "swan song" in the Senate in May 1966.
Victoria Daily Colonist, 28 May 1966

A Political Century

Introduction

Tom Crerar was moulded by the wheat boom of the early years of this century – that "golden age" (at least in memory) of prairie agriculture, with immigrants pouring in, new acres going under the plough, profitable wheat prices, and the long trains of laden boxcars snaking their way across the flatland eastward towards the head of the Great Lakes. The struggles and triumphs of the wheat economy hardened and inspired him and nurtured in him a conception of Canada that never really changed. The sturdy liberalism of his youth – a mix of personal freedom, self-reliance, and the virtues of cooperation – still shone through in his farewell speech to the Senate of Canada six decades later, however dated it then might seem.

But if his values changed little through the years, the country that he served for so long became a very different sort of community indeed. When Crerar entered public life, he was a typical westerner. He expected little from a national government that rejected any responsibility for the welfare of individual Canadians. Ottawa's duty was to ensure order and to provide a fair playing field, and Crerar reacted sharply when special interests seemed to be favoured. By the time he retired, he was roundly condemning the federal government's creation of a culture of dependence, as he saw it, that was undermining the values of the early part of the century and making clients and supplicants of Canadians and their institutions. There were few people better placed to record these momentous changes than T.A. Crerar, though at the end he greatly feared that his country had lost its way.

Whatever the benefits of the National Policy of the late nineteenth century, the result had been an artificial national economy. It created powerful vested interests that depended on the state to maintain their competitive position and ensure their future – manufacturers who demanded protection, railways that insisted on subsidies, and agriculture that sought regulation of its economic environment, while vigorously proclaiming its commitment to free trade. When Crerar and other western leaders were challenged about the Crow's Nest Pass subsidy, which underpinned the grain transportation network, they defended it as a justifiable quid pro quo for the tariff that increased production costs.

Crerar was one of the leading prairie apostles of cooperation among grain growers, both for buying and for selling, arguing that farmers could do for themselves far better than any government could. As president of the Grain Growers' Grain Company (GGGC) and subsequently founding president of its successor, United Grain Growers (UGG), he made his dream come true, as the farmer-owned enterprise went from strength to strength. The Farmers' Platform, which Crerar helped to draft early in the Great War, was a political manifesto designed to redress the national economic imbalance that allowed industry, commerce, and transportation to exploit prairie agriculture – all, of course, in the name of "fair play."

Public office had never attracted Crerar prior to the First World War. He was vaguely a Liberal, like his friend John Dafoe, editor of the *Winnipeg Free Press*, but hardly an enthusiast. When the passions of the war dramatically realigned the politics of the nation, however, he did not hesitate in accepting an invitation to enter Sir Robert Borden's Union government as minister of agriculture and spokesman for the grain growers. It all seemed so simple then to most westerners. National government and conscription were patriotic, sensible, and fair methods to meet the gravest of challenges.

Attempting to help turn that simplistic ideal into practice would teach Crerar much about his country and its politics. But he made it clear at the outset that his political loyalty was to the Farmers' Platform, not to the Tories who dominated the wartime coalition. He was there to help fight the war, he said at the time, not to launch a new career or condone a badly flawed fiscal policy. He was soon put to the test. Less than two years after he entered the cabinet, when the Union government brought down its first postwar budget with the conventional Tory concern for protection, Crerar resigned his portfolio.

But he did not leave politics, though he continued as president of United Grain Growers. Almost willy-nilly he became leader of a political attempt to implement the Farmers' Platform directly. The Progressive party won sixty-five seats in the dominion election of 1921, thus rupturing Canada's two-party system irreparably. But it failed in its main purpose: there was no significant lowering of the tariff. The Progressives were able to defend the Crow's Nest Pass rates but otherwise had only mixed success. More interesting and more revealing was the story of their demise – the sum of internal contradiction, Liberal opportunism, and Crerar's own personal conflicts. He resigned as leader of the new party a year after the election of 1921.

During most of the following year he was in Winnipeg, attending to the fortunes of UGG. The company weathered a brief recession in the wheat business in 1921 and 1922 but otherwise flourished during the decade. This was the case despite the challenge of the wheat pools – the marketing phenomenon of the time. Crerar tried at first to cooperate with the pools, but they would have none of it. Even though both UGG and the pools were farmer-owned, there was constant sniping throughout the twenties. But UGG survived the initial shock of the Depression unimpaired; the pools did not.

Surrounded by his close friends – a group known facetiously by themselves and suspiciously by others as the "Sanhedrin" – Crerar kept a discerning eye on Ottawa. From their point of view, what the Liberal party needed most was a dose of real liberalism – the western variant, which they urged on Prime Minister William Lyon Mackenzie King at every opportunity. Finally, late in 1929, Crerar re-entered politics by accepting King's invitation to join his cabinet. A few months later Crerar was back on the sidelines again, when the government succumbed to the Depression and the Bennett sweep. But like every government in Canada save one – John Bracken's coalition in Manitoba – R.B. Bennett's ministry fell victim to the economic hard times of the "dirty thirties."

When the Liberals returned to office in 1935 the Depression had not lifted, and they were forced to address the most fateful question in Canadian federalism. Was the national government in Ottawa responsible for the welfare of all Canadians? If it accepted this obligation, it would distort relations with the provinces permanently, as well as revolutionize the fiscal policies of the nation. The economics of John Maynard Keynes and the recommendations of the Rowell-Sirois Commission abetted the dramatic shift in political responsibilities. Conditioned by the devastation on the prairies during the Depression, Crerar gave support to what became a system of equalization payments, a redistribution of national income by Ottawa. He would later recant. Crerar was also in the vanguard in cabinet, recommending budget deficits to stimulate and encourage economic growth. But unlike almost all other politicians of the day and later, he took Keynes literally, expecting government to restrain an expanding economy with reduced spending and higher taxes to recover its stimulative deficits.

The exigencies of the Second World War confirmed the trend towards an activist state. The need to act swiftly and purposefully justified invocation of the War Measures Act, allowing the government to rule through orders-in-council and, as well, to increase taxes six-fold. Freed from legislative restraint and a jealous House of Commons, the dominion civil service demonstrated a praiseworthy professional competence but at the same time acquired, at least in Crerar's opinion, a habit of command that led to an unfortunate assumption of omniscience. His favourite target during the war was the Department of National Defence, and especially its military bureaucrats. Their handling of the military manpower problem, which he steadily opposed, made him permanently suspicious of the senior civil service and its support for innovative government, especially in social policy.

Crerar chaired the cabinet committee preparing for the vital dominion-provincial conference at the end of the war that would plot the country's future. He very much feared that the signpost marking the road to that future had been the legislation creating the family allowances program. When the issue had been before cabinet, he had demurred, thus acquiring a reactionary reputation, according to the current conventional wisdom, which grew with the years.

Senator Crerar, as he became in 1945, had not set himself against helping people in need. He felt, for example, that the federal income tax could provide a perfectly satisfactory method of protecting the disadvantaged. His fundamental objection was to the principle of universality, as applied to family allowances or pensions or any other of the social programs being bruited about at the time. It simply made no sense to him to have the federal government give money to people who did not need it and were quite capable of providing for their own requirements, and then taxing it back. The result, and a bad one as far as Crerar was concerned, was a steadily growing and expensive legion of functionaries issuing benefits and then taxing those who did not need them in the first place. If this was the future, he wanted none of it, and he said so, loudly.

For twenty-one years the unreconstructed liberal used his position in the Senate to fire volley after volley at federal governments, especially Liberal ones, for distorting Canada's federal system. How had we reached such a pass, he exclaimed in exasperation at one point, that the national government in Ottawa was building a curling rink in rural Manitoba? When he finally stepped down in 1966, Crerar's liberalism *was* anachronistic; indeed, he positively glowed when the newspapers described him as a "Gladstonian Liberal." That, for him, was not an anachronism but the true faith.

T.A. Crerar was a politician of the second rank, but that does not make him second rate. Crerar, Edward Blake, W.S. Fielding, H.H.

Stevens, Ernest Lapointe, C.D. Howe, and Jimmy Gardiner – an eclectic lot, surely – were bound by the fact that they never became prime minister, yet all left an indelible mark on their country. The enduring success of United Grain Growers is testament to Crerar's leadership of twenty-two years, his faith in the cooperative ideal, and his skill as a businessman. His political longevity was the result of several factors. Not least was his reputation in the agricultural community, and it was as its spokesman that he was invited to join Sir Robert Borden's Great War coalition. He later became its champion – albeit briefly – as leader of the Progressive party.

But it was as a Liberal (and a liberal) that he made his political mark. As a member of Mackenzie King's cabinet through Depression and war, he shared responsibility for some of the most serious decisions the country has faced. He was willing to risk the displeasure of his leader and the much-desired seat in the Senate when his convictions were tested. During his years in the upper house Crerar was both witness and commentator as the country changed, often to his dismay. He remembered the Canada of the early twentieth century, and he had helped to change it. The simple liberal trust in the beneficence of progress had, he believed, brought not fulfilment and prosperity but rather a culture of dependence. Yet the disappointment he felt at the end of his long journey never quite extinguished Tom Crerar's hopes for Canada.

PART ONE

A Liberal in
the Grain Trade,
1876–1917

Trading Floor, Winnipeg Grain Exchange, c. 1908. Courtesy Archives and Special Collections, Dafoe Library, University of Manitoba

CHAPTER ONE

Grain and Cooperation, 1875–1915

Russell, Manitoba, was not exactly a window on the world. Its quiet rhythms were determined by the seasonal demands of the early wheat economy, and there was no reason to suspect that any of its residents would play a significant role on the national stage. But in the spring of 1907, the little agricultural service town near the Saskatchewan border was hosting a picnic. A surprise visitor at the customary baseball game was E.A. Partridge, a charismatic agrarian leader – "the man from Sintaluta," as he was known. Partridge had been the inspirational founder of the Territorial Grain Growers' Association, the first producer cooperative among prairie wheat growers. The movement had spread rapidly, and for several months now he had been caught up in the much-riskier venture of cooperative marketing. As president of the fledgling Grain Growers' Grain Company (GGGC), Partridge was trying, not very successfully, to make the transition from cooperative evangelist to business manager. Part of the strength of this attractive and complex man was his recognition of his own limitations. It was this realization that had taken him to Russell.

It was not the local team, but a particular player that Partridge was scouting – the manager of the Russell Farmers' Elevator Company, Thomas Alexander Crerar. He was "Sandy" to his family and "Alex" to his local friends, but it was as "T.A." or "Tom" Crerar that he would be known for the next fifty-nine years in the commercial and public life of the prairies and Canada. The tall, athletic young man could hardly know the long career stretching ahead of him. Partridge's visit would change his life remarkably.

Since 1881, the Crerar family had farmed in the Russell area, to which it had migrated from Molesworth, near Stratford, Ontario, when young Tom was only five. His people, on both sides, were

Perthshire Scots, hard working, ambitious, strong in their Presbyterian individualism, and possessing a deep love for their new country. Tom's father, William Crerar, was a successful farmer in the Silver Creek area near Russell and served as reeve of the township for fifteen years.

T.A. Crerar, born 17 June 1876, was the eldest of eight children. His education, by today's standards, was rather sketchy. He went to the local primary school, then spent one year at the collegiate at Portage La Prairie and, later, one term at Manitoba College in Winnipeg. Until 1895 he worked on the family farm as well. At nineteen, he began a sporadic, five-year teaching career that was not especially distinguished. Crerar was granted third-class, non-professional standing in September 1895. Two years later he received his professional certificate; but the following year he failed the departmental examination for second-class standing. At its best, the teaching profession was unrewarding: Crerar's highest salary was $30 a month, in 1900.[1]

That same year he bought his first quarter-section, near Russell, from the Hudson's Bay Company, for $155.30 on instalments and began homesteading. Though he abandoned teaching, his academic status, somewhat ironically, was augmented many years later when he received honorary degrees from the University of Manitoba and from Queen's University. Crerar enjoyed farming. Within five years, he had acquired two additional quarters and even indulged in some profit taking when he sold some of his original quarter at $1 per acre for a railway station and townsite in 1906.[2]

During this period, he also acquired an interest in and then control of a sawmill. So he spent his summers in the field and his winters on the slopes of Riding Mountain. He had some success at his new venture, since local demand for sawn lumber was incessant. But, as an inexperienced young entrepreneur, he also had his problems; the J.I. Case Company claimed that it held a lien on his mill, the dominion Department of the Interior warned him to stay out of crown timber reserves, and the North-West Mounted Police seized timber in his yard in 1905, alleging that it had been illegally cut. When the mill burned in 1906, Crerar had quite lost his enthusiasm for it.[3]

At age twenty-nine, he had moved into Russell in 1905 to take up a new position as manager of the Farmers' Elevator Company. He had earlier bought stock in the locally owned enterprise, and he followed its progress with interest. The new job paid $75 per month, and since the elevator company did not buy grain, Crerar was able to earn another $50 by sending occasional lots of grain to the firm of Graves & Reilly in Winnipeg, for which he acted as representative.

For the next twenty-four years he would be active in the grain business.[4] The move to town was also preliminary to his marriage. On 21 January 1906, T.A. Crerar wed Jessie Hamilton of nearby Solsgirth at "Glendale Farm." Their long life together, though marked by the tragic loss of a daughter, was serene and fulfilling.[5]

Crerar's youth and early manhood had not been untypical of the eclectic life of the agricultural frontier. After an indifferent schooling, he had been teacher, farmer, and lumberman, and now he was involved in the grain trade. But, perhaps untypically, he remained a student. Throughout his life, Crerar read constantly – history, biography, politics, and economics. Especially, in those early years, he was learning all he could about the grain business. He and his father shared these interests. The elder Crerar had been president of the local elevator company and of the Russell Liberal Association as well. He had run, unsuccessfully, in the dominion election of 1900. But their primary concern was the fate of the grain grower. William Crerar was currently a director of the Russell-area unit of the Manitoba Grain Growers' Association. Together, father and son had watched the emergence of the Grain Growers' Grain Company (GGGC) and its near-demise in its immediate clash with the Winnipeg Grain Exchange. So when Partridge turned up at the local baseball game in June 1907, T.A. Crerar was a knowledgeable and avid listener.

He had first come to the attention of the company in the autumn of 1906, when Vice-President John Kennedy visited Russell to sell stock in the new cooperative venture. Crerar was one of the few individuals who committed $25 for a voting share. During a long conversation, Kennedy was drawn to the young man. He encouraged him to attend the first general meeting of the company in February 1907. Accompanied by his father, Crerar went to the gathering and played a mildly active role, making the sensible suggestion that direction of the enterprise should be kept separate from leadership of the Grain Growers' Association.[6] He returned home and began to send carloads of grain to the GGGC whenever possible, as well as trying to induce other farmer elevator companies to do the same. "They are both agencies working toward the same end – Justice to the men who grow the grain," he wrote in a circular letter. "Why not work together and give help one to the other?"[7]

Crerar's growing interest led Partridge to cultivate their friendship and to indicate that he was "very desirous to see young men like yourself come to the front in the conduct of the Company's affairs." Probably prompted by Kennedy, Partridge wrote to Crerar that he was thinking of withdrawing from his active role and hoped that

Crerar would consider joining the board of directors.[8] Whatever he may have thought of this overture, there is no evidence that Crerar answered the letter. Partridge persisted, however, and the two had a long talk at the Russell-area picnic in June. The president urged Crerar to attend the first shareholders' meeting of the Company, to be held in Brandon on 16 July in conjunction with the Provincial Exhibition.[9]

It is difficult not to conclude that Partridge and Kennedy carefully managed the sequence of events that July day, which so determined the future of the company and of Crerar. It had become evident that Partridge would probably have to step down as president. The bitter struggle with the Winnipeg Grain Exchange about the company's seat – its right to do business in the grain-trading institution – had been resolved. Two essential compromises had been required. The GGGC agreed to abandon its cooperative scheme of distributing profits to its members on a patronage basis, which violated the by-laws of the exchange, and it announced that it would adopt the approved method of making returns to shareholders on the basis of stock held. It seemed at the time that the GGGC had no other choice. But its decision to surrender this vital principle of cooperative organization would bedevil the enterprise for years and raise occasional suspicions about its commitment to the interests of prairie farmers. As well, and less well known, the members of the exchange had had quite enough of the mercurial and vituperative Partridge. The company held its seat on the exchange in his name, but he was clearly no longer acceptable.

The GGGC's first annual meeting lasted only a day. The most important news for members was that the company had even survived the struggles of its first year. Partridge was able to announce a modest profit of $797. If the future was not secure, at least it was now a distinct possibility for the farmer-owned marketing agency. When the meeting turned to selection of the board of directors, John Kennedy nominated Crerar, who, despite his protestations of inexperience, was easily elected.

The bombshell went off that night when Crerar attended his first board meeting. Partridge announced that he was stepping down for the good of the company and to placate the grain exchange, though he would remain on the board. When he recommended that Crerar succeed him, there was general approval from all the other directors except one, Crerar, who was understandably stunned. He impulsively rejected the proposal but was pressed by Kennedy and the others to "sleep on it." After talking the matter over with Jessie, Crerar agreed the next day to accept the offer.[10] However swift and surprising the turn of events, Crerar was not unambitious, and he had considerable confidence in his own abilities. His lack of experience, he was convinced, he could overcome with hard work, caution, and steady devotion to cooperative action by prairie producers.

During his first few years as president of the GGGC, Crerar won more battles than he lost; but the tests, for himself and the company, were severe. When he took over in the summer of 1907, the enterprise was preparing to handle its second crop, and it immediately faced a crisis. The GGGC was a commission house – that is, it took grain on consignment from farmers, both members and non-members, at a commission of one cent a bushel. In order to pay farmers promptly for their grain, it needed a substantial line of credit. In its first year of operation, the GGGC had secured credit from the Bank of British North America in Winnipeg, which had demanded personal pledges of security from the directors. The following year, the bank refused it credit under any conditions. Farmer-members immediately suspected a clandestine attack on the new company by "the interests" – a combination of private grain traders, the Canadian Pacific Railway, and the established, chartered banks.

But there was no time for recriminations as grain began to move in early autumn. The grain company had to handle nearly five million bushels that year.[11] Fortuitously as it appeared at the time, there opened in Winnipeg that summer a branch of the Home Bank – a fifty-year-old, Toronto-based savings and loan company, which had just recently gone into commercial banking. Anxious for new accounts, it eagerly took the business of the GGGC.

During the autumn of 1907 a permanent arrangement emerged. Partridge was appointed a committee of one by the directors to conduct negotiations. The result was that the Home Bank became official banker to the grain company, which in turn became exclusive agent to sell the bank's stock throughout the west. GGC agents sold stock as well as memberships in the grain company to the extent that the two institutions became closely identified. Most of the directors, including Crerar, and the grain company itself took significant amounts of stock in the Home Bank.[12] When the bank collapsed in 1923, the GGGC, and especially Crerar, would be greatly embarrassed by the arrangements that Partridge had made. But the financial support of the Home Bank was critical in 1907. When Crerar made his first annual report in 1908, the grain company had grown to 2,953 members, with paid-up capital of $20,385, and he was able to announce an annual profit of $30,190 – a respectable beginning.[13]

The following year brought another major test for Crerar and the young enterprise. The relative success of the 1907–08 crop year was a spur to new memberships as the GGGC seemed to promise stability, fairness, and satisfactory returns. Between July 1908 and June 1909, paid-up capital skyrocketed from $20,000 to $120,000, as wheat growers' confidence in the venture increased.[14] Crop forecasts for 1908 were optimistic; with membership booming, the company handled 7,643,146 bushels of the 1908 crop and declared a net profit after expenses and reserves of $52,902.[15]

This success did not go unnoticed by private grain dealers. Abruptly in August 1909, the Winnipeg Grain Exchange, as an experiment for one year, suspended commissions. Many in the grain growers' movement interpreted the change as a direct attack on the GGGC. From commissions – the only revenue that the company received – it paid its business expenses, built reserves, and paid annual dividends to member-shareholders. Without them, it would be out of business. The large elevator companies (or "syndicates," as the farmers called them), which dominated the exchange, made most of their profits from their line and terminal elevator operations and could afford to lower or even forgo the customary commission, which was calculated on grain delivered to the line elevators. The fate of all the commission houses hung in the balance. The GGGC's only defence was the loyalty of its membership.

In a circular appeal, Crerar laid out the options and asked members if they wished the company to lower its commission, maintain it at one cent, or leave the decision to the board. Overwhelmingly, members rejected the first choice.[16] When the 1909 crop year ended, the company had handled over 16 million bushels and made a net profit of $95,663.[17] The exchange ended its "experiment," and the grain company emerged stronger than ever. But Crerar was convinced that the continuing struggle with the elevator companies would be resolved only by public ownership of elevator facilities – both line and terminal – an opinion he would soon modify.[18]

Despite the rapid progress the GGGC was making, Crerar was not beyond criticism from some members, and the annual meeting of 1912 featured a direct challenge to his leadership. There were many reasons for this, but at root was fundamental disagreement between him and Partridge over the role that the Company should play in prairie society. Founding of the enterprise had been a defiant blow struck for liberation of the grain growers from the "corporate enemies" that beset them on all sides. He had been the inspirational leader, a role that Crerar freely acknowledged.[19]

As the GGGC grew in membership and the amount of grain that it handled increased rapidly, the two men began to differ sharply on policy. Crerar's determination to build a strong cash reserve fund was criticized by Partridge, who felt that the money should be returned to the members. When the company began to deal in futures to even out the risk of price fluctuations, Partridge (and some others) accused Crerar of speculating with the members' money. Crerar rejected the criticism, arguing that Partridge "has very largely failed in recognizing what must be a plain fact to [any] person, that the business of the Company has now grown to such proportions that care must be taken in conducting it on sound lines."[20]

There were other criticisms. The business manager, A.M. Blackburn, had made heavy commitments on oats futures in the spring of 1911. It was a highly speculative bid, an attempt to capitalize on a temporarily depressed market, and it was apparently made without the knowledge of Crerar and the directors. When delivery was taken, the oats found a satisfactory market, and there was no financial loss for the company. But it was patently evident that there had been a failure of control, or inadequate supervision, or both. There was also widespread discontent with the company's performance over the winter of 1911–12. The harvest was wet and large, so a great deal of damp, tough grain began to pile up, exacerbating a shortage of cars. Much grain went "out of condition," and disputes over grading seemed endless. The staff had not grown sufficiently to handle the rapidly increasing volumes of grain, and the GGGC marketed almost 28 million bushels that season in cramped quarters with inadequate resources. But these problems were met, however tardily. Blackburn was replaced as manager by J.R. Murray, who would have a long and distinguished career in the grain trade. And the GGGC acquired its own building with excellent facilities.

All these issues, and the underlying conflict between Crerar and Partridge, came to a head at the annual meeting of July 1912. Partridge and three other directors published an attack on Crerar's record in the *Grain Growers' Guide* in June, without making any specific accusations. In the same issue, Crerar retorted that the real point of dispute was that he refused to be led by Partridge and his friends on the board.[21] As one supporter of Crerar pointed out in a letter to the *Guide*, Partridge had revealed his dwindling enthusiasm for the cooperative movement in a recent letter to *Cotton's Weekly*, a radical sheet, confessing that "I think I may prove to be more at home among the Socialists."[22] In a letter typical of many that he wrote drumming up support before the meeting, Crerar reiterated his faith in the movement but added: "My four years experience in the Company have sobered my judgement considerably" and future development must be based "on a sane policy." The present difficulty, he continued, "is very largely due to the fact that Mr. Partridge could not use [me] as he wanted to."[23]

In the event, Crerar won overwhelming support at the annual meeting. He boldly stood on his record as president, pointing out that paid-up capital was now over $586,000 and that over 27 million bushels had been handled that year, at a net profit of $121,000.[24] Partridge then spoke, and there followed a long debate, which ended with a ringing endorsement of the president. The next day, Partridge's three dissenting colleagues were denied re-election to the board, and he himself won the last seat available. He then withdrew, declaring himself quite out of sympathy with the company.[25]

The two strong-willed men were not through with each other. Partridge organized a competitor, the Square Deal Grain Company, which gained a seat on the Winnipeg exchange, thanks to Crerar's behind-the-scenes support. But the new enterprise soon collapsed and had to be taken over by the GGGC. When Partridge found himself in financial trouble in 1916, the directors authorized a grant to him of $5,000. A further $1,500 was approved in 1924, and Partridge was subsequently granted a life pension of first $50 and later $75 a month.[26] His mercurial personality and his passion to build a more equitable world along socialist lines put him outside the mainstream of the farmers' movement, though his inspirational early leadership was not forgotten and not unrewarded.

Crerar emerged from the 1912 annual meeting in firm command, but with his idealism tempered. Cooperative action, for him, had become a tool to advance the economic interests of the grain growers. It was a pragmatic, hard-headed philosophy, enabling farmers to compete successfully. Crerar did not eschew reform, and his interests were still wide; but more and more, he was coming to see the farmer as a businessman. Success would come only if calculated and planned for, not as a result of unbridled enthusiasm and zeal. As he wrote to one correspondent, "I feel we are not always making progress when we are quarrelling with other interests, and if our business is to succeed finally it must be built on the solid reason of our shareholders, and not on appeals to passion and prejudice." His stewardship was serving the farmer-members well, he claimed, and he pointed to " ... the present strong position and respect that [the company] occupies in the business and communal life of the community."[27]

Expansion had been steady, and Crerar was carefully raising his sights. The GGGC began publishing the *Grain Growers' Guide* in 1908 and the following year established The Public Press Limited, a wholly owned subsidiary, to publish it. The GGGC as well made annual educational grants to the three prairie grain-grower associations. The next few years would be dominated by two great issues, grain elevators and central marketing, and the company and Crerar would have to adapt to the dislocations caused by the Great War.

For years grain growers had felt victimized by private elevator companies. Many suspected that the latter combined to extract excessive storage and handling fees and bilked the producers through duplicitous mixing and grading practices. Government supervision had only partially allayed these fears. The elevator companies continued to draw heavy criticism. E.A. Partridge, not surprisingly, was quick to point the way. The 'Partridge Plan,' as it became known, was simplicity itself. It considered storage and handling of grain a matter of public interest. Provincial governments should own and operate all the line elevators within their jurisdiction, and the dominion government should take over the terminal elevator facilities. The scheme was picked up with great enthusiasm by the provincial associations, but the governments were at best lukewarm. Only in Manitoba, where earlier experiments with publicly owned power and telephone utilities had proved successful, was there willingness to go this route.

The GGGC saw distinctly favourable possibilities in such a program. Producers would be issued certificates of weight and grade on delivery of grain. They could sell enough for immediate needs and release the rest according to price. The scheme would also provide an opportunity to establish a government-supervised sample market in Winnipeg, which would enable producers to sell at the milling value of their carloads.[28]

Sir Rodmond Roblin of Manitoba was the only prairie premier willing to implement the proposal of government-owned elevators. In response to Roblin's request, Crerar, his vice-president, John Kennedy, and officials of the Manitoba Grain Growers' Association (MGGA) submitted a draft bill. The essential feature of the proposal was that the provincial elevator system must be run by an independent commission responsible to the legislature. The Roblin government characteristically declined to accept this advice and set up a system that was virtually an arm of the public works department. The experiment was a dismal failure. Within two years, the government wanted out, and negotiations took place between Crerar and Roblin to find a solution.[29] Both Alberta and Saskatchewan had rejected public ownership; the governments there provided financial assistance to allow producers themselves to create cooperative elevator companies.

With his brief flirtation with public ownership ended, Crerar proposed that the GGGC take over the government elevator system on a lease basis.[30] In July 1912, a two-year deal was struck, and the company entered the elevator business.[31] There were subsequent leasing arrangements until, in the mid-1920s, the company bought the system outright. It began as well in 1912 to construct its own elevators at shipping points in all three prairie provinces. By 1916 it had sixty elevators of its own, in addition to 135 leased from the Manitoba government. The program was rounded out in 1913, when the GGGC leased two large terminal elevators at Fort William from the Canadian Pacific Railway.[32]

Crerar was still not content. His goal was a completely farmer-owned system of grain delivery. That meant that the company must begin marketing grain directly – a venture that would not be as easy or as immediately successful as the elevator business. From the outset, the GGGC had experimented with sporadic direct sales to exporters and eastern Canadian flour mills. It seemed appropriate to take the final step – to establish a formal selling agency that would enable the company to handle grain from farm gate to foreign consumer. This occurred late in 1911 with creation of the Grain Growers' Export Company Limited, as a department of the GGGC, with capitalization of $50,000.

As we have seen, the 1911 crop put much tough, wet grain on the market. The new selling agency was off to a very inauspicious beginning, and this situation added to Crerar's problems at the 1912 annual meeting. In fact, the company lost some $230,000 in its first formal trading venture and suffered a further loss the following year.[33] Though the loss was easily covered from reserves, Crerar's board wanted the company to give up direct selling.[34] But he was not so easily discouraged, and he was consoled by the editor of the *Financial Post*, who advised him: "Most of the big houses in the export business have at some time in their career had similar losses."[35]

The GGGC prepared more carefully for its next venture in marketing, which, while financially encouraging, would not be entirely consistent with the cooperative ideal. It would also lead to increasing friction with the Saskatchewan Co-operative Elevator Company (SCEC). Crerar had made a business connection with T.A. Springman, a principal of Messrs. Shipton, Anderson and Company, a large British grain importer which had handled much of the company's grain sold through the grain exchange.[36] Together, in the spring of 1914, they agreed on a new format. A new Grain Growers' Export Company Ltd. would be created, separate from the GGGC, but with the company and Shipton, Anderson each putting up $50,000 to launch the new export firm. Crerar hired an experienced grain dealer, Henry Stemper of J. Rosenbaum Grain Co. in Chicago, as manager. Stemper was to receive 10 per cent of net or a guaranteed minimum of $10,000, whichever was greater. The Bank of Montreal, now reconciled to the company, and the Home Bank would finance the Canadian sales, and Guaranty Trust, New York, foreign exchange. Shipton, Anderson, for its part, received sole British distribution rights in return for putting up half the initial capital and would handle continental European sales on a commission basis.[37]

In the spring of 1914, Crerar took the charter of the new enterprise over to London to settle final details, despite one major disappointment.[38] It had been Crerar's hope that all the farmer-owned companies on the Canadian prairies would cooperate in the new scheme. Certainly, the three provincial associations favoured closer cooperation. The Alberta Co-operative Elevator Company (ACEC) was quite agreeable to moving its grain through the new company. The SCEC, however, was not at all amenable. Crerar met with manager Charles A. Dunning, George Langley, and other of its officials in Regina in March 1914. The conclave ended in failure when the Saskatchewan people insisted on capitalization of at least $500,000, preferably $750,000. In a long account of the meeting, Crerar concluded that the SCEC was "not very anxious to go ahead upon the basis suggested. It struck me as if they were laying down impossible conditions with the purpose in view that if criticism of them should arise later because of their disinclination to work with us, they would be in a position to say 'we were willing to go ahead and cooperate with the GGGC in that matter of exporting grain but they were unable or unwilling to meet our wishes in the matter'. I do not think there is any genuine desire upon their part to get together. I am convinced there is not on Mr. Langley's part at least."[39]

Over the next few years, Crerar endeavoured to gain Dunning's cooperation in marketing, but the manager of the SCEC, while always encouraging, would never be pinned down.[40] Saskatchewan, by far, produced the most grain of any of the prairie provinces, and it seems, from all the evidence, that a spirit of provincialism deterred the SCEC. It feared losing its identity in any close collaboration with the GGGC, and its intimate ties to the provincial Liberal government acted as a further brake.[41]

The new export firm was an immediate, indeed startling success. The first year of the Great War quickly inflated demand and price for western grain. By early 1915, the somewhat-reduced crop of 1914 had been sold and Stemper was dispatched to New York to pick up what business he could. With a line of credit from Guaranty Trust, he immediately began dealing in American grain, to great advantage. The export company was established on the New York, Chicago, and Winnipeg exchanges and, in its first year, made a profit of $375,000 on the handling of 40 million bushels of grain.[42]

Crerar's enthusiasm was only slightly tempered by his realization that, while his board would not be upset by the profits, "the Winnipeg end of the business [must] be kept well to the front." He revealed his concern in a letter to Springman when he cautioned that "in order to carry out the purpose for which the Company was organized, and avoid criticism, it is necessary that the Winnipeg and Canadian end of the business be in no way neglected."[43]

Springman, however, sought to dampen Crerar's satisfaction even further. He and his associates applauded Stemper's achievement but "[a]ll of us here," he added, have "become considerably scared at the business [he] is doing and we are all agreed that, unless considerable curtailment takes place, we are running the serious risk of spoiling what otherwise is a magnificent institution."[44] He pointed out that the large profit masked some significant losses on individual transactions; in his opinion, Stemper "has over-taxed himself and the business and ... over-traded." He urged that the business "should be cut back, since Stemper lacked adequate assistance." In a gentle remonstrance, Springman reminded Crerar: "You have already gone through the mill with the old Company and must surely have learned the lesson of caution." He suggested that the export company be recapitalized at $300,000, with Dunning and the SCEC taking one-third – a scheme that would prove illusory.[45]

Smarting from Springman's admonitions, Crerar defended the operations of the export company. He implied, as well, that making profits for the shareholders redressed any criticism that the GGGC was moving away from the cooperative ideal. In a quite uncharacteristic outburst, Crerar retorted: "Personally, I see no reason whatsoever, why ... the Company should not attain to the position of being the largest export house in America, and I will quite candidly confess that my ambition, for one, is to see it attain to this position."[46]

Perhaps Crerar's head had been turned by the instant success of this second venture into the export business. If so, his aggressive stance did not last long. There was widespread comment about this new departure from the original purpose of the GGGC, and Crerar soon reverted to his more cautious business ways, as shown by an exchange of letters with W. Clifford Clark, then a young economist at Queen's University and later Ottawa's most powerful mandarin.

Clark had written to request a copy of the GGGC's 1915 annual report. After congratulating Crerar on the success of the company and its export business, Clark asked "if this does not seem to be getting away from your old Co-operative ideal. Or perhaps this is only a temporary phenomenon due to the war. How would you answer such a criticism, which must have already been made?"[47] In his reply,

Crerar's business caution was reasserted. He played down the profits of the export business, attributing them to the very large volume of grain handled. The New York office had been considered "of a temporary character" and was being maintained largely as a convenience. No decision had been taken to continue it after the war.[48] As a consequence, however, in order to deflect such criticism, the GGGC had set up the Grain Growers' Export Company Incorporated, which was chartered in New York state in 1916, to handle American business. The GGGC acquired Shipton, Anderson's stock in the Grain Growers' Export Company in Winnipeg, and exporting became a less prominent and controversial aspect of the GGGC's operations.

In any case, in December 1915, under the authority of the War Measures Act, the Canadian government commandeered the wheat crop and transformed the rules of the game. The impact of the war would, at least temporarily, disturb the open market in wheat, and thus the fortunes of the GGGC. It would also involve Crerar directly in national affairs. But in 1916 he was hoping to bring to fruition his scheme of coordinating the activities of all the producer-owned grain companies on the prairies. In the spring, representatives of the three farmer-owned companies and the three provincial grain growers' associations met in Regina to consider Crerar's scheme. Essentially, what he proposed was a general federation. The GGGC would become the central selling and purchasing agent for all the organized prairie farmers. As a pre-condition, Manitoba farmers would have to form their own cooperative elevator company, using, presumably, the elevators of the GGGC. The central agency would export all the grain of the provincial elevator companies, manage the terminal elevators, and purchase all supplies. The provincial companies would handle grain initially and distribute farm supplies. Crerar pointed out that, since the interests of all prairie grain growers were similar, the dream of a great, united farmers' cooperative could at last be achieved.

While the grain growers' associations, including that of Saskatchewan, were inclined towards the proposal, the SCEC was not willing to surrender its independence, which was not too surprising. Saskatchewan was the paramount grain producer, and its cooperative company had a flourishing commission and sales business, complete with its own terminal elevator and seat on the Winnipeg Grain Exchange. It was not content to accept a minor role in a prairie federation.[49] When the scheme foundered on the rock of Saskatchewan provincialism, Crerar, with the active support of Henry Wise Wood, president of the United Farmers of Alberta (UFA), sought a more modest, but significant objective.[50]

Delegates to the 1916 UFA convention shook off their disappointment and directed their president to gain whatever measure of cooperative action was still possible. Negotiations between the ACEC and the GGGC proceeded quickly, and the two companies amalgamated under the name of United Grain Growers (UGG) on 1 September 1917. T.A. Crerar was unanimously endorsed as president and general manager of the new enterprise. The demise of the Grain Growers' Grain Company coincided almost exactly with the end of Crerar's first ten years as president.

What had begun as a modest commission business to serve farmers on a cooperative basis had grown and changed since 1907. Its first subsidiary, The Public Press Limited, published for many years the *Grain Growers' Guide*, the bible of western producers. The firm flourished, until quite recently, as a large job-printing house in Winnipeg. The Grain Growers' Export Company Limited, after a shaky beginning, was now firmly and profitably established. War conditions meant a temporary, but spectacular, burst of activity for the New York office of the Grain Growers' Export Company Incorporated. It was now managed by Jimmy O'Donohoe, who had succeeded Henry Stemper after the latter's untimely death in an automobile accident. In 1917, for example, the New York office had been named sole buyer of U.S. oats for the British, French, and Italian governments. O'Donohoe expected that this would mean business of ten million bushels a month.[51]

At the end of 1913, the GGGC had opened a Co-operative Department, purchasing supplies of various kinds and distributing them directly to farmers. The department grew very quickly and handled "Apples, Coal, Flour, Fence Wire, Fence Posts, Lumber and Binder Twine."[52] The GGGC also operated a sawmill and held valuable timber limits in British Columbia. One of its most profitable ventures began in 1916, when it set up a livestock department on a commission basis in the stockyards in St Boniface, Manitoba. This department handled several thousand carloads of livestock a year on a cooperative basis.

While Crerar was understandably satisfied at the progress the company had made, he was equally pleased with the benefits distributed. There had been a steady and substantial return to farmer-members each year. But beyond that, the company was able to provide $35,000 to support the *Grain Growers' Guide* in its expansion drives.[53] Even more satisfying was the record of support for the three prairie grain growers' associations. Between 1909 and 1914, the GGGC gave $25,000 to the associations for operating grants and a further $60,000 to aid in their educational programs to foster cooperative activities.[54]

The years since 1907 had been eventful for Crerar, and he seemed to thrive on the work. The yearly rounds were broken only by brief August vacations at Lake of the Woods. He and Jessie and their two young daughters, Audrey and Dorothy, seemed to share a happy home life despite his many business trips away. Indeed, in the summer of 1916, the board of directors expressed some concern at his heavy schedule, advising him to get out into the countryside more often, and purchasing an automobile for him to encourage him to take more leisure.[55] His salary had advanced with the company's fortunes – from $4,000 in 1911, to $9,000 in 1915, and to $16,000 the following year.[56] He was offered and refused twice that amount to join a larger Minneapolis grain company. The steady, gratifying progress, like much else in the world, however, would be radically altered by the Great War.

When the Canadian government confiscated what was left of the 1915 crop in December of that year, the days of the open market were clearly numbered. But the final push would come from Canada's major customer. Wheat prices, which had been hovering around the eighty-cent mark early in the war, began to advance. In June 1916, wheat was selling for $1.09 (basis No. One Northern at Fort William). By November, it reached $1.98. The reaction from Britain was swift. A Royal Commission on Wheat Supplies was established and recommended central purchasing to stabilize the price. The royal commission became purchasing agent for all grain imported to Britain, France, and Italy and, later on, smaller Allied countries as well. With only one purchaser in the field, the open market collapsed, and trading of futures on the Winnipeg exchange was suspended in May 1917. With the United States now in the war and only one European purchaser, there had to be virtual integration of North American supplies.

The response of the Canadian government was to appoint a Board of Grain Supervisors in 1917 "to determine fair prices for wheat and to regulate its trade" because of the creation "of an importers' monopoly which placed the competitive trade in jeopardy."[57] It was assumed that the purchaser's (that is, the royal commission's) wish to secure supplies at a price as low as possible consistent with production stimulation and ensured supply would also work to protect the Canadian consumer. The eleven-member Board of Grain Supervisors included Crerar (who had in fact recommended against ending the open market) and Henry Wise Wood to represent the farmer-owned companies. Crerar's stature in the grain trade of Canada was thereby recognized, but his service on the board would be brief. Close control of price, however, required not only balance between producer and consumer but coordination of price with the United States. In its first major price decision – with which prairie farmers could not have been unhappy – the board in September 1917 fixed the price at $2.21 (basis No. One Northern, Fort William) for the entire crop year. This price was, of course, coordinated with that of a similar government-appointed selling agency in the United States.

Crerar played his full part in the discussions leading up to the decision on price, and his experience lent much weight to his opinions. But it would be unnatural if he had not had other things as well on his mind. Canada was passing through one of the great political crises of its history. The debate over compulsory military service and Union government reached its climax just as the Board of Grain Supervisors began its tasks. Crerar, as well as the GGGC, had accomplished a great deal in ten years; he had gone from manager of an obscure country elevator to adviser to the government of Canada. The month after the Board of Grain Supervisors set its benchmark price for wheat, Crerar was sworn in as minister of agriculture in the Union government of Sir Robert Borden.

CHAPTER TWO

Political Apprentice,
1909–17

There is a remarkable similarity between T.A. Crerar's business career and his entry into active politics. He served no apprenticeship in either, nor did he ever languish in minor roles. On the same day he joined the board of directors of the Grain Growers' Grain Company (GGGC), he was offered the presidency of the enterprise. The first political office that Crerar held was minister of agriculture in Sir Robert Borden's national coalition government in late 1917. The two events were not unconnected.

Throughout his long public career, stretching over six decades, Crerar was never a consistent partisan. Ostensibly a Liberal, his politics was originally shaped by the philosophy of cooperation and the economic needs of the grain growers. His liberalism, which he always thought of as progressive, was rooted in belief in the worth of the individual and a commitment to personal liberty. His Liberalism, in contrast, was defined as much or perhaps more by his view of the political alternatives than by faith in the Liberal party. Voluntary association was his operative principle of democratic action, and throughout his life he maintained a scepticism about the efficacy of the state and an aversion to the power of an aggressive bureaucracy, however imaginative and talented.

There were, of course, some inconsistencies in his political beliefs, and trial and error were sobering teachers. But at the end of his public life, as Canadians celebrated the nation's centennial and many accepted willingly, indeed demanded, an activist government, Crerar rejoiced in the newspapers' description of him as the last of the nation's Gladstonian liberals. His Canada had changed dramatically, but Crerar, very little. Thus his view of Canadian development and his own role in the country's affairs can serve as a measure of our distance from those late-nineteenth-century, essentially agrarian, values to which he clung.

Crerar's political formation took place in the heady years of progressive reform prior to and during the Great War. He sampled, and often supported for a time, many of the political nostrums of the day, but always in the context of prairie farmers' desire for fair treatment and against the tradition of unblinking and unthinking party loyalties. In the Manitoba election of 1909, Crerar solicited support for the Liberal candidate in Birtle, not because of his party affiliation but because the candidate favoured provincial government ownership of line elevators. There was an engaging naïveté in his argument: "[T]he old fetish of partyism is I believe slowly breaking down and none too soon. When our farmers cast their votes for honest men whom they respect and trust, a brighter day will be dawning for purity in public life and honesty in the administration of public affairs."[1] His flirtation with public ownership, as we have seen, was short-lived. But his lack of concern for party fortunes, indeed for party itself, was a continuing theme in his political life. His liberalism – however dated it might become – was for Crerar a philosophy of life, and the Liberal party merely a vehicle.

Liberal ideas and methods were a mixed bag in those bustling years before the Great War. Like most of his prairie contemporaries, Crerar's interests were inspired by the conviction that western Canada was being exploited by a wicked triumvirate. In a letter to Louis Post, editor of the progressive journal the *Public* in Chicago, he complained: "The Money Interests [banks], Transportation Companies and Manufacturing Power are rapidly developing into a strong trinity in this country, in fact, they are already strongly established. Signs are not lacking, however, that the people are awakening to a sense of their danger."[2]

Some of the danger signs were the newly imported ideas circulating throughout the west. Crerar was intrigued by the simplicity and alleged fairness of the Single Tax movement of Henry George and spoke publicly in its support.[3] He was even more attracted by the potential of the Direct Legislation League, which he judged to be both appropriate and congenial for any movement for prairie reform. He served on its advisory board, raised funds, and enthusiastically supported the league's activities.[4] As a prominent Winnipegger, he worked for the Social Service Council of Manitoba. As an avid learner, he joined and became active in the local unit of the Round Table Society, though he soon lost his keenness for imperialism.

The *Round Table*, which beat the imperialist drum throughout the white British Empire, took a close interest in western Canada and often reacted snidely. In one issue, for example, it criticized the western farmer because "[h]e too often regards the Canadian cities above a certain size as hostile garrisons planted in the land, inhabited wholly by vicious and greedy middlemen and parasites who treat the toiling farmer as helots and serfs and out of the proceeds of their exactions lead lives of Sybaritic luxury and Babylonian iniquity." Much more directly, it roundly condemned the resolution passed at the January 1913 convention of the Manitoba Grain Growers' Association rejecting the naval policy of both Liberals and Conservatives, aimed at bolstering Britain's Royal Navy, and bristled that "grain exporters are more vitally interested in the Empire's naval supremacy than any other class in Canada." Crerar and his fellow delegates could have been only bemused, if not outraged, by the *Round Table*'s claim that there was no good reason "why the Grain Growers should not be as good imperialists as the directors of the Canadian Pacific Railway ... "[5]

But there were more enduring values, convictions, and relationships that emerged in those early years. Crerar's commitment to the cooperative ideal was conditioned by his role in the business aspect of the movement. He certainly seemed at times more businessman than agrarian idealist, and this often drew criticism, as we have seen. But that does not mean that he was any less convinced that free association, in both the spirit and the institutions of the cooperative movement, was the route to progress for prairie grain growers. His business experience made him cautious; but the zeal, if muted, remained with him even after he left United Grain Growers in 1929. In his early years it had flared brightly. In a long letter to a well-known Alberta cooperator, W.J. Tregillus, Crerar wrote: "We must – as far as possible – surround our people with a healthy environment, physically, mentally and spiritually and I know of no surer method of bringing this about than by the development of a fine spirit of co-operation, which unconsciously brings home to the individual the fact that he cannot live to himself and that his happiness is bound up in the happiness of those around him; and that he can best attain to true happiness by extending the helping hand and by having it extended to him."[6] Crerar's simple eloquence was not part of his public image, but no less sincere for that.

This desirable spirit of free cooperation, to the minds of most western farmers, was hampered most by restrictions on trade imposed by a remote and insensitive dominion government. So for the first third of this century the dominant political issue for westerners was the protective tariff and their demand for its reduction or abolition. Crerar was a doctrinaire free trader in his early years, and though he would later modify his views somewhat he quickly became a prominent antagonist of protection. When angry farmers descended on the nation's capital in what was colourfully dubbed the "Siege of Ottawa" in 1910, Crerar informed Henry Vivian, a leading free trade MP in Britain, that it was a result of "the Free Trade sentiment that exists among practically all the farmers of Canada. The justice and equity of the principle of Free Trade is taking a strong hold." The immediate objective was an increase in the British preference to sixty-six per cent and free trade with the United States in farm implements and natural products.

Even this early in his career, however, Crerar was conscious that farmers could not have it both ways – that is, a significant lowering of tariffs and direct help in whatever form from the government. (This awareness would later condition his attitude towards the Wheat Board.) "The Canadian Farmer, as a class," he confidently assured his friend Vivian, "wants no protection for his own products."[7] His reputation among free traders in Britain was that of a welcome ally, and he was made an honorary member of the Cobden Club, the rallying point of free traders there.[8]

Not surprisingly, as president of the GGGC and leading figure among all prairie farmers at the advent of the Great War, Crerar's advocacy of sharply reduced tariffs gave him a political persona whether he wished it or not. Yet he seldom failed to take advantage of any opportunity to advance the cause or embellish its virtues. In 1916, he attacked the *Winnipeg Tribune*, which had ridiculed a free-trade speech in Winnipeg by Dr Michael Clark, MP for Red Deer. Crerar especially rejected the *Tribune*'s claim that the war would force Britain into protection. Not so, he cried, as he praised the gallant struggle of that "little free trade kingdom." Its sturdy resistance "has justified the claim of those who support it that freedom of trade is the soundest fiscal system any nation can have."[9] In his early public years, Crerar was uncompromising on the issue of the tariff.

The two primary requisites in the long struggle of the farmers against a protective tariff, which in their view favoured central Canada at the expense of the other regions, were organization and method. There have been several accounts of this campaign for tariff reduction.[10] Crerar had decided opinions on both aspects of strategy and played a conspicuous role in their development. He steadily abetted the capacity of strong farm organizations to mobilize the potential power of the agrarian interest. But organization must be thorough at all levels. The provincial associations of grain growers were simply the general expression of the collective will of the prairie farmers.

In one of many letters that he wrote on the subject, he urged F.W. Green, secretary-treasurer of the Saskatchewan Grain Growers' Association, to encourage his association to avoid the appearance of centralized control. There must be emphasis on the local units (which Crerar called "counties," by which he meant, perhaps significantly, electoral divisions). Special attention ought to be given to the social dimension, including concerts, debates, libraries, and a wives' auxiliary to attract and hold members. County executives would elect to the provincial associations members, who would in turn choose representatives to an interprovincial organization. This body, which ultimately took form as the Canadian Council of Agriculture, could be, Crerar argued, an effective lobbying agent, not only with rural-based provincial legislatures but also with the dominion authorities who controlled the tariff.[11]

He also encouraged emergence of a farmers' organization in Ontario, which he rightly felt was essential to the achievement of any strong national pressure. "[I]t is very necessary for the farmers of Ontario to get thoroughly organized," he wrote, "and get themselves into a position where they can make their voice heard in demanding legislation, particularly on the tariff at Ottawa." He arranged financial assistance for the United Farmers of Ontario (UFO) and kept in touch with E.C. Drury, W.C. Good, and J.J. Morrison, its leading spirits.[12]

Crerar, even after the outbreak of war, still saw the farmers' movement as a lobbying group rather than a nascent political party; indeed, it was precisely its apolitical character that he felt would buttress its effectiveness. The national organization of farmers would produce a national program that farmers all across Canada of all political persuasions could endorse with enthusiasm and urge on both dominion political parties. Thus were born the Farmers' Platform and its successor, the New National Policy. They advocated the general goals of Canadian agriculture – lower tariffs, selected free lists, public control of utilities, cheaper credit, and lower freight rates – the familiar catalogue of agrarian reform. Crerar helped to write and promote the platform.[13]

The commitment to non-partisanship, however, had never meant eschewing of the political process, simply rejection of party. Crerar had often sought by political means to advance the interests of farmers generally and cooperatives in particular. It was a thinly disguised exercise in application of power, and he and the organized farmers had little difficulty convincing prairie governments that farm interests might be ignored only at great political peril. At the dominion level, he lobbied hard before the war with Arthur Meighen, the Conservative solicitor general, concerning lake and ocean freight rates and a general incorporation law for cooperative societies. He was very successful, indeed, in gaining the aid of Robert Rogers, the arch-Tory Manitoba member of Borden's cabinet, in the matter of British purchases of Canadian oats during the war, ensuring a sizeable share for the Grain Growers' Grain Company.[14] By the mid-point of the Great War Crerar was considered, certainly in Ottawa, as one, if not the leading, representative of western agriculture.

But there were also other influences at work in moulding Crerar's attitudes and outlook. Before and during the war he built up a network of intimate friendships in Winnipeg that would persist for decades and greatly influence his ideas. In addition to Crerar himself, the core of this group – often referred to by outsiders suspiciously, and members facetiously, as the "Sanhedrin" – comprised John Wesley (Jack) Dafoe, who had been editor of the *Manitoba Free Press* since 1901; A.B. (Bert) Hudson, a gifted Winnipeg lawyer, attorney general in the Manitoba Liberal cabinet of Premier T.C. Norris (1915–17), MP 1921–25, and, finally, a justice of the Supreme Court of Canada; and, much less well known, Frank Fowler, manager of the Grain Exchange Clearing House and briefly mayor of Winnipeg, who was rather the paterfamilias of the quartet. During the early years, they lunched together in Child's restaurant, but later, as they all acquired a greater degree of prominence (and affluence), they ate together at the exclusive Manitoba Club. They were all nominally Liberals at the outbreak of the Great War, but their political allegiance was fragile.

Over the years, other members drifted in and out of the group – H.J. Symington, who went on to a successful career with the Canadian Pacific Railway; J.B. Coyne, a Winnipeg lawyer (to whom members referred affectionately as "Bogus"); Edgar Tarr, a Winnipeg insurance executive and an active supporter and organizer of the Canadian Institute of International Affairs; and an occasional visitor and inveterate letter writer from Montreal named A. Kirk Cameron, a businessman and self-proclaimed confidant of Sir Wilfrid Laurier, Ernest Lapointe, and many others. Crerar, in fact, maintained an extensive and remarkable correspondence for nearly fifty years with Cameron.

But the dominant influences on Crerar were Dafoe and, to a lesser extent, Hudson. Many, many times, this tightly knit group, tied to Winnipeg in a variety of ways, would affect the course of Canadian affairs, and Crerar would be its political expression. This does not mean that he was in any sense a puppet; but he trusted Dafoe and the others, trusted their judgment and their values, which he shared. He did not always take their advice, but he usually sought it and always considered it very carefully.

The war undermined their commitment, such as it was, to the national Liberal party. Crerar had not hesitated to support non-Liberal candidates for office, and his analysis of the party's policies and methods was never simply emotional. In a letter to H.B. Cowan, then the editorial voice of the UFO, he explained: "We have a strong 'Whig' element in the Liberal party in Canada, whose natural place is in the 'Tory' camp; and personally, I strongly hope that when a few more years have rolled by they will be found where they properly belong."[15] His political education was proceeding apace.

By the end of 1916, Crerar's political position was ambiguous in the extreme. A sometime Liberal whose closest confidants were Liberals, his significance to others, especially in central Canada, was as the presumed (if not always acknowledged) leader and spokesman of the organized grain growers. This made him very attractive to political recruiters. Yet he himself, admittedly in private, was receiving suggestions that organized farmers should enter politics as a "balance wheel" to influence trade and taxation policy. He did not immediately reject the proposal.[16] Publicly, he supported the resolution passed at the 1917 convention of the Manitoba Grain Growers' Association in Brandon which declared that the resources of Canada could be organized for war only "by a National Government in which the interests of the political parties will be made entirely subservient to the interests of the State."[17]

A good part of that winter saw Crerar in and around Ottawa and Montreal on business; but in that hot-house atmosphere of wartime pressures, politics dominated almost all discussions among public men. He was in demand as a speaker, presumably to facilitate political assessments as to his potential value. Just prior to Christmas, he addressed the Ontario Liberals. More important, he agreed to appear at the influential Montreal Reform Club (a Liberal bastion) after the holidays. It was at this time that he began his enduring friendship with Kirk Cameron, who arranged the invitation. The latter wrote to Crerar that he had dined with "Sir Wilfrid Laurier the other evening and took occasion to advise him you were to address the Club, and he expressed himself as delighted."[18] Subsequently, Crerar met with George Graham and E.N. Macdonald, two prominent Liberals.

He must have passed muster, for Sir Wilfrid wrote to Crerar shortly afterward, inviting him to become a Liberal candidate in the anticipated dominion elections because he could do "more than any other man to reconcile Western and Eastern opinion on fiscal questions, on sane economic grounds." There is a certain coy ambiguity to Crerar's reply, as if he did not wish to close this Liberal door completely. He told Laurier that his colleagues on the board of the grain company would probably be averse to his entering politics. (This consideration certainly did not inhibit him a few months later.) In any case, he continued, if he did enter the House of Commons, he would feel obliged to further "by every legitimate means the policies which the organized farmers have promulgated in the recent statement [i.e. the Farmers' Platform] ... on public questions, policies which to my mind are in accord with the traditional principles of Liberalism."[19]

It seems, however, that this exchange was mere fencing. By early 1917, the question of national government – and, behind it, the much more volatile problem of compulsory military service – were preempting all other political concerns. And Crerar, like many western Liberals, was beginning to consider the idea of a coalition government. When Arthur Hawkes, a well-placed Toronto journalist, travelled west in February 1917 on a sounding mission for Ontario Liberals leaning towards coalition, Crerar sent him on to Henry Wise Wood and Cecil Rice-Jones, his manager, in Calgary with his endorsement.[20]

But western Liberals were cautious and sceptical; they remembered the loss on reciprocity in the dominion election of 1911 with bitterness and focused much of their animosity on Clifford Sifton, owner of the *Free Press*, opponent of reciprocity and now a proponent of coalition government for Canada, along with his Toronto colleagues. The westerners seemed more interested in forging a progressive alliance for radical goals and disinclined to consider any type of union before an election. Feelers were also being put out in the opposite direction. When Henry Wise Wood made a swing through central Canada as president of the Canadian Council of Agriculture in May, Crerar introduced him to Andrew McMaster, the free-trade Liberal MP from Montreal, as "one of our good Progressives in Western Canada and a personal friend of my own."[21]

CHAPTER THREE

Turning-Point, Summer 1917

Crerar spent much of the spring of 1917 in Ottawa in connection with the wheat emergency and later as a member of the Board of Grain Supervisors. When Robert Borden returned from Europe and recommended compulsory military service, the widely anticipated political crisis began. After Wilfrid Laurier refused Borden's invitation to join a national government, the prime minister, despite objections from some members of his caucus, shifted his attention to unhappy western Liberals. By the end of June, Crerar's name was common currency in the speculation.[1]

Much has been written about the events of the summer of 1917, which culminated in formation of Union government in October. Most accounts have been by biographers of the major players involved, advancing the reputation of their subjects, and by historians whose view, somewhat understandably, is Ottawa-centred and tends to see the prairie provinces as a homogeneous unit and western Liberals as undifferentiated, secondary figures. A closer look at the ideas and activities of Crerar and his friends and colleagues will not change the conventional story radically; but it may perhaps reveal a much richer and more varied texture in the political drama of that summer and avoid centralist oversimplification.

It has traditionally been argued that the Military Service Act and, especially, the Wartime Elections Act left western Liberals in an untenable position; they must either go along with conscription and coalition or be defeated in a general election. This may have been true of many, if not most, of the incumbent Liberals from the prairies. It does not necessarily follow that it applies to those westerners whom Borden sought as potential cabinet ministers. They were not members of Parliament, and they thus had no dominion seats to lose. In fact, at least until late September 1917, the concerns and goals of the Winnipeg Sanhedrin were little connected with the worries of the prime minister.

That is not to say that the Winnipeggers were uninterested in vigorous prosecution of the war. They certainly were. But they were also concerned with the reviving strength of Henri Bourassa in Quebec, resulting largely from the bitterly fought school and language issues of 1916 in Manitoba and Ontario, and they resented any attempt by dominion politicians to intervene. They were also unhappy over what they regarded as Montrealers' reactionary control of the Liberal party, and they felt a growing determination to radicalize the party or leave it. The notion of an independent western pressure group was already well planted. But there was, as yet, no unanimity of opinion or purpose, even within the Sanhedrin.

Shortly after the Military Service Bill was introduced in the House, Crerar wrote to a sometime Ottawa lobbyist for the Grain Growers' Grain Company asking if the measure would "lead to the creation of an almost solid French-Canadian Bloc in the Commons? I would like this information for personal reasons."[2] The reasons were evident in a letter from Dafoe to Sifton at the end of June analysing the rumours about Premier Norris of Manitoba and A.B. Hudson's being courted by Ontario Liberal conscriptionists, who, Dafoe felt, hoped to dominate any coalition government, probably under the leadership of N.W. Rowell, Liberal leader in Ontario. Crerar, at this time, according to Dafoe, was very cool to any such idea and more radically inclined. He was urging, Dafoe went on, that it was "time for the Libs & the farmers to get together and capture the entire west, sending a wholly independent group to Ottawa."[3]

The occasion to move, for Crerar, would be the meeting of "Western Liberals and Progressives in Winnipeg" in early August, called by the MPs and senators from the region. He did not indicate any political attachment, but he sought the help of an old friend in Russell to secure appointment as a delegate from Marquette constituency, even though "my relationship with the Liberal Party has not been very active during recent years. I have had several talks with Dafoe and Frank Fowler and Hudson. They want me to assist in drafting a tentative platform." There is no mention of coalition or conscription in the letter, only concern about the reactionary influence on the party in the east. He sought creation of "a progressive wing that would study Canadian problems from the point of view of all the people rather than from the point of view of the manufacturing, transportation and financial interests." He concluded that such a platform – in effect, the Farmers' Platform – would isolate and cripple the Tories in the west for many years.[4]

A gathering of Ontario Liberals in late July did little to clarify the position of the party; rather it made Crerar and the others even more suspicious of central Canadian motives. Any coalition government might very well buttress protectionist forces. That was certainly the position of J.J. Morrison of the UFO, admittedly a most unsympathetic witness, who informed Crerar: "The same crowd that defeated reciprocity now want to seize the reigns [sic] of Government, not the Torys but the bolting Grits. We are indeed a gullible people if we put up with this." The same resentful response came from a well-known and rather dyspeptic Toronto Liberal lawyer, Gordon Waldron, who saw the Liberal meeting as nothing but a scheme to make Rowell prime minister. In such an event, Waldron complained, the western farmers were sure to be the losers.[5] Protestations of loyalty and support for the war effort in Ontario were not accepted uncritically in the prairies, especially when associated with their least favourite public figure. The fact that Clifford Sifton, now living in Toronto, stumped western Canada that July to rally support for conscription and coalition did little to reassure prairie opinion and nothing to influence it.

In a reply to Waldron a few days before the Winnipeg convention, Crerar noted the Ontario Liberal enthusiasm for conscription but seemed content to leave the issue to the delegates, though he judged that the decision could go either way and that support was not at all certain. He seemed much more worried about other matters and expected that the convention would accept much of the Farmers' Platform. There would, of course, be a strong statement on the tariff. More surprisingly, Crerar was very keen on state ownership of railways, telegraphs, and express companies. On practical grounds, he argued, "if the people of Canada are to take over the lame ducks in the form of the Canadian Northern and the Grand Trunk Pacific, they should take over the fruitful lines represented by the Canadian Pacific as well." Furthermore, like most westerners, Crerar wanted heavy taxes on land held for speculation, especially property close to railways. "Personally, I would not be too considerate of the parasites who hold them." He played down Waldron's suspicion of Sifton: "In the west, [he] is, I think, as dead as a door nail. The people don't trust him." And he was convinced that there was "no possibility whatever of any Western Progressives or Liberals going into a Union Government with Borden or for that matter considering Union Government until after the election is over." His own strong preference was "for the formation of an independent parliamentary group from the West."[6]

Henry Wise Wood and the United Farmers of Alberta (UFA) suspected that conscription was a Machiavellian attempt to seduce western Liberals into a disastrous coalition. Then the Conservatives and the westerners, with conscription as a bond of union, could quite believably form a coalition to prosecute the war, and, since Borden would be unacceptable to the west, Sifton would emerge as compromise leader. Any rejection of Laurier at the convention would simply advance the plot. The safest route, Wood urged Crerar, would be to "neither endorse nor condemn either conscription or Laurier." Let the election come, and the west would guard its own interests. "Nothing could be more dangerous," he concluded, "than for this Convention to be caught in the net of the Conservative party; that net is conscription. Whatever you do, keep out of it."[7]

Crerar sought to reassure Wood about Sifton's lack of influence, the happy prospect of the convention's virtually adopting the platform endorsed by the Canadian Council of Agriculture, and the slim chances of coalition. "The sentiment against uniting with Borden is very strong, and the general feeling is that nothing should be done in this until after the election is over." He said little of conscription itself, except to note that the question at the convention would be much in doubt.[8]

Meanwhile Dafoe was playing his usual, active role behind the scenes, though his was a different concern. He and many other Liberals less wrapped up in agrarian demands than Crerar were watching the drift of events that summer with some dismay. After the meeting of Ontario Liberals, which did not repudiate Laurier, Dafoe wrote sharply to George Graham that westerners were tired of being advised that their actions must be considered in light of French-Canadian opinion to avoid throwing Quebec Liberals into the arms of Bourassa. "After one has been told twenty five times in succession, as I was in Ottawa, that our national course on the war must be determined by the consideration that it is preferable that Laurier instead of Bourassa should control Quebec, the dose becomes nauseating." What Dafoe meant, of course, was that Bourassa was the real master, and it was better that this was out in the open.

Dafoe was still smarting over the language flare-up in May 1916, "which was a wanton affront to English Liberal sentiment." There was no room in Dafoe's liberalism for minority-language rights in the west; indeed, he and the *Free Press* had led the attack on bilingual education in Manitoba. He concluded his angry outburst to Graham by asserting that Laurier ought to have accepted Borden's offer of a coalition and the principle of compulsion, applied only after a thorough trial of the voluntary system of recruiting by a national government.[9] His wounded regionalism was little disguise for his lack of sympathy for Laurier's position.

The convention of western Liberals that met in Winnipeg on 8 and 9 August 1917 was dominated by more than the question of conscription. There was a perceptible determination by the organized farmers to achieve adoption of a radical economic program that suited their interests. Urban delegates, especially those prominent in Winnipeg Liberal circles and members of Liberal governments in all three provinces, were more concerned with coalition government, compulsory service, and Laurier's leadership, on all of which the farmer delegates were reluctant to commit themselves. Crerar found himself in both camps, to some extent, torn between western agrarian demands and the anxieties of his Winnipeg cronies.

There were a thousand delegates at the convention, including fifty women finally beginning to play a role in public affairs in the west. A.B. Hudson was chairman, and C.A. Dunning, now in the Saskatchewan government, secretary of the Resolutions Committee. The economic and fiscal demands of the farmers were shoved into the background as debate raged over the issues generated by the alleged manpower crisis in the armed forces. In order to avoid an open rupture, particularly on the questions of national government and Laurier's leadership, there was a reluctant move towards compromise.

Crerar himself proposed a resolution that attempted to paper over the obvious divisions between rural and urban delegates and between supporters and opponents of Laurier. It indicated that there was no sympathy for a coalition government *before* an election – this to satisfy Laurier loyalists. Hope was expressed that the campaign would avoid "all appeals to passion and prejudice in matters of race and creed" and that "whichever party is returned to power the business of the Government of Canada should be carried on by a truly National Government." Compulsory service was not mentioned at all. The urban Liberals, especially those from Winnipeg, were bitterly disappointed. A public protest that favoured both conscription and national government was quickly organized and included Frank Fowler, J.B. Coyne, and Crerar.[10]

By mid-August 1917, Crerar's ambivalence had ended, and he was prepared to enter politics directly. There is no evidence now to date precisely when he made this decision, but the swirling gossip in Ottawa that spring about coalitions in which his name had been mentioned had certainly opened the possibility. He had many private reservations – about Borden's leadership, about Sifton's influence in the movement to coalition, and, most of all, about the potential effect that his own involvement would have on his reputation among western grain growers. But he had reached two firm conclusions. The demands of the war on Canada must shove partisanship aside in favour of a broadly representative government, and within that government organized farmers must have a voice. By the time the western Liberals gathered at Winnipeg in early August, Crerar was deep in political negotiations.

The first overture had been made by a delegation from his old home of Russell, Manitoba, in the dominion constituency of Marquette. The group went to Winnipeg led by J. Allison Glen, a Russell lawyer and long-time political collaborator of Crerar's (who eventually succeeded him in the cabinet in 1945). It had, apparently, little difficulty in persuading Crerar to accept its support in seeking the nomination for Marquette in the widely expected national election. Crerar immediately sought approval from the board of United Grain Growers. Not only was his intention endorsed, but the board agreed that he should retain his position (and his salary) as president and general manager. It was assumed that his would be only a temporary absence, until the end of the war.

One week after the inconclusive Winnipeg convention, Crerar replied to Glen that he would seek the nomination in Marquette as an Independent Liberal Grain Grower, which seemed to cover all the bases. He planned to run on the Farmers' Platform, committed to none of the current leaders and, following the majority opinion of the convention, favouring a renewed effort at obtaining voluntary enlistments for the armed forces, only after which he would support conscription. But he asked Glen to proceed with some discretion; he was about to leave for Ottawa in response to a telegram from Borden inviting him to an urgent meeting.[11]

Borden had abandoned hope by this time of any useful alliance with sitting Liberals from the west and was looking beyond the House of Commons for coalition support, despite strong misgivings in his own party. The two-day meeting in Ottawa has been much discussed by historians. It was apparently organized by Sir Clifford Sifton, upon whom Borden was relying as a conduit to the west, and included A.L. Sifton, Clifford's brother and premier of Alberta; J.A. Calder, Saskatchewan's minister of public works and political manager of the provincial Liberal party; Henry Wise Wood, president of the UFA; and Crerar.

There was no possibility of Wood's entering any coalition government. He detested Clifford Sifton, suspected all Tories, and, in any case, shied away from political office (and responsibility) throughout his career. He much preferred to remain an *éminence grise*, much like

Sifton. So Borden concentrated on attracting the three other westerners – Premier Sifton, for his Alberta support; Calder, for his acknowledged political talents; and Crerar, as representative of the organized
farmers. Indeed, throughout all these negotiations, Crerar wore a
rather apolitical mantle and, unlike the others, drew little resentment
from worried Tories.[12]

After two days of discussion, the westerners, without Wood,
returned to Winnipeg to consider their position in talks with Hudson
and the rest of the Sanhedrin.[13] On 26 August Calder, Crerar, Hudson, and A.L. Sifton sent off their well-known telegram to Borden
indicating their readiness to enter a coalition government, but insisting on a change of leadership. They recommended Borden's colleague Sir George Foster, Adam Beck of Ontario Hydro, or Sir
William Mulock of the Ontario Exchequer Court as a suitable
replacement for the prime minister.

This abrupt communication has been described by some historians
as the sheerest effrontery – presumptuous, arrogant, and mischie-
vous. But six years of Borden's government had earned the prime
minister considerable hostility in the west. The litany of grievances
included failure of reciprocity and Tory defence of the tariff, misman-
agement and corruption in the war effort, concentration of war contracts in central Canada, the baneful and unwelcome influence of
Clifford Sifton, and the continuing presence in the cabinet of Robert
Rogers of Manitoba, the arch-Tory and political manipulator.[14]

Borden, according to his biographer, was willing to step aside, if
the way would then be opened to Union government and compulsory service, but his cabinet and caucus angrily rejected any such
suggestion and endorsed his continuing leadership. In fact, anti-
coalition Conservatives considered the telegram a godsend, arguing
that the whole idea should now be killed.

Crerar, blissfully unaware of the reaction that the telegram might
(and did) provoke, wrote to Glen the following day, suggesting that
nothing need yet be done in Marquette: "[T]here appears to be a
reasonable expectation that a [Union government] will be formed. I
have been asked to go in and will probably do so, provided the
colleagues I would be associated with would be satisfactory."[15] He
may have been stunningly naïve, but he really seemed to believe that
a Union government could be formed that would ensure adequate
military reinforcements overseas, suspend partisanship, and end
political corruption.

Such a government, Crerar wrote to H.B. Cowan of the *Farm and
Dairy Review* in Ontario, would "not last beyond a year after the war
is over, since they would be practically certain to split on domestic

issues." That would provide the opportunity "to create a really Progressive Liberal administration free from the reactionary influences that operate within the Liberal Party."[16] Borden's departure would relieve western anxieties and draw general support.

Equally important, the prospective western members of a Union government feared the influence of Sir Clifford (presumably these did not include his brother Arthur), and Crerar explained to Glen that he did "not like the thought of going into a government with Clifford Sifton behind pulling the strings unless I had the strongest colleagues possible." Crerar very much feared that the Tories, "while shouting their heads off about winning the war, are as much concerned about playing politics as the Liberal Party from the East are."[17] The only honest men left, it would seem, were on the prairies. Crerar and Calder then joined a party touring the new mining area of northern Manitoba for ten days, as much for a holiday as for information.

The prime minister also took to the woods to consider his next move, accompanied by a reluctant Arthur Meighen, who was no lover of the outdoors. The rankling hostility among his fellow Tories, however, had not dissuaded Borden from the coalition project nor cooled his enthusism for bringing in the westerners, despite their rebuff. Meighen, the dominant westerner in his cabinet, was not at all pleased about bringing three or four well-known western Liberals into the government, especially Calder and, to a lesser extent, Hudson, who might threaten his pre-eminence. So concerned was he that, unknown to Borden, he tried to induce Isaac Pitblado of Winnipeg to join any coalition that might be formed. Pitblado was a prominent Liberal, a man of much political sagacity but little public ambition. He would have suited Meighen much better. But Pitblado's strong sense of duty would not overcome his reluctance to enter public life, especially if Crerar and the others were still in the field. Meighen's scheme fizzled; but it is questionable if Borden would have agreed in any case.[18]

Shortly after Calder and Crerar returned to Winnipeg, Arthur Sifton turned up there (probably at the instigation of his brother) with a renewed request from Borden that they return to Ottawa to resume negotiations – this time with the clear understanding that Borden must lead the coalition. Arthur Sifton, Calder, and the Sanhedrin gathered to canvass the outlook. One obstacle had been removed when Borden dropped Rogers from the cabinet, but the recently passed Wartime Elections Act gave them pause. None of them liked it. But they now considered the political and manpower situation so critical that they cast their doubts aside. Crerar, Calder, and Hudson, at least, considered their entry into the government a short-term, non-partisan commitment to get the country through the war honourably and safely. They wired Borden that they would travel to Ottawa immediately on the understanding that they would deal only with the prime minister and that questions of cabinet membership, distribution of portfolios, and the general principles of Union government be agreed to in advance of any announcement. Borden concurred the next day.[19]

The negotiations in Ottawa were tense but fast-paced and concluded early in the morning of 12 October. In the end, Hudson did not go in, to Dafoe's annoyance and, probably, to Meighen's satisfaction. The latter was further mollified by being appointed minister of the interior, the titular position of western leadership. Arthur Sifton took Customs, Calder went to Immigration and Colonization, and Crerar to Agriculture. That all three were willing to accept minor portfolios, apparently without dispute, is in itself an indication of the limited nature of their commitment. Calder indeed would have readily forgone the obligation of administering a department. Expression of solidarity and determination to prosecute the war effectively and honourably were their primary motivations. The new Union government was announced on 12 October, and it soon began to prepare for the upcoming election, which would be fought, as Borden later made clear in his *Memoirs*, to gain the confidence of the electorate "to administer Canada's affairs during the remainder of the war."[20]

Not everyone was pleased with the new government. French Canada was now quite isolated: Laurier Liberals outside Quebec were in political jeopardy. W.L. Mackenzie King, as always, found conspirators everywhere. He managed to convince himself that the real purpose, directed by Clifford Sifton, had been to serve "[Sir William] Mackenzie & [Sir Donald] Mann [of the Canadian Northern Railway] & the plundering interests they represent."[21] But most of the English-language press was well satisfied. The *Manitoba Free Press*, not surprisingly, lauded the new personnel "as disinterested and capable and believed that it would give a united nation far-seeing, high-minded and patriotic leadership." Privately, Dafoe regretted Hudson's absence, "but his presence is not indispensable. Crerar will be accepted as a suitable representative of Liberalism. Opportunity knocked loudly on Hudson's door but he would not draw the bolt."[22]

Crerar probably would not have agreed with Dafoe's narrow definition of his role in the new government. He was, somewhat ironically in view of later events, most anxious to be seen as an occupational representative in the cabinet. Two days after public announcement of formation of a Union government, he telegraphed George Chipman, editor of the *Grain Growers' Guide*, asking him "to make it clear," in any published reference, "that I am not severing my connections with Company or organizations and that I am not entering party government but am going into Union as representative of organized farmers." To his supporters in Marquette, he explained "that it was desired to have representation from the great farmers organizations of Western Canada to complete as far as possible a truly national government."

But Crerar felt at the outset that old party lines might never reform, and he expected "the development of a Progressive Party somewhat later." He rejected R.J. Deachman's fear "that I might not be found in the Progressive element when that time comes. I have not sacrificed one iota of my belief in freedom of trade and the general principles of taxation."[23] His explanations generally found acceptance, but there were isolated criticisms, and one writer in the *Alberta Non-Partisan* felt that he had been "brought over to the ranks of the enemy."[24] The proof would have to await the end of the war.

Before the election campaign began, Crerar wrote to the chairman of the Board of Grain Supervisors tendering his resignation. But since he saw his new position as apolitical and probably of short duration, he had no intention of neglecting the affairs of United Grain Growers. When thanking Springmann in London for his congratulations, he assured him that he was not "severing my connection with the Company here or its business, and I still hope to be able to attend Directors' Meetings and advise and counsel with the other members of the Board in all matters of policy."[25] His resolve, however, would be compromised to some extent by the pressures of government duties. His first obligation now would be to get himself and the new Union government elected.

PART TWO

Upheaval in Ottawa, 1917–22

United Grain Growers' Elevator, Drumheller, Alberta, 1923. Courtesy Archives and Special Collections, Dafoe Library, University of Manitoba

CHAPTER FOUR

Minister of Wheat, 1917–19

The Unionist campaign of 1917 in western Canada began in Winnipeg on 22 October. At an enthusiastic gathering of five thousand people, Crerar, Calder, and Meighen described the negotiations that had led to the coalition and dedicated themselves and the Union government to the war effort. Crerar carefully confined his own "practical" remarks to indicating his determination to encourage all branches of agriculture in an effort "to produce at a maximum rate." The three repeated their performance the following night in Regina and then split up to work their separate spheres. Crerar spent most of his time in Manitoba but made one extended speaking tour of rural Ontario, during which he appeared with Borden at London.[1] Only sporadically was he in Ottawa and in touch with his Department of Agriculture.

Support for Union government was strong in the west, but it certainly was not unanimous. The Military Service Act was an unpredictable variable. Labour leadership was restless and volatile; farmers were concerned about their labour supply and expected relief from compulsory service; and many grain growers were anxious about the direction that the new government would take in domestic fiscal matters. And underneath all was a righteous assumption that conscription was quite properly aimed at the French Canadians. Crerar would walk a fine line in devoting himself closely to the interests that he claimed to represent.

The southwestern Manitoba constituency of Souris offered him a nomination (and probably the election) by acclamation, but he declined.[2] He was set on running in Marquette, his home district, but on as broad a political base as possible. Local Liberals and Conservatives were approached as farmers and asked to suppress their traditional party loyalties for the common cause. In one of many letters to acquaintances in the riding, he talked of the new government and national unity, by which he seemed to mean a unity of disparate economic groups of which he represented one. He made no mention of the isolation of French Canada.[3]

Crerar assured potential voters that his "whole sympathy and interest is with my fellow grain growers in the West." He was still a member of the Canadian Council of Agriculture, had helped to draft its program, and would campaign on it. He acknowledged that some aspects of it would have to be put aside until the war was over and demobilization complete. But he hoped that the Union government would at least eradicate patronage, reform the civil service, and levy fairer taxes on the wealth of the country. But if it ever came "to the time when I have to make my choice between my political and administrative work in Ottawa, and the work with which I have been associated for the last ten years, I shall certainly choose the latter."[4]

In his formal address to the electors of Marquette, he reiterated his responsibility to represent the interests of the grain growers and announced that "I was not asked to, nor do I accept one iota of responsibility for what the preceding government did, nor do I abandon any of the principles that I have believed in and advocated in the past."[5] It seemed enough for most of Marquette. On 15 November a nomination meeting of Liberals, Conservatives, and Grain Growers acclaimed Crerar as its candidate.

During the campaign, he was in and out of Ottawa occasionally but had little opportunity to become familiar with his new ministry. His first impressions reflected his business experience. It was rather like "entering a museum," he wrote to an Alberta friend, " ... the whole atmosphere of the place tended to stifle or depress initiative rather than encourage it."[6] It was his political role, however, that first drew public attention. He was immediately beset by requests for exemptions from the Military Service Act, a problem that would bedevil him (and the other cabinet ministers) until the end of the war. Crerar shared the general presumption of the prairies and rural Ontario that food production was as vital to the war effort as military service at the front. In one of his first presentations to cabinet he noted that farmers were not applying for exemptions in great numbers for their hired help. "The great advantage of selective conscription," he pointed out, is "that those who can best contribute by staying home may be kept there." Farmers should be urged not to hesitate to ask the tribunals for exemptions for their experienced farm labour. A politically sensitive cabinet did not think it advisable to publish such a notice.[7]

Crerar tried to reassure farmers that the men needed for farm work would not be taken, and those who had been called up he would try to have returned. But the requests poured in. The president of the Manitoba Agricultural College, J.B. Reynolds, sought exemptions for his faculty and entire student body.[8] It was a touchy business. Crerar secured an exemption for Jimmy O'Donohoe, manager of the New York office of the Grain Growers' Export Company, but refused to consider similar requests for any other staff members. Rather sharply, he told O'Donohoe: "I do not desire to leave myself open to any misrepresentation in the matter."[9] To a correspondent overseas, he remarked on the dissatisfaction among farmers with the tribunals and the growing pressure on the government. The problem was eased, for a time, by the order-in-council of 23 December 1917, which authorized exemptions for farmers' sons. But the issue would return with a vengeance in the spring.[10]

Meanwhile, his own campaign in Marquette had taken an unexpected twist. He was not concerned by the charge of the *Labor News* in Winnipeg that he had joined the "grafters" in government. He had, as well, expected sniping from the remaining Laurier Liberals, but no formal opposition. In this he was right; but a challenge did come from a quite surprising quarter. Late in the campaign, James Weir, a Non-Partisan League member of the Alberta legislature and second vice-president of the United Farmers of Alberta (UFA), entered the contest against him. Crerar's entry into the Union government, Weir charged, was neither in the farmers' best interests nor representative of western agrarian feeling. He offered no specifics.

Henry Wise Wood, UFA president, immediately repudiated Weir's action as unauthorized by the association and stated that he, Wood, "supported Crerar as the representative of the farmers of the west." He offered to come to Marquette himself to lend his aid and to denounce Weir publicly.[11] The whole affair was more nuisance than danger, but there was one benefit. Weir challenged Crerar to a debate that took place in Minnedosa and allowed the latter to assert once again his devotion to the Farmers' Platform and restate the conditions of his entry into the government. Privately, Weir told Crerar that he was not opposed to him. It seems that his resentment was really directed towards Arthur Sifton and the *Guide*.[12] It was the only excitement in an otherwise smooth and easy campaign.

When the election took place on 17 December, the Unionists swept the west, despite a surprisingly strong vote for Laurier and the straight Liberals. All the blandishments and tub-thumping patriotism had not overcome old loyalties and lingering suspicions. In Marquette, Crerar took every poll but one. Prominent Winnipeg Liberals had spoken throughout the riding, including Premier Norris, R.S. Thornton, the education minister, and even Isaac Pitblado, for whatever good they would do in a rural riding except to comfort Liberals voting for a heavily Tory government. But Crerar was especially pleased that the campaign had been locally financed. Rather sententiously, he wrote to Hugh Lockhart, one of his organizers: "[W]hen we have an interest like this taken by the electors it conduces to a much higher standard of purity in our elections." His own expenses, at least as reported by his official agent, Allison Glen, had been $77.20![13]

It was now up to Crerar and the Union government to deliver on all the pious and patriotic rhetoric. He soon came to see his own role rather narrowly, realizing that he and his western colleagues were in the government as much for effect as for any contribution they might make. Whatever he thought about conscription – and he did support it then as being the fairest method of ensuring an adequate flow of replacements – he knew that they were there to make it more palatable. But he took as a personal mandate the obligation to represent agricultural interests, especially those of the grain growers, in cabinet. He felt as well a necessity to interpret and explain western attitudes to his cabinet colleagues.

Crerar had no illusions about his political future; indeed, he would last only twenty months as a member of the government. He did not seem to develop any close affinities to other cabinet members, though he did come to have a sincere admiration for Borden's vigorous Canadian nationalism, which he very much shared. While they were never close personally or on matters of fiscal policy, Borden would recollect that he "frequently found [himself] more in agreement with [Newton] Rowell and Crerar, the most advanced among the Liberal element, than with my former colleagues." And despite their noisy political battles of the next few years, Crerar and Meighen hit it off so well that the latter's biographer would write that "for Thomas Crerar, [Meighen] acquired a lasting genuine liking and respect."[14]

To give a refurbished image of renewed dedication to the great effort, the prime minister divided the senior cabinet members into a War Committee and a Reconstruction and Development Committee. Crerar's appointment to the latter well suited him. Not only would the committee deal with demobilization, in which he was greatly interested, but it was also asked to plan for land settlement, revenue and taxation, and labour, among other matters. In addition, he was frequently at meetings of the War Committee when matters of food production and control were being discussed.

One of his first concerns, however, was to try and allay the emotions provoked in the west by the election campaign, which he very much regretted. The anti-French and anti-Catholic animus that underlay the conscription issue made quite evident what many westerners expected from the Military Service Act and the conception of Canada that they held. A friend and subsequently a member of the Winnipeg Sanhedrin, Edgar J. Tarr, wrote to Crerar the day after the election expressing his "hope that in dealing with the Quebec situation now the Government will use a very firm hand and will unswervingly and promptly enforce [conscription] ... whatever the threatening consequences may be." Such action, he went on, "is absolutely essential to the future unity and well-being of Canada." A rural Manitoba business acquaintance was even less subtle and probably more typical. He congratulated Crerar on saving the country from "the plots of the French Jesuit Priests."

In replying to the many such letters, Crerar carefully avoided commenting on the virulent anti-Quebec sentiments. It was his first official brush with the "primary antithesis" of Canada, and it immediately began to affect his attitude towards conscription and, more profoundly, his understanding of the complexities of governing the country. He was not as hopeful as Norman Lambert, who worked for the *Guide*, that Union government could lead Canada "out of the darkness and bitterness of the racial strife that has been raised to the nth degree during the past month."[15]

Nor was the victory so complete. As Tom King, editor of the *Toronto World*, pointed out to Crerar, "the Liberals are not beaten much worse on the conscription issue than they were on the reciprocity issue in Ontario, and not much more discredited thereby." The unanimous support of six Toronto newspapers for the government would not last. Opposition would return with little delay, and "as a mere business proposition some newspapers will have to turn Liberal."[16] Perhaps the political culture itself would help to repair the rupture, but Crerar carried this anxiety about ethnic tensions for the next three decades.

He had little time for reflection, however. The daily rounds and pressures of a cabinet minister – especially a new one – crowded in on him. He tried to remain true to long-held convictions and the motives that had led him into the government. But he would soon learn that Ottawa had an intense political life of its own, and he would have to struggle against the isolation that it subtly but dangerously imposed. He was routinely advised, for example, by Martin Burrell, secretary of state, that the *Manitoba Free Press* "has been added to the list of newspapers authorized to receive Government patronage" –

the presumption being obviously that this was "his" newspaper and now part of the team. He replied, rather stiffly, when Burrell sought further suggestions, that it seemed to him "that the papers that could best supply the service that is required should be used," without regard to political affiliation.[17] And when he learned that he had the disposition of postmasterships in Marquette, he wrote to one of his contacts there for a recommendation, assuring him that "I do not care what his politics are as long as he is qualified."[18]

It was easy enough to be high-minded when it came to minor patronage matters. It appeared, however, that there was a significant difference in Crerar's attitude when it came to appointments to the bench. Throughout his many years in politics, judicial promotions merited his close attention. For him, the courts represented both the rule of law and the protection of individual rights; but they were also an essential part of government. Proper legal qualifications were always a prerequisite, but this does not mean that he disregarded political allegiance in such cases. Appointment of judges was not only proper, as opposed to an elected bench, but highly symbolic as well. The future intentions of government could often be read in these actions.

Thus, in the late winter of 1918, when an appointment became necessary to the Court of King's Bench in Manitoba, the relative strength of Meighen and the Tories in the Union government and of Crerar would be tested. The benchers in Manitoba had recommended E.L. Taylor. Hudson, recently Manitoba's attorney general, and Isaac Pitblado both hurriedly contacted Crerar, who replied: "You can rest absolutely assured that Taylor, or any other old line Tory in Winnipeg will not get this position – before, at any rate, a good sized row develops over it." Taylor's appointment was blocked.[19] For Crerar, "patronage" comprised distribution of minor offices, contracts, and favours. Positions on the bench (and to a lesser extent in the Senate) were reflections of high policy.

As a westerner and a grain grower, Crerar was vitally concerned with transportation policy. The Canadian Northern Railway had already failed, and the Grand Trunk Pacific was about to be taken over. Arthur Meighen had the difficult task of developing the government's policy. Despite the kicks and screams from many of his fellow Tories, he was moving towards creation of a publicly owned and operated national system. Crerar had little direct influence in the ongoing struggle, which would not be fully resolved for several years. But he certainly represented the attitudes of the organized farmers of the prairies whenever he had a chance. "My views of the railway situation have not changed in any respect," he wrote to Education

Minister Thornton in Winnipeg. "To my mind there is only one way out of it and that is by an entire nationalization of all Canadian railways."

The grain traders in Winnipeg had mixed views. His old friend Frank Fowler complained to him about the lack of rail cars to move grain and urged nationalization of all but the Canadian Pacific Railway, which he claimed was the most efficient in the world. Crerar did not see "eye to eye" with him on the question. "It might be well to mention that the rotten conditions you speak of [lack of cars] have arisen from private ownership."[20] He would become intimately connected with railway affairs in much of his subsequent political career, and the problems would not change much.

Whatever his concern with consistency, he would soon be caught up in a precarious political situation. Despite Meighen's symbolic role of western leadership as minister of the interior, it was to Crerar that the prairie farmers turned as their particular champion. In addition to his duties as minister of agriculture – itself an equally symbolic appointment – he was also wartime food controller and directed by the cabinet to do his utmost to increase food production, especially in cereals. It was precisely for his presumed influence with the grain growers that he had been recruited by Borden. His broad western constituency was quite happy to comply, especially with the advance in wheat prices and the Board of Grain Supervisors doing the marketing. To respond effectively, it expected Crerar and the government to reduce tariffs on farm implements and to protect their labour supply from compulsory military service. Given the dominance of friends of protection in the Union cabinet and caucus and the commitment to conscription, his political skill and determination would be quickly tested. So also would his current convictions about fiscal policy.

The question of farm labour had been met partially (and, as it turned out, quite temporarily) by exemptions from conscription promised to farmers' sons during the election campaign. The tariff issue, in contrast, brought immediate pressure. One of the many letters that Crerar received came from Cecil Rice-Jones, now acting general manager of United Grain Growers: "The first thing that 80% of the farmers that you talk to regarding increased production bring up is the tariff on implements and there is no getting away from the fact that the position is very hard to explain." In other words, Crerar should do something.

Crerar couldn't agree more, and he used all such letters to score an early, small victory. He was able to persuade cabinet, in the interest of encouraging production, to remove the duty on imported tractors valued at under $1,400, though he quickly learned that such victories were scarce. He told Chipman that he "would like to see ploughs and seeders [and] a great deal more on the free-list. However, a person cannot get everything he desires in that direction at the present time."[21]

The reaction of the manufacturers was swift. A delegation of forty descended on the cabinet in early March 1918. It complained of course about the concession on tractors but was even more disturbed that the exemption might be extended to other agricultural implements. It wanted to know, as Crerar recounted to Henry Wise Wood, if manufacturers were now regarded as "undesirable" people. It pointed out to cabinet, quoting extensively from the *Grain Growers' Guide*, the current high prices of wheat, the rising income of the west (including the many automobiles), and the many references to prosperity.

Crerar was not impressed by the group's argument and accused its members of having "come to look upon their tariff protection as a divine right." He was, however, very much aware that they were "strengthening their organization in every way they can – as they have a perfect right to do." He concluded by urging Wood to stir up the Canadian Council of Agriculture to demonstrate the strong position that the west had come to occupy in Canadian affairs."[22]

Crerar was shrewd enough to see the danger implicit in the protests of the manufacturing interests. Farmers could appear to be (and many probably were) just as self-serving as any businessman. Crerar told Chipman that he had to deal constantly with the charge that "[n]othing will satisfy your farmers. When the farmer urges that the duty be taken off agricultural implements to increase his prosperity, he is taking a narrow, selfish view." He acknowledged that there was "considerable force in this criticism." Arguments against the tariff must therefore be placed on higher grounds, such as that taken by "Cobden and Bright seventy-five years ago."[23] Tariffs generated revenue as well as providing protection, as Crerar well knew. His experience in the wartime cabinet, as the government's debt steadily mounted, was slowly modifying his free-trade faith and leading him to an altered view of the best methods of raising the needed revenue.

Meanwhile, his campaign for increased production was having some success, not only in cereal crops but in meat and dairy products as well. He continued to be concerned, however, about labour supply on the farms. He received many suggestions, some more helpful than others. One urged that half a million horses in Alberta be bought, killed, canned, and sent over to Europe for food. Another argued quite forcefully that a million "Manchurian Chinamen" should be brought in to till the prairie lands. "The people who try to get at you with all sorts of schemes," he told Chipman, "and the wires they pull to meet you, is wonderful. I had no idea there was so much human ingenuity in the world."[24]

Crerar's bemused reaction was dispelled by the government's decision to cancel all future agricultural exemptions under the Military Service Act and to review those already granted. The last desperate assault by the German army in the early spring of 1918 broke the British front and provoked the crisis. Borden considered the situation so serious that he felt that the Canadian army must be supported by full reinforcements, whatever the cost. On 19 April the prime minister announced that exemptions would be removed, not by amendment of the Military Service Act, but by issuing of an order-in-council, following parliamentary approval of a government resolution to do so. Reaction was strongest among the farmers of Ontario and, to some lesser extent, Quebec, and they came to Ottawa five thousand strong to insist on continuing exemptions for farmers' sons. They were refused access to Parliament, and at an angry meeting at the Russell Theatre Borden rejected their demands in view of the military emergency.[25]

Not surprisingly, Crerar, as minister of agriculture, became the focus of much agrarian resentment. He considered the action "very drastic" and "arbitrary." Every day, for six weeks, the telegrams and letters of complaint poured in. "Frankly," he confided to his old friend John Kennedy, "the thing is commencing to get on my nerves and I just feel like running away from it." He continued to argue that the government had not done enough to protect food production. As a member of cabinet, he did what he could, but he was clearly peripheral to decisions on manpower policy. In a long memorandum to cabinet in mid-May, he tried to make the case for agricultural production: "Today thousands of farmers, whom a few weeks ago we were urging as strongly as we could to grow more food, are largely helpless. They naturally cannot understand it." He urged cabinet to reinstate some exemptions and authorize a generous leave-of-absence policy to assist farmers in seeding and harvest. But it was to no avail; the cabinet's decision would stand.[26]

Though most of the complaints were coming from Ontario farmers, Crerar was very concerned about the unfavourable image that the issue was creating for the government across the country. He acknowledged that during the recent election campaign Unionist candidates in Ontario had promised that the government would not take farmers' sons and experienced help, and he regretted that the impression had been left "that the Conscription Measure was

directed against Quebec." The result was that "many of them feel a
good deal like the man who is swindled on a horse trade." To Cowan
at the *Farm and Dairy Review,* he confided that *"privately* I think the
whole thing has been poorly handled. The Militia Department have
acted in a stupid manner and a good many of the Judges before
whom the re-hearing of the exemptions granted last Fall are going
on, are acting in an equally stupid way." But he could not resist
pointing out that "scarcely a complaint has come in from the Province of Quebec."[27]

The delegation to Ottawa, he felt, had been ill-conceived as well,
creating a widespread impression of agrarian selfishness. Crerar and
his colleagues in the Canadian Council of Agriculture greatly feared
a backlash. When Morrison and the United Farmers of Ontario (UFO)
called another protest meeting in Toronto in June, Henry Wise Wood,
the council's president, was dispatched to try and cool down the
hotheads, but with little success. Norman Lambert, now secretary of
the council, reported to Crerar that Wood had a difficult time when
he addressed the meeting in Massey Hall. Lambert feared that the
farmers' movement would be stigmatized throughout Canada "as a
narrow, selfish and unpatriotic institution." He blamed Morrison and
"the hard-shell, partisan mind of rural Ontario." The long-range danger, as they both agreed, was that Morrison's actions could jeopardize any hope of attracting the war veterans and the Labor party to
a general political movement.[28] The seeds of the "broadening out"
controversy of the 1920s were planted during the Great War.

The passions aroused by the issue of exemptions began to cool as the
end of the terrible war seemed finally in sight in the autumn of 1918.
So also did Crerar's enthusiasm for staying in the government. His
duty, as he had seen it, was done. And he knew that he would have
little influence on the government's fiscal policies, and that, as a
consequence, his reputation in the agrarian community would suffer
more than it had already. Indeed, the whole drift of the Union government was making him increasingly unhappy. The failure of the
government to tax the interest earned on Victory Loans was widely
criticized in western Canada. When Crerar tried to persuade the
finance minister to do so, he received a sympathetic response, but no
action, since the people of eastern Canada, according to Sir Thomas
White, "take a narrower and more selfish view."

Crerar tried as well to win more understanding for the plight of
conscientious objectors, suggesting a program of alternative labour
service. He fought stoutly against aspects of the government's ban
on "subversive" organizations and publications. With support from

Newton Rowell, he was able to have the Social Democratic party explicitly excluded from the ban. He was increasingly conscious that central Canadians were badly informed about the west. As he put it, the Social Democratic party "has two men on the City Council in Winnipeg. I have never thought that they constituted any menace to society and certainly do not think so now."[29]

Ottawa itself was beginning to depress him. He felt closed in and isolated. He had to cancel a speaking tour of Marquette when a virulent influenza epidemic struck the country in the autumn of 1918. "As usual," he told Chipman, "the poor districts are the ones that have suffered most. Perhaps we will realize some day that decent housing accommodation and open air spaces are matters of national importance." To J.R. Murray, now general manager at United Grain Growers (UGG), who had inquired about his Winnipeg house, he replied that he was not particularly anxious to sell "as I may require it before long."[30]

Despite the pressures of his position at Ottawa, Crerar had tried to keep abreast of UGG affairs and the activities of the organized farmers. He took a direct hand in dissolving the partnership with Shipton, Anderson & Co., which had been the basis of the Grain Growers' Export Company Incorporated in New York. With there being only one central purchaser in Europe, its operation had become temporarily redundant. UGG simply bought out its London partner and maintained the incorporated company with the expectation that the end of the war would bring return of the open market. Both parties anticipated, after the amicable settlement, that peace would also make possible resumption of their business relationship in some form.[31]

A somewhat trickier problem arose in Winnipeg. Discussions had taken place between the board of the *Grain Growers' Guide* and the Saskatchewan Co-operative Elevator Company (SCEC) over the possibility of the Saskatchewan company's acquiring a fifty per cent share of the *Guide*. There were, of course, advantages to such a move. The *Guide* would speak for all the organized farmers of the prairies, and perhaps the arrangement would lead finally to full cooperation between the two great farmer-owned companies. Crerar, however, was not very hopeful. The *Guide* was a wholly owned subsidiary of UGG, and Crerar was president of both. He had nurtured the newspaper from its inception, through lean financial years, until now it was profitable and influential. Any such change would probably result in a board divided equally between the two companies, and Crerar feared "the narrow sectional view that some of the Saskatchewan men have almost invariably adopted." His experience in negotiating with them on marketing questions had been disappointing, and he remained deeply suspicious of their motives. Nothing came of the proposal, probably to Crerar's relief, but the organized farmers remained divided.[32]

He was equally exercised by a proposal for a conference between farmers and manufacturers. The idea was being pushed by Sir John Willison, imperialist and newspaperman, who, Crerar charged, was "being retained at a large salary by the Industrial and Reconstruction Association." Crerar suspected that the whole effort was a front for the Canadian Manufacturers' Association to proselytize for continued tariff protection. He warned Henry Wise Wood and Lambert to keep the Canadian Council of Agriculture clear of its schemes.[33]

Such preoccupations were symptomatic of Crerar's increasing restlessness in Ottawa. His sense of being a spectator, an outsider, came through frequently in his correspondence, and he knew that his reputation was suffering in the west. "One's motives and intentions can be so easily misunderstood," he wrote to Wood, but "if my being here is of any assistance at all, I can come to no other conclusion than that I have followed the plain path of duty." Virtue, in this case, would certainly have to be its own reward.

But he was learning. "My experience in Ottawa convinces me more every day that we must have a new deal all around," he told Lambert. Strong differences in matters of policy could not be endlessly compromised. Lambert expected Crerar not to stay in the cabinet much longer, he informed Wood, but "to come out from amongst that crowd in Ottawa ... I shouldn't be surprised to see him withdraw before the next session is over."[34]

The comment was prophetic. When the war ended in November 1918, Borden was obliged to travel to England. Concerned for the future, he canvassed the former Liberals in the Union government as to their intentions. All of them were willing to stay in the cabinet but Crerar, who only "agreed to stay until after demobilization."[35]

During his last six months in the government, Crerar devoted less and less time to its activities and more and more to a burgeoning political correspondence. As far as he was concerned, his obligation to Borden had been fulfilled, though he recognized the need for a period of relative stability to facilitate return of service people to civilian life. He had to consider not only his own future but the increasing politicization of the organized farmers, which he attempted to restrain and direct. But he was quite aware that his influence would wane the longer he remained a member of the cabinet and shared the responsibility for its record.

He apparently took little interest now in the cabinet's delibera-
tions, unless his department was directly involved. On matters of
more general policy, Crerar often found himself at odds with his
colleagues. He, along with a few others, steadily urged that the Wartime Elections Act be rescinded and a new, fairer Franchise Act put
in place. In this he was eventually successful.

But he was largely alone in his struggle in 1918 against sending
Canadian troops to Siberia. He held out to the very last and was
persuaded to go along only by the arguments that it was necessary
to reopen the Eastern Front and that failure to cooperate would constitute a virtual breach of promise to Britain. But once the war ended,
he became adamant. Before leaving for a Canadian Council of Agriculture meeting in Winnipeg, he laid out his position to Sir Thomas
White, acting prime minister. The question was due to come before
cabinet again, and Crerar asked White to present his position: "I am
absolutely opposed to sending any additional forces to Siberia, and
the Forces there ... should ... be brought home."

His reasons then followed. With the war over, there was no longer
any need for an Eastern Front. The question of how Russia, in the
throes of revolution, should "settle her internal affairs is her concern
– not ours." If Britain and France chose to maintain forces in Russia,
that would be their decision. There was absolutely no justification for
Canadian troops to be on Russian soil, especially troops raised under
the Military Service Act.[36] He was in a distinct minority, but he was
now much less concerned with cabinet disagreements. It would be
events in western Canada that would determine his future course.

The most significant decision of the meeting in late November 1918
of the Canadian Council of Agriculture (CCA) was to reissue the
Farmers' Platform of 1916, renamed A New National Policy For Canada, with the obvious implication. Crerar did not have a direct hand
in the action, but since it varied little from the original platform,
which he had largely written, he was well content. The intention, the
CCA stated, was to bring the document up to date. Since 1916, some
of the original objectives – prohibition, female suffrage, personal and
corporate income taxes – had been partially or fully adopted by the
dominion or provincial governments. Now it was time to consolidate
these gains and focus on the other issues.

The revised document began with a commitment to a new British
Empire composed of free and equal nations and a statement of opposition to any attempt to centralize imperial control. Most attention,
however, was directed to fiscal policy. The CCA urged general and
substantial reduction of all tariffs, free trade with Great Britain, reciprocity with the United States, and an expanded "free list" to include

agricultural implements and the raw materials for their manufacture. This stance forced the council, of course, in view of the huge war debt, to address revenue as well. To this end, it advocated a tax on all unused land, including all natural resources, and graduated income and corporation taxes. It concluded with demands for repeal of the Wartime Elections Act, proportional representation, women in Parliament, and an end to the granting of titles in Canada.[37]

Not surprisingly, this renewed offensive sparked demand throughout the prairie west that MPs force the tariff issue in the next session of Parliament. The meetings of the provincial Grain Growers' Associations in early 1919 endorsed the platform and increased pressure for action on western members.

But the western farmers were divided on another issue, which would in fact disrupt the grain growers' movement for years. Early in 1919, the annual convention of the Saskatchewan Grain Growers' Association passed two resolutions: the first requested that Ottawa establish a fixed price for wheat for the new crop year; the second asked for a central selling agency, to be operated or regulated by the dominion government. Both would continue the emergency marketing practices put in place because of the unusual conditions of the war. There was little objection to the second request, as it would take a year or two to re-establish the open market. For Crerar and others, however, the demand for a fixed price involved not only practical difficulties but, more important, a cardinal principle of the farmers' movement. European customers, who had suffered high wartime prices, would certainly seek to return to pre-war levels, especially when Argentinian and Australian wheat again became available to world markets. To maintain a fixed price anywhere near that paid out for the 1918 crop would, in Crerar's estimate, mean a dominion subsidy of at least $100 million. Since the U.S. Congress was already committed to such a price-maintenance system, it was a perplexing situation.

When Chipman sought advice as to the *Guide*'s editorial policy in the matter, Crerar, sobered by wartime expenditures, pointed to the state of the country's finances. That was not his primary concern, however; it was the subsidy itself. "The Saskatchewan Convention," he lectured, "placed itself not far from the level of the selfish attitude of our Canadian manufacturers." He advised Chipman to hold off taking an editorial position until the forthcoming meeting of the CCA.

Meanwhile, he wrote the CCA's President, Henry Wise Wood, to make his own position clear, since he would be unable to attend the meeting. He was opposed to a fixed price for several reasons. If the dominion government guaranteed wheat prices, why not prices for stock raisers or any other commodity producers? Their claims would be equally valid. He also pointed out the drain on the dominion treasury. But his most important objection was that such a guaranteed price would constitute a special consideration to grain growers, thus violating the very principle for which the organized farmers had been contending over the previous ten years. "Public opinion in Canada," Crerar warned, "is quick to note inconsistencies." A guaranteed price to grain farmers was no different in principle than the tariff that protected manufacturers. Such action "would tremendously weaken the position that the farmers of Canada have attained." He concluded by urging that western farmers seek the best price they could get for their wheat and that "the matter should end there."[38]

The CCA met in the first week of April and shelved the issue because it was unable to reach an agreement. Both the Manitoba and Alberta conventions had opposed a fixed price, and Crerar was accused by some of the Saskatchewan men of influencing their decisons, which he denied.[39]

Whatever satisfaction this course of events gave Crerar it was short-lived, for there was another side to this coin. With wheat prices sure to decline, agitation to reduce costs through substantial reduction in the tariff became more insistent, and pressure on the western MPS to take action at the present session of Parliament increased sharply. It was obvious to Crerar that this question involved the very future of Union government. He was not opposed to the growing sentiment in favour of political action among the grain growers; indeed, he supported it, with some reservations. But he was not at all keen on the resolution adopted at the Manitoba convention that sought to pledge MPS to convention direction on the tariff question. He was even more concerned that demands for action on the tariff by western members would precipitate an immediate election. The government, in his view, would accept only token measures on tariff reductions in the new session. Even worse, if an election were forced, it would not be fought on the tariff but would reawaken the ethnic controversies of the war and allow a spurious loyalty cry to dominate the contest. Better to wait until passions cooled. The farmers, in any case, lacked any political organization and needed at least a year to create a political structure. The worst possible result would be to force the issue and lose.[40]

But Crerar was not in a position to control events, and he would soon have to declare himself. Throughout the early months of 1919, he wrote many letters to local associations of grain growers, stating his position on various matters, but especially the tariff. He reiterated his support for the Farmers' Platform and, though never explicit, seemed to be preparing the ground for his resignation from the cabinet.

The issue was joined, however, in late March. Andrew McMaster, the free-trade Liberal MP from Brome, in Quebec, proposed an amendment to a motion to go into Supply. It attacked the government's fiscal policy and was a clear want-of-confidence motion. It was designed – so McMaster told Crerar privately – to commit his fellow Liberals to tariff reduction, but it placed all the prairie members in a vexing position. When the government was sustained, a great deal of confusion resulted. As Crerar had argued all along, however, the real test would come on the budget to be brought down in June – and so the *Guide* advised its readers.[41] There would be no ducking the issue then.

The Union government, as Crerar had predicted, was willing to make only minor tariff concessions. He had almost no personal impact on the budget discussions – his views were well known and unacceptable to his colleagues. If he resigned in protest, which he fully expected would be the case, he would immediately become a rallying point for western dissatisfaction. He would also become a target. To forestall criticism of a personal nature, he had instructed the board of United Grain Growers to rescind a salary increase that had been authorized without his agreement late in 1918 and continued to draw the same amount as he was receiving when he entered the government in 1917. It was the action of a man who planned to continue in political life.[42] But it would soon be as a private member.

When Prime Minister Borden returned from Europe and the peace conference in late May 1919, he knew that there would be problems over the budget. He discussed the situation with some of his close advisers, considering "principally the views and intentions of Mr. Crerar whose free trade instincts have been aroused and who does not like the financial arrangements which Sir Thomas White has submitted to Council." He agreed to speak with both men.[43] There was no resolution.

On 4 June 1919, Crerar submitted his resignation to Borden. "As you are aware, I am not in accord with [the budget] and therefore cannot support it, either in the House or in the country." He went on to thank Borden, whom he genuinely admired, for his past courtesies and to commend him for "the fine manner in which you have represented Canada overseas." Borden expressed his regret in accepting the resignation but appreciated the "sincerity of the convictions which have impelled you to take that course."[44] They parted as friends and would remain so, but they clearly were finished politically.

The announcement was received with satisfaction by Crerar's confidants in Winnipeg and, with a Liberal leadership convention in the offing, was widely interpreted as the beginning of a reorganization of Canada's political alignments. "This is a time of radical change," the *Ottawa Citizen* mused. The next prime minister "may well be called to office from Western Canada, and in Mr. T.A. Crerar … are the qualities of national leadership."[45] It was the beginning of an exciting thirty months that would indeed remould Canadian political life.

CHAPTER FIVE

Leading the Progressives, 1919–21

Crerar had not taken lightly his decision to resign from Borden's Union government, but he had few regrets. In June 1919 successful prosecution of Canada's war effort and repatriation of the overseas troops were now virtually complete. As representative of the organized farmers of the west, Crerar had been witness to their support of the government's determination and played a public, if minor, role in its activities. But he had harboured a secondary, less well-known, and apparently futile hope for the Unionist movement – that it might be the vehicle for a regeneration of Canadian politics. It might have brought to "the country a new spirit and a new ideal. I feel that it is hopeless to expect this. The old methods and expedients will govern." He had concluded that the Unionist party would "be substantially the old conservative party." Dafoe, who had abetted Crerar's entry into the government, very much shared his disappointment, and they both concluded that, even if any remaining liberal elements in the government were able to influence fiscal policy, it would never be sufficient to attract significant support from a restless west.[1]

It did not appear that Liberals offered any better prospects. They had scheduled a policy convention for the summer of 1919, which, by necessity after the death of Laurier early in the year, would choose a new leader as well. Perhaps the liberal spirit of the west, drawing inspiration from the Farmers' Platform, could capture the convention, ally itself with the more radical Liberals of the east, and drive the old, stand-pat Liberals into their true home with the Tories. Crerar much preferred this outcome to any attempt to create a farmers' party. The obstacles to such a result were simply too formidable. According to Dafoe, Crerar felt that a purged and radical Liberal party would be possible only under Fielding; but the latter had broken with Laurier on compulsory service and thus would have difficulty attracting support in Quebec, especially that of Ernest Lapointe, from whom Crerar expected much.[2] Besides, Fielding at heart was a protectionist.

Crerar's own immediate future remained unclear. He would have to await the result of the Liberal convention, the expected reorganization of the government and its new policies, and the outcome of the Ontario election, planned for September and certain to attract a large number of farmer candidates. But of one thing he was certain – the dominion government was in for a rough ride, and Crerar cheerfully passed on some current wit to Jacques Bureau, another Quebec Liberal whom he was cultivating: "[L]iken the Union Government to a ship on which the captain is sick and the engineers are fighting down below; the crew is infected with pox and scurvy, mutiny is rife and both anchors are gone; a tempest is raging and she is beating up against a rockbound coast which is lined with savage tribes (i.e. farmers, labor, G.W.V.A., French Canadians, etc) waiting to plant their assegais as she beaches."[3]

Despite his disappointments, Crerar's twenty months in the wartime cabinet had been something of a political education, and it led him to certain conclusions that would guide his future public positions. In spite of his earlier convictions, he was now convinced that conscription had not been worth the price in national divisiveness, and he would not forget the lesson. Borden's greatest wartime accomplishment, in Crerar's opinion, was his insistence on an increasing degree of Canadian autonomy within the empire – his demand that Canada be more an accepted partner than an acolyte. Like Dafoe, Crerar became a strong supporter of the League of Nations, and he hoped that it would lead to both an international police force and a world court. He rejected any notion of a centralized imperial foreign and defence policy. "I am a Canadian, first, last and all the time," he wrote to the editor of the *Ottawa Citizen*, "and my hope and ambition is to see Canada grow to fuller and more complete autonomy rather than to become involved with any scheme of Imperial Councils or Cabinets or Parliaments."[4]

Watching the Canadian cabinet wrestle with the country's railway mess led Crerar to an equally firm conclusion as to future policy in this area. In October 1919, he addressed the problem in a speech in the House of Commons, which indicated that he was becoming more selective in his attitudes to government activity in economic life. The Canadian Northern Railway, which had already failed, and the faltering Grand Trunk Pacific should be merged into the national railway system. He cited the successful examples of Winnipeg City Hydro and Ontario Hydro in public ownership and argued that "all democratic peoples are coming to believe in it." He still clung to the notion that the "function of government is not to do for people in their private lives what they can do well enough for themselves"; but major "natural" monopolies such as transportation and power were best left to governments. He also wanted the new national railway to have a fair trial and insisted that the valuation of the debt-ridden Grand Trunk Pacific be written down. Like most westerners, he always had a weather eye cocked towards the Canadian Pacific Railway and its ambitions. The new, truly national railway would remain an article of faith for Crerar and his western colleagues.[5]

But in the immediate aftermath of his resignation from cabinet his public position was identified above all else with the tariff. He was still adamant that "tariff protection is not only economically unsound but morally wrong." In a "Message to Women Voters," he asserted that "the amount of taxes a country raises is not so important as the manner in which they are raised." But the war had made him increasingly conscious of the government's need for revenue. When he spoke during the debate on the budget that had provoked his resignation, he addressed only the tariff. He estimated that the government required $300 million annually and that that sum should be raised through taxes on income, inheritance, and the value of unimproved land. The tariff, by implication, was unnecessary as a source of government funds.[6]

Increased revenues would also be generated by expansion of trade and incomes, and Crerar repeatedly reminded correspondents and colleagues that the old Reciprocity Agreement of 1911 was still on the American statute books and should be actively pursued by Canada. This was a matter of some moment, as the u.s. Congress was considering a motion to repeal the long-standing offer. In an interview with the *New York Evening Post*, Crerar pleaded that "rejection of Reciprocity by the Canadian electorate in 1911 was an error of the first magnitude. It was not a considered verdict." The old bitterness still burned in the west. Hence though the future was full of uncertainty, Crerar hoped that the region would somehow be the catalyst of national revival.[7]

The aftermath of the budget debate of June 1919 found the House of Commons in a novel configuration. There had, of course, been independents there previously, both by the result of election and by the force of political circumstance, but the basic two-party alignment had persisted since Confederation. Now there was an incipient third party on the scene. Crerar and the eleven other western Unionists who had opposed the budget were now definitely separated from the government, and nine of them, including Crerar, moved to the cross-benches. But without any formal constituency sanction or extra-parliamentary organization, they were a rather self-conscious group in a restless House.

In any case, politicians and the rest of the country were obsessed with more immediate events. For almost a month a dramatic general strike had been paralysing Winnipeg. The decision of organized labour and its thousands of supporters in the Manitoba capital to resort to mass economic action had polarized the nation and drawn exaggerated comment, mostly unfavourable, throughout the industrialized world. Like most observers beyond Winnipeg in that year of the "Red Scare," Crerar disapproved of the strike, but not blindly. He tried to reassure an anxious correspondent in Britain: "At no time was the civil authority directly challenged, or in any way in danger. The unfortunate thing," he went on, "is that the general discontent – much of it well founded – gave the extremists an opportunity of which they took full advantage." To another he pointed out that it must be recognized that the old order was changing, and he quoted John Bright's remark – "Force is no remedy for social ills."[8] But there was general relief among the country's political and economic elites when the weakening resolve of most of the strikers was delivered the *coup de grâce* by the intervention of the dominion government. The politicians, especially, were eager to turn to more familiar, and for them less frightening, preoccupations.

There was some expectation that the Liberal convention scheduled for late summer would help to clarify the jumbled political situation at Ottawa. The party of Laurier, so badly battered and divided during the war, was at a crossroads. The two likely contenders for the leadership – W.S. Fielding and William Lyon Mackenzie King – represented the stale and the untried, respectively. But for Crerar and much of the west, it was the platform – the future direction of the party and its policies – that was of primary concern. A rejuvenated and radical Liberal party might attract the unhappy westerners; but a stand-pat, or worse, a reactionary policy would surely provoke political revolt on the prairies. The test would be the tariff resolution adopted by the convention and, to a lesser extent, the choice of leader.

There was a flurry of activity during July on the prairies, instigated by Crerar, Hudson, and Lambert, aimed at coordinating efforts of the three prairie Liberal governments, grain growers' associations, and delegates to the convention. It became evident during discussions that unless the westerners could forge an alliance with eastern radicals (among whom Crerar counted Lapointe and Andrew McMaster of Quebec the most influential) nothing could prevent the west from following its own line of action, probably in step with Ontario's farmers. Even then, there was some doubt that Alberta's farmers would stay in line.[9]

But Crerar was not willing to risk his own position just yet. He resisted the blandishments of highly placed Ontario Liberals such as Charlie Murphy and Arthur Roebuck, who urged him to attend the convention himself. The advantages to the Liberals of having Crerar take a public position with them were obvious. His decision not to attend, however, was not simply coyness on his part. He wrote quite openly to Andrew Haydon of the National Liberal Federation, who was party manager and one of the posse trying to corral him, that his position among the people of western Canada had never been stronger. He suggested to Haydon, somewhat enigmatically, that he "might be in a position to contribute more to the building of a real Liberal party by refraining from attending the Convention rather than by attending it." He had first to gauge the strength and direction of the rising temper of the prairies.[10] From Crerar's point of view, it was the right decision.

It was probably in the cards that the results of the convention would never satisfy the more forward spirits in the west or head off the political rupture that was building. The careful compromises implicit in selection of King as leader and the progressive gloss on the new program adopted at the convention were sufficient to reconcile most Liberals in central and eastern Canada, but they were clearly inadequate for the prairie west. As Dafoe had noted wryly to Sifton, however, the enthusiasm for independent action in the west involved a "certain amount of hypocrisy, for some of the most influential leaders of the Grain Growers – Crerar and Dunning, notably – hope to make a deal with the Liberals; but the fact is they have started something they cannot control."[11] For the next two and one-half years, the implications of Dafoe's forecast would be the focus of Crerar's political life.

Crerar also had a living to make. After he left the cabinet, he was able to spend much more time in Winnipeg at his desk at United Grain Growers (UGG). The company, like scores of other businesses, had done very well out of the war and, despite experiments with government-controlled marketing, would continue to flourish until the collapse of wheat prices in late 1921. The general well-being of UGG, plus the fact that Crerar had a splendid and loyal number two in Cecil Rice-Jones, meant that there had been little pressure on Crerar to curtail his political activities. Indeed, most of the company's senior officers took a close and often active interest in agrarian politics. They were all keen cooperators as well as aggressive businessmen. By the end of 1920, the enterprise had spawned a number of subsidiaries – the two export companies based in Winnipeg and New York, the Public Press and the *Grain Growers' Guide*, a parallel grain company in British Columbia, a securities firm, sawmills, and flour mills. Crerar was president of all but the flour mills.

The end of the war brought as well lifting of the freeze on Crerar's UGG salary, which freeze he had insisted on for obvious reasons. In November 1919, his stipend was increased to $15,000. To help with his political activities, now that he was out of the cabinet, the board hired Tommy Wayling as an Ottawa-based secretary. So Crerar was, for the moment, in the happy position of not having to worry about his tenure with the company and enjoying some assistance in pursuing his political manoeuvring.[12]

When Crerar and his little band of Progressives, as they were becoming known, took their places on the cross-benches at the new session of Parliament in September 1919, the political situation, in his words, was chaotic. Borden's firm wartime hand had relaxed. The government appeared to be drifting, and the prime minister seemed listless and indifferent. There was considerable speculation as to his ability or will to carry on. The Liberal convention had not opened the possibility of a major realignment of political forces. Indeed, in Crerar's opinion, it had been a great disappointment. There had been no clear declaration against the principle of protection; its handling of the railway question "was stupid and meaningless"; and Crerar very much doubted that King, the new leader, had the strength to drive out those who "had clogged Laurier's progress."[13] There was no longer any hope of heading off a western revolt. The challenge would be to try to control and direct it. There was so much uncertainty that probably only a dominion election could clear the air. It could also confuse matters even further.

More immediately, the political movement among the farmers and his own relationship to it were Crerar's primary concerns. On the prairies, there was no common pattern across the provinces. Though the Liberals were in power in all three, the farmers' political movements did not deal with them uniformly. In Saskatchewan, the farmers created a formal political action organization in September 1919 – a meld of the Grain Growers' Association and prominent Liberals, intending to devote its energies to economic reform at the national level. The preoccupation in Alberta, where the movement was dominated by Henry Wise Wood, was with democratic organization at the constituency level, both provincial and dominion. From Crerar's point of view, it was even more alarming that the Albertans refused to recognize any interest but agriculture and rejected as members all but working farmers. This, and their rhetoric, brought the inevitable accusation of "class exclusiveness," even though there was little agreement on what that meant. Given the anti-radical impulse of 1919 following the strike in Winnipeg, however, it was likely to bring trouble. The direction of Manitoba's grain growers was not yet clear, but there was considerable sympathy for action at both provincial and national levels.[14]

Crerar had hoped that all three prairie governments would work closely with the grain growers, but they were no more in a position to control events than he was. He dreaded entry of organized farmers into provincial politics. For one thing, it was not really necessary. Given the political demography and the structure of representation in prairie legislatures, no government could afford to ignore the wishes of the grain growers and hope to survive. For another, the great issues of the day – the tariff, the railways, and Canada's position in the world – could be influenced only at the dominion level. More subtly, an open break between farmers and the Liberal governments would threaten the longer-term goal of a radicalized Liberal party "through the infusion of the Graingrowers' ideals and policies."[15]

Implicit in these dynamics was the danger of regional and/or occupational isolation. Whatever the problems of prairie farmers, their major concerns required national solutions, and Crerar always considered the farmers' movement an integral part of the national polity. Organized political action by the grain growers must take place in a national context. Even a "third party," however, must reach out beyond the exclusive concerns of the farmers for nation-wide support, if it wanted a sympathetic hearing in all regions.

There was little that Crerar could do yet. He was the temporary "Leader of our Group in the House. I have neither right nor authority to assume leadership for the Farmers generally. Each province is pretty well minding its own affairs."[16] Yet in much of the country's press, he was touted as the leader of the farmers and even considered a possibility as the next prime minster. The ambiguity was frustrating.

There was, of course, more to the farmers' movement than the prairies. Ontario was on the eve of a provincial election. The United Farmers of Ontario (UFO) was in the field with excellent prospects. Crerar was even more isolated from it, but that did not stop him from trying to influence its decisions and keep it conscious of the importance of dominion politics and the need to avoid a narrow, occupational appeal. The UFO's financial needs gave him his opportunity. The *Farmers' Sun*, its organ, was partially financed by the *Grain Growers' Guide*, and George Chipman, editor of the *Guide*, expected that the UFO paper would duplicate the *Guide's* role and style. Crerar, as president of the *Guide*, had to approve the arrangement.[17] This brought him into regular contact with J.J. Morrison, secretary-treasurer of the UFO and its most dynamic, if erratic, spirit.

Prior to the Ontario election, Crerar urged Morrison to modify the image of the UFO as a purely occupational and constituency-conscious movement, but he had little success. At the very least, he advised, it ought to recognize the need for coherence and able leadership. "No matter how much enthusiasm there is in a body of men," he wrote, "if there is not planning and intelligent leadership that co-ordinates the whole and turns it into an effective working machine, failure is bound to come."[18] Morrison paid little heed.

After the election in late October 1919 resulted in a plurality for the UFO, Crerar was present in Toronto when the neophytes gathered to face the responsibility of choosing a leader, forming a cabinet, and running the province. It appears that they were as surprised as anyone else. Crerar hoped – and privately urged – that they would turn to Sir Adam Beck, the champion of public power in Ontario, but he realized that the new members would want one of their own as leader. Their choice of E.C. Drury did not displease him, but he was anxious that the new premier go beyond the ranks of the farmers in choosing his colleagues. Only in that way could the new government "effectively meet the criticisms that are being made and will be made with increasing volume that the farmers' movement is purely a class movement."[19]

Morrison thanked Crerar for his interest (and his wire and letter), even if we "do not see eye to eye with you in all your advice." Somewhat condescendingly, he went on: "[S]ome of us feel that you are the great central figure when the Federal fight comes"; but he added, rather ominously, that "it is unfortunate that we are not in perfect agreement."[20]

The political success of the farmers in Ontario was repeated in dominion by-elections in late October 1919. Of the eight contests, two went by acclamation (probably an arrangement of courtesy), to W.L. Mackenzie King and to Sir Henry Drayton, the new finance minister. Lapointe took over Laurier's seat in Quebec East, and the farmers won all four contests that they entered. The additions to the cross-benches, especially O.R. Gould from Assiniboia and T.W. Caldwell of Carleton-Victoria (a breakthrough in the Maritimes), who brought considerable strength and debating skill, pleased Crerar of course.[21] But he was not at all surprised. The tide was flowing strongly, and he felt that he would have to intervene or the entire agrarian movement would be rent by centrifugal pressures.

The gravest danger came from Wood and the United Farmers of Alberta (UFA). The party had entered and won a provincial by-election in Cochrane, Alberta, and Wood used the occasion to trumpet his views. In Winnipeg in November, he asserted that "government by economic groups was inevitable." Two days later, in Regina, Crerar struck back in a speech in which he denied Wood's contention. "We do not want class movements in Canada. We do not want them in the making of our laws or administration of the governmental business of the country."[22]

With the emerging dispute thus public, there was, as Crerar had hoped, an attempt made to defuse the situation. The Canadian Council of Agriculture (CCA) scheduled a meeting in Winnipeg on 6 January 1920, with Wood in the chair. Despite his objections, the meeting not only agreed on political implementation of the CCA's New National Policy but also approved a resolution on "broadening out" to attract labour and war veterans. It was not a complete rejection of Wood, however, since political organizing was left in the hands of the provincial associations and Crerar was denied a national organization.[23]

When Wood returned home he moved quickly to ensure that Alberta farmers "owed their loyalty to him and the UFA and not to Crerar and the Progressives." A crucial resolution at the UFA convention of 1920 declared that "all activities of the UFA – social, educational, economic and political [– would be] under the direction of the central executive."[24] So the chasm opened, and thus began an intense, three-year struggle between the two leaders for the political soul of the farmers' movement.

Crerar had been the keynote speaker at that same convention, and careful observers had noted signs of future difficulties. He pointed out, with some pride, that there were now 125,000 members of farmer organizations across the country but reminded the audience that numbers and influence also brought great responsibilities. Their bond was the New National Policy, which was a national platform addressed to dominion issues in which the farmers were vitally interested. The new national railway system must be guarded attentively; Canada's growing autonomy must be nurtured; and, reflecting western bitterness with the wartime experience (and his own disillusionment), Crerar declared, "[T]he Canadian people will make the profoundest mistake they have ever made if in any way we commit ourselves to any form of compulsory military service."

The balance of his speech, predictably, he devoted to the tariff. His argument presaged a dispute that would soon divide the western farmers bitterly and finally remove the tariff as a western issue from national politics for good. The protective tariff was wrong, Crerar asserted, because it increased production costs, and only lower costs would ensure the prosperity of the wheat economy. For the moment this statement brought cheers.

Crerar concluded with a ringing call for a strong representation of farmers in the next Parliament, but one willing to broaden out its concerns to include other groups, in the interest of the nation. This was the image of the agrarian movement that he hoped would spread across the country, and the applause of the delegates masked the important fact that it was Wood who controlled the resolutions that were passed.[25]

Despite Crerar's reluctance about launching a new national farmers' party, the die was now cast. The older parties were naturally alarmed, though they could hardly have been surprised. For the Union government – soon to be reorganized under Arthur Meighen as the National Liberal-Conservative party – the threat was immediate. Its prospects in Quebec, still embittered by conscription and the election of 1917, were poor at best. If it lost the west and rural Ontario to the farmers, it would be out of power. For their part, the Liberals were equally concerned at this potential danger to their revival, and Crerar was besieged by Haydon, Charlie Murphy, and others seeking some grounds of cooperation. But the apparent strength of the farmers still had to be moulded into a cohesive instrument if they were to influence those national policies they sought to change.

This would be Crerar's primary preoccupation throughout 1920. He and his little group in the House were the focus of much attention. On 3 March 1920, eleven strong, they held their first formal caucus meeting, appointing a whip and two deputy whips. "We are now looked upon in the House as a third party," Crerar wrote to Chipman.[26] But it was as yet a political head without a body, since there was no organization in the country to support it.

Two of the group's strongest members, Chief Whip Levi Thompson from Saskatchewan and Dr Michael Clark of Red Deer, were not farmers, and there was already considerable doubt that they could win another nomination in their constituencies, because of their occupations. This narrow view of representation did not bode well. Crerar was convinced that "no group can get along in the House without lawyers and they should be good ones." He made this point continually to R.M. Johnson, secretary of the Saskatchewan Political Committee, and to Chipman at the *Guide*.[27] The fact that Gould, of Assiniboia, had agreed to a recall arrangement with his constituency committee sparked a lively debate in the House, obliging Crerar to try and calm the alleged fears of the spread of radical populism imported from the United States. His posture was continually defensive.

Meanwhile, Crerar and Wood danced a careful ballet, with neither man willing to force the disagreements between them to the point where the movement would be publicly threatened. Indeed, Crerar often defended Wood from the charge of wanting to inject class politics into Canadian life. He hoped to blunt the criticism more directly by persuading Wood to issue a denial that the farmers' movement was a "class" movement or that it sought only its own selfish ends. Wood warned Crerar that such accusations were motivated by fear that the farmers were on the brink of political success and that their opponents would try desperately to divide them. Nevertheless, Crerar continued to insist that Wood, as president of the Canadian Council of Agriculture (CCA), must assure Canadians that the farmers were willing to work with anyone who shared their goal of a truly liberal society, free of powerful special interests. While he professed continued loyalty to the national movement, Wood gave no indication of surrendering his tight control of the Alberta wing to any central organization.[28]

Conditions in Ontario were not much better. A widening rift was developing between Morrison and Premier Drury. The ostensible issue was a proposed pension scheme for Ontario's public servants, which Morrison and many others in the UFO opposed. By letters and visits, Crerar attempted to persuade them both to call a truce in the interests of the farmers' ambitions in the dominion field, where solutions to their major problems must be sought. The deeper issue, however, was Morrison's resentment of Drury's not leading a purely farmers' government and the premier's conviction that any such limited government must inevitably fail.[29]

Norman Lambert, secretary of the CCA, was anxiously watching events and suggested to Crerar that a meeting of the agrarian leaders, under the Council's auspices, might help to ease tensions and deflect the growing threat to the national movement. He arranged a gathering in Winnipeg in early July to consider the general political situation and the coming dominion campaign. Wood, Morrison,

Johnson of Saskatchewan, Caldwell from New Brunswick, and Crerar were among those attending.

The meeting was a mixed success. The attempt to create a central coordinating body to direct activities in the three prairie provinces was opposed by the Albertans, and it became rather distressingly clear, at least from Crerar's point of view, that even the provincial committees would have little influence at the constituency level. He was also unable to persuade the meeting to issue a statement that the farmers were not a class movement and would welcome anyone who accepted the positions outlined in the New National Policy. His colleagues feared that such a statement would be misunderstood in the west and dampen support for political action. It was a discouraging business, he reported to Levi Thompson, warning him that he must expect opposition to his renomination in Qu'Appelle, since he was not a farmer. Enthusiasm for the dominion cause would require an external public focus.[30]

The dominion government was the unlikely agent. During the week following the CCA's meeting in July 1920, Borden finally resigned, and Arthur Meighen, the choice of the Tory caucus, became prime minister. The civilities of the day were observed, and Crerar offered his compliments, even though he did not "pretend for a moment that I shall be able to support your public policies; indeed, quite the reverse will likely be the case, but that does not prevent me simply and sincerely offering to you my congratulations." Meighen sent his thanks, recalling their period as cabinet colleagues and trusting that "in the future if it is impossible for me to earn your support, I shall never forfeit your respect." In fact, after years of political battles, they became warm friends when Crerar went to the Senate.[31]

After reorganizing the cabinet and deciding for the moment against a general appeal to the electorate, Meighen set the date for a series of by-elections in the autumn. The most significant politically was that in Ontario's East Elgin, and most of the political heavyweights took part. The by-election there was considered by the national press to be variously a test of the new prime minister's popularity in this traditionally Tory riding, an opportunity for Mackenzie King to stimulate a Liberal revival, and a chance to determine whether the agrarian movement was anything other than a prairie phenomenon. Its importance, Crerar told Morrison, was that it was not "local in its character but national" – an opportunity to find out if the electors "with their votes [will support] the national reforms of the Council of Agriculture." But a three-cornered contest might divide the opposition and allow the government candidate to slip in. However, to win such a contest would be an enormous coup.[32]

Morrison had urged Crerar to visit East Elgin, but he hesitated. He feared that he might excite local animosity or raise the spectre of centralized organization. But he could hardly stand aside and surrender the field to the other party leaders. The prime minister himself spoke for the government candidate, as did Sir George Foster, Senator Robertson, and even the renegade grain grower R.C. Henders. The Liberals sent in their new leader but tried as well to persuade Crerar to stay out. Both Haydon and Charlie Murphy worked on him, implying that the Farmer candidate should withdraw in the interest of some future alliance.[33] That, of course, would have been fatal to Crerar's pretensions of leadership. In late November, he made a last-minute swing through the riding, apparently to excellent effect. In what was considered a stunning upset, the Farmer candidate romped home winner.[34]

In the excitement of the victory, little notice was taken, except by those who followed such things closely, that Crerar was quietly shifting ground. He had pretty well abandoned his earlier devotion to a tax on land values and was also modifying his tariff stance, moving towards favouring a tariff for revenue rather than outright abolition.[35] But the result certainly increased his national reputation. A month later, he was formally endorsed as leader of the National Progressive party by the Canadian Council of Agriculture (with Wood seconding the motion), and Tom King, editor of the *Toronto World*, thought that Crerar "is going to be the next Prime Minister of Canada."[36] It was heady stuff, but Crerar was fully aware that East Elgin was but the first step through a political minefield.

A national election was widely expected in 1921, but Arthur Meighen had his own worries. He had to secure his hold on the party, firm up its programs, and attend the first postwar Imperial Conference, which would deal with the tricky problem of renewal of the Anglo-Japanese alliance. King's first eighteen months as Liberal leader had been at best a mixed success. In the winter of 1920–21 *Maclean's Magazine* gave Meighen and King space to outline their programs – a sort of preview of their coming platforms. The issue of 1 February contained Crerar's "Confession of Faith" – put into final form by John Stevenson, a journalistic ally – and it stuck quite closely to the New National Policy.[37]

In Ontario, Drury's popularity did little to mollify Morrison, and the sniping continued. Morrison's exclusiveness, Crerar feared, could seriously cripple the UFO's efforts in a national campaign. A strong showing in Ontario would go far to erasing the agrarian movement's image as simply a western party. Hence, in letter after letter, he urged Morrison to consider the interests of the national struggle and hoped, even if there could be no reconciliation with Drury, for some sort of interim neutrality. "Drury and Morrison must get together," he wrote to Cowan of the Ontario *Farm and Dairy Review,* "otherwise our whole cause will be hurt."[38]

In the west, political developments were more focused. The untimely death of Arthur Sifton, Sir Clifford's brother and Crerar's former cabinet colleague, had opened the constituency of Medicine Hat, where a by-election was called for June 1921. Meighen was attempting to muddy the political waters by instigating a formal inquiry into the grain business, the major purpose of which seems to have been almost purely political – to discredit the farm organizations in general and Crerar and United Grain Growers in particular. After acrimonious public hearings, strident editorials, and court injunctions, it petered out by the end of the year.[39] And it had little effect on the outcome in Medicine Hat.

According to Dafoe, Henry Wise Wood would have preferred to make the by-election a UFA affair exclusively and not even invite Crerar to speak. Wood was "on record," he told Clifford Sifton, "as saying that a head-on collision between him and Crerar was bound to come." But the managers of the campaign for Farmer candidate Robert Gardiner were not about to decline outside help, especially among the labour voters in the city of Medicine Hat.[40] Given his protestations about constituency autonomy, Wood could hardly intervene. Crerar, and Norman Lambert as well, spent four days in the riding, presumably to good effect. Gardiner won by over nine thousand votes, and the government candidate lost his deposit.

The most heartening part of the result, for Crerar at least, was the composition of the majority. Gardiner lived in the far north of the constituency and was running against Lieutenant-Colonel Nelson Spencer, the Tory candidate, who had been a popular mayor of the city and MLA, yet the Farmer candidate swept the city as well as the rural polls. "Every town in the constituency," Crerar crowed to Cameron, "I think [but one] gave Gardiner a majority, in some cases the vote being five or six to one." In congratulating the winner, Crerar emphasized the breadth of his support and rejoiced that this could not be interpreted as a "class" victory. And to Morrison, he wrote: "[T]he plain fact of the matter is that the cities and towns are as much interested in good policies and sound administration as the farmers are."[41] He hoped that the message would be taken to heart by all.

But it wasn't. Subsequent events in Alberta that summer were much less satisfactory. A provincial election in July swept the UFA into power and, according to Wood's biographer, "made it clear that not all farmers were willing to go along with Crerar and his doctrine of the new liberalism."[42] Crerar tried to put the best face on it. To his friend Cameron he explained: "H.W. Wood's peculiar theories doubtless appealed to some but there was a good deal of dissatisfaction with a few of [Premier] Stewart's ministers and there was not a due regard being shown for economy."[43]

Both Crerar and Dafoe were convinced that Wood should come out from behind the scenes and face his responsibilities. The former wrote to J.E. Brownlee, United Grain Growers' solicitor in Calgary, who would enter and eventually lead the UFA government, "[T]here is no doubt in my mind that Wood should accept the leadership of the government. His personality has undoubtedly been one of the strong factors in producing the result that has come about in Alberta. ... I certainly think it is Wood's duty. If Wood remains out and endeavours to direct the government from outside no doubt the same condition of affairs will be brought about within a year that now exists in Ontario between Morrison and Drury."[44]

The second jolt came in September, but it was not unexpected. Dr Michael Clark, who had strongly supported Crerar and the Farmers in the House, was denied renomination in Red Deer and published a bitter letter denouncing Wood and "class government." Crerar of course feared the effect that this turn of events might have in eastern Canada, where it surely would be misunderstood. "The curious thing is," he informed Cameron, "that Wood does not believe in class legislation or class domination. He execrates both in private and is really convinced that [his] new method of organization [namely, group government] will make class legislation and class domination impossible in the future."[45] But he would have little time to worry about Clark.

Meighen had grasped the nettle and announced an election for December 1921. Crerar did not expect that any party would receive a majority, though he forecast that the Progressives would win from seventy-five to eighty seats. While there was concern in government circles about the possibility of an alliance of Progressives and low-tariff Liberals, Crerar worried about a possible arrangement between protectionist Liberals and the Tories. Post-election manoeuvring promised to be as important as the vote itself, since Crerar's forecast was pretty accurate. King received a plurality of 116 seats, the Progressives gained sixty-five seats, and the Tories were reduced to fifty. The unfamiliar politics of sectionalism was now the order of the day.

If central Canada was surprised at the strong showing of the Progressives, Crerar was rather disappointed. He had expected a minimum of seventy-five seats and felt that the United Farmers of Ontario (UFO) had let the side down, returning only twenty-four Progressives. The reason, for Crerar, was very evident. "The narrow nature of the appeal ... largely stamped our movement as a class movement in that Province," he wrote to J.B. Musselman in Saskatchewan, "with the result that ... our candidates did not get more than ten per cent of the vote of the cities, towns and villages." Since the next electoral redistribution would reduce rural Ontario's political strength even further, the strategy of J.J. Morrison and the UFO was hopelessly self-defeating.

Even before the election Crerar had told Morrison that when it was over, "it will probably be found that no party has a majority." This would result in a "general demand from all over Canada that a strong government be formed and we will be in a position where we will necessarily be an important factor in the reckoning."[46] It is unlikely that Morrison really understood Crerar's concern; if he did, he did not believe or accept it.

To Crerar, an inconclusive election would create the opportunity of "getting the policies we have advocated made effective." Throughout the entire election period and its aftermath, it was the policies of the movement that were vital to him, not the narrowly political aspects of cabinet formation and the party's role in the House of Commons. As he recalled long afterward to W.C. Good, "I was not mainly concerned at all with the triumph of a party as a party. ... I was interested then, and still am, in sound policies of development for Canada."[47] Thus he rejected, even before the election, Morrison's strategy of using a balance-of-power situation to extort concessions. He considered such a policy quite irresponsible, he recalled for Grant Dexter: "[It] was wholly impossible since it was contrary to our whole concept and theory of democratic Government."[48] Parliamentary cooperation must be founded on agreed policies and only secondarily on political advantage or personnel. Crerar would find, however, that belief and practice would be difficult, if not impossible, to reconcile in the absence of political discipline.

CHAPTER SIX

A Divided House,
1921–22

Long before the election of December 1921, the possibility of a Liberal-Progressive alliance of some sort was being considered. On three separate occasions between late 1920 and mid-1921, King had suggested to Crerar and Drury a coalition of the two groups before any dominion election; presumably, King saw no insurmountable differences of policy.[1] Nothing came of these overtures, perhaps because of the others' suspicion of King's sincerity. During the course of the 1921 campaign, Crerar met secretly in Montreal with W.S. Fielding, at the latter's request. Fielding was seeking to keep open the lines of communication and also urged Crerar to hold his party committed to reciprocity with the United States, whatever that implied.[2]

Consequently, Crerar was stunned during the last three weeks before the election when King several times denounced the Progressives, scorned the idea of coalition, and seemed even to reject the possibility of any post-election cooperation. To the editor of the *Globe*, Crerar acknowledged that "he was at a loss to understand [King's] attitude." The Liberal leader "was foregoing the opportunity [of creating] a real Liberal Party in Canada."

Both Cameron and Dafoe, however, suspected that the political "fix" had already been arranged. In a letter to Clifford Sifton on the day after the election, Dafoe, using information from Cameron, suggested that the Canadian Pacific Railway (CPR) and the Montreal faction of the Liberal party, led by Sir Lomer Gouin, had gotten to King, thus explaining the latter's surprising statements during the last days of the campaign. King's willingness to negotiate after the fact was the result entirely of his minority position.[3]

Crerar was still willing to give King the benefit of any doubt – an attitude that caused some consternation among his intimates. Dafoe felt that the Progressive leader "is of a trusting nature," and it would be up to his friends to save him ... from putting his head in the noose."[4] There was certainly no shortage of advice forthcoming. Two days after the election, Sifton, who seems to have been congenitally incapable of resisting any temptation to meddle, however unwelcome his interventions, told Dafoe that Crerar should stay clear of King unless he were offered a fifty–fifty cabinet share and definite agreement on policy. Dafoe passed the message on to Crerar the same day, but the latter was politely noncommittal.[5] Of much more concern to Crerar was a letter written to him that day by Tommy Wayling, his secretary in Ottawa, who was in touch with Morrison. Wayling warned Crerar that the UFO was "unanimously opposed to alliance of any kind" but added that Morrison nevertheless would try to keep it loyal to the ostensible leader.[6] In other words, Crerar was aware before any overtures were made that the UFO, driven by Morrison, would accept no deals with King and the Liberals.

The story of the not-so-secret negotiations between King's emissary, Senator Andrew Haydon, and Crerar is well known. But in many accounts the chronology of events is misleading, and the question of motivation deserves to be explored further. Such an analysis may also help to resolve the confusion created by some players and observers who have left conflicting, often self-serving accounts of the delicate game that took place after the election. It does appear that King's anti-Progressive outbursts had been intended very much for effect – designed to quell any anxiety in Montreal – and that Crerar's confidence in him was not entirely misplaced. Certainly, King's first post-election instinct was to create as broadly based a government as possible. On 8 December he told Haydon that he was willing to take both Crerar and Drury into the cabinet, and he later informed Fielding that he would be able to meet their policy concerns, to which he was generally sympathetic. This was before any consultation with the Quebec Liberals.[7]

Haydon had wired congratulations to Crerar on the day after the election. In his reply, Crerar emphasized King's opportunity to remodel the Liberal party and warned against over-reliance on the Quebec bloc, which, he argued, "was not good for Liberalism, nor Quebec nor the country. A solid Quebec now will inevitably mean a solid Ontario a few years from now."[8] His fear derived primarily from his wartime experience and partly from the fact that he had avoided Quebec during the election campaign and knew little of its politics. But Quebec was not as solid as Crerar believed and would shortly discover.

After instructing Haydon to contact the Progressive leader, King summoned from Quebec City Ernest Lapointe, who stopped in Montreal to see Cameron on his way through. According to Cameron, Lapointe was quite anxious for an arrangement with "the farmers" and spoke of "six to seven Cabinet posts," but the government must be a "Liberal Government."[9] This would of course eliminate the Montreal interests. Lapointe seems to have had his own plans at this time.

Cameron's message made Crerar "a good deal more hopeful." Crerar greatly feared that if "King forms a Government out of his present supporters ... dominated by the Montreal end ... he will bring on racial and sectional animosities fiercer than anything you or I have ever seen in this country. Ontario will be full of smouldering resentment." The only solution was a truly liberal party that included the Progressives. The crucial matter was policy. "While I cannot go further than I can take my supporters with me," Crerar went on to Cameron, "I feel certain that we can go a long way to meeting King on a thoroughly Liberal programme. I am thinking of Canada before everything else at the present time."[10] This would all sound smug and pretentious in a public statement, but Crerar was always candid in his letters to Cameron and almost never wrote for effect.

Lapointe reported back to Cameron that King was trying to have it both ways and was considering a cabinet that would include Crerar, Drury, Fielding, Gouin, and himself (Lapointe).[11] Haydon meanwhile was en route to Winnipeg to see Crerar, but his preoccupation with cabinet positions was quite inappropriate. It was for the Progressive leader a matter never of men but rather of measures.

Crerar was being pressed from several quarters. Fielding was working through Cameron to induce Crerar, Drury, and Hudson (elected as an Independent Liberal in Winnipeg South, but really the sixty-fifth Progressive and generally recognized as such) to join the government. J.J. Morrison, after learning that Haydon was heading to Winnipeg, feared that Sifton was now involved and excitedly wired Crerar to "remain steadfast to your principles. You are master of the situation. See that you maintain this position." Wisely, Crerar did not react to this peremptory message but tried to reassure Morrison after the first meeting with Haydon, who claimed that King was proposing a low-tariff policy and elimination of the Montreal interests – "but I want satisfactory guarantees before taking matter up with my support."

Advice from other sources was probably more to Crerar's liking. The editorial board of the *Globe* was concerned primarily with protecting the infant national railway and feared the power of the CPR in Montreal. The *Globe* was convinced that if King were surrounded by "such a trinity as Fielding who can speak with authority for the Maritimes, Lapointe, who is the successor of Laurier in the affections of Quebec, and Crerar, with his mandate from the west, Canada will enjoy good government."[12] Cameron was pressing King directly to take in the Progressives, arguing that such a move would free the prime minister from the Bank of Montreal and CPR group led by Lord Atholstan of the Montreal *Star*, who seemed determined to wreck the national railway.[13]

But King's attitude towards cabinet positions was (and would remain) a severe obstacle. He saw them as means of control rather than as instruments and symbols of policy, and he resented Crerar's insistence on prior agreements on a program. He complained to Drury, whom he considered more reasonable – by which he meant more malleable – that "Crerar was making a mistake and asking too much to suggest terms *re* tariff, railway rates, natural resources etc. that he should have faith in men proposed [,] not exact conditions." Crerar and the others would "have to come in on the same conditions as other ministers."[14] This was precisely the sort of coopting that Crerar was determined to avoid.

The discussions in Winnipeg lasted four days, and telegrams flew back and forth between Haydon and King. Crerar took his counsel from his small group of intimates – Dafoe, Hudson, and Frank Fowler. During the talks with Haydon they were never far away, especially Hudson, and Crerar's position began to harden. Dafoe only thinly disguised his role when he wrote to Sifton: "I have no direct personal knowledge of these conferences but Crerar kept in touch with me and on Saturday night [after Haydon returned to Ottawa] there was a small gathering which I attended." The Winnipeg "Sanhedrin" already knew that the UFO would spurn any deal with King and that the latter was very reluctant to make any guarantees in advance. It feared, and rightly, that if Crerar and Drury went into the cabinet without firm commitments, "they would find themselves in a hopeless minority" and "the whole Progressive Movement could be headed off and destroyed." Its conclusion was that there could be cooperation only on the basis of a formal coalition, with public guarantees. The Progressives, to protect themselves (and Crerar), must maintain their separate identity. This was the message that Crerar would take to a meeting of western Progressives in Saskatoon on 20 December.[15]

By coincidence there was another gathering in Winnipeg that same week. The executive of the Canadian Council of Agriculture was in town for its regular meeting, presided over by Henry Wise Wood of

Alberta. He told the secretary, Norman Lambert, that the Alberta members of Parliament had met in Calgary before proceeding to Saskatoon to meet Crerar and that they were unanimously in favour of cooperating with Crerar and King on a coalition basis, "feeling that they have more to gain by emphasizing issues than the personal equation." They would hardly have taken such a position without consulting Wood. Lambert was also aware that Hudson was being sent to Ottawa immediately to make it clear to King that "the political traditions of Western Canada have always placed issues before men."[16]

Crerar went to the Progressives' conclave in Saskatoon with a firm plan of action and expected an endorsement there, given what Wood had indicated to Lambert, and perhaps he hoped that this would soften the attitude of the UFO members. He got what he wanted: "Resolved: If an invitation is extended to Progressive members to enter Hon. Mr. King's Cabinet as individuals *upon conditions they feel are satisfactory* we give our tacit approval ... including the Hon. Mr. Crerar."[17]

There have been many distortions made about this meeting. E.J. Garland, Progressive MP and later member of the "Ginger Group," for example, claimed in his recollections some years later that Crerar "wanted us to endorse his acceptance of a Cabinet position ... [A]t once we began to draw away from him and that was the beginning of the later separation of the UFA group from the Progressive caucus."[18] This statement can be regarded only as post hoc puffery. Crerar wired the result to Hudson in Ottawa that night and set out for Toronto to meet the Ontario members.[19]

When Hudson passed the information to King, the latter seemed to feel that a deal was still possible, even though he had been made aware that the Progressives would retain their separate identity. But he was not ready to cut his connection with Gouin and the Montreal Liberals.[20] Even before Crerar met with his Ontario colleagues, the new prime minister was coming under tremendous pressure from Montreal. Cameron made it clear that Gouin was now determinedly hostile to any arrangement with the westerners and "had thrown in his lot with the others," who included Atholstan of the *Star*, Sir Herbert Holt, and the CPR.[21] While Crerar was closeted with the UFO in Toronto, King called Hudson in once more and tried to persuade him to convince Crerar "not to bargain for terms, but to come in on the basis of men in Govt to work out policies together."[22] The prospects of any agreement were already fading rapidly.

Crerar's hand was certainly not strengthened by his reception in Toronto. The *Farmers' Sun*, which spoke for Morrison, warned shrilly that Sifton and the *Free Press* were behind the whole nefarious scheme to deliver the Progressives into the hands of King. Drury, who was Crerar's only real hope for Ontario support, had already taken himself out of the game. So it was no great surprise to Crerar that the UFO flatly refused to consider cooperation of any kind, even on matters of legislation that the Progressives favoured. He regretted the UFO's "narrow and uncompromising spirit," since its position would endanger any chance to forward Progressive policies on the national railway and the tariff.[23] (Norman Lambert, in a letter to J.D. Atkinson of the *Toronto Star*, claimed that the UFO's decision was the clincher, since the Saskatoon resolution had to be approved by the Ontario group.[24] No evidence has been found to corroborate this assertion, and Crerar certainly did not feel constrained by any strings on the Saskatoon resolution.)

On Saturday 23 December Crerar met with King, and it was evident that any formal agreement was now beyond reach, whatever the intransigence of the UFO. According to Crerar, "a considerable change had taken place. The activities of the Montreal Star and Gazette had made anything in the nature of an understanding impossible."[25]

There were few recriminations – only some regret and self-delusion in the wake of collapse of the negotiations. Crerar's view was that King, through a failure of will, had missed an opportunity to forge a truly liberal party based on a national railway, lower tariffs, reinstatement of the Crow's Nest rates, and more autonomy from Britain – all of which could be supported by King, Lapointe, Fielding, and the Progressives.

There is considerable irony in King's immediate reflections on the events of December 1921. Where the UFO believed Sifton was pushing Crerar into a deal with the Liberals, King was convinced that it was Sifton who was behind Crerar's refusal to join the cabinet. But he never, of course, blamed himself. To his diary, he confided, "I see Crerar's position. I admire him for considering his following's wishes, but it is real lack of leadership which prevents him from inspiring and dominating his following"! His satisfaction came from the conviction that Crerar was a lesser man than he. "I feel genuinely indignant at Sifton. What poor fools men are who will permit themselves to be the puppets of such a man."[26]

Others saw things differently. Kirk Cameron was depressed by the breakdown, and he blamed King: "He should never have made the move unless he proposed to see the thing through ... He has delivered himself into the hands of the Montreal crowd." Norman Lambert was more hard-headed. "The fact that Mr. King was unable to give the assurances to the Western men ... was offset by the fact that Mr. Crerar would not have been able to guarantee to Mr. King the solid support of 65 Progressive members." Perhaps the most acute observer in Ottawa, J.K. Munro of *Maclean's Magazine*, argued that when Crerar came to see King after the election, Gouin had already ensured that there would be no alliance with the Farmers. As for Crerar, the cabinet question was secondary. He wrote to Cameron afterward: "I have been subjected to a good deal of criticism because I even considered any suggestion from King. It does not worry me in the slightest. If King had adhered to his original programme I think I would have gone in anyway. As for the future, we shall have to wait on events."[27] The most immediate issue would be the role of the Progressives in the new Parliament.

With sixty-five members of the House of Commons, the Progressives could have claimed the position of Official Opposition, but they did not. The usual explanation has been their inexperience and their inability or unwillingness to act cohesively. While both factors affected the situation, it was not nearly that simple, especially in Crerar's mind. There were other, more important, elements involved. Neither Crerar nor King had completely abandoned hope for some future arrangement. Crerar's conception of the party system and parliamentary stability influenced him greatly. And above all, there was the desirability of certain public policies that had brought the Farmers into politics in the first place.

Despite his disagreement with Crerar, W.C. Good was not far off the mark when he reflected that Crerar "honestly believed that the two-party set-up or system was the best, and that we would be well advised to get back to it as soon as we could ... [T]he Progressives should go into the Liberal Party, drive out the reactionary Liberals, and create a new Liberal Party."[28] Rather surprisingly, given the conventional interpretation, Henry Spencer, MP, a future member of the Ginger Group, blamed Crerar for not forcing the issue: "We had the right to be the official Opposition. Crerar at that time advised us not to be. I think now that was a great mistake, that it would have been a great thing for us to be the official Opposition." This stance at least rejects the balance-of-power strategy that many radical Progressives were said to favour and which Crerar explicitly condemned in a speech to the United Farmers of Manitoba convention after the election. The *Canadian Forum* had endorsed such a policy, arguing strangely that it would have the effect of driving Grits and Tories together. Paul Sharp, in *Agrarian Revolt*, somehow persuaded himself that because Crerar could think only in terms of legislative objectives, the Progressives were "wedded to a balance of power concept."[29]

The historical record, however, is not so contradictory. In early 1922 Crerar was primarily concerned with the legislation to be advanced by the new government. King's program, drawn substantially from the Liberal convention of 1919, was encouraging. And there were signs of his willingness to accede to some of the Progressives' legislative wishes. Not only was King now making conciliatory speeches, but a direct overture came from Fielding, the new finance minister, who regretted "that you are not with us. But while officially I have no right to ask your assistance, I wish to say that I am still anxious to be favoured with your help ... in matters to which western folk attach importance."[30] It may be that the Liberals feared the result if the Progressives became the Official Opposition, since that might necessarily limit cooperation, threaten King's minority position, and build in a structural rigidity that might thwart any future union.

Crerar seems to have made up his mind on the party's role at least by mid-January 1922. In a personal and private letter to an old friend in Neepawa, he pointed out: "If we become the Official Opposition we are expected to oppose. If we fail to do that and support the government when it is right, Meighen, whether he occupied the position of Official Opposition or not, would come to be so regarded in the country." And there was also the inexperience of his new members. He continued: "[I]t is difficult for a man who is past middle life, and has had little or no public experience, to adapt himself effectively to the requirements of Parliament. I think, then, that the best place for our group is on the side lines."[31]

What remained unresolved for Crerar was the vital question of legislation, and he expected the Liberals to move in his direction. When the new Parliament opened, the Progressives had several meetings to consider their options. Their most immediate concerns were the tariff, the Crow's Nest rates, and Canada's relations with Britain. He later summed up the situation neatly for Grant Dexter:

It was clear that if the new Liberal Government under King moved substantially in the direction of tariff reductions, we would not be opposing them but would be supporting them. Likewise, if they decided to let the Crow's Nest pass rates be restored when the statutory limitation of three years had expired, we would also be supporting them; and also if they moved to a really Liberal position in the matter of Canada's relations vis-a-vis Great Britain, we would be supporting them. We expected that in all these matters if the Government took a forward position, the Conservatives would be opposing them. It can thus be seen that as an Official Opposition the Progressives would have been in an impossible position.[32]

It is also very possible, of course, that the Progressives as a party would never have accepted the discipline inherent in being Official Opposition, and disintegration would have been immediate. Crerar thought it necessary to nurture his forces: "While I think we have a few men who will develop good ability, the great majority will be ordinary, some of them perhaps very ordinary, members. If we become the Official Opposition we are expected to oppose."[33]

That status for his party made little sense to him in such a divided House. When Crerar spoke in the throne speech debate in early March, King must have been pleased indeed to hear him say that the Progressives intended to further their own principles, and not to oppose the government for the sake of opposing.[34] Crerar's disclaimer allowed his Progressive colleagues to plunge into the proceedings with much enthusiasm and few inhibitions. J.K. Munro informed *Maclean's* readers: "[E]very gap in the conversation finds a Farmer to fill it. The end of the first awful week showed that the sixty-five devoted followers of the Hired Man's Hero [Crerar] had furnished fifty per cent of the speakers while a score of others has scented the battle at close quarters and were displaying symptoms of a great desire to get in closer and garner a mouthful for themselves."[35]

Despite Munro's amusement, the session of 1922 would be the only one at which the new Progressive party could look back with any sense of accomplishment. The House grappled with issues of central concern to its very presence in politics, but the struggle also exposed its internal incoherence and, in the end, contributed to Crerar's resignation as leader.

The Progressives' one conspicuous success was restoration of the Crow's Nest rates. The origin of the issue dated back to 1897. In order to pre-empt any further extension of American mining and railway interests into western Canada, the Laurier government agreed in that year to subsidize expansion of the CPR into the Crow's Nest Pass area of southwestern Alberta and southeastern British Columbia. In return, the CPR guaranteed a flat rate, in perpetuity, for transporting prairie grain to Lake Superior, as well as lowered rates for carrying settlers' effects to the west. The new Canadian Northern Railway of William Mackenzie and Donald Mann, with its bonds guaranteed by the Manitoba government in return for regulated rates, lowered even further freight rates on grain moving eastward.

The CPR, not surprisingly, had never been happy with the arrangement. During the Great War, the Crow Rate (as it was popularly known) was suspended by order-in-council, but it was to come back into effect automatically in the summer of 1922, unless otherwise determined by Parliament. The CPR (and the Canadian National, for that matter) sought to make the suspension permanent; the Progressives were equally committed to protecting what the westerners considered by this time almost a birthright – a justifiable trade-off for the benefits that central Canada gained from the protective tariff. "I have let it be known," Crerar wrote to an old friend, "that as far as the Progressives are concerned we will oppose as strongly as we can the setting aside of this agreement for any further period."[36]

The CPR offered a package of reduced rates across the country in return for abolition of the Crow Rate. Presumably this would attract enough central and eastern MPs, perhaps even a few Ontario Progressives, to carry the day.[37] The issue was referred to a special committee of the House, which included Crerar, Hudson, and three Liberals who turned out to be key players – Malcolm (South Bruce), Euler (Waterloo), and Cahill (Pontiac). The CPR's case was supported by the other Liberals and the Tory members of the committee, which wrangled for a month to little purpose. Crerar finally proposed a compromise that attracted the three sympathetic Liberals: reinstate the Crow Rate on grain but deregulate the other rates on goods moving west. His motion was lost to the casting vote of the committee's chairman.

The question would now turn on the attitude of King and the Liberal caucus. It was described as the stormiest caucus in years; the lines were drawn sharply between Gouin and his colleagues and those Liberals who resented and were determined to resist Gouin's influence and sought better relations with the Progressives. King intervened with his view that Crerar's compromise was the only realistic solution. A combination of low-tariff Liberals from southwestern Ontario and some from eastern Quebec and the Maritimes routed Gouin and the "Montreal crowd." They refused, it was said, to be dictated to by the railways.[38] The possibility of an alliance between these Liberals and the Progressives was again much talked about. But the outcome on the Crow Rate was the high point of the session for the Progressives.

Another vital issue was re-establishment of a compulsory Wheat Board. Crerar was not in favour of a national, compulsory system for marketing wheat; he regarded it as impractical and found the compulsory aspect offensive. But the steady decline in wheat prices during 1920 and 1921 made the idea attractive to many western farmers. The government had controlled marketing after 1917, established by order-in-council under the government's emergency powers as a result of centralized purchasing by the British government on behalf of itself and its allies. Because of wartime conditions, Canadian producers enjoyed a high price for all the wheat they could produce, guaranteed by the dominion of Canada.

But neither the government of the day, nor King's, had any intention of being in the wheat business permanently. It was simply assumed that the open market would return as soon as possible. For one year after the war the government had had a Wheat Board handle the transition until the private markets reopened. There was little possibility, however, that the high prices of the war period would continue, and the postwar depression made the guaranteed prices of the old Wheat Board look better than ever. Consequently, in the session of 1922, Crerar and the Progressives were under great pressure to have the board re-established. It proved a divisive battle.

The Canadian Council of Agriculture's (CCA's) proposal for a new Wheat Board was taken to the House by the government and sent to the Agriculture Committee. There it was stalled and, according to Henry Wise Wood's biographer, "the government, with Crerar's support sought to sidetrack the whole question by referring the constitutionality of the proposed bill to the Supreme Court of Canada, but the Progressive members of the Committee, aided by the Conservatives, rejected this suggestion."[39] The implication is not entirely fair. Indeed, Crerar urged Lambert, secretary of the CCA, to prepare the strongest case possible to present to the committee in favour of the proposal and gave him several useful suggestions to entice the necessary support from beyond the Progressive group on the committee. To his colleague Jim Murray at United Grain Growers, he expressed the hope that "Lambert is aware that I am working for the re-establishment of the Wheat Board."[40] It was, however, a reluctant commitment and would never have extended itself to include a compulsory board.

The question that bedevilled the committee's hearings concerned whether or not Parliament had the power to establish such a Wheat Board, now that wartime emergency powers had lapsed. Enforcement of civil contracts had always been a jealously guarded right of the provinces. Government members of the standing committee had suggested that the question be referred to the law officers of the crown for opinion. Crerar argued that this might be inconclusive and preferred to "have a stated case placed before the Supreme Court and a decision handed down that would have some finality to it." He was apparently supported in this view by the Progressive caucus, and the Agriculture Committee gave its unanimous agreement.

When the recommendation went to the House, Meighen opposed it, claiming that it would mean interminable delay – an argument that drew the agreement of some of the Progressives and Henry Wise Wood, who was in Ottawa at the time – and Lambert, less directly, also opposed it. Crerar, very unhappily, concurred in sending the issue back to the committee, as suggested by King.[41]

There was some very plain speaking in the Progressive caucus next morning. Crerar pointed out that if the party forced the issue on the government, disaster might follow. The result might be defeat of the government, "another election at once, no Wheat Board, and the Government back with a majority which would enable it to carry on independent of the Progressives or anything else." The Wheat Board was of importance only to the west; for the rest of the House it was a local issue and, in the opinion of many, likely to result in higher prices for flour and bread. Crerar said: "It is quite enough to get carping letters from people forty miles from the railway in Saskatchewan or Alberta. One looks for that, but hardly from Norman [Lambert], or from H.W. Wood either."[42]

On the recommendation of the Agriculture Committee, the government endorsed enabling legislation that allowed any two of the prairie provinces to pass legislation to set up a Wheat Board themselves. Alberta and Saskatchewan did so (Manitoba later refused), but they were unable to find anyone competent and willing to run it, and the scheme foundered. Crerar took much of the public blame in the west.[43]

In private, there seems to have been considerable relief at the outcome. Neither Premier Dunning in Saskatchewan nor A.J. McPhail of the Saskatchewan Grain Growers expressed much regret. According to Dafoe, Crerar was probably "quite pleased that the scheme blew up; and that he is no more pleased than Premier Dunning, Premier Greenfield, most of the farm leaders and most of the Progressive M.P.s."[44] As Dunning put it to Motherwell, a Saskatchewan Liberal and King's minister of agriculture, "on a falling market the farmers would never believe the Board had honestly dealt with them" – a position with which Crerar agreed.[45]

But the failure to achieve the Wheat Board was the occasion for the drawing away of that stubborn band of Progressives who owed their allegiance to Henry Wise Wood, rather than to Crerar or, of course, to the Progressives or to any other party.

The end of the session was to bring Crerar little respite. Though he took no direct hand in the Manitoba election of early summer 1922, he was not able to distance himself completely from its implications.

The United Farmers of Manitoba (UFM) conducted what turned out to be the last great incursion of the grain growers into political action, but it did so without a recognized leader. As early as March, Crerar's name had been mentioned as a possible leader and, assuming victory, next premier. He expressed little interest in the position and open hostility to the suggestion that any resulting government be organized on the basis of group representation. "I am going to fight the group idea of Wood and Morrison, and fight it without gloves on." He greatly feared that it would do infinite harm to the Progressive cause outside the prairie west.

In the event, the UFM won a plurality and could hardly reject the responsibility of forming a government. According to Dafoe, "the first thing the farmers did was to ask Crerar to come and give them a little advice. Thereafter they tendered the leadership to Professor [John] Bracken." While his opinion may not have been the critical factor – Bracken was available and Crerar was not – the latter certainly approved of the choice.[46]

The national field was, if anything, more ambivalent. The initial curiosity about the avalanche of Progressives onto the Ottawa scene was giving way to a sense of impending collapse. The agrarian impulse might prove remarkably short-lived. As J.K. Munro remarked, "Crerar is liked generally, and sympathized with by many. For his trials are greater than those of Job of old. Like our biblical friend, he suffers from boils, while unlike the latter, he has to lead sixty-five Progressives and of these it has been said that they 'do their progressing by jumping sideways.'" The image was becoming widespread. Roebuck sent his good wishes from Toronto when there was a minor Progressive split concerning the budget, commiserating " ... with the great difficulties under which you labor with your unlicked crew. They remind me of the deck-hands of H.M.S. Pinafore who expected their orders sugar-coated with an 'if you please.'"[47] It was all very dispiriting, and Crerar's resolution was waning. The intervention of an external crisis, however, would quickly refocus his attention.

When Turkish troops in the summer of 1922 menaced the British garrison at Chanak in Asia Minor, the British government, without any warning, called on the dominions for support. King immediately summoned Crerar and Hudson to Ottawa. They and almost all the Progressives supported King's stand against any participation in European affairs. Indeed, all three considered the issue so important that it might be the occasion to bring the two parties together. But it would have to be on King's terms. He was more than willing to bring Crerar into the cabinet, but he refused to drop Gouin, which

Crerar had made an absolute condition.[48] Discussion dragged on for two weeks, the emergency passed, and the chance was lost.

A final, and ultimately decisive, worry for Crerar that summer was his relationship with United Grain Growers (UGG). The virtual collapse of wheat prices in 1920–21 had placed severe strains on the company, and while it did not miss paying a dividend, it was dipping into its reserves rather heavily. Crerar was being pressed either to return to his position as manager, which UGG preferred, or step aside for someone else. It could be fairly said that he had built UGG, and he was deeply interested in its continuing success, especially in view of the rising challenge of the pooling movement. The prospect of remaining as leader of "that restless and unreliable band" (as W.L. Morton described the parliamentary Progressives) on the salary of an ordinary MP was not all that attractive. In addition, as he wrote to Cameron, the "possibility of any Liberal-Progressive alliance coming to fruition in the near future is, I think, remote."[49] The discussions with King at the time of Chanak seemed confirmation enough.

In mid-October 1922, Crerar set out for Winnipeg to attend a critical meeting of the board of United Grain Growers. En route, he received news that his younger daughter, eight-year-old Audrey, had died suddenly of diphtheria. It took the heart out of him. Still in shock, he wrote his friend Cameron that he had no will to go on in public life at present.[50] He resigned the leadership of the Progressive party a week later. It was not any single issue, but the total of all these factors – the state of the Progressives, his position in the company, and his grief at Audrey's death – that induced him to resign. He found much support and sympathy from his friends in the Winnipeg Sanhedrin. But Dafoe "did not think it means in the least the elimination of Crerar from politics."[51]

PART THREE

Working from Winnipeg, 1922–34

Crerar in 1924. Courtesy Archives and Special Collections, Dafoe Library, University of Manitoba

CHAPTER SEVEN

Wheat Pools and the Home Bank, 1922–25

In both private correspondence and public comment, there was much sympathy because of Audrey's death but little note of finality about Crerar's resignation as Progressive leader. The prime minister was certainly not disheartened. He confided to his diary that it meant the end of the Progressives as a separate party and added, perhaps hopefully, that Crerar's announcement "was a very good, fair & honorable one. I spoke well of him in interviews given the press." *Maclean's* columnist J.K. Munro summed up Crerar's year as leader quite defiantly:

He refused to be diverted from his purpose by the minions of H.W. Wood who bore down on Ottawa howling for a Wheat Board. Nobody knew better than Crerar that any kind of a Wheat Board Montreal would give to the West would not be worth paying the freight on. Nobody knew better than Crerar that with Sir Lomer Gouin helping the little grey Nova Scotian [Fielding] to make his budget any concessions in the tariff wouldn't yield enough money to buy a Christmas box for the hired man. The freight rates were his one and only choice, so he waited – and he won. That means millions of dollars in the pockets of western farmers – and just because Tom Crerar concentrated on one thing and got it.

While he claimed that his own plans were indefinite, Crerar acceded to the request of his constituents and did not resign his seat in the Commons, even though "it would be impossible for me to be in the House more than a few days this Session ... [F]or the next year or so anyway I must give my attention pretty much undivided to our business here."[1]

There were two problems facing Crerar when he resumed the active presidency of United Grain Growers (UGG) – the immediate financial position of the company and the more general question of the future of wheat marketing in Canada. The two were, of course, inextricably related. The price of wheat, which had stood at $2.82 per bushel in September 1920, had suffered a long, frightening slide to $1.11 per bushel in December 1921. The decline prompted great pressure from the shareholders and directors of UGG for Crerar's return. It had also occasioned, as noted above, a demand for establishment of a new Wheat Board, which had failed of realization.

The situation at UGG was serious but certainly not desperate. Early in his tenure, Crerar had insisted on creation and maintenance of a substantial financial reserve, a policy that now served the enterprise well. When the profit-and-loss statement for the crop year ending 31 August 1922 was approved, it had been necessary to draw on the contingency reserve for $100,000 and to write back $158,312.10 of depreciation charges. Even so, the company showed a loss that year of $118,350.31 and for the only time that decade had to forgo paying the customary 8 per cent dividend.[2]

Part of the difficulty, however, was managerial. In addition to the parent company with its several departments, there were six subsidiaries of which Crerar had been, at least nominally, president. Thus "it is an easy thing," he wrote Cameron, "for a big business institution to travel a good distance on the toboggan slide if once it starts." According to Dafoe, this structure made UGG "particularly subject to internal friction and there has been a lot of this during the past few years while Crerar has had his attention concentrated upon politics. It looks as though Crerar is the only man who can administer this company." It seems that the shareholders and directors agreed. He received such a resounding welcome at the annual meeting in Calgary in late November that he felt that "his position had never been stronger."[3]

Crerar's first move was to take control of the grain and supply end of the business, leaving the acting general manager to handle the livestock, securities, and sawmill operations. Later in 1923, he also resumed the general manager's duties and took full control of the company's many interests.[4] It does not seem to have taken him very long to turn matters around, which indicates probably the essential soundness of UGG and the fact that the agricultural depression of the early 1920s was drawing to an end. By late February 1923, he felt that "we have recovered pretty well from the reverses of last year and expect this season the Company will have a very good result." It was a matter of considerable satisfaction. While commenting on Crerar's reawakening political interest, Dafoe informed Sifton: "He has pulled the United Grain Growers out of the hole in which it found itself and is, I think, very happy in being able to concentrate upon its management." But, he went on, Crerar "is by no means out of politics and is constantly consulted on matters of Progressive policy."[5]

The end of the crop year brought confirmation. The largest wheat crop ever – upward of 450 million bushels – was harvested across the prairies. Prices had advanced modestly, and a smaller-than-average American crop made Canadian prospects that much better. Farmers were still cautious and still mightily concerned about marketing problems. But when the representatives of the 36,000 shareholders of UGG gathered in November for the annual meeting, Crerar described the year "as the most successful in every way in our whole experience." Volume of grain handled was well up, and profits for the year were over $500,000. The corner clearly had been turned.[6]

Despite his popular image as a prairie Progressive, Crerar's business ability did not go unnoticed. Indeed, it caused him some embarrassment. In September 1924, Vincent Massey invited him to join the board of directors of Massey-Harris of Canada. One can only imagine the discussion on tariff protection that might have occurred with Crerar present on such a board. He politely declined the invitation, but it was not the only one that he received. He felt obliged to take the matter up with his board at UGG, informing it that he "had several opportunities in the past year to go on Directorships of other Companies, – a Trust Company, a Bank, Life Insurance Company and an 'Implement Manufacturing concern.'" The board was divided on the issue, and Crerar did not push it, simply indicating that at some future time he might wish to accept such an offer and would consult the board again.[7]

The board was quite adamant, however, on the matter of Crerar's political career. It very much feared a repetition of the attacks of 1921 on the company and was convinced that the business had suffered as a result. In addition, the shareholders included supporters of all political parties, and for Crerar to become publicly identified with any party could have obvious and unfortunate repercussions. Thus Crerar spent little time in the House for the balance of that Parliament and, at the insistence of the board, took little part in the election of 1925, in which he declined to run.[8]

As we see below, the muzzle was effective only on Crerar's public, political activities. But he was also deeply engaged during these years with a potential threat to the company from another front. Failure of the attempt to re-establish the Wheat Board in 1922 had sparked interest in a new marketing phenomenon on the prairies – the pooling movement.

There had been some discussion of the technique of pooling in the grain growers' locals and in the *Guide*, but the critical moment came in the autumn of 1922. Price recovery had not yet begun, and the farmers had to accept the disappointing news that there would be no new Wheat Board. Crerar was urging that cooperation could accomplish more than any government board. Yet many of the grain growers set out to do for themselves what the government had declined to do – create an alternative to the futures marketing system and the influence of the private grain trade.

Enter Aaron Sapiro, the hot-gospeller of the pooling movement. He was much like E.A. Partridge, the first charismatic leader of the western farmers – energetic, innovative, glib, and utterly fearless. But he had many of Partridge's less admirable traits as well – a consuming ego, a mercurial temper, and an inability to translate ideas, however inspired, into practical administration. But Sapiro's reputation as a successful organizer of commodity pools in the United States and his dynamic, indeed evangelical campaign style had a messianic impact. He turned up first in Ottawa, where his enthusiasm for the pooling cause impressed Prime Minister King, but not to a point where King was willing to concede Sapiro's request for government guarantees for a line of credit for the pools. But he wished him well on his trip "to the west to speak on the subject at the instance of Crerar & others."[9]

Initially, Sapiro went from strength to strength and received an enthusiastic response wherever he appeared. Support for a wheat pool was building quickly, despite the often-negative aspect of the exhortations.[10] Attacking the Winnipeg Grain Exchange, Canadian home of the open market, and particularly trading in wheat futures, became a central feature of the campaign to drum up support for the pooling technique. The futures market clearly protected grain buyers, millers, and to some degree even consumers by hedging the risks of a fluctuating grain price. Producers would also benefit, despite Sapiro's rhetoric, since buyers, with risks diminished, could afford to offer a higher initial price. They could do so only because their purchases and their sales were hedged – that is, grain dealers used futures to protect themselves against rises and declines in the world price.

It was not a case, as Sapiro charged, of buying low when farmers were forced to sell and then enjoying an unearned increment. Two royal commissions on grain marketing demonstrated that the price spread between autumn and spring sales of wheat was equal to the costs of storage and carrying charges. The grain grower may be forgiven for missing this advantage in a marketing process that could not function without a significant degree of speculation, which provided the necessary liquidity. But this was theory; what actually happened was more interesting. In condemning speculation, grain growers also eschewed hedging as a legitimate business tool to reduce risk in an uncontrollable world marketplace. The repercussions would be dramatic.

The main features of a commodity pool are not complex. Producers agree by contract for a fixed period of time to deliver all their crop to the pool. In return, they receive an initial payment, based on the pool's expectation of the world price for the crop year; an interim payment, usually just before seeding time; and a final payment, when the year's business has been concluded and final accounts have been rendered. The total figure is the average price received over the year minus the costs of handling the operation. Financing was done through the chartered banks, the major requirement being the cash for the initial payment, which was secured by the contracts held by the pool. The pool would of course require an extensive elevator system as well.

It all sounded simple enough – deceptively simple. Producers everywhere in the pool area would receive the same price for the same grade over the whole crop year. The traditional rush to market, which allegedly so distorted supply, would be replaced by orderly marketing. And it was assumed that the pool would quickly create a central selling agency for direct sales both at home and abroad, thus eliminating at least two sets of middlemen. But there remained dangerous ambiguities and important unresolved problems.

First, for any possibility of success a commodity pool must sign up a significant number of producers in a geographic area; the considered viable minimum was at least half. So a dispute quickly arose between proponents of a voluntary pool and those who argued for a 100 per cent compulsory pool, enforced by legislation. This was much more than an economic question. Second, there does not seem to have been any consensus on the meaning of the term "orderly marketing." At its simplest, it ensured regular distribution of deliveries and sales over the year, intended to achieve a satisfactory average price for pool members. But to others, it meant matching supply to demand at best advantage – price manipulation through controlled selling, or so-called supply-side economics at its crudest level. It also entailed the undesirable likelihood of carry-overs. In both senses, it meant at least cooperative marketing. But there were already two successful farmer-owned companies in the field, with chains of elevators and their own experienced selling agencies. Third, success would depend upon the skill of pool managers and especially the central selling agency in predicting grain prices and achieving large, regular sales without hedging. But whatever the doubts and potential pitfalls, the pool movement would have its day.

In July 1923, the Canadian Council of Agriculture met to consider the implications of the prairie provinces' failure to establish a new Wheat Board. There seemed to be no alternative left but cooperative action of some kind, and the pooling technique touted by Sapiro offered a chance to escape the clutches of the private grain trade. At the meeting, Crerar proposed a prairie-wide voluntary pool based on short-term contracts. He offered the proven experience of his company, its extensive elevator chain, its selling agency, and its considerable financial strength to help to launch the project.[11]

But his scheme was a non-starter, even though he was willing to envisage the eventual take-over and disappearance of UGG by a flourishing pool such as he had proposed. The Saskatchewan Co-operative Elevator Company would not face such a prospect with comparable equanimity. And there were other difficulties. Crerar's liberal instincts set him against a compulsory pool, which he found inherently offensive, and against long-term contracts, which he deemed unnecessary.

Practically, the scheme foundered on the rock of internecine Saskatchewan quarrelling, which by now seemed endemic. Growing anger was marshalled by the fledgling Farmers' Union of Canada (FUC), Saskatchewan Section, and directed against the more-than-cosy relationship among the Saskatchewan Grain Growers' Association, the Saskatchewan Co-operative Elevator Company (SCEC), and the Liberal provincial government, with their overlapping leadership and interests. The FUC crowd, with a fine sense of non-discrimination, also disliked the farmers' commercial companies, as well as Crerar, and hated the Winnipeg Grain Exchange. It was largely its animosity that accounts for the persisting notion that Crerar was implacably opposed to the pooling movement. He wasn't; but he did oppose compulsion and government regulation of the marketplace.

In the event, three separate and voluntary provincial pools were organized – with UGG financial aid – and, at least in Alberta, a government guarantee. They combined to form a Central Selling Agency (CSA) with a seat on the Winnipeg Grain Exchange (paid for by UGG) under the managerial control of A.J. McPhail and experienced grain traders helpfully supplied by UGG. The direct selling policy of the pools was implemented through a network of agencies that grew quickly to twenty-eight offices in fifteen countries. Within three years the CSA was handling over 50 per cent of the prairie wheat crop, which made up two-fifths of the world export total. After a brief but lively fling with coexistence, Saskatchewan Pool took over the SCEC and all its elevators. UGG, after some hesitation, declined very properly to sell its chain of elevators to the pools when they refused to agree to handle non-pool grain, thus freezing out UGG members, of whom many chose not to join the provincial pools.

The pools appeared to be off to a flying start, but all was not rosy. McPhail fought a continuing and draining rearguard action against the ideologues of the FUC, who sought a 100 per cent compulsory pool and castigated McPhail and the CSA for their limited (but timely) use of the futures market. The most enthusiastic supporters of the pools, and specifically those who recruited and signed members to contracts, raised expectations unduly with their inflated claims. Formation of the pools, they boasted, would immediately raise the world price by 10 cents per bushel. They bravely, and foolishly, implied that once the pools were firmly established their great market influence would ensure prosperity for all prairie grain growers.

During the first three full years of pool operations – crop years 1925–26 to 1927–28 inclusive – there were few clouds to cool their ardour. The pools on average handled over half the prairie wheat crop, at prices of $1.45, $1.42, and $1.4225 per bushel, respectively. While gratifying, the prices were a far cry from those of the war years, though that was hardly the fault of the pools. Not surprisingly, there were fierce debates, often based on extremely dubious figures, about whether pool or non-pool growers were better off. They were, of course, quite inconclusive. Total producer income, however, was high for those three crop years, largely because of world conditions – a stable gold price, heavy European imports, high levels of international investment, and heavy yields on the prairies – none of these the doing of the pools, either. Only in the first year was the CSA obliged to protect its margin with the banks by entering the futures market, and then only briefly, albeit effectively.[12] But even that brought howls of protest from the purists.

But there were other factors that ought to have been considered and should have prompted a greater degree of caution, even though McPhail's selling policy could hardly have been considered radical. In order to get as much cash into the hands of their members as soon as possible, the pools operated on very narrow projections of the spread between initial and final price. The only charges that the CSA levied against the final price were for administrative expenses, which were kept admirably low; for a special reserve of 2 cents per bushel, to meet the costs of elevator purchases and construction, which were extensive; and for a commercial reserve of only 1 per cent, which would prove completely inadequate in a crisis. All the pool grain was unhedged and thus immediately vulnerable to fluctuations in the world price.

Pool supporters argued that their system of initial, interim, and final payments over the crop year was itself a sufficient hedge against price variation and adequate to maintain the required margin of 15 cents per bushel with the banks that supplied the credit. True enough, though this was so only if the world price remained relatively stable. But the pools, with roughly 20 per cent of current world export production, were not in a position to ensure a stable price themselves by managing the flow of grain to market. And their narrow spread would then be put in grave danger if price fluctuation occurred.

In addition, wheat was a difficult commodity to control effectively by pooling, unlike, for example, raisins, the supply of which could be closely managed. Wheat could be grown in any of the temperate zones of the world. Rising demand or sharp price increases could bring a vast acreage into production from Canada's major competitors, such as the United States, Argentina, and Australia, or even occasional exporters such as the Soviet Union, which, desperate for hard currencies, was at the time dumping wheat on the European market. Those importing countries of Europe, as well, were under increasing pressure from their own farmers to protect their position against foreign imports by tariffs, quotas, or other trade restrictions.

The stable prices of the mid-1920s masked the danger that the pools' selling policy, while virtuously avoiding the speculators in the futures market, constituted a gigantic and unprotected speculation on the cash market. A sharp downward price break could erode their reserves, wipe out their margin with the banks, and throw them into chaos. Their testing time was not far in the future; but in the meantime they were a stern challenge to the stability of UGG.

Crerar was also facing an additional challenge, which dated back to the origins of the company and its early banking arrangements. His identification with the Home Bank lasted long after he had severed his relationship with that troubled institution. United Grain Growers and the Home Bank had grown up together in the prairie west, and both had been seen as upstarts, challenging the large banks and the private grain trade. For several years, the arrangement that Partridge had negotiated back in 1908 had been mutually satisfactory, and the two institutions seemed equally to flourish. And from the very beginning the reputation of the bank drew heavily on the credibility of Crerar and the company. "This is no fakir's scheme," announced A.B. Hudson, then solicitor to UGG, "but a sound, safe, profitable investment ... I advise every western farmer to take stock in the home bank of Canada."[13] They did by the hundreds. So also did UGG, Crerar, and other officials of the company. What they did not, and perhaps could not, know was that the Home Bank was, at least according to one analyst, rotten from its inception.

The Home Bank had developed from the relatively prosperous Savings and Loan Bank established by the Catholic bishop of Toronto in the mid-nineteenth century. It subsequently fell into the hands of Colonel James Mason and his militia crony Sir Henry Pellatt at the turn of the century. After incorporation in 1903 with dubious secu-rity, the Home Bank doubled its capital stock in 1907 without the necessary authorization from the Department of Finance, and the whole share issue was technically illegal. The following year the fatal arrangement was made with the Grain Growers.[14] When the bank eventually failed in 1923, Crerar was immediately accused of all manner of heinous crime, and there is some evidence that the attacks were politically motivated.

When news of the bank's collapse began to circulate in May 1923, Cameron wrote rather excitedly to Crerar that it was being claimed that, in return for promoting sale of bank stock among western farm-ers, Crerar had received 125 shares of stock, which he later sold for $12,500,00 and that he had used his position as a director of the bank to advise UGG to unload its stock before the bank failed. "You may be sure nothing will be left neglected that will in any way contribute to your undoing," he warned his friend.[15] Crerar took the news phlegmatically, commenting: "The Home Bank failure was very unfortunate. Many of our staff, including myself and Mr. Kennedy [vice-president of UGG] had money on deposit there."[16] But Crerar's reputation was to suffer more than his bank account before the affair was laid to rest.

The dominion government quickly came under pressure from angry depositors and stockholders. In January 1924, Crerar wrote to James Robb, acting minister of finance, pointing out that there might be at least "a moral obligation upon the government, in view of the representations that were made to Sir Thomas White [then finance minister] in 1916 by the three western directors," of whom Crerar was one.[17] The government's response was to set up a commission of inquiry under Judge McKeown of Nova Scotia to consider all aspects of the bank failure. Extensive hearings took place in Win-nipeg in May 1924.

In view of the widespread concern among bank stockholders on the prairies, Crerar's testimony about the relationship of himself and UGG to the Home Bank attracted considerable interest and was followed closely by the press.[18] The company held about one thousand shares of Home Bank stock, and Crerar himself had purchased sixty-six shares on the open market at $133 per share. In 1910, Crerar, John Kennedy, and John Persse of Winnipeg, who had no connection with the grain growers, were made directors and responsible for western operations of the bank. They seldom attended board meetings, which were held in Toronto.

After 1911, the company ceased to act as sales agent for bank stock in the west. The Winnipeg manager of the bank, W.M. MacHaffie, continued to work closely with the western directors and, late in 1914, informed them that he was very distressed at the bank's loan practices. Together, they forced a reference to Sir Thomas White, who appointed Zebulon Lash to investigate the bank's affairs. Cosmetic changes that resulted – including appointment of Mason's son as general manager – did not correct the offending lending policies approved by the eastern members of the board, who constituted a majority.[19]

When he entered the Union government in late 1917, Crerar resigned his directorship, since, as he announced, he felt that no cabinet minister should sit on the board of a bank. Kennedy had resigned the preceding year because he was unable to attend director's meetings in Toronto. In 1916, as well, UGG became unhappy with the Home Bank's attempt to limit its line of credit. The company switched its account to the Union Bank and sold off its Home Bank shares in 1918–19 (when the Home Bank seemed to be doing well) to raise money for elevator construction. Crerar sold part of his holdings in 1919 and the balance early in 1923 – at a loss, he claimed – before there was any public indication of trouble. His personal bank account remained with the Home Bank. The difficulty for Crerar was that none of this was known to most of the hundreds of farmers in the west who had purchased Home Bank shares. What they remembered was that their company had encouraged them to buy, then later sold out its own holdings without informing the membership.[20] Much of the odium became attached to Crerar personally and was great ammunition for the Farmers Union and the more vociferous of the pool supporters.

The *Winnipeg Tribune* in particular harried Crerar endlessly about his connection with the Home Bank, implying that he had both profited from his directorship and misled the membership of the company. Early in 1925, after an especially nasty attack, he wrote a long, angry letter to the editor of the *Tribune*, setting out in detail the whole history of the relationship of the bank to the grain growers. But sensibly, he accepted the advice of Dafoe and Symington and never sent the missive. They claimed that it would do little good and only keep the controversy alive.[21] The issue would not die easily, however; rather it festered away and was used effectively by the Tories in the election of 1930, as we see below. Despite his retirement from the Progressive leadership and his preoccupation with the affairs of UGG, Crerar had never really left politics.

The letter of resignation that Crerar had addressed in November 1922 to T.W. Caldwell, chairman of the Progressive caucus, had run to nineteen pages. Cited as the primary factor was his obligation to UGG, but Crerar was not satisfied to leave it at that. He re-examined the difficulties of the Progressives in the parliamentary session of 1922 and offered his diagnosis of the movement's political ills and his prescription for the future. Norman Lambert was sure that it had been drawn up with the aid of Hudson and Dafoe, but the latter told Sifton that, while he had been shown the letter the day prior to its release, it had been written by Crerar himself: "He had made up his mind that it was necessary to force a showdown in various directions and this letter was the result ... [H]e believes that in some respects he will have more freedom to make suggestions than when he, as leader of the party, had to placate various factions." In particular, Dafoe went on, "he is planning to make things pretty warm during the next year or so for Mr. H.W. Wood of Alberta." There was, Dafoe suspected, some element of calculation in his action.[22]

Without mentioning his personal and business reasons for resigning, Crerar informed Caldwell and the caucus that his continuance as leader was problematic in any case in the absence of a clear resolution to the vital question of whether the Progressives "shall descend into a purely class movement or not." The disappointing outcome of the election of 1921 was the result of "widespread fear in the hearts of thousands of electors in Canada, who were in general sympathy with [Progressive] policies, that it would become purely a class movement."

The blame for this he laid squarely at the feet of Morrison and Wood, whose views he considered impractical and irrelevant, respectively. Morrison's proposal was that farmers, where possible, should elect to Parliament one of their own, who should remain resolutely independent in order to be able to voice farmers' interests. This stance would lead nowhere, according to Crerar, since by remaining isolated they would be unable to influence legislation.

He considered Wood's ideas more baneful. It was not just that Wood was proposing representation in Parliament by occupational groups, which would presumably be able to act cooperatively to develop generally acceptable legislation – a proposition that Crerar found extremely dubious As well, the UFA was becoming more insistent that MPS be guided and directed by the UFA locals in their constituencies. That same right, Crerar argued, must logically be extended to all other constituencies in Canada. "You would have two hundred and thirty-five Members, each guided and directed by his constituents, some of whom were thousands of miles away, attempting to seriously carry on the work of Government. The absurdity of the thing requires no further comment." In classic Burkean terms, he insisted that an MP "is not a delegate from his constituency to act only as someone in it pulls the strings. He is a representative of the whole Dominion." He represents not only farmers or labour or business or professional men, but all of the electorate. Wood's visionary scheme, he concluded, would lead only to class antagonism, the very thing that Wood professed to deplore.

Turning to the future, Crerar asserted the need for the party to broaden out, to welcome all who shared its principles as applied to public policy. He argued as well for the absolute necessity of effective organization and adequate financing for the party's survival.

His advice on the policies to be pursued indicate some interesting developments from the Farmers' Platform on which the Progressives had fought the election of 1921. The most startling departure was that he now gave primacy of place to Canada's changed status in the world as a result of the war, which "made it forever impossible that this country can longer be regarded in any sense whatever in the colonial status." The new relationship with Britain must now be clearly defined by the Canadian Parliament: "Personally I do not subscribe to the doctrine that when Britain is at war Canada is at war." The only remaining bond was common allegiance to the sovereign. It would be for Parliament to decide what engagements the country should assume, and Crerar urged steady support for the League of Nations.

On fiscal policy, Crerar's ideas had matured greatly. He was no longer the doctrinaire free trader (though a tariff-free trading world would remain a dreamed-about nirvana), and he had quite abandoned his earlier notions of the importance of the Single Tax. The protective tariff, however, remained "unsound, unjust, and indefensible, and not in the best interests of Canada." The tariff must henceforth be based on the requirements of revenue, not on the principle of protection. But despite the need for revenue, he advised the Progressives to insist on free entry of implements and machinery for production in agriculture and other natural resources. His other suggestions included a fair trial for the national railway on a fair basis of capitalization, a system of proportional representation, and, even before the Home Bank mess, effective government inspection of the banks and perhaps some form of deposit insurance.

In concluding his long letter, Crerar referred to the cooperation the previous year between the Progressives and some of the Liberals, which had led to restoration of the Crow's Nest Pass rates. Such continuing work together, he pointed out, was stoutly resisted by the reactionary element in the Liberal party and by those Progressives who, from honest but mistaken motives, wished to see the movement rest on a class basis or who insisted that it must have no cooperation with any other group. He left the caucus to draw its own conclusion.[23]

There is little to indicate in Crerar's letter of resignation that he had lost interest in the future of the Progressives or that he planned to abandon political life. Norman Lambert, after reading the document, observed to Morrison that he reckoned that Crerar "appreciates the situation fully, and in getting out at the present time, anticipates the breaking up of the present Progressive party and the absorption of it into both of the old parties, thus clearing the way for himself to return at a later date to the House of Commons as possibly a member of a new Liberal Government."[24] He was not far off the mark.

CHAPTER EIGHT

Rethinking Canada, 1923–24

While Crerar stuck pretty close to his desk at United Grain Growers in Winnipeg in 1923 and 1924, he had not lost any of his keen interest in public affairs. In particular, he devoted what spare time he had to considering the national status of Canada in the aftermath of the Great War. His thinking was shaped by his brief membership in the Union cabinet, Canada's entry into the League of Nations, and the shock of the recent crisis over Chanak, but even more by his business experience in the west.

Despite his support for the war and Union government, he had never been much of an imperialist, and he had crafted the clause in the Farmers' Platform that looked forward to greater Canadian autonomy. The Chanak affair had galvanized many, including Clifford Sifton, who went hareing off on a round of Canadian Club speeches, urging an unambiguous declaration by the House of Commons that Canada was no longer to be associated with British policies. He clearly hoped that Crerar would be his parliamentary champion, if not his stalking horse, but Crerar was not prepared to go that far. There was no doubt where Dafoe stood on the issue, and the Sanhedrin in Winnipeg often discussed the long-term implications of Sir Robert Borden's initiatives taken during and after the war.

The western grain growers, as we have seen, had been chastised more than once by the *Round Table* for their lack of enthusiasm for imperial solidarity. Hence Crerar, Dafoe, and Sifton were regarded as an insidious cabal, seducing Canadians from their proper allegiance.[1] But if the three were in advance of English-Canadian opinion, they were not that badly out of step, and they were determined. In December 1922, Dafoe informed Sifton of "the hullabaloo that followed Crerar's statement about Canada & imperial wars" at a public meeting in Winnipeg.[2] This was just in advance of Sifton's tour of the Canadian Clubs in Ontario, during which he wrote to Crerar and suggested that he introduce an appropriate resolution to the House. But Crerar urged caution, for he feared that any attempt at formal constitutional revision of the relationship might provoke a union of opposites.

He agreed with Sifton that his proposed resolution had the merit of putting "the issue squarely and clearly" before the House and the people of Canada and that it would appeal "to the national spirit and self respect of Canadians, very necessary factors, if this country is ever to amount to anything." But he warned Sifton, with whose ideas he was quite familiar, that any such resolution must "have some statement ... protecting any existing rights the French Canadians at present enjoy." It was not so much the Catholic religion that concerned Quebec, in Crerar's surprisingly perceptive view for that time, but the French language. The leadership of Quebec, political and otherwise, saw the Privy Council in London as its ultimate line of defence, and its concerns must be accommodated. He had discussed all this with Lapointe and was convinced that "no matter how people may feel about it the French language is in Canada to stay." He concluded by warning Sifton that his resolution was, "in effect, a declaration of complete sovereignty on the part of the Canadian Parliament." Unless it passed the House almost unanimously, Britain would probably decline to pass any necessary declaratory consent to a new constitutional relationship, thus throwing the issue into "the field of practical politics" and "the hectic atmosphere of an election."[3] He did not feel it necessary to elaborate further.

Dafoe, as well, was trying to restrain Sifton. He told him that Crerar was willing to go as far only as he felt "that he could command a support in Parliament that would make it worth while." The Sanhedrin was of the view that it would be best "to seek and obtain from Parliament formal approval of the doctrine that Canada is at war only when the Canadian Parliament says it is." This, it felt, would be a practical and useful first step. In addition, as Crerar suggested to Sifton, "Canadian representatives in any future Imperial Conference of any kind [should] take no part in any discussions of foreign questions where Canada was not directly concerned."[4] In the event, Sifton's initiative died aborning, as King prepared to attend yet another Imperial Conference later that year.

Concerned about the apparent centralizing tendency of British rhetoric (with support from New Zealand) and the ambiguous position of Australia, Crerar was relieved at the outcome. "King seems to have done pretty well in London by refusing to do nothing [sic]," he wrote to Cameron. This happy outcome he felt was the result of the influence of Dafoe and O.D. Skelton, King's deputy minister, who had accompanied the prime minister. These conferences, he went on, were "becoming something of a joke. It would be better for all concerned if they cut them down to one in five or ten years."[5]

It is difficult to tell how representative of western opinion Crerar was on relations with Britain, but a wider degree of autonomy had been popular on the prairies for years. To some extent, this sentiment had been driven by the *Free Press* and the *Guide*, and the organized farmers had steadily endorsed this evolution. Greater autonomy was ultimately a utilitarian objective, and Crerar defined its elements: Canada's judges were more competent to interpret Canadian law than the Privy Council, treaties affecting this country should be shaped at home, and the right to amend the constitution and any decision to go to war must be Canadian decisions.[6] He did not recommend "actively asserting our nationhood" but warned that any movement towards imperial centralization must be resisted. It would never work and, worse, would sunder the existing unity of spirit that at present obtained "through a common language, common traditions in government, law and literature, and everything else, that are the things, intangible but strong as steel, that hold the British peoples together."[7] If this sounds confused and mildly contradictory, so also was the state of Canadian opinion in the 1920s, as the country groped its way to a revised connection with the empire.

There was, of course, an obverse side to the question of Canada's imperial relations – dealings with the United States – and on this matter, Crerar clearly spoke for most prairie folks. Freer trade had been a by-word for the grain growers for decades, but emphasis on the American market was intensifying during the 1920s for both practical and emotional reasons. The sharp decline in wheat prices early in the decade prompted more than the pool movement. In the wake of the Great War the traditional British and continental markets could no longer be relied on. "The staggering burden of debt in European countries, the lowered standard of living and the absence of purchasing power due to paralysed industrial conditions ... is bound to have a momentous effect on this country. Whether we like it or not, our future is bound up more and more with the United States."[8]

Crerar saw great possibilities for shipping prairie cattle for finishing in the American corn belt and for increasing exports of wheat and flour, despite American tariffs, since the United States was and would increasingly be a food-importing country. What was needed was an energetic policy by the dominion government to widen trade, even if that meant unilateral tariff reductions by Canada. In his continuing argument with his friend Cameron, he allowed that "I may be wrong but my basic consideration is that Canada has much potential wealth, that that wealth lies in her agricultural lands, her forests, her fisheries and her mines, that it does not help us to develop this wealth by creating industries that are more or less artificial." Canada's future prosperity depended on increased access to the American market for natural products, which goal the government must not fear to promote. "I am not much for building up cities, people deteriorate in cities, morally, spiritually and physically."[9] Throughout his long career, Crerar never really lost this physiocratic view of life, which was so typical of the west and predisposed him against Canada's traditional economic policy.

To give effect to these aspirations, the most pressing need, in the opinion of Crerar and many others, was adequate representation for Canada in Washington, and he urged it at every opportunity. "Why in Heaven's name doesn't King send a Canadian representative to Washington," he complained to Cameron, and "give him all the power he can give him, a house of his own and a sufficient allowance so that he can acquaint Washington with the fact that there is such a country as Canada?" The British embassy "does not bestir itself very much to helping Canada's trade." Cameron forwarded Crerar's complaints to Finance Minister Fielding, who promptly rejected the implication. But Crerar kept up his campaign, badgering Charlie Murphy, Frank Cahill, and Andrew McMaster, all prominent MPs, pointing out that few congressmen realized "the fact that Canada is one of Uncle Sam's best customers. Our own prosperity is largely bound up with better trade relations with the United States, and we are doing practically nothing whatever to aid in bringing this about."[10]

Early in 1923 Crerar tried to enlist Loring Christie in the cause. Christie was an officer in External Affairs, attached to the British mission in Washington. When it was rumoured that he was about to leave the service, both Crerar and Dafoe tried to impress upon him the importance of Canada's relations with the United States and urged him to stay on. When Christie replied that he could not continue on his meagre salary, Crerar's low opinion of the government's intentions was simply confirmed.[11]

Crerar's hectoring had one, rather mysterious result. W.L. Mackenzie King was at least tepidly interested in exploring the possibility of a trade deal with the United States. He seems to have authorized Crerar to set up a meeting with Herbert Hoover, the American secretary of commerce, through the good offices of a prominent New Yorker, Julius Barnes. According to Crerar, King "welcomed [Barnes's] suggestion that a few members of the Canadian Government with myself should meet Mr. Hoover and another representative of your government with yourself, quietly in New York," to discuss matters of mutual interest. King's interest was limited to the free exchange of pulpwood, livestock, fish, vegetables, and forage.[12] Given this agenda, it is not surprising that the meeting never took place. But it was not untypical of King's methods and indicates that the prime minister continued to foresee a political future for Crerar with the Liberal party, as long as he found him useful.

But Crerar's active role in elected politics, through the balance of the fourteenth Parliament (1921–25), was tightly constrained by the demands of the company, and there is little doubt that he was discouraged by the political prospects. The election of 1921 and its aftermath had not only exposed the prairies' deep regional suspicion of central Canada but had as well disguised the confusion that underlay it. "The thousand miles of wilderness between East and West has a political significance that should not be overlooked," Crerar wrote to Cameron. Even the western business community, which he knew intimately, shared the regional discontent. "They don't like Wood and they don't like Morrison and they don't like some of the things that the Progressives have in their platform, and yet at bottom that is the attitude of mind."[13] The difficulties within the movement that he had led would prove as intractable as the geography of the country.

In Crerar's view, the farmers of the west must be brought back to the unity of purpose they had in 1916: "At the present time, they appear to be wandering off into the bogs of Wood's cloudy philosophy and pinning their faith to Wheat Boards and other fancied shortcuts to relief." But they could not be effective in isolation, he insisted; nor could they remain simply a party of protest, attempting to force their views on others and renouncing the responsibilities of power, as Wood and Morrison enjoined. The Progressives are "sort of stranded between heaven and earth – no organization for pushing its programme in the country and no means to do it with if there were such an organization. It must go ahead or it will go back."[14]

In addition, the Alberta notion of exploiting a balance of power in the Commons must be rejected. When Robert Forke, his successor as House leader, sought his advice on the wisdom of submitting a budget proposition to Finance Minister Fielding early in 1923, Crerar pointed out the obvious implications. If Fielding accepted Progressive wishes on the budget – wishes that a section of the Liberal party would surely oppose – then he could quite rightly ask if the Progressives would continue to support the government on other matters.

He could hardly be expected to place his party in a weakened position to satisfy the Progressives on the budget alone. Such a balance-of-power strategy would be "as ineffective in getting our programme realized as it had been in the past in maintaining the peace in Europe."[15] The long-term goal for the Progressives must be "broadening out" and eventual realignment of Canadian politics. The defeat of the narrowly based United Farmers of Ontario (UFO) government in June 1923 seemed to bear out his claim.

Prime Minister King, in his hesitant, tentative way, was thinking along the same lines, and he continued to see Crerar as central to any such realignment, despite his continuing unwillingness to make any really radical reconstruction of his cabinet. In March 1923, he was pressed by Sifton to create a Department of Immigration with its own minister. King was amenable and agreed that Crerar would be the best choice, confiding to his diary: "I would take Crerar if I could get him." He authorized Sifton to make the approach through Dafoe.

Given his situation at United Grain Growers (UGG), there was no prospect of Crerar's accepting any appointment at that time. According to Dafoe, Crerar felt that the time had passed for cooperation between Liberals and Progressives during the present Parliament but looked "forward to a showdown which may bring [the two parties] together as the only alternative to a Conservative government." But he would never enter any cabinet that included Sir Lomer Gouin, though that did not mean that Crerar was uninterested. Dafoe fully expected him to return to political life in "two or three years ... and he is constantly consulted on matters of Progressive policy."

Crerar seems to have been quite disgusted with King's vacillation. He complained to Hudson: "The Big Interests always have had a mental reservation about the Liberal party, and yet the latter is sitting on their doorstep, seeking to get what favors it may be able to secure in the way of support." The time was clearly not yet ripe for any move on his part. Any initiative would have to come from King and would have to be dramatic.[16]

A chain of events that began with the fall of the UFO government would provide King his opportunity, and once again he would fumble it. The key to much of what happened was the public perception (shared, presumably, by King) of Crerar as the leading spokesman of the west. Despite his resignation and the internal problems of the movement, J.K. Munro could still write in *Maclean's* in February 1924 that "where [Crerar] sat is still the head of the Progressive table."[17] But the internal difficulties were nearing the breaking point.

After the Ontario election, Morrison bitterly attacked Crerar in an angry letter. "I consider that your action and Drury's action have done more to destroy the power to do good that lay at our door than any other cause," he charged. "I am sorry to say these things, but at my time of life it is a great disappointment to see our work wrecked, not from without, but from within." Crerar replied that he must "emphatically dissent" from such a view. It was not goals that divided them – for they both agreed on the Farmers' Platform – but the means to achieve them. Wood's chimaera of group government and Morrison's insistence that farmers should elect their own representatives who would hold themselves apart and press the interest of "their class" had created an unfortunate effect in the public mind, Crerar argued, and frightened off many who might have given the Progressives much-needed support. He did not doubt the sincerity of either Morrison or Wood, but he could not refrain from pointing out that the Canadian Council of Agriculture had never approved either position.

Despite this angry exchange, they continued to correspond and finally came to a significant agreement – that the farmers' organizations must cut their ties with any political party – an action that Crerar had advocated as early as mid-1922.[18] What Crerar did not say was that he hoped that such separation would end the dominance of the United Farmers of Alberta (UFA) over the Alberta MPs and the disruptive policy of constituency independence and delegate control. The issue flared up at the UFA convention in early 1924 and led to the final break-up of the parliamentary party after the budget debate in Ottawa in the spring.

The prime minister watched these proceedings with some complacency, feeling that the bulk of the Progressives would come his way, since they could hardly support Meighen and the Tories. But he was not able to await events. The loss of a by-election in Halifax in early December 1923 led him to press the cabinet to look to the west for support and to bring Crerar into the government as witness to the new departure. Then, in quick succession, Fielding suffered a stroke and was forced to leave politics, and Sir Lomer Gouin resigned from the cabinet, ostensibly for reasons of health, but more probably as a protest against any courting of the west.[19]

Reconstruction was now not only possible but mandatory, and the two stoutest Liberal supporters of protection were now gone from the cabinet table. A flurry of political activity, both public and private, seemed to indicate that King might finally seize the nettle: "I am inclined now to take the bold course and link up at once with the farmers," he confided to his diary, and "taking in of Crerar is a means to that end."[20]

After a visit (apparently unknown to King) from Ernest Lapointe, Cameron wrote excitedly to Crerar that he should expect an overture from the prime minister and inquired if Crerar would consider entering the government as minister of finance. Crerar was visiting the UGG's sawmills on the west coast, and when he returned to Winnipeg he replied cautiously: "If a satisfactory basis of personnel and policy can be definitely reached," he would consider the suggestion. But he added that inclusion of Hudson would be an absolute condition.[21]

After Lapointe reported these exchanges to him, King invited Crerar (and Dunning as well) to Ottawa for discussions early in January 1924. But he was by no means committed and rather inclined to "let matters work out in a natural manner – it is apparent to me the west is now coming our way."[22] Crerar was of much the same mind. He had been back at the company full time for little more than a year, and much remained to be done; but he clearly was not quit of politics. Both his ambition and his vanity were piqued.

Even so, Crerar was careful to consult the "Sanhedrin" and heeded advice from other quarters as well. His friend T.S. Lyon, editor of the Toronto *Globe*, wrote a long letter to Cameron to be passed on to Crerar. In it he argued, quite sensibly, that the only basis for a successful understanding between Liberals and Progressives depended almost exclusively on tariff policy. The only way the Progressives could be assured of a more favourable tariff was to control fiscal policy. Ergo, Crerar must become finance minister; if not, "he ought not to enter the Government at all. In almost any other department he would have responsibility without power."[23] Crerar took the message to heart.

When he arrived in Ottawa, he and Dunning met with King together, separately, and then with Lapointe and Haydon as well. The contrast between the two guests, at least to King, was fascinating. Crerar gave the impression that King needed him more than he needed a return to active politics, and he was thus inclined to deal with the prime minister from a presumed position of strength. At King's invitation, he spelled out his policy positions – a tariff for revenue, maintenance and support for the national railway, the alternative vote and proportional representation in the cities, regular bank inspections, and appointment of a representative in Washington, who would, among other things, forward joint development of a St Lawrence seaway. Dunning apparently insisted only on a revenue tariff, which led King to reflect: "He is a stronger, saner and sounder man than Crerar." Dunning argued that Crerar would "not be good for finance" and – ironic, given their futures – that he was "not a good administrator, too visionary & lacking the physical health, likely to weaken under close application."[24]

King was aware that both men were after Finance and that appointment of either would surely limit his flexibility on the tariff. The next day, at a private luncheon, King demurred at Hudson's entry (which would necessitate dropping McMurray of North Winnipeg), and Crerar then said that he could go no further. Later that day, "Both Dunning and Haydon agreed Crerar was inclined to be arrogant – & putting too much stress on his own virtues and values. Of the two men, I believe Dunning to be the abler, – Crerar the more pleasing personality, & better platform presence and manner."[25]

To some extent, Crerar had misread the political situation. He felt that King had no choice but to reconstruct his cabinet and that the west would get the influence it deserved – all to the good of the country. But King would not be pushed – on policy or personnel. In his view, the moderate Progressives had little option other than to support the Liberals. He could wait. The meetings ended with a polite press release from Crerar about a frank exchange of views, and then he left Ottawa.[26] It would now be some time before he would join King at the council table.

There does not seem to have been any sense of personal disappointment on Crerar's part – rather, regret that King had missed a splendid opportunity to remake the Liberal party. This opinion was shared by Lyon of the Toronto *Globe* and Atkinson of the *Toronto Star*, and even more so by the Sanhedrin, especially Hudson (unaware of Crerar's demand concerning him), who considered that King's timidity now guaranteed Meighen's victory in the next election.[27]

Crerar returned to his duties at UGG and kept a weather eye on Ottawa, for there was never any lack of issues. He grumbled to Cameron that it was ill advised for the government to seek the opinion of the Canadian Pacific Railway (CPR) as "to the advisability of building certain branch lines of the C.N.R. [Canadian National Railways]." The Tories were ever anxious to make political capital out of the problems of the public railway, and King was only playing into their hands. When Sir Henry Thornton, the CNR's president, complained to Crerar that his railway should be subject only to the same audit as other railways and not to the "super-audit" being rumoured about Ottawa, he received a sympathetic response, and Crerar tried to enlist Hudson and Forke on the CNR's behalf. Crerar was convinced, however, that

the people of Canada would never let the national railway fall under
private control, and he would certainly oppose such a move.[28]

Legislation before Parliament proposing to create a United Church
of Canada drew only sceptical interest from Crerar. Church union
was already a way of life in the small towns of the west, forced by
pragmatic and financial reasons. Crerar seemed concerned only that
the dissenting minorities among the congregations be treated fairly
in the division of property. Doctrinal differences were of little
account to him, and he doubted very much that "when we come to
the Pearly Gates St. Peter is going to inquire whether we are Presby-
terians, Baptists, Methodists or Catholics. Our passport to the bliss
that is supposed to reign supreme in Heaven will not be measured
by these yardsticks."[29]

He found time to write an article for MacLean's following a series
by Grattan O'Leary of the Ottawa Journal on "An Orgy of Extravagance." Crerar largely agreed and recommended more productivity
from the civil service, fewer members of Parliament and cabinet ministers, and a solution to the railway mess. "Businesslike government"
was his panacea.[30] His liberalism was becoming very hard-headed.
He continued as well to advocate greater and freer trade with the
United States. Almost in anticipation of such a development, he and
his brother Peter bought a farm near Clandeboye, Manitoba, for
stock raising.[31] It would prove a handy retreat in a few years.

Crerar did not attend the House very frequently in the session of
1924, though he was acutely aware of the significance of the budget
debate for his party's future. It would mark the first of two ruptures
within the Progressives that would ensure their political demise.
King appeared convinced (with some reason) that minor tariff concessions would speed their dissolution and bring many of them his
way. But he received a boost from an unexpected source.

During the debate on the budget, which had included reductions
on farm implements, J.S. Woodsworth, Labour member from Winnipeg, posed the Progressives a cruel dilemma. He moved an amendment that would lower duties on the "necessities of life," thus
leaving the Progressives, according to J.K. Munro, "the choice of
voting against their own platform or turning out the Government
they were fast learning to love."[32] Most chose the safer option and
supported King, but fifteen defied Forke and joined Woodsworth on
the amendment, though all but one supported the budget and its
tariff reductions on third reading. Prime Minister King could hardly
have planned it better himself. Most of the Progressive dissidents

were now permanently alienated and soon coalesced in the House as the Ginger Group.

Crerar was not at all surprised. He thought that the dispute over the budget was the occasion for rather than the cause of the division. It had been festering a long time, and the defection of "the 'so-called Ginger Group' was due to dissatisfaction with Forke as much as anything else." Though "Woodsworth's capacity is not fully appreciated in the House," Crerar doubted that the farmers would make any permanent alliance with labour. But the departure of the dissidents obviated any need for King to call an autumn election. "Why should he? If he and his friends think that the Progressives are breaking up, have they anything to lose by waiting?" On this score, at least, the prime minister was right.[33]

For Crerar, the real significance of the defection of the Gingerites became clear at the next convention of the United Farmers of Alberta (UFA) in Calgary in January 1925. He did not attend, but he was thoroughly briefed by Chipman of the *Guide* and Murray of UGG, who had been at the Calgary meeting. At issue was an attempt to reconcile the Gingerites with those Alberta MPs who had remained with the majority of the Progressive caucus on the Woodsworth amendment, as well as some means of keeping the dispute off the convention floor.

After a conciliatory resolution had been proposed, according to Crerar's information, Henry Wise Wood was behind a further resolution, introduced and passed after many delegates had left, that would have placed Alberta's Progressive MPs under the control of the UFA. They "must be known as UFA Members and must not consort with other ill-conditioned folk" who come from "[p]rovinces where the true gospel has not been preached." They were further enjoined, Crerar went on, "to accept no other creed than that enunciated by the UFA, which up to the present ... is confined to a reform of the monetary system via the route of the printing press." Despite the somewhat "comic opera" appearance of the whole performance, Crerar warned Forke that the split was probably final and that most Alberta Progressives would be tied to Wood and the UFA.[34]

Whether or not the Progressives could have survived the defection of the Ginger Group is at best a moot point. After all, there were only a dozen Gingerites from an original parliamentary group of sixty-five. Their significance has been enhanced by the fact that they themselves survived for a time and went on to help found the Co-operative Commonwealth Federation. A deeper concern for Crerar, Forke, and others was the fact that there was a serious division among the

remaining Progressives, much of which centred on Forke's leadership and involved most of the Ontario Progressives. Once again it
was a budget that marked the occasion for further division.

The budget introduced by the King government in the spring of
1925 contained almost no revisions to the tariff, except an increase in
the duties on coal demanded by three provinces – including the UFA
government of Alberta. Seventeen of the Progressives (many of them
from coal-producing Alberta) supported the Liberals and defied
Forke, who had not even called a caucus to determine a budget
position. When Crerar arrived in Ottawa to take part in the debate
on a new Grain Act, he found Forke disconsolate, the caucus unable
to find a chairman, and the party in a shambles.

"The two factions exclusive of the Gingerites are about evenly
divided," Crerar wrote to Chipman. The Ontario Progressives, badgered by Morrison and estranged by the western bias of their colleagues, were slipping away. The movement in Ontario was "pretty
well shot to pieces," he informed Glen in Marquette; " ... the scan-
dals and the personal feuds of Morrison and Drury have brought
this about." Crerar was now ready to concede that the combination
of the regional demands of agriculture, the failure to "broaden out,"
and the baneful influence of Wood and Morrison had brought the
end of a farmers' party in Canada. "There is no leadership except in
name. Everyone is a law unto himself with an eye only as to what
will please his constituents, a confusion of tongues worse con-
founded."[35] It did not necessarily follow that the national vision of
the Progressives was dead, and Crerar was prepared to make one
final effort to salvage what to him was most important.

Early in August 1925, Progressive MPs were scheduled to meet in
Regina. None of the Ontario members attended, nor did most of the
Ginger Group, which was a good indication of the way things were
going. Convinced that occupational politics had been fatally discredited, Crerar proposed the calling of a western convention, "along the
lines of the Liberal Convention of 1917." The intent would be to
crystallize western opinion among all groups and interests. Such a
convention would define a purely national program, which would
deal with railways, immigration, wider markets, tariff for revenue,
banking reform, and reductions in spending and taxation. The convention would then elect a leader and "state as its definite policy its
willingness to co-operate with all other parts of the Dominion in the
carrying out of the programme thus laid down." It would be, he
boasted proudly to Cameron, "the slogan of the Liberals of sixty
years ago in Britain, – 'Economy, Retrenchment and Reform.'" His
Gladstonian outlook, in which he would later revel, was already

fixed. If his scheme miscarried, he told his old friend, he would not stand in the next election.[36]

Crerar's proposal was not accepted by his colleagues. As the agricultural depression lifted and the farmers of the west abandoned politics for economic nostrums, the old grain growers' associations went into decline. Crerar continued to claim that western opinion could be marshalled behind a national program, but "some of our Saskatchewan friends opposed it. The Progressive Party is cursed with narrow-minded bigots."[37]

The only one who seemed to pay any attention was King, whose suspicions seldom slept. In July, the prime minister was contemplating reconstructing his cabinet with the inclusion of Crerar, Dunning, and Brownlee, holding a short session, and then calling an election in October. A month later, he worried that "Crerar doesn't know his own mind. Is a little jealous of my having captured leadership. His desire to form a western party & he the leader reveals his ambition and want of fair play."[38] The ambition was at least temporarily banked, however, for Crerar had determined to leave active politics, partly through inclination, but largely at the behest of United Grain Growers (UGG).

When the election was finally called in September 1925, Crerar had already informed the Progressives of Marquette that he would not stand again. The board of UGG, fearing the sort of adverse publicity that had occurred in 1921, would have preferred Crerar to stay out of the contest entirely, but it did authorize him to speak in support of the Progressive candidate in Marquette. That was all he was inclined to do anyway.[39]

In his observations during the campaign, there was a general air of indifference. Relying to some extent on Grant Dexter, the *Free Press*'s man in Ottawa, Crerar predicted to Cameron that Meighen would do well in central and eastern Canada and thought "it almost certain that [Meighen] will form the next government." The prospect did not upset him unduly. "Perhaps the best thing we can have is five years of Tory rule," he went on, "and if so, I hope it will be Tory with a vengeance. This might make possible the bringing about of a real Liberal party."[40]

The campaign performance of the prime minister quite depressed him. In one of his western speeches, King promised "a tariff for revenue, which at the same time gave adequate protection to established industry." Crerar expected that thousands of western voters would give this double-talk the answer it deserved. In his opinion, the most significant development in the campaign on the prairies was the decline of the Progressives. While there was still some enthusiasm, they were having difficulty meeting their expenses. They "may elect quite a few candidates in the west, but I see no future for them as a party." He spent the last three days of the contest in an unsuccessful attempt to save Marquette for the Progressives.[41] The result was much the same in the rest of the grain belt. The euphoria of 1921 was gone, as the Progressives dropped from thirty-eight to twenty-two prairie seats.

It had all been so unnecessary, according to Crerar. The spectacle of three-cornered contests where Progressives fought Liberals and allowed Tories to win with small pluralities testified to the political wrong-headedness of prairie folk. "The Conservative gains in Manitoba," he wrote in a personal note to Fred Livesay of the Canadian Press, " … were straight gifts. In Marquette, Neepawa, Selkirk and Springfield either a Progressive or a Liberal running in a straight fight would have won easily."[42]

The Canadian people once again had failed to elect a majority government; Meighen had 116 seats against a combined opposition of 129. With only ninety-nine seats, the Liberals' tenure as governing party was in jeopardy. All would depend on the twenty-four Progressives (including nine UFA men from Alberta), whose dubious party discipline would give neither King nor Meighen much comfort. Robert Forke, the erstwhile leader, would be at best an uneasy king maker.

Before consulting any of his elected colleagues, Forke talked to Hudson, who had also declined to run, and at length to Crerar. They both advised him that in any choice between King and Meighen, the west would much prefer King, and so presumably would almost all the Progressive members. Crerar was very detailed in his recommendations to Forke and seems to have expected that they would carry weight. Since Meighen had fought the election over protection, he must be kept out of office. But King, in return for Progressive support, must be held to terms. Crerar's presumption was that the government, whoever formed it, would not and should not last beyond one session. Accordingly, he advised Forke to give King informal assurances of Progressive support for certain purposes – the election of a Speaker; any motion of confidence on the address; the budget, provided that no protective features were included; a supply bill; and no contentious legislation. Another election would be called as soon as convenient after the session.[43]

For Crerar, it was a question of tactics. He wished the Liberals to have the advantage of power when the next election was called. In his view, the determining races would be in the agricultural ridings in the west, and, if certain preparations were made, Meighen would never be able to hold his prairie seats. King's strategy should be to get through a short and non-contentious session. He should then reorganize the government and add a few Progressives, effect specific tariff reductions long sought by the west and otherwise openly proclaim a tariff for revenue as Liberal policy, introduce a firm and aggressive scheme for immigration, reduce public expenditures, and appoint a representative to Washington and improve trade relations with the United States.

If King did all these things, Crerar argued, there would be no three-cornered contests on the prairies. King "would probably lose some seats in Quebec, ... gain a few in the Maritime Provinces, possibly gain a few in Ontario ... and come back to the House with a majority of twenty or twenty-five." Since his business experience told him that "the country is on the eve of better times," a reorganized and re-elected Liberal party could claim the credit. Such a program "would make Western Canada a stronghold of Liberalism in the Dominion and this is in the natural order of things." All this he pressed on Forke, and "when we discussed it he was in agreement with me."[44]

So Forke went off to Ottawa full of advice. Much of what Crerar had predicted came to pass, but in a manner that neither he nor anyone else could have foreseen.

CHAPTER NINE

Progressive Absorption, 1925–29

John Dafoe had missed the election of 1925. He returned to Winnipeg from a trip to Australia shortly thereafter, and the Sanhedrin (Dafoe, Crerar, Fowler, Hudson, and Symington) met to consider the implications of the inconclusive results. Crerar communicated their discussions by letter to Cameron and by telephone to Dunning in Regina.

Generally, they agreed that the outcome was a result of lack of confidence in King and his ministry, rather than of the appeal of Meighen's call for greater protection. Despite the decline of Progressive support in the west, Dafoe especially argued strongly for an open coalition with the Liberals and an attempt to carry on for a year or two. Such a ministry could deal with immediate problems and adopt a tariff for revenue. There was little apparent sympathy for King, whose ambivalence on the tariff was seen as the critical factor in the Liberals' difficulties.[1] Much of this was similar to Crerar's advice to Forke, and all would turn on the success of King's decision to meet the House and attempt to carry on, for which, in the view of the Winnipeg group, a thorough reorganization of the government was essential. Despite Meighen's plurality, the Winnipeggers were adamant that power should not be handed over to the Tories.

Crerar continued to believe that the Progressives held the key to the future, despite their electoral decline. In his opinion, the voters were dissatisfied with both the Progressives and the Liberals and voted against the incapacity of the government and the futility and class posture of the Progressives. It was not the policies of the latter that they rejected. Thus eastern Liberals must agree to a firm policy on tariff for revenue, the national railway, immigration, and expanded trade with the United States: "The policy must be definite, advocated in all parts of Canada, and carry conviction that it will be implemented."[2] Failing this, he argued, the west would be alienated from the Liberals and the Tories.

But Crerar's influence on events was much more limited than he would care to admit. His decision to drop out of the House meant that he was no longer a central player in the developing courtship between Progressives and Liberals. Furthermore, his earlier battles with Henry Wise Wood and his criticism of the pooling movement made him suspect among many politically active prairie folks. Dafoe, in a letter to Sifton, reported a conversation with Forke, who quite firmly believed that Crerar was no longer acceptable to many of the Progressive members: "[Crerar] had undoubtedly made enemies among the Progressives ...[Forke] regretted this as he realized Crerar was the best equipped of them all for public office."[3] Now out of active politics and out of sympathy with the popular pooling movement, Crerar was in imminent danger of being eclipsed as a western leader.

King was now cultivating Dunning as the key to rebuilding Liberal fortunes in the west and attracting Progressive support. Dafoe felt that Dunning's decision to enter King's cabinet was momentous; if the Saskatchewan premier could secure definite commitments on policy from King, he could quickly "make himself the leader in fact of both the Western Liberals and Progressives." Dunning, seeking additional support, asked Crerar if he would enter as well, "if satisfactory terms were offered to him." Crerar, according to Dafoe, remained noncommittal. The long and usually friendly rivalry between Dunning and Crerar was entering a new phase as the former entered the dominion field.

But Crerar was not completely forgotten. Once King was assured of enough Progressive votes to carry on, he continued to seek ways of increasing prairie support. And once again he hoped to include Crerar in his plans. His method was to attempt to defuse the perennial problem caused by tariff levels at budget time. Since he could never reconcile the interests of high- or moderate-tariff Liberals in central Canada with Progressive (and western Liberal) demands for lower tariffs, he hoped to depoliticize the issue by creating a three-member Tariff Advisory Board. To have any credibility, the body would have to include a westerner whose views were consistent with those of the grain growers. King sought Dunning's approval, as his new western Liberal leader, for appointment of Crerar to "offset any concern in the minds particularly of the Progressives as to the possible protectionist leanings of Daoust [a Montreal shoe manufacturer] or Bowman [an Ontario insurance executive]," the other proposed members.[4]

Vincent Massey was the prime minister's emissary to Crerar, and
Charles Stewart, minister of the interior from Alberta, also applied
heavy, if clumsy pressure. Crerar saw the scheme for what it was –
a rather transparent ploy to obscure the government's tariff decisions
behind a public cloak of objectivity, or taking the tariff out of politics
but not politics out of the tariff. In his polite but firm rejection of the
offer, Crerar cited his reasons: that he was too busy to do the job
justice, that "tariff policies must be settled by Parliament and that a
Tariff Commission would therefore largely be futile," and that the
board's proposed mandate would make it little more than a research
arm of the Department of Finance. To Stewart, Crerar made it plain
that he felt that the whole scheme was an attempt to use him and
that he was not at all interested.[5]

In the end, King's plan fizzled. Bowman declined to serve as chairman, and Daoust injudiciously announced that he thought tariff
levels inadequate and was fired. A board was eventually set up to
satisfy the promise in the speech from the throne, but it was isolated
and ignored.

Beyond the ill-conceived tariff board, Crerar found the rest of the
speech from the throne satisfactory. While he did not wish the Progressives to appear to be "for sale," a Meighen coup among some of
the Progressives was always a possibility. On the first, crucial test of
confidence, a few dissidents did support Meighen's amendment, but
most Progressives sustained King. Dafoe was urging an open coalition in the *Free Press*, and Crerar told Forke that he shared this view.
But "one thing is certain to my mind, and that is that the Progressives cannot continue to be the arbiter of what Parliament shall do
without taking responsibility ... and if persisted in, will without a
doubt complete the ruin of the Progressives." The only course to
follow, he concluded, was to offer principled support to the government, which really meant that Meighen must be kept out – on the
face of it, a rather narrow view of responsibility.

Crerar's vehemence grew from his conviction that the United
States would see its next presidential election in 1928 fought on the
tariff issue. (He could hardly anticipate the anti-Catholic outburst
that followed nomination of Democrat Al Smith.) This could provide
the opportunity for a broad Canadian–American trade agreement –
a possibility that a Meighen government would certainly reject. Even
just for this reason, the Progressives should continue to support
King.[6]

The prime minister was still attempting to solidify western support
through a cabinet reorganization. His great prize was Charles Dunning, and King hoped to secure an equally prominent Manitoban. On

a trip west in late January 1926, King held a meeting with Crerar and Hudson and inquired if either would be willing to come in. Hudson was firmly opposed, but, according to King, Crerar was willing to think it over. After discussing the matter with Hudson, with whom there "is no rivalry whatever," Crerar informed Cameron that the "prospect was not very inviting."[7]

But there was another factor of which Crerar could not have been unaware. In an interview with the prime minister, Forke informed him that the "Alberta men" would be opposed to Crerar's entering the cabinet and advised against such a move. This prompted King to consider Hudson and Symington as possibilities, but neither was interested. Dafoe was quite concerned and grumbled to Forke: "I think it is unfortunate that there is this prejudice against Crerar, but while it remains it probably would not be wise for him to attempt to re-enter public life."[8]

In the end, the new cabinet members were Dunning, William Eccles of Ontario, and Vincent Massey. The possibility of Crerar's inclusion had to be dropped. King, as an afterthought, asked Hudson to tell Crerar, who had gone south to escape some of the winter: "Time may be required to satisfactorily work out the political situation, but it is, I believe, only a matter of time."[9] If this was intended as consolation, Crerar does not seem to have reacted.

The situation seemed to be working out for King. The bulk of the Progressives were now persuaded that the only way to avoid an unwelcome election was to maintain the Liberals in power; so the blandishments of the Conservatives had little effect, even on the most reluctant of the Progressives. But, in Crerar's view, this was a rather dangerous game, acceptable only for a short time. He warned Forke that an impression could quickly form that "the Progressives are calling the tune and the Cabinet's dancing to whatever they call." Since the Progressives had polled only a small percentage of the total vote, the Tories would leap on the situation. The best solution, Crerar advised (as did Dafoe), was "to accept co-operation with the Liberal party" and "a definite share of the responsibility of governing the country by accepting seats in the Cabinet." He seemed genuinely concerned that Parliament itself was becoming a subject of growing contempt and regretted that all the manœuvring would probably detract further from its prestige. This was hardly a letter written by one no longer concerned with or interested in public life; but its effect on Forke was minimal, since King offered the Progressives neither a coalition nor cabinet seats.[10]

The prime minister, however, hoped to secure his own future with the budget of 15 April 1926 – Minister of Finance James Robb's "prosperity Budget," as it was trumpeted by Liberal enthusiasts. It contained only one tariff change, a very popular reduction from 35 per cent to 20 per cent on American automobiles. Since the price of Canadian cars was also 35 per cent higher than American domestic prices, the reduction seemed to pose little threat to the Canadian industry, despite howls from General Motors and a march of angry auto workers on Ottawa. The budget also revised the income tax, raising the basic exemption and lowering rates on taxable incomes to benefit lower-paid workers. Since few Canadians paid income tax, and almost no farmers did, the practical result was limited, but the symbolic and political dividends were indeed rewarding.[11]

Crerar felt compelled to congratulate the prime minister, praising the budget as a "bold undertaking" and "well-warranted." He was especially pleased by the change in income taxes (since he was hardly in the low-income bracket). He implied, however, that such a budget was long overdue. The country was prosperous, and government revenues would probably decline little as a result. He urged King to apply "sound Liberal principles in the matter of public expenditure," by which he meant keeping them down. King must have been heartened by Crerar's prediction that the budget would be accepted by progressives throughout the country and certainly "should have the undivided support of Progressives in the House." Crerar ended by saying that "progressives and Liberals must work together and when the next election comes along they should appeal to the Country as a united force."

In his reply, King assured Crerar that relations between the two groups, "short of a complete fusion, are at the moment all that could be desired." Things could only improve, according to King, and he expressed the wish that Crerar could join Dunning in Ottawa to share the future.[12]

Crerar left immediately afterward on a business trip to Ottawa, New York, and Washington. On his last stop, he met for a few minutes with President Calvin Coolidge, finding him a man "lacking a vision and capacity" that one would expect in a president; "in short a thin-haired, thin-lipped New England Yankee." Crerar was more taken with Herbert Hoover, the commerce secretary, who possessed "force and organizing power," but he doubted "if he has ever read any political economist of standing." He noted that decorum in the House of Representatives suffered by comparison with the Commons at Ottawa. A two-hour debate on farm relief reminded him "of a Grain Growers' Convention."[13]

Crerar returned home, however, to find his own national legislature in an uproar over a customs scandal, leaders talking of constitutional crisis, and an election a near certainty. The revelations of widespread violations of customs and excise regulations opened a long-simmering cesspool. The department had been badly administered for years, and smuggling from the United States so rampant that Canadian merchants were protesting loudly about this illegal competition. King had removed one minister, Jacques Bureau, but his successor, Georges Boivin, had been given little support in cleansing the stable. H.H. Stevens, who led the attack for the Conservatives, not only exposed the details of corruption but indicated that the government knew of the situation and had failed to act.

King was on the defensive, and his erstwhile allies, the Progressives, were in a quandary. Could they swallow their pride (and their principles) and sustain King in the looming motion of censure? The alternatives were either Meighen and the Tories or an unwanted election – more probably, both. But King was determined to avoid facing the music and went to Governor General Lord Byng and recommended dissolution of Parliament. Byng quite properly declined to follow the advice, preferring first to await the decision of the House on the censure motion. King then resigned, leaving Byng without an adviser and the country without a government. The governor general, with little alternative, asked Arthur Meighen, leader of the largest group in the Commons, to form a government. Meighen did, and was then summarily defeated in the House.

Meighen sought and received a dissolution from Byng, and Mackenzie King realized that he had an appealing, if trumped-up, issue for the forthcoming election – that Byng's refusal to grant King his dissolution was a constitutional affront and unwarranted interference in the rights of Parliament and, presumably, the prime minister. But it was a sham. Many years later Meighen recalled that King's "minions far and wide, especially in Quebec, lambasted 'Downing Street domination', and King all the while concealed from the Canadian people the fact that he was the only one seeking Downing Street intervention in any way."[14] This was a reference to the little-known fact that King had urged Byng to consult the British government on his request for a dissolution.

The so-called constitutional crisis did not appear to be the leading issue in western Canada in the election of late summer 1926. Though the Liberal press, especially Dafoe, exploited the alleged interference in Canadian affairs, other matters were equally important on the prairies. Curiously, Crerar made little comment on the issue, except remarking to Cameron that "if [Meighen] had acted wisely he would have refused to have formed a Government under the circumstances."[15] Even so, he gave vigorous support to King, as we see below.

There was considerable speculation as to Crerar's personal intentions. Ralph Maybank, leader of the Manitoba Young Liberals and soon to launch a twenty-year run as a member of Parliament, consulted Hudson to see if Crerar might accept the vacant position of leader of the provincial Liberal party – a rather unlikely possibility. There was also much public discussion as to whether Crerar would be the Liberal candidate in Winnipeg South Centre.[16] He was offered that nomination, as well as joint Progressive-Liberal nominations in both Selkirk and his old riding of Marquette. He was clearly interested in Marquette and hesitated for three or four days before declining with obvious regret.[17]

The reasons had not changed much. The board of United Grain Growers (UGG) was flatly opposed to its president re-entering politics, fearing damage to the company. In any case, if he ran and remained with UGG, voters who belonged to the Manitoba Pool would be incensed. If he resigned and ran, he might be accused of abandoning the company during its crucial struggle against the pools. But the real reason was financial. He simply did not care to exchange his president's salary for that of a private member of the House of Commons.[18]

But whatever the misgivings of his board, Crerar took a rather active part in the campaign. He worked hard for Allison Glen in Marquette, spoke for fusion (Liberal-Progressive) candidates in other constituencies, and, at Mackenzie King's request, campaigned against Arthur Meighen in Portage La Prairie.[19] He could be facile for the cause when necessary. To a wavering friend in Marquette, he explained that all Canadians condemned the scandal in the Customs Service, "but you cannot indict a whole party because of wrongdoing in the administration of one Department."[20] He could conveniently avoid the issue of responsibility when it was politically necessary.

King saw in the Liberal victory of 14 September personal vindication. But the sweep on the prairies – R.B. Bennett in Calgary was the only Conservative elected – can be attributed to other factors. Most important was the willingness of Liberals and Progressives to work together, either by supporting each other's standard bearers or by nominating fusion candidates. Robb's spring budget had been very popular out west. And King's clear commitments on completion of the railway to Hudson Bay and the Crow's Nest grain rates (both of which Meighen opposed) were appealing inducements.

Crerar was greatly pleased by the results, especially in Manitoba, and his own efforts seem to have had some influence. None the less they hardly justified his rather sanctimonious observation to Cameron that it "was not only a decisive turndown of Tory policies, but a stern rebuke to the scandal mongering of those who sought to crawl into office by attacking the reputation of honorable men."[21]

Immediately after the election, Crerar set out once again to instruct Robert Forke, who had been re-elected easily in Brandon. The United Farmers of Alberta members from Alberta had announced prior to the election that they would sit in the House as a distinct group. Crerar urged that what remained of the Progressive party should sit on the government side of the House, though he did not yet go so far as recommending that they attend the Liberal caucus: "They should maintain their identity, but should make it clear that they are there to co-operate in every possible way with the Liberals."[22]

This is what happened, and with the support of his colleagues, Forke entered the cabinet as minister of immigration. Crerar's fondest political dream – to make the prairies a bastion of liberalism – seemed now to be possible. And he was quick to rebuke J.J. Morrison when the *Farmers' Sun* criticized the Manitoba Progressives for supporting the Liberals. Because of the failure of the United Farmers of Ontario to act as a party, Crerar wrote, there was now nothing ahead for the Progressives "but disintegration and this has been steadily going on for the last four years."[23]

There was only one sour note. There was some pressure from Montreal to have successful Liberal candidate Sam Jacobs included in the cabinet, and Cameron had asked Crerar to try to influence Dunning in favour of their mutual friend. Crerar agreed that politically "it might be well to give the Jewish population some recognition," even though "rightly or wrongly there is a good deal of antipathy to the Jewish fraternity" in the west. His personal opinion was that "the Jew should be treated the same [i.e., accepted] in Canada as he is for instance in Great Britain."[24] The suggestion of Jacobs for the cabinet did not go anywhere, and the problem of anti-semitism in Canada was one that Crerar would have to face in a direct and painful way a few years later.

But for now he could relax somewhat his political activity. The Liberals had a safe majority, the Progressives were on their way to absorption, Meighen and Tory protectionism had received a severe reverse, and the increasingly prosperous prairies could look ahead with confidence. Crerar could now direct his attention elsewhere. The UGG, in its struggle with the wheat pools, would require much close attention. His personal finances, always an obstacle to his return to active politics, were becoming more than adequate. And in a very few years and in a surprising manner, his long battle against the tariff would be over, and protection would no longer be a crucial issue for western farmers. The tariff would largely be out of politics, and Crerar would be back in.

Despite the relative prosperity on the prairies in the late 1920s – based on good, stable grain prices and above-average yields – there was no sense of complacency at UGG. The company did well, and healthy dividends went out each year, though Crerar's stewardship was cautious, always ensuring maintenance of substantial reserves. But the animosity of the pools was constant, especially in Saskatchewan, where the Farmers' Union of Canada (FUC), the pools' most fanatical enthusiast, conducted a virulent campaign against the Saskatchewan Co-operative Elevator Company (SCEC), UGG, and Crerar himself.

The animosity was misdirected, since Crerar was no enemy to the pools or to pooling techniques. After a meeting in 1925 with Andrew McPhail of the pools' Central Selling Agency and two representatives of the SCEC, held in Crerar's office, McPhail recorded: "There was the utmost frankness and plain speaking on the part of Crerar and Rice-Jones [of UGG] while there was the usual fencing and ferreting and stalling on the part of the Co-op. men. Crerar is willing to discuss anything even to amalgamation while the Co-op. men would not get down to seriously discuss anything."[25]

Nevertheless, the attacks clearly stung Crerar. He urged George Chipman to go after the FUC in the *Guide* "with a club." It was the leadership of the Farmers' Union (and not the pools) that he blamed, and he asked "what single constructive idea the Leaders of the Farmers' Union had put up outside of their adherence to the wheat pool, and that their claim there was unjustified since Alberta had started the first pool without even a shadow of assistance from anyone connected with the Union." It was only fair to point out, he concluded, that UGG had given timely and important assistance to the pools, including some of its best people.[26]

Crerar's attitude towards the provincial pools is reflected throughout his correspondence in these years, as well as in the actions of the company. He was rather fearful of the evangelical fervour of some pool supporters (especially the organizers), claiming often that one could not build a sound organization on drum beating. More specifically, he preferred cooperation to compulsion. Thus he found the pools' insistence on binding, five-year contracts and demands for a compulsory 100-per-cent pool unacceptable. Equally, he was opposed to the pools' policy that their elevators would handle only pool grain – a position that created great inconvenience and expense, with thousands of elevators scattered among small country shipping points. Competing farmer-owned elevators made no sense, so a policy of exclusiveness was both unfair to non-pool shippers and economically ruinous to both.

His real quarrel, however, was with the prevailing assumption among pool supporters that market control was the best way to ensure good returns to grain growers. The pools, they assured everyone, could use their supply power to influence prices by advancing or withholding grain at appropriate times. In Crerar's view, this scheme would not work, even in the middle term, for reasons we see below. In his opinion, the most effective means of maintaining farm income was through lower production costs; hence his long struggle against the protective tariff. But he never opposed the technique of pooling itself. Indeed, he continued to hope that the pools and UGG could cooperate effectively, even if they could not find an acceptable basis for amalgamation. And Crerar made much of one final point. Pool members received nothing tangible from their membership except the service; members of UGG always had their shares (and their dividends) in the company.[27]

The grain-handling system on the prairies was rationalized somewhat during Crerar's last years with the company. The SCEC disappeared, taken over by the Saskatchewan Pool. After much difficulty, UGG came to mixed lease/sale arrangements with the Alberta and Saskatchewan pools for their control of its elevator system on the western prairies, protecting the delivery rights of its members.[28] But cooperation in the marketing of grain was never achieved, much to Crerar's regret. In his view, the answer to the developing marketing dispute between the pools, on the one hand, and UGG and the private traders, on the other, lay with the major customers for Canadian grain.

So in April 1928 he went off to Europe to see for himself. Staying almost two months, Crerar made a thorough canvass. In Britain, he visited Liverpool and London, consulting both merchant importers and millers. In Copenhagen, he met representatives of the grain and flour business of Denmark, Norway, and Sweden. He then went on to Hamburg, Berlin, and Dusseldorf in Germany, and finally to Paris, Brussels, Rotterdam, and Edinburgh.[29] Everywhere he met great interest in the pool movement and considerable anxiety about the pools' selling methods. The Central Selling Agency (CSA) of the three provincial pools hoped to eliminate European middlemen by avoiding merchant importers and selling directly to large millers. The millers were happy to acquire Canadian grain at a lower price, but they had to depend on the merchants for their grain imports from other countries, so it did not serve them well to alienate the merchants. By the end of the 1920s, as a result, the CSA was pretty well obliged to sell through merchants.

The merchants and millers told Crerar that at times they found the CSA's offers puzzling. If the price went down a few cents a bushel, the CSA's offers did not follow suit; neither did they fully follow a price advance. But the greatest apprehension concerned the pool movement's future. Crerar's notes indicate that some interviewees feared that the pools might get control of practically the entire Canadian crop and use the resulting power "to hold up the consumers in Europe in the price of their bread." If this happened, the merchants predicted, it would lead to agitation in Europe for nationalizing the importation of wheat.

Crerar found European merchants otherwise generally hopeful, and he returned to Winnipeg early in June 1928 fairly sure that UGG's future was, if not secure, at least favourable.[30] He continued to believe that the pools were going in the wrong direction. In 1930, after wheat prices had begun their disastrous slide and the pools were in serious distress, he repeated his long-held conviction that farmers must "keep production costs down and I got a good deal of unfavourable criticism a few years ago for holding the view that the Pool idea of compelling Europe to pay a price commensurate with our cost of production was wholly fallacious."[31]

Up to late 1929, when he left UGG and entered King's cabinet as minister of railways and canals, Crerar was attempting to bring the pools and the company together. After the stock-market break in October, he sensed that wheat prices would decline, though no one expected the collapse that ensued. He attempted to consolidate the position of prairie grain growers. He wrote to his old antagonist Henry Wise Wood to enlist his support in making some marketing arrangement between UGG and the pools. Wood seemed at least willing to talk, but it was already too late for any such amalgamation to be effective.[32] The pools were in desperate straits.

Crerar's brief stint in King's ministry (see chapter 10) did not get him away completely from issues of grain marketing. He was considered to be the minister for Manitoba and was thus expected to aid the province in its distress.[33] This task would prove difficult, as "opinion in Eastern Canada has swung pretty strongly against the Pools. They are blamed for not selling wheat and thus bringing about more or less of a business depression and unemployment." Crerar felt this assessment both incorrect and unfair; yet the banks were urging the pools to persuade the prairie governments to guarantee the pools' margin with the banks.

Crerar, within the cabinet, was inevitably drawn into the dispute. He wrote to the prime minister that "any delay in moving our grain to foreign markets has not even in the most remote degree affected the stability of our financial institutions." Early in each crop year the banks had always made substantial advances against Canadian grain (including that of UGG and the pools). In any case, Crerar explained to King, the risk was insured by the grain itself and the pools' tangible assets of $25 million in fully modern elevators.[34]

But the pressure continued. Premier Bracken of Manitoba sought Crerar's intervention with Dunning, now finance minister, to see if Ottawa would cover half of the margin guarantees to the banks for the provincial governments – a move that he claimed would do great political good. Crerar did what he could but reported that Dunning's view was that the dominion government would intervene only if the costs of the guarantees exceeded the provinces' resources. In addition, as Crerar pointed out to Bracken, it was "commonly held in Eastern Canada that the Pools had rather messed up the selling of their grain," and the government would be criticized for "coming to the relief of people who had gotten into the position they were in as a result of their own mistakes."[35] Despite Crerar's jabs at the pools, the situation was so desperate that governments at both levels were inexorably drawn in, and the Canadian wheat trade changed for ever.

Crerar sensed that something quite profound was happening to the industry in which he had spent his adult life. In a letter to his old friend R.A. Love in England, he explained that until late 1928 the "business interests of Canada generally were pretty solidly behind the Pools." Manufacturers cheered them on because the pools took the farmers' minds off decreases in the tariff, and bankers were happy because the farmers no longer pressed for amendments to the Bank Act. Even so, Crerar considered much of the current criticism of the pools somewhat unfair, "because I doubt if the Pool could have sold much more wheat at any time during the last few months." He conceded that the pools were probably right in their contention that "if they had offered wheat at even lower than market prices, the chances are that they would have got counter offers still lower."[36] Known surpluses have a nasty habit of strengthening the buyer's hand, especially in Europe, where there was much suspicion of the pools.

By March 1930, rumours spread widely that the second payment from the pools would not be forthcoming that spring and that there would be little money even for seeding. Increasingly worried prairie premiers asked Ottawa to guarantee wheat prices – say, at seventy cents a bushel. Rather dispirited, Crerar wrote to King that he doubted the wisdom of their request, yet he had to concede that logic was with them: "If Bennett is going to assist the manufacturers by protective tariffs; if he is going to assist the unemployed labor in the cities by the expenditure of money to relieve unemployment, why should he not guarantee the farmer at least 70 cents a bushel for his wheat. When I consider all this I sometimes wonder wither [sic] we are drifting." UGG, however, was weathering the storm. It got through the crop year with a credit at the bank and paid a 6 per cent dividend. "Wheat we had left in the stocking proved useful."[37]

The most alarming trend in all this for Crerar was that western Canada was losing interest in the tariff: "One of the most regrettable things in the last few years is that the low tariff forces have been by far too quiescent … [S]ince the beginning of the Pool that agitation has in a large measure died down, largely because many people got the wholly fallacious notion that the remedy for their ills lay in making the world pay a price for our wheat that would give us an adequate return."[38]

Once the government began to guarantee a floor price for wheat, the trend was irreversible. It was then obliged to buy up surpluses to maintain the floor price, which it did. After a few years R.B. Bennett's Tories abandoned these efforts and brought back the Wheat Board, in 1935. For western farmers, the tariff was out of politics for good. As long as they were guaranteed minimum prices and costs of production, lobbying to raise the floor price became the focus of political action. This attempt to compensate for high production costs would eventually jeopardize Canada's marketing position. By the time the pools failed, however, Crerar had been in and out of active politics again, and his long career in the grain business had ended.

Crerar had changed a good deal over the years, though his political ideas remained generally constant. Since 1907 he had lived in Winnipeg and briefly in Ottawa, and he was now a long way from his rural roots, more businessman than farmer, despite owning a farm north of Winnipeg. And even with the challenge of the pools he was clearly becoming dissatisfied, if not bored, with his work at UGG. To an old company colleague, he confessed in 1930: "I was not particularly happy in my work in Winnipeg in the last year or two, simply because we seemed to be in the grip of circumstances that seemed to be continually narrowing our field of usefulness and action. Standing still is not a thing that I enjoy very much."[39]

Even the company's membership in the Canadian Council of Agriculture (CCA), which it helped to found and continually financed, had to be surrendered in 1928 in the face of criticism, mostly from the Saskatchewan Pool. But Crerar still continued monetary support for the CCA for a year, after which the council soon collapsed. His great regret concerning the loss of the CCA was that the educational work among farmers, which the company had sponsored for twenty years or more through the CCA and the Grain Growers' Associations, came to an end. It was not at all likely that the pools would fill the void.[40]

But at bottom, his restlessness in the late 1920s was the result of his desire to return to active politics. And the great obstacle to his return, which had led him on several occasions to reject nominations and the overtures of Mackenzie King, was now in train to being resolved. Earlier in the decade, when forced to choose between the House of Commons and UGG, he had preferred the financial security of the company. At each succeeding opportunity to get back into politics, financial circumstances always dissuaded him.

By the late 1920s, all this had changed. His salary with UGG had advanced steadily with the fortunes of the company. In September 1926, it was raised to $24,000 per annum, and the following year, Crerar informed the company that he wanted only $21,000, which figure the board then implemented.[41]

His investments were now standing him in good stead. During the Great War, he had put what he was able into Government War Bonds. This was in addition to the stock he held in UGG and in the Home Bank (which he sold well before its failure in 1923). After his return to Winnipeg in 1922, he acquired some land around Winnipeg and Fort William. He invested in a local automobile agency and joined the Richardson family in the Manitoba Cattle Company. In 1924, he made his first venture in mining stock in a company working the Peace River country. He began to concentrate on mining stocks, frequently with the helpful advice of his friend Kirk Cameron, chairman of the Mines Bureau of the Montreal Chamber of Commerce. It was Cameron who introduced Crerar to Noah Timmins, who developed Noranda Mines, in which Crerar invested early.

In the spring of 1927, Crerar accompanied Timmins on a tour of the Rouyn-Noranda districts. When he returned he told Cameron how much he had enjoyed (and profited from) the trip and thanked him for "what you say as to the opinion the members [of the party] had of my visit with them. I was particularly glad to have met them, especially Mr. Timmins." He was fulsome in his praise of Timmins, whom he felt was doing great and important work in developing northern Ontario and Quebec. He looked forward to the same scale of mining development in northern Manitoba, which he felt would be an important factor in creating a mutual interest of east and west. He was especially pleased that Timmins had acquired control of Noranda, since he disliked seeing "Canadian resources pass into the control of Americans. I like to see Canadians obtain control of their own resources." He also asked Cameron to keep him apprised of Timmins's other interests; if stock were issued to the public "I should like to get a little of it, if possible."[42]

Crerar was also buying shares in Central Manitoba Mines, which owned the Sherritt-Gordon property. When Cameron wrote to Crerar to tell him that Timmins was interested, Crerar acted as intermediary with John Bracken and arranged a meeting between the premier and Timmins. The latter wanted the same sort of exemption from royalties that had been granted to the Flin Flon mine by the dominion government (which still controlled prairie resources), and he felt that Bracken must therefore agree to it. He was also involved in the discussions between the Flin Flon developers and Sherritt-Gordon to undertake a joint power development to serve the proposed smelting plants. On the advice of Timmins, Crerar eventually sold his shares in Sherritt-Gordon and put the money into Noranda, on whose board of directors Timmins had invited him to serve.[43]

He was also elected a director of the Great West Life Assurance Company. Such was his reputation as a businessman (and his new financial independence) that UGG apparently made no objections. Even the *Russell Banner* still took approving note of his achievements.[44]

Crerar's interest in politics, in these busy years, had not flagged. He applauded the movement of most of the Progressives closer to the Liberal party, and even of their decision to begin labelling themselves Liberal-Progressives. He displayed occasional grumpiness at some of the government's activities, but generally he found its performance acceptable.

He also had more time for reading, reflection, and conversation in these years. In Winnipeg the Sanhedrin met regularly and discussed events of the day, especially the aftermath of the Imperial Conference of 1926. Despite the long-term significance of the Balfour Declaration, Crerar was not overly impressed: "We are still at war when Britain is at war and liable to have our coast cities or commerce attacked ... [T]his is still the essential nature of our relationship." Members shared and discussed the latest books and kept Cameron in Montreal involved in their activities by mail and during his irregular visits. Crerar disliked Woodward's iconoclastic treatment of George Washington, was fascinated by Trevelyan's social history of England, and was enthralled by T.E. Lawrence's *Seven Pillars of Wisdom*.[45]

The Sanhedrin followed major patronage appointments closely, and all the members got involved, even pressuring King and Lapointe, when it was rumoured that E.T. McMurray would be named to the Court of King's Bench in Manitoba. They were relieved when the appointment did not take place. It was on this occasion that Crerar first urged naming of Hudson to the Supreme Court of Canada; but neither Hudson nor King was ready for such a move.[46]

The diamond jubilee of Confederation in 1927 was the occasion for the first Dominion-Provincial Conference, an event much scoffed at privately by the Winnipeg group. In a prescient moment, Crerar observed to Cameron that it was all very well to make sentimental appeals in a "Jubilee Year" and attempt to "justify the handout to the Maritimes [as a result of the Duncan Commission] on this ground," but he predicted that the conference would provide an opportunity for a concerted raid by the provinces "on the Federal Treasury for more cash subsidies, but it won't work. In the declining days of Rome the central power made frequent use of handouts to allay discontent in the more distant Provinces."[47]

Crerar's opinion of the Conservative party had changed little. He attended its leadership convention in Winnipeg in the autumn of 1927 "and knocked around the hotels for two or three hours the night the Convention closed." He was not surprised that R.B. Bennett had been selected but agreed with many observers that "Meighen could unquestionably have had the leadership by an overwhelming majority if he stood for it." The Tories, in his view, "are surely facing difficulty unless King throws them the trump card."[48] The prime minister was doing his best to solidify the position of the Liberals in the minds and hearts of westerners.

King still had misgivings about his western prospects. The policy of pressing ahead with the Hudson Bay Railway was very popular, despite Dunning's last-minute (and sound) decision to change the terminus from the mouth of the Nelson River to that of the Churchill. Equally promising, the long dispute about transfer of natural resources to the prairie provinces was almost resolved. Yet King deplored the hostility between Dunning and James G. Gardiner, Liberal premier of Saskatchewan, and the fact that Charlie Stewart of Alberta "has no grip on his province." Manitoba "has no leadership in Forke."[49]

So King began again to entice Crerar back to Ottawa. His first step was to name Crerar to a royal commission set up to arbitrate the financial settlement between Ottawa and Manitoba for lands alienated by Ottawa until that time, minus the subsidies that had been paid in lieu of control of resources. Crerar was present at the final meeting that resolved the issue, along with King, Lapointe, Robb,

Forke, and Mr Justice Turgeon of Saskatchewan, who chaired the commission. The settlement continued the subsidies and compensated Manitoba for past losses.[50]

Turgeon and Crerar were then joined by C.A. Bowman to adjudicate the amount of compensation, and the three sat frequently in Ottawa. Manitoba was represented by A.B. Hudson. Work went forward quickly, and an amicable and acceptable agreement gave Manitoba upward of $4 million. The question of personal compensation can scarcely have influenced the commissioners. Crerar received $30 per day, plus $20 for expenses.[51] But the appointment did bring him back to public notice, which is what King desired, and he was convinced now that "Crerar would come into the Gov't. any time."[52]

In the autumn of 1929, King and Haydon made a lengthy trip to western Canada. At a private meeting in Winnipeg King formally asked Crerar to enter the cabinet, "at a time to be decided later on." Crerar expressed cautious interest and suggested that King discuss matters with Dafoe, Fowler, and Hudson. Haydon jumped at this opportunity to have "these Liberal Unionists ... get back into line." The prime minister found "the regular Liberal Executive ... a disgruntled lot wanting more say in patronage & ready to knife Crerar." He ignored them, since clearly he was more interested in getting the Winnipeg Sanhedrin on side.[53]

The following day, King discovered that there would be no time for a lengthy courtship. The health of James A. Robb, the minister of finance, had become critical, and he would have to be replaced. King had for some time planned to move Dunning from Railways and Canals to Finance. Now he had an opportunity for more general reconstruction of his government. When he returned to Winnipeg from the west late in November, he met with Crerar, Dunning, Fowler, Hudson, and, of course, the ever-present Haydon; here it was agreed that Forke should go to the Senate and Crerar should join the cabinet and seek election in Forke's Brandon seat.

The next day, Crerar agreed to enter, but there was some unfortunate confusion about which portfolio he would take. Crerar wanted to succeed Dunning at Railways and thought that King understood this; but the latter somehow was thinking that Crerar would replace Forke at Immigration. For the moment they were both enthusiastic, however, and Crerar "said he would get Dafoe, Fowler, Hudson and all that group to work with him. He thought they could do their own [election] financing." It was also made clear that Crerar would have a free hand to organize Manitoba in the next election.[54]

When the prime minister returned to Ottawa, his hesitation over Crerar's portfolio became understandable. He was concerned that the appointment to the then important post of Railways and Canals might upset Quebec Liberals and create the impression that they would be relegated to minor offices. For that reason, he wanted Crerar to accept Immigration until Lapointe could be consulted and his agreement secured. Crerar meanwhile was engaged in a survey of Brandon constituency, but he made it clear to Dunning that all activity would cease if he did not receive Railways. King wrote in his diary: "I learned Crerar wants Railways at once (perhaps he is right, but he shows little faith at any time)." But King still hesitated until Lapointe returned, "with the chance of losing Crerar in interval." The Quebec ministers finally agreed a week later, and the announcement was made of Crerar's appointment as minister of railways and canals.[55]

Among the many notes of congratulations that Crerar received was one from Colonel H.D.G. (Harry) Crerar, with whom he would be connected off and on for many years. Though no direct relation, Colonel Crerar considered himself "as one of the clan."

As the year came to a close, King seems to have been just as gratified as Crerar. He claimed to be sorry to lose Forke from cabinet "but have immeasurably strengthened it by securing Crerar, & Finance by getting Dunning in there – this will all help to hold the West." He was particularly pleased as well that Crerar, as a former member of the Union government, represented a healing of that old rupture of the Liberal party. The addition of Crerar also ended the division between Progressives and Liberals on the dominion level in Manitoba, just as the recent merger of the parties on the provincial level had ended the local split. "This is an achievement," he exulted in his diary. "It has taken 8 years to get Crerar," but King obviously felt the effort justified.[56] The two men would be colleagues a long time, but there was little warmth between them.

The new minister had little time for self-congratulation. Only three weeks remained until the opening of the new session of Parliament, and he had a large, bustling department with which to become familiar. But even that had to wait until he had secured a seat in the House of Commons. Robert Forke had managed Brandon successfully, largely because he had maintained the support of all the Progressives, including pool members. How Crerar would fare with the pool voters was another matter.

His public announcement that he would resign as president of United Grain Growers and from its board helped somewhat. It was also encouraging to hear from an old acquaintance, R.H. Cobb, assistant grand chief of the Brotherhood of Railway Engineers. Cobb offered to help among the railwaymen in Brandon and Souris and saw "no reason why they should not give you their support." Another informant in the constituency wrote hopefully that there was little opposition to Crerar as an outsider or from the pool.[57]

The Tories chose not to oppose Crerar, and he won the seat by acclamation. While this eased his immediate problem, an extensive working of the constituency and a solid local organization would have served him well a few months later.

CHAPTER TEN

Rethinking Liberalism,
1929–34

Crerar had been out of the House of Commons for five years, but he had not been forgotten. When he took his place on the ministerial benches in late December 1929, R.B. Bennett, now Opposition leader, immediately twitted him on leaving his old Progressive associates and joining those he had earlier criticized. And one of those old associates, Gingerite Robert Gardiner welcomed Crerar back but insisted that he no longer spoke for western agriculture, since he had been so long away from the farm, having lived in Winnipeg for twenty-years.[1] It was a nice point. Crerar was widely known and respected and considered a fine administrator and business executive. He had become in many people's eyes, including King's, a spokesman for Manitoba and the prairie west rather than the grain growers. But he still considered their interests carefully.

His appointment to the Railways portfolio, then considered a senior cabinet post, indicates as well as anything else that it was his general administrative ability that was being recruited. However, he would have little time to put his mark on the department. He was immediately plunged into a session of the House, which would end with an election call. He had for many years been a staunch supporter of the national railway and on close and friendly terms with Sir Henry Thornton, its president. And he agreed with Thornton's suggestion that the personnel of the Board of Railway Commissioners and the Select Committee on National Railways should remain the same, ensuring a fair, if not favourable, hearing for Canadian National in Ottawa.[2] It was not expected that Canadian Pacific would be pleased with his appointment.

In the House, Crerar went to some lengths to protect the reputation of the Canadian National Railways (CNR). On one occasion, when asked how many CNR employees had been laid off at central region shops in recent years, he declined to supply the figures, claiming that it was "not in the public interest to bring down information of this character."[3] He was able to make some progress on the rights of bondholders who held stock in subsidiaries of the old Canadian Northern system, which the government had taken over during the Great War. In a new CNR Amalgamation Act in 1930, he placed these charges against the physical assets of the old companies and thus protected the revenues of the CNR, which, like most other businesses in 1930, was struggling.[4]

The deteriorating economic situation began to assume paramount importance for Crerar and his cabinet mates. He was especially concerned with the west, where falling wheat prices, a large carry-over from the harvest of 1929, and the difficulties of the pools were causing consternation.

Worsening prospects in the west also had unfortunate social repercussions, as so often happens. When pressed by an acquaintance in the Press Gallery about the activity of the Ku Klux Klan, he replied: "The big drum of anti-Catholic and anti-French cry is still being vigorously pounded in Saskatchewan," but he expected "a very considerable reaction against it." He felt obliged to write to the prime minister objecting to a petition in British Columbia demanding that the provincial government prohibit owning or leasing of land by "Orientals or persons of Oriental descent" and arguing that they should be denied the dominion franchise. He professed to be unconcerned when warned that the Klan would fight him in the election, believing that J.J. Maloney, the Klan leader, would stay out of Manitoba, but he forwarded the warning to Dunning.[5] While disturbing, these manifestations of social unrest were partly symptomatic of the real problem, the deepening depression.

The government was now in the fourth year of its mandate, and King had soon to decide whether to call a summer election or wait and hope for conditions to improve in 1931 – a prospect becoming ever more dubious. His decision was influenced largely by two factors, both related to External Affairs, his own department. First, the Smoot-Hawley tariff adopted by the U.S. Congress early in 1930 raised American rates to unprecedented levels and virtually excluded all Canadian agricultural produce. It would be politically damaging for King not to react vigorously. He had Dunning prepare a budget that increased Commonwealth preferences, to the obvious disadvantage of the Americans. Second, this opening to the empire/Commonwealth fitted nicely into his desire to attend the Imperial Conference set for the autumn of 1930, which would complete the devolution begun in 1926 and, as well, seek cooperative means to combat the economic slump in the trading world, more and more beset by high-tariff psychology. It would, he believed, put Bennett in an impossible position if the Liberals were seen to be reacting against the United States by increasing both Commonwealth economic preferences and unity.

Crerar was not enthusiastic about the prospect of an election, and not simply because he had just arrived in Ottawa. He felt that Liberal chances in Manitoba would suffer badly because of difficulties in the wheat belt and the consequent general business decline. The Sanhedrin certainly agreed and through Dafoe tried to dissuade the prime minister from an early election. King noted Dafoe's advice, "written evidently at Crerar's insistence," strongly against an appeal but took heart at Dafoe's "fine spirit ... truly friendly and complimentary." He was delighted to have the *Free Press* back in the Liberal fold, despite its old "determination because of conscription never to support a non-conscriptionist leader, no small triumph in itself."[6] But he did not take Dafoe's advice seriously. By early spring, King decided on an appeal to the electorate.[7]

But he blundered badly in an impatient retort in the House while discussing relief measures. There are several versions of this angry exchange with Bennett. Crerar was mildly critical when he wrote to Cameron: "King made a rather unfortunate break in his speech ... when he intimated that he would not want to give five cents to any Tory Provincial Government for unemployment relief purposes." Neither correspondent realized the potential damage of such a petty and partisan outburst. Crerar was rather complacent in this letter, arguing that Tory demands for increased protection could not be squared with the fact that the United States, which had among the highest tariffs in the world, had an unemployment rate "two or three times as great as it is in Canada."[8] But he had little else to offer.

In cabinet, Crerar reluctantly went along with a bonus scheme for Nova Scotia coal, though he knew that it would draw fire in the west. He balked openly in the House, however, at the suggestion of dominion support for highways as a matter of policy, reminding his colleagues of the debt burden left by the Great War and claiming: "We must have some regard to the taxpaying capacity of the Canadian people."[9] But he shared the party's hope that the economy would soon right itself and its fear that government tinkering would probably do more harm than good. Retrenchment until the storm passed seemed to be his watchword. It was a position that he would abandon later in the Depression. King, in contrast, was prepared to risk the government's fate on a clever budget and then run on the record. It would not be good enough.

Despite the fact that Dunning's budget of 1930 contained more specific tariff reductions than increases and expanded the British preference, it generally sought greater protection for the Canadian economy. It seemed rather weak-kneed to argue that Tories would raise tariffs even higher. Crerar was in no position to take an active part in defending the budget in the House. He was bitterly attacked by opponents who cited his own anti-protection speeches given in the chamber in the early 1920s. He was thus obliged to suffer in silence. His old friend and colleague Chipman of the *Guide* summed up Crerar's evident embarrassment when he wrote, rather sadly: "It is pretty difficult for a person engaged for 20 years on a low tariff campaign to become very enthusiastic about the present budget." But like most government supporters, he saw little alternative, with the Tories out for more protection and the Progressives pretty well shot to pieces.[10]

But King was determined, and the day after the budget he informed the cabinet that he had decided on an election. With mixed feelings, they all went along, including Crerar. Most of them sensed that a year's delay would probably do little good.[11] Crerar was responsible for his own constituency of Brandon, but he also had general supervision of the campaign in Manitoba. Members of the Sanhedrin stood ready to assist as advisers, sounding boards, speakers (or editorial writers), and fund-raisers. Despite their political experience and sources throughout western Canada, however, they had little sense of the tide rising against them.

Crerar still carried the odium of the failure of the Home Bank. Despite all the evidence revealed by the royal commission that had investigated the collapse, it had been Crerar and the Grain Growers' Grain Company that had urged farmers to purchase bank stock in the first place. And now, twenty years later, he was still being held responsible. As recently as early May 1930, he had been sharply attacked in the House by Peter McGibbon of Muskoka (Ontario), who claimed that one thousand of his constituents were still suffering.[12] It simply would not go away. Neither would the resentment of dairy farmers across the country over the issue of New Zealand butter, which was entering the country in vast amounts under a treaty that Canada had negotiated with Australia.

Despite these specific and obvious difficulties and the general pall of depression settling on the country, there was a rather startling air of unreality about Crerar's role in the 1930 election. At a campaign stop in Winnipeg, King met with Frank Fowler, who told him: "The situation throughout Manitoba is good ... Crerar evidently has succeeded in welding different groups together." The next day the prime minister talked with Crerar, who had just returned to the city and reported that "all is well with the situation in Manitoba, is not concerned about his own seat." They were both pleased that all Progressive and Liberal difficulties had been ironed out.[13]

Crerar seemed equally blind to the problems facing him in Brandon. Presumably, he had hoped for a straight fight with a Conservative. He had written to his old friend R.H. Cobb of the Brotherhood of Railway Engineers, "They have nominated a pretty strong man against me," and he asked Cobb to come to Manitoba and "give me a lift with the boys in Brandon and Souris." Cobb responded willingly and also circulated a letter to union members in the riding describing Crerar as "a personal friend for a number of years" and telling them that they would have a minister of railways from whom "we may always expect a square deal." Unfortunately, he could not prevent the local Labor party in Brandon from fielding a candidate, though Crerar continued hopeful.[14] But the election was a rout.

There was only one government in Canada, provincial or dominion, to survive a Depression election – that of John Bracken of Manitoba in 1932 (and again in 1936) – and it was a coalition. In the 1930 dominion election the Tories elected 137 members to ninety-one for the Liberals. The popular vote was not as unbalanced, 45.8 per cent for the Conservatives to 45.2 per cent for the Liberals. But the defeat was decisive. On the prairies the Tories won twenty-three seats, a stunning gain of twenty-two. The Liberals and their Progressive allies, except the United Farmers of Alberta, dropped from thirty-two to eighteen seats. Crerar lost Brandon by a disappointing margin; his almost effortless election seven months previous obviously meant little.

King tried to put a brave face on the results. He wrote to Crerar expressing his regret at the loss in Brandon and thanking him for "strengthening the Government, helping the Party, and serving the country. Please have no concern regarding the future. All will work out for the best in the future." His advice did not include any practical measures.[15] When they met a few days later, King found Crerar pained and disappointed, for "he would like to be back in Parliament." He felt that this must be arranged somehow. "He (Crerar) and Dunning are most necessary." But there was little that could be done immediately.

When King and Bennett had an unexpected post-election talk, King conceded that he might have overestimated Crerar's influence with the farmers. Bennett agreed but added that discontent against Crerar and the Liberals on the prairies was the result of old hurts from the Home Bank's collapse and current resentment at the easy entry of butter from New Zealand.[16]

Crerar's return to politics had been brief and hardly spectacular, and he no longer had the company on which to rely. While disappointed, he was not ready to abandon public life and begin something entirely new. He could be content (and financially able) to wait for another opportunity. And prospects for the Liberal party might not be as bleak as the results might indicate. In the view of the Sanhedrin, it was not the Liberal voters who were stampeded, but the former Progressives. According to Dafoe, the Liberals were "stronger in numbers" on the prairies than "at any time since the disruption of the party in 1917."[17] This was at least an analysis from which to take heart and look ahead. After all, it was now Bennett and the Tories who had to deal with the worsening depression.

Crerar soon established a new rhythm of life in Winnipeg. He and Jessie moved into a house in the west end, about a twenty-minute walk from downtown. Dorothy was now enrolled at the Normal School. Crerar was able to devote personal attention to the stock farm that he and his brother Peter had purchased a few miles north of the city. So he still had some loose connection with the rural community.

There was as well the Sanhedrin, from which he always drew support. The group met two or three times a week, he informed Cameron, "but do not seem to be making much progress in solving the nation's affairs."[18] It would sustain him over the next few years, as he awaited another opportunity. An indication of the changed status of all the members was that their frequent lunches now took place at the exclusive Manitoba Club, rather than at Moore's restaurant. They were very concerned about the international situation, especially as it affected the economic prospects for prairie agriculture, for they remained convinced that the grain trade was still a major factor in the national economy. They also followed the doings at Ottawa closely.

Within a few months, Crerar was back to political activity. He maintained his extraordinary correspondence with Cameron and was in frequent contact with Mackenzie King. At King's request he arranged a meeting in Winnipeg to revive Liberal spirits by launching attacks at Bennett's tariff hikes. He kept urging the Opposition leader to tackle Bennett on his economic policies, fearing that the national government would become committed to the principle that "we will relieve unemployment by spending public monies that we collect from the taxpayer; and that we will find markets by loaning foreign countries [China, in this case] the money with which to buy our goods." Such a policy was the first fruit of protectionism.[19]

It was not only Canadian policy that Crerar regretted, but the nationalistic economic impulse that was sweeping the trading world in reaction to the Depression. The Sanhedrin found the root cause of the difficulties in the Treaty of Versailles. The nations of Europe had been guided by "stupidity and cupidity," and reparations had led largely to tariffs, "which are economic warfare in the international field." By its vengeful attitude, France was forfeiting the sympathy that it had been shown. The United States, in insisting on repayment of war debts, was exacerbating the situation.

Crerar saw little hope of improvement. "Laval talks debt reduction, Hoover talks disarmament and Laval replies with security." There could be no real peace in Europe until France and Germany established their relationship on mutual confidence and goodwill, a not-very-likely prospect. "Have we not pretty much a state of mind between the nations where each wants to beggar his neighbour and has this attitude of mind to change before we can get started to real recovery?"[20] None of this was profound, but it did indicate a keen interest in events.

Crerar was surprisingly different in his attitude to the Soviet Union, which he always referred to as "Russia". In letters to King he opined that the Russian experiment was going to be a success and would have a powerful influence: "The commercial and industrial forces in Canada should recognize it and put their house in order." Later, he complained that the "big business" people of Canada "don't realize that the capitalist system (so-called) is in danger." He was unusually adamant in urging King to be aware of the situation the world was in:

I am not a communist and I am very far from being a socialist, but that does not blind me to the fact that there are grave abuses in the body politic so far as business is concerned, and the way to meet the communist or even the radical socialist is not to shout at him as a dangerous agitator, but to survey our own structure and cure the defects. We have placed the emphasis altogether too largely on the materialistic side of life and not enough on things that have to do with the spiritual and cultural side of our existence.[21]

This was a remarkable analysis from a man now "clipping coupons." One can only wonder at King's reaction.

Crerar gave considerable attention to the political situation in Manitoba. The election of 1927 had returned John Bracken to the premier's office, sustained by a loose, informal alliance between Liberals and Progressives. Now Bracken was seeking an organic union. King was urging Crerar to assist the project as well as he was able, and Crerar used what influence he had. He conferred several times with Bracken and the Manitoba Liberals. His own view was that the Progressive party as such was now an anomaly and that a merger of the two groups would be the best means of reorganizing provincial politics into the forces of light and darkness. So both he and King were pleased when the two united to fight and win the 1932 election, defying the Canadian pattern of government losses in Depression elections. Clearly fusion had been the key. Crerar's intervention was hardly the crucial factor, but both Bracken and the local Liberals saw him as representing the wishes of King, as well as his own.[22]

The most startling news of 1931 for Liberals, including the bemused Sanhedrin in Winnipeg, was the Beauharnois scandal, which tainted King and his closest confidant, Andrew Haydon. The Beauharnois power syndicate had made a campaign contribution of over half a million dollars to the Liberals, after they had authorized an order-in-council in 1929 that allowed diversion of the St Lawrence River to the advantage of the Beauharnois power scheme. The scandal destroyed Haydon's reputation, as his law firm had received a $50,000 retainer, subject to passing of the vital order-in-council.[23] He was rather callously left to "swing in the wind," while King made brief expiation in his "Valley of Humiliation."

The Sanhedrin seized the event as an opportunity to reform the party – a goal that King now piously shared. Crerar was somewhat sceptical, however; he sensed "that the general feeling was that the Liberals were found out and that the Tories were not, but were equally guilty, if not from Beauharnois then from somewhere else." He was forced to agree that the Liberals had been badly compromised, and "a great many electors would be willing to consign both the old parties to the devil."[24] The Sanhedrin was alarmed at the rumour that King was contemplating resignation. With no other possible leader on the horizon, it swallowed any doubts that it might have had about King, and Crerar communicated its apprehension, as well as his own considered advice, in a long and rather frank letter to King.

He began by regretting that the revelations had pushed Bennett's record into the background. Defeat of the Liberals a year earlier had been due not to "weakness or graft in the administration, but to the spectacular appeal of Bennett" in depressed conditions. The people opted for change, any change, though "it has taken only one short year to wholly disillusion them." He went on to argue that "your personal integrity is not, and will not be challenged"; but he had to concede that the party had suffered badly and that Haydon's political usefulness was over. He urged King to put any thought of resignation out of his mind, since he and the Liberals must stand ready to save the country from Bennett. The latter's extravagant promises had perverted the public's mind as to the proper function of government: "We are building up an army of mendicants in Canada who sit on the doorstep of the public treasury."

Crerar suggested that King turn the situation to advantage by appealing to the imagination of Canadians on the whole business of public policy: "I would like to see the party come out with a clear cut announcement that it was not going to accept campaign contributions from corporations or individuals who might in any way be looking for government favours." There should also be a regular accounting given to the public of all party receipts and disbursements. It was strong stuff, and Crerar also made belated amends for his support of Dunning's budget the previous year. There should have been no concessions, however small, to the principle of protection. He concluded by advising King to put it all behind him and look forward with hope.[25]

King was in a mood to listen and anxious to put as much distance between himself and party funds as possible. He replied to Crerar that he had "grown nearly desperate over the matter of party organization." He sought Crerar's help in a move that led the following year to creation of the National Liberal Federation. A meeting of the National Liberal Organization was to be held in Ottawa in late November, and he appointed Crerar Manitoba member. The latter was happy to accept and attended the meeting that set in train a major party overhaul.[26]

But there were some things other than politics in Crerar's life. He spent much of the summer of 1931 on the farm, "getting my muscles toughened and physically feel in tip top shape." (He was now fifty-five.) Around the city, he took a hand in various activities; as a board member of the YMCA, he took on the task of fund-raising. And he kept in touch with many of the friends he had made in Ottawa. Ernest Lapointe wrote him a curious letter, informing him that he was not practising law in Quebec City and inquiring whether Crerar, as a director of Great West Life, might ask if that company would like a French-Canadian director on its board.[27] The appearance of Dafoe's book on Sir Clifford Sifton kept the Sanhedrin buzzing, most of its members agreeing with Dafoe's interpretation in general, though Cameron, a warm partisan of Laurier's, objected to many of Dafoe's accounts of the relations of the two colleagues. Long exchanges between Dafoe and Cameron form an interesting supplement to the book.[28]

This seemed a pleasant, undemanding period in Crerar's life, and it would continue for the next three years, until the political call came once again. He took on several tasks of a more or less public nature, and he travelled extensively, especially throughout northern Manitoba. His interest in mining development drew him there, but he slowly began to cultivate the area politically. To "Armulree," the farm north of Winnipeg, he and Jessie moved in the summer of 1932 – by choice and because they could live there and rent out the house in the city. He was in Winnipeg two or three times a week in any case, so he missed few meetings of the Sanhedrin. And with his extensive correspondence, he was not at all isolated.

Late in 1931, Crerar took on the chairmanship of a Citizens' Committee in Winnipeg to coordinate the unemployment welfare activities to which he devoted considerable time. The welter of public and private organizations that sought jobs, recreation, and entertainment for the unemployed had created "a complex and difficult problem."[29]

He also became involved with an issue that seemed never to die in Manitoba – the Catholic schools. Catholics of Winnipeg paid public school taxes and supported their own parochial schools as well. As the Depression worsened, the Catholic community could no longer bear the costs of its six schools, with some twenty-four hundred pupils. Archbishop Sinnot so notified the mayor, and plans had to be made to accommodate this sudden influx into the public schools. Crerar met with Sinnot to discuss a scheme whereby the public school board would rent the Catholic schools for $1 a year, leave the pupils where they were, and use the contributed services of the teaching nuns, who would wear ordinary garb and remove religious symbols from the classrooms. The former parochial schools would then operate as public schools.

Sinnot felt that if Dafoe and the *Free Press* supported the scheme, there would be little difficulty, a strategy with which Crerar agreed. So off he went to see Dafoe, who had always been rather intransigent on this question, and the latter was not willing to compromise the public schools in any way. In recounting the issue to King, Crerar said: "Frankly, I was rather disappointed in his attitude. ... I quite sympathize with the desires of the Catholics, at any rate in the early grades, to have their children taught by Catholic instructors." Crerar feared any revival of denominational controversy in such difficult times, though he felt that Sinnot's offer could be construed as falling within the provisions of the Public School Act. The scheme failed to be adopted, however, and some schools had to be closed. Crerar found the whole business distasteful and disappointing.[30]

During much of 1933, he served on a committee to investigate the affairs of the privately owned Winnipeg Electric Railway – a large, local transportation and power utility created by Mackenzie and Mann, the Toronto-based international traction entrepreneurs. The company had defaulted on the bond interest of one of its subsidiaries, and several others were financially shaky. The work, which he thoroughly enjoyed, took him to Toronto frequently, which allowed him to keep in close touch with political affairs.[31]

Such varied assignments, in combination with his political activities, mining interests, and the farm, kept him busy and often in the public eye. And he took seriously the obligation of those who had been successful in business to assist the community from which they had profited.

In public affairs, Crerar and the Sanhedrin remained preoccupied with international trade, the problems of the Canadian National Railways, the rise of the Co-operative Commonwealth Federation (CCF), and the fate of the Liberals. They held out little hope of good results from the imperial economic conference that Bennett convened in Ottawa in mid-1932. Crerar saw some perils for Canada. The only means of influence open to him and his colleagues was through King. Crerar was arranging a visit by King to Manitoba, which included a lunch with the Sanhedrin that Crerar hosted at the Manitoba Club. In briefing King, he laid out the danger as he saw it. The supporters of imperial trade were looking to some kind of imperial *Zollverein*, which Crerar saw as folly. He pressed on King the argument that this would only provoke retaliation in the rest of Europe. Then he turned to simple arithmetic. Canada and Australia produced annually from 450 to 500 million bushels of wheat for export. Britain's needs did not exceed 140 million. "We must sell the rest mainly on the Continent of Europe." Since the only answer to Canada's economic woes was an expansion of markets, a closed imperial trading system would completely beggar Canada.[32] It was a theme to which he returned throughout the coming months.

As the conference approached, Crerar grew more gloomy. "I have no faith whatever in Bennett's judgement"; and he feared that the prime minister would try simply to make political capital of imperialist sentiment. He regretted that economic nationalism would probably ruin the conference. Bennett would never run the domestic risk of making serious reductions in trade barriers, even against British goods. Only bold action would help, he told Cameron. If the assembled statesmen had "[t]he vision and courage to wipe out tariff barriers within the Empire excepting for purely revenue needs" and at the same time announce that all the dominions and Britain were willing to make favourable trade deals with any other country that would reciprocate, "the Conference would achieve something worth while. But the prospect of their doing this is very remote." He was convinced that selfish nationalism would prevent any beneficial result, and to give the impression that the empire was even considering a tariff against the rest of the world "would simply accentuate the fears and suspicions and jealousies that today lie at the roots and feed the roots of the world's troubles."[33]

During the course of the conference, late in the summer, Crerar was again highly critical of Bennett, claiming that "he could not harmonize the Canada First policy with a general empire trade policy." All the dominions were far too aggressive, in his opinion. Only Baldwin of Britain was acting in an admirable spirit. "The thing, of course, cannot be allowed to fail," so some cosmetic accomplishments would be trumpeted. Bennett spoke proudly of a wheat preference from Britain, but "it is not worth a hoot." Canada and Australia were faced with nearly 550 million bushels of wheat to dispose of; so even if Britain took all its needs from them, they would still be left with some 400 million bushels. Only really smashing blows at trade barriers would be of any significance.[34]

It was the firm opinion of the Sanhedrin that the conference had been a failure; its most advertised agreement – that of competitive tariffs – would never really be honoured by Bennett. There was a round of letters and meetings with King and Norman Lambert (who was now working for the party) to devise a proper Liberal response. Despite Hudson's contrary view, they agreed that King should hold back on his criticism until the full impact of the rather hostile reaction of the British press became familiar to Canadians.

So King waited until Parliament was again in session before announcing a formal party position. His indictment came in a long speech in the House in October 1932. Crerar was delighted with it and quickly sent his congratulations. It was especially apt, he felt, to point out that the marginal shifts in trade within the empire had had no effect in expanding total trade. King's strongest criticism was that a great opportunity had been missed for launching a general lowering of tariffs and an invitation to the rest of the world to follow suit. Failure to achieve such reductions would probably lead to further economic nationalism throughout the trading world. Crerar could not have phrased it better himself.[35] The unhappy fact remained, however, that all the hopes that the conference had aroused had been dashed. And the Depression wore on.

One of the potential casualties could be Canadian National Railways (CNR), burdening the government with huge annual deficits, now including operating losses as well as bonded debt. There were persistent rumours that the Montreal business community and a large

section of the Conservative party favoured some form of amalgamation with the Canadian Pacific Railway (CPR) as a solution – a move
that would certainly be denounced in western Canada. Bennett had
set up a commission in 1931 under Sir Lyman Duff to consider the
best method of meeting the railway situation. The Sanhedrin, and
Dafoe especially, were convinced that the commission "are out to
hamstring the national railways." Their fears were heightened when
Sir Henry Thornton resigned the presidency of the CNR before the
commission reported. Crerar's reaction was that "C.P.R. influence at
Ottawa is paramount" and that Thornton "had been thrown over-
board." Dafoe in turn wrote a long, detailed letter on the railway
problem to Grant Dexter, the (now *Winnipeg*) *Free Press*'s man in
Ottawa, in which he said that he anticipated further attacks on the
national railway and made Dexter aware that Dafoe was going to
fight any move to undermine the national road.[36] But the Winnipeg
group, and the Liberal party, could only await Mr Justice Duff's
report.

The document appeared just before Christmas 1932, and Vincent
Massey, at King's instruction, immediately dispatched it to Crerar,
requesting that he bring the Winnipeg group together to discuss it.
In two long meetings, he, Dafoe, Fowler, Hudson, and Edgar Tarr, a
new member who ran a successful insurance business, examined the
report carefully. They were assisted by Norman Lambert, who was
in Winnipeg, as well as by Harry Sifton, Sir Clifford's son. So it
received a thorough canvass, but from a decidedly western point of
view.

Duff's report, apparently with some reluctance, recognized the
political difficulty of any attempt at amalgamation of the two railways. But it chose to fasten on the alleged extravagance of the CNR,
which had resulted largely from political interference to satisfy
regional pressures. The CPR, which had spent just as freely in the late
1920s, was dealt with lightly. The commission proposed to abolish
the board of directors of the CNR and replace it with three trustees
to oversee operations. It also recommended a board of arbitration to
settle disputes between the two railways, with binding decisions.
Clearly such appointments as trustees and arbitrators would be crucial, and the Sanhedrin feared that any appointees proposed by the
Bennett government would favour the CPR. Much worse, from
Crerar's point of view, control would be removed from Parliament.

On behalf of the Sanhedrin, Crerar wrote a lengthy assessment after
the discussions and sent copies to King, Lambert, and Massey. Members agreed that public confidence in the management of the national
railway had been eroded but shared the public apprehension about

a railway monopoly. So amalgamation under CPR control was quite unacceptable; it would lead to deterioration in service and creation of a power so great as to be able to make and unmake governments. Therefore the "Liberal Party should set its face unalterably against amalgamation ... as is now proposed and urged in Eastern Canada."

Instead, Crerar wrote, the present system of management of the CNR should be abandoned and replaced by a board of trustee shareholders, which would stand in relation to the CNR as any set of shareholders would to a private company. It would elect a board of directors, chosen geographically, which would in turn select an executive committee, which would oversee operations and include the deputy ministers of Railways and of Finance. The government would appoint the president, who would hold office at the pleasure of the board of directors. The system would be a bit cumbersome, but it would guarantee public and parliamentary control. The problem of cooperation between the railways would be resolved by application of the conciliation and arbitration provisions of the Industrial Disputes Investigations Act.[37]

Mackenzie King was generally delighted with the report. He demurred only at the recommendation that the initial board of trustee shareholders be chosen by a judicial panel in each province. He was probably quite accurate when he replied: "You know what the attitude of labour is towards the courts and just how far railway employees and, indeed, the working classes generally, or the farmers, would be prepared sympathetically to view any control which traced its origin to the mind of the judiciary." A sad, but practical objection. Otherwise, he told Crerar, he would take the opportunity of an impending visit by Dafoe to shape the report into Liberal policy.[38]

Early in the new year, the Bennett government brought legislation to the House based on the Duff report. The Liberals feared that it would pass; and after its being in effect for a year, they suspected, the government would announce that the two railways could not operate this way and must be amalgamated – and only a truly national government could do that. Rumours of interest in a coalition to meet the emergency of the 1930s had been rife. To the Liberals, of course, such an idea was preposterous and simply a desperate Tory ploy to hang on to power.[39] But King, armed with the Sanhedrin's proposals, was ready. His attack in the House presumed that the government's real intention was to destroy the national railway. He scoffed at the hope that the two railways would submit disputes to arbitration, but he devoted most of his efforts to denouncing such a brazen attempt to subvert the rights of Parliament. Despite the hyperbole, he did score heavily.[40]

Bennett's majority ensured passage of the bill, but it came to little; indeed, it proved unworkable. And as King's biographer points out, the deficits continued. The CNR was saved, to go on losing more money.

The Sanhedrin had made its contribution to two critical policies of a reviving Liberal party – opposition to protection and defence of the national railway. It was also asked to help shape Liberal policy on a central bank, an issue in which it took considerable interest, but to which it gave more enthusiastic support than useful advice.[41] More effectively, it, and Crerar most of all, attended to political organization throughout the early 1930s, looking to a dominion election.

National success would depend heavily on reconstructing the Liberal party of Manitoba, through a firm alliance with John Bracken and the Progressives. In this endeavour, Crerar would play a major role. Liberals and Progressives had been steadily moving closer in Manitoba, except for a group of "die-hard" Liberals, mainly in Winnipeg. With a provincial election due in 1932, there seemed some urgency in institutionalizing the courtship. National Liberal headquarters watched events closely. King intervened directly. He told Crerar that he had "been thinking a good deal over the Manitoba situation and your own relationship to it. I really feel that it would be a great help to all, both provincially and federally, if you could see your way at once to enter the Ministry." This extraordinary suggestion also included Joseph Thorson, a rising young lawyer of Icelandic descent. King added that he hoped to see Crerar and Thorson in Ottawa after the next dominion election but did not think that a brief period in provincial politics would prevent them from jumping to the other field. He urged this course of action, even though there was no indication of how Bracken would react. King's only real concern was the fortunes of the dominion party.

There was also another sub-theme. National Liberal headquarters was concerned that a confrontation might be brewing between Crerar and Thorson over the constituency of Selkirk. Crerar's farm was in the riding, and he considered himself an established resident; but it was a natural area for Thorson, with its large and politically sensitive Icelandic population. The Manitoba situation was considered so vital that Lambert travelled to Winnipeg for a meeting at the Manitoba Club with Crerar, Dafoe, Fowler, Hudson, and Thorson. It turned out, however, to be an inconclusive discussion, focusing on Bracken's position.[42]

Crerar's reaction was to delay his reply to King. But he was not inactive. When Bracken formally invited the Liberals to join his

Progressives in fighting the next provincial election, Crerar took a hand in creating a Liberal-Progressive committee to organize Manitoba constituencies; he expected that it would carry over into the national field. A group of Winnipeg Liberals balked, however, despite the agreement of the Liberal Association of Manitoba, and announced that it would run straight Liberal candidates in the election, expected that summer. It did so, according to Crerar, out of dislike for Bracken, who, "with the best of intentions in the world, often displays a lamentable lack of tact. He is too much the school master in politics." Though Crerar felt the move sound and remained hopeful, he argued that the present was not the moment to discuss personnel.[43]

Events worked out much as he had hoped. By the time the Manitoba election was called for mid-June 1932, a firm coalition had been effected, except for a few Liberal malcontents who insisted on nominating a handful of nuisance candidates. Crerar kept a watchful eye on Bracken during the campaign, telling him early on that "no government could win on its record no matter how good it was, in these times, but that if the coalition could get the idea across to the people that the parties in it had sunk party differences to serve the province," and hammer the Conservatives for not joining in, he could win. "But Bracken is a school master by profession and the temptation lies heavily upon him to justify everything that the government has done."[44] It was much to Bracken's advantage that the Tories ran a poor campaign, and the voters apparently accepted the coalition as a fresh start. And he did switch his position from defence of his record to an attack on Ottawa. As a Tory friend of Crerar put it, "the people of Manitoba didn't vote for Bracken but they voted against Bennett."

After the election, which Bracken won handily, Crerar finally replied to King's suggestion of January. He had mulled over the idea of going into Bracken's government, he told King, but his personal affairs quite engaged his attention. He was rather abrupt: "I discussed this pretty carefully with [Dafoe, Hudson, and Tarr] and they were all agreed that it was inadvisable for me to go into the administration. The reasons I need scarcely trouble you with now."[45] There was little prospect that he would be deflected from his intention to return to Ottawa. His problem now was to convert the successful provincial coalition into a similar national Liberal organization.

King was of course immensely pleased at the result in Manitoba, which demonstrated the wisdom of his support for a union of Liberals and Progressives. He hoped that Crerar would have equal success nationally and that the Winnipeg "die-hards" could be discouraged.[46] But for the future King and Lambert were anxious to avoid a battle between Crerar and Thorson over Selkirk. The summer after the provincial election, Lambert arrived in Winnipeg for a round of meetings with Crerar, Thorson, and the Sanhedrin, alone and severally; and Crerar and Thorson met to discuss Selkirk. Thorson was adamant, and Lambert was inclined to go along with him, since Crerar was known throughout the province and should have little difficulty in finding another riding. He even suggested to Crerar that he think of running in South Winnipeg.

Only the Sanhedrin was aware that Crerar was considering a surprising alternative.[47] When Crerar attended the small gathering of prominent Liberals, which included Dafoe, that Vincent Massey hosted at Port Hope in September 1933, he discussed the situation with King and Lambert. His long interest in mining and his many visits to northern Manitoba were about to bear political results. He was contemplating running in the vast Churchill constituency, with its major centres the mining towns of The Pas and Flin Flon. According to Lambert they also discussed cabinet rank, and "King said while [Crerar] stood on good ground, he could not say anything that might be interpreted as a promise." King's customary oblique caution became more pronounced as the prospects of a return to power improved. It was not evident that Crerar was in any manner discouraged. As soon as he returned to Winnipeg he agreed to head up the election finance committee for Manitoba, with help from Fowler and Hudson.[48]

His organization work went on apace. As a member of the Liberal-Progressive Executive Committee, he was able to help steer it to a position "wholly sympathetic to Liberal-Progressive organization for federal purposes," and he was sure "the thing will work out all right." At a general meeting in Brandon in June 1933, the Liberals and Progressives had "unanimously agreed to co-operate for the federal election" and had formed the requisite organization. Lambert was urging Crerar on, especially in organizing the rural constituencies, but warned him to keep Bracken strictly out of these matters because of his unpopularity with the old die-hards of Winnipeg, who could still cause trouble. Crerar preferred to seek advice elsewhere. By the spring of 1934, the die-hards were a spent force, and a lively convention of Young Liberals enthusiastically endorsed cooperation with the Progressives. In fact the result was closer to a fusion, and by the time Bennett called an election in 1935, Manitoba Liberals and Progressives would be firmly united and ready.[49]

Their optimism was tempered somewhat by the appearance in 1933 of the Co-operative Commonwealth Federation (CCF), with its

Regina Manifesto. Crerar was inclined to take the new party seriously and sensed danger for the Liberals. Late in 1932, when asked
to address the convention of the United Farmers of Manitoba in Dau-
phin, he found that nearly twenty-five per cent of the delegates
present were already strong supporters of the embryonic movement.
If this were true across the prairies, and one added in the old Gingerites and their supporters who were already included in the movement, it surely gave cause for concern. At the same time, Crerar
informed Lambert, "There was a very considerable opposition" to
the new socialist party. The best line for the Liberals to take, in his
view, particularly in the local weekly press in the west, was that
support for the ccf would lead nowhere. There would be no support
in eastern Canada, and even if the new movement "carried forty
seats in the west, they would be up against a blank wall in getting
results." The Progressive experience still rankled, but the ccf would
bear watching. Desperate times often fostered desperate measures,
but Crerar advised a temperate response.[50]

The Conservatives felt no such inhibitions. They were doing the
Liberals "a good turn by describing the efforts of Agnes MacPhail
and Woodsworth as 'Communist,'" according to King. Crerar was
shrewd enough to realize that the Liberals must not be backward in
advancing imaginative resolutions in the House, or a major initiative
would be lost.[51]

There is little doubt that the traditional view of the ccf as the prod
urging the Liberals leftward is true. In mid-February 1933, a general
meeting of the Manitoba Liberal Association discussed the new
group and concluded that only "a sane, advanced programme for the
Liberal Party" would turn back the threat. Crerar was rather amazed
"to see the radical attitude taken by men like [J.B.] Coyne and Walter
Lindal."[52] But he was convinced that any appeal based on "Marxian
Socialism" would fail, largely because "not one in a score of those
supporting [Woodsworth] understands what it means, and Agnes
[MacPhail] is among the twenty."

Woodsworth would never succeed, Crerar argued, in uniting
labour and farmers, because their interests were antithetical. He
derided Woodsworth's socialism, claiming that it was based purely
on materialism – "the same kind of materialism that has dominated
big business." He recounted a story about a ccf orator in a rural
Ukrainian district of Manitoba who promised his audience that its
debts would be readjusted. An old Ukrainian farmer rose during the
questions and said: "You are going to cancel my debts. I like that; but
at the same time you are going to take my land. I don't like that. I
think I would rather keep my debts and my land." Crerar concluded:

"That old bird of an [sic] Ukrainian put his finger squarely upon the weak spot of the Woodsworth programme." For all that, Crerar was quite aware of just how crucial debt adjustment was to suffering prairie farmers.[53]

There was little point in attacking the CCF on theoretical grounds, Crerar advised King, as the latter prepared to visit Manitoba that summer. The Liberals must offer appealing alternatives. He urged King to state clearly his support for a central bank "and the functions it could perform in currency and credit control." Woodsworth, he went on, was on excellent ground in attacking the big corporations, and that was making him "more friends than anything else he does or says." So the Liberal party must present a credible plan to "control the corporations and make them behave." It must be conceded that "[t]here has been a great deal of financial buccaneering carried on in the last fifteen or twenty years." The great task for the Liberals was "to convince the people of their good faith." Simple condemnation of the CCF would not be enough. King took the advice. On his western tour, he did not rant against the CCF, or "denounce its supporters as enemies of the state," but tried to offer effective alternatives.[54]

The provincial elections in Ontario and Saskatchewan seemed to confirm Crerar's estimates. He had argued that CCF support was 80 per cent labour, 15 per cent intellectuals, and 5 per cent farmers. "The poor showing made by the CCF in Ontario, and especially in Saskatchewan, affords pretty certain evidence that the farmers in both these Provinces are quite a distance yet from accepting the Socialistic programme." For the moment, at least, the threat seemed to have abated.[55] But now the battle would shift to the dominion level, as Bennett could not delay much longer in calling an election.

As far as Crerar and his Winnipeg cronies were concerned, the major elements of national Liberal policy were set – expansion of markets through reciprocal tariff reductions, support for the national railway, and a central bank to control currency and credit. But the overwhelming issue would be the Depression. In political terms, it was better to be out of office than be obliged to justify one's stewardship, especially in the drought-stricken west.

Crerar kept King advised of prairie conditions and opinions: "When a man has worked hard all summer to produce a crop; when his wife has slaved twelve or fourteen hours a day to help him, and they find when it is marketed there is little left, the iron enters their souls."[56] Above all, King must remain positive and hopeful. Care must also be taken not to give any encouragement to the sporadic references to a national government to meet the emergency. Both

Crerar and Dafoe had supported Union government in 1917 but denied any parallel now. As Dafoe put it to Crerar, following an inquiry by King, conditions were entirely different, since in the earlier case "all parties at that time were supporting the war." But in the 1930s, there would be no possibility of reconciling two wholly divergent points of view.[57]

As the parliamentary session of 1934 opened, the Sanhedrin was alarmed at Bennett's proposal to bring back the Wheat Board and pass the Natural Products Marketing Act. It denounced both. Dafoe instructed Dexter to keep a sharp eye on the demand for a new Wheat Board. He was sure that the pools were behind it, since that would be the only way to have bulk selling, as they had been forced out of it. Crerar remained opposed to what would in effect be a compulsory national pool. His own panacea remained the same – a sharp reduction in the costs of wheat production through lower tariffs. Only in that way could prairie farmers compete. But the Sanhedrin had little to offer in the way of suggestions as to how to dispose of the roughly 300 million bushels that the government now held, following the continuing bail-out of the pools.[58]

The Marketing Act was, according to Crerar, "altogether bad in every way, but I fancy in these disturbed times, it will find quite a few friends." Most of those allies, he warned King, would support the CCF in the election. He feared that the powers of a marketing board would be virtually unlimited. He complained to Cameron: "Bennett has shackled the consumers of Canada pretty completely to the protected manufacturer. He now proposes to shackle the farmers to a Government bureaucracy in the marketing of their products."

Like Dafoe, Crerar suspected that the pool leaders were promoting both ideas. Assumption of arbitrary economic power by the government could lead, as it had in Europe, to assumption of arbitrary political power. Increasing government intervention and control could "carry us a long way indeed from the conceptions of liberty and freedom that we once looked upon as our proud heritage." He advised King to oppose the Marketing Act in principle but not to attack the government on the wheat surplus or the holding back of grain. If prices were to rise because of climatic conditions elsewhere, the surplus would be cleared out and Bennett vindicated. But the Wheat Board legislation should be opposed in principle, and he wrote to Lambert for reassurance that King was holding to that line.[59]

As 1934 drew to a close, the political prospects of the Liberal party seemed fair indeed. There had to be an election by the following summer, and Bennett's policies seemed to be in disarray and his government in general disfavour. The country and most of the world were in desperate straits, but for the Liberals the new year almost certainly would bring a return to power, and Crerar expected to be included in a major role.

PART FOUR

Ministry of Talents, 1935–45

Crerar on his way to Buckingham Palace, November 1939.
Copyright Associated Press, Winnipeg Tribune Collection,
University of Manitoba

CHAPTER ELEVEN

Mines, Wheat, and Keynes, 1935–39

The campaign of 1935 began unofficially with Prime Minister Bennett's radio broadcasts early in the year, in which he announced the proposals that became known as the "Bennett New Deal." This broad (and vague) program of massive government intervention into the social and economic life of Canadians brought a mixed response from Conservatives, cries of hypocrisy from most Liberals, and an expression of mild interest and heightened expectations from the people. All would have to wait for the legislation to come to Parliament before the content of the proposed reforms could be fairly judged. But clearly Bennett had caught the attention of the country and briefly rekindled the flickering hopes of his party.

In Winnipeg, Crerar and his cronies were sceptical. By the end of January, he felt that the impact of the broadcasts was receding and the public would now see them in their "proper" perspective – "a desperate throw to retrieve a desperate situation." He argued, however, that immediate hostility by King would probably bring on a snap election and leave the Liberals open to charges of being opponents of reform. When the legislation finally appeared, it fell far short of the drastic revisions intimated in Bennett's broadcasts. The Liberals in the House tried to treat each issue on its merits, so as not to give credence to an accusation of obstructionism. They supported some measures and opposed others. The Prairie Farm Rehabilitation Act, for example, was actually quite useful once this agency was adequately funded by the Liberals in later years. Yet Crerar was still rather distressed. He grumbled to Cameron that "all this Reform legislation so-called is having a very disturbing effect, and I have a doubt upon the wisdom of the Liberals acquiescing in it so completely." However, he had little alternative to offer to King's careful strategy of defusing the effect of Bennett's initiatives. In any case,

Crerar became convinced that "the veneer has largely worn off RB's radio addresses."[1]

In the run-up to the election that summer, the major issues in the west were the alarming carry-overs of wheat and the government's intention to shift this burden to a new marketing agency – a revival of the Wheat Board of the Great War period – which many grain growers would undoubtedly welcome. Crerar was deeply suspicious of Bennett's intentions. John I. McFarland, appointed by the prime minister to liquidate the carry-over when the pools failed, now had some 240 million bushels of wheat to sell. It was Crerar's view that McFarland was intentionally keeping the price so high "that we are selling less wheat at this time of year than we have done for 20 years."

He feared that this was simply a tactic and "that when the election is called Bennett intends to come out with a raging tearing campaign against the organized grain trade." Such a strategy amounted to a huge speculation that could be capitalized on politically. This wicked scheme must be exposed, he insisted to King. The best method would be a parliamentary inquiry, which Crerar urged King to demand. Only then could McFarland be obliged to present his monthly accounts for the past eighteen months and defend his operation. Crerar even travelled to Montreal to brief J.L. Ralston, whom he felt would be the most effective Liberal to lead such an inquiry.[2]

Despite Crerar's rather Machiavellian interpretation, the wheat situation was indeed pressing. Through the spring, McFarland announced several widely different forecasts about the carry-over at the end of the crop year. But the situation could be disastrous if there was anything like a normal, 400-million bushel crop in 1935. "Of all the experiments in lunacy that Bennett has undertaken," Crerar fumed, "the red ribbon easily goes to his handling of the wheat situation."[3]

Bennett's final attempt to deal with the issue involved a new Wheat Board, proposed late in the session of 1935. Crerar's reaction was predictable. He wrote a long letter to King urging that the party squarely oppose it. "The principle embedded in the wheat board legislation," he declared, "is opposed to every principal [sic] of liberalism." What he feared most was the application of "Woodsworth's theories" and regimentation of wheat producers and other farmers. It was the same argument that he had used years earlier against the compulsory pool.

Yet he did not oppose creation of a Wheat Board with limited power. He acknowledged that an agency of some sort was necessary to liquidate "the mess the Government and McFarland had made of the situation." But it should be only a temporary device, preceding restoration of a free market, under such regulations as might be necessary in the public interest. The real problem, he remained convinced, was to find buyers. His own long experience in selling wheat led him to the position that markets for wheat and other natural products of Canada could be secured and held only if the country were "to make real trade concessions." The concern of the farmer was not past government policies but whether or not he could market the 1935 crop, which in June looked promising.

So he pressed King to have the party support a non-compulsory board to liquidate the surplus. But a complete Liberal program should include policies to reduce farmers' costs of production, recover markets, and re-establish the free market, with appropriate safeguards, under the administration of the Board of Grain Commissioners. He was gratified to learn that King accepted the bulk of his recommendations.[4] And the Liberals were able to force significant changes in the original bill during its passage through committee. The compulsory feature was eliminated. Farmers would be offered a minimum price and left free to sell their wheat to the board or to the private trade. Only wheat was to be included in the board's mandate, not oats and barley, as had been proposed. Crerar was delighted with the result.[5]

During these months, he had been very active in his new constituency of Churchill, which sprawled over the northern half of Manitoba and was very different from Marquette, for which he had sat as an Independent Liberal Grain Grower turned Unionist (1917–19) and a Progressive (1919–25), and his more recent seat in Brandon, as a Liberal (1929–30). He concentrated on the larger communities of Flin Flon, The Pas, and the Swan River Valley. At the convention in mid-April he easily defeated Daniel Baldwin for the nomination, but Baldwin promptly announced that he would run as an Independent Liberal.[6]

Churchill was vast and home to a wide variety of people. Crerar had to learn to play ethnic politics very quickly. He was helped to some extent when Winnipeg's flamboyant and determinedly reactionary mayor, Colonel Ralph Webb, came to The Pas and bitterly denounced communists, Jews, and others, ostensibly to assist the Conservative candidate. Leader Tim Buck canvassed the riding to assess the prospects for a communist candidate but decided against it.[7]

Crerar worked the constituency actively and well. It was really a series of frontier communities, which, he conjectured, "did not wish to be represented by the losing side." He was still realistic enough to recognize that if the people in Churchill and elsewhere voted heavily against the government, it would indicate not so much any great faith in the Liberals as resentment against the Conservatives, and then "the Liberal party will have one more chance but if it does not rise to the occasion it will probably pay the penalty if there is no return to prosperity."[8] Happily for him, the situation had clarified in Churchill by the end of June. Baldwin withdrew, and Crerar faced the incumbent Conservative, Barney Stitt, and a CCF candidate.

He was quite hopeful about his own riding and Manitoba as a whole. He spent much of his time organizing the province, though there was some friction between him and the ambitious Joe Thorson in Selkirk. King, when he wrote to thank Crerar for his letter about the Wheat Board, acknowledged his help effusively and expressed his wish "to have you at my side in the House of Commons, for today, more than at any moment in years past, we need the combination of political wisdom and practical experience."[9] King's words would ring hollow after the election.

On 14 October 1935, the voters of Canada chose King over the allegation of chaos. It was a decisive victory. The Liberals gained a solid majority, having taken almost 45 per cent of the vote. The Reconstruction party of Tory dissident H.H. Stevens received 8.7 per cent of the vote but only one seat. The CCF, with its 8.8 per cent of the vote more concentrated, took seven seats. On the prairies, the Tories won only one seat in each province; the Liberals took thirty-one and the CCF four, and in Alberta the new Social Credit party swept fifteen of seventeen seats. Crerar was particularly pleased by Manitoba's showing, where the Liberals won fourteen of seventeen seats, as he had predicted. He himself won easily in his new riding and then returned to the farm in Clandeboye to await events.

William Lyon Mackenzie King's attitude towards Crerar before and after the election of 1935 confirms many of the criticisms of King's often-fickle sense of obligation. Prior to the voting – indeed, for several years – he seemed to be depending on Crerar for advice on policy, especially on western matters, and relying on him (and his friends) to organize Manitoba for the Liberal party. His letters to Crerar were always friendly, encouraging, and full of goodwill and protestations of how much he wished Crerar was still beside him in the House. Perhaps it was simply a reflection of his insensitivity, but King always appeared to be most influenced by immediate and future demands and prospects. Loyalty seemed a one-way street with him.

Crerar had handled Manitoba extremely well, raising funds, conciliating constituency disputes, and speaking constantly throughout the province. In the interests of party harmony, he had not insisted on running in Selkirk, where he lived, but took on the different and more difficult riding of Churchill. He was batting on a good wicket in 1935, but he had reason to be pleased at the Manitoba results and to expect to be asked to join the government.

With the election over and a Liberal majority safely ensconced, King felt unburdened by past achievements and obligations and guided by considerations of future advantage and liability. It was simply assumed in Manitoba that Crerar would represent the province in the cabinet, but King hesitated before extending the anticipated invitation. Almost thirty years later, Crerar sought the details of what had transpired from Professor Blair Neatby, who was writing his excellent volumes on King. Crerar then wrote an *aide-mémoire* based on excerpts from King's diaries, which Neatby had provided him. When canvassing the Manitoba situation, King had noted that "Crerar had little hold on Manitoba" and had referred to criticisms that Crerar had been connected "with Union Government, Home Bank," and now was "representing Grain Exchange against the Pool."[10] To King these were now all apparently handicaps, though they had not dissuaded King from assiduously courting Crerar in the 1920s, when these issues were much more current, or from bringing him into the cabinet in 1929. They certainly do not seem to have influenced the electoral result in Manitoba in 1935.

In any case, King first offered the Manitoba cabinet post to J.W. Dafoe, with little expectation that he would accept but, he hoped, ensuring the continued support of the *Free Press*. When King then asked Dafoe who should come in from Manitoba, Dafoe replied, "Crerar, of course."[11] This may explain the rather cryptic and suspicious entry in King's diary a few weeks later: "This little group in Winnipeg keep close together & watch each other's interests above all else."[12] Perhaps King simply did not understand such friendship and loyalty. Norman Lambert was probably right when he noted much later in his own diary: "T.A. Crerar was chosen as the Manitoba representative, despite his own clear perception that King did not like him personally."[13] Yet even a cursory reading of King's diary for these years reveals that, with the possible exception of Ernest Lapointe, there was not a member of King's cabinet whose personal standing with the prime minister did not fluctuate wildly with circumstance.

Crerar was eventually summoned to Ottawa a few days after the election and arrived at King's home, Laurier House, on 21 October. He was "a bit surprised to find Lapointe and Dunning there."[14] Lapointe he respected and liked; but there had never been much love lost between him and Dunning. Crerar simply did not trust him on the railway issue, since he had always suspected him of leaning towards the CPR and against the national railway. It was not a good omen, since the Railways portfolio was the one that he wanted again.

There is some confusion as to what exactly occurred at that meeting. According to Dafoe, who was perhaps not a little blinded by friendship, Crerar was reluctant to push himself after the election and "made no attempt to promote his interests at Ottawa." If he would not say anything for himself, "he had friends who saw that his case was not overlooked." And the Sanhedrin had given him a happy sendoff from the Manitoba Club on 18 October.[15]

Neatby, as well as Bothwell and Kilbourn in their study of C.D. Howe, assert that Crerar did press his claim for the Railways portfolio. Bothwell and Kilbourn also note: "Dunning had already reminded King that Crerar had been particularly weak as railways minister," implying that Crerar's friendship with Sir Henry Thornton had led to lax control.[16] Since Crerar had held the office for only a few months, this was hardly a fair assessment. But it was not untypical of Dunning.

Crerar has left only a brief account of the meeting, recorded twelve years later. When the congratulations were over, Crerar recalled, King said: "I think I should tell you there is much opposition to your coming in from Manitoba" – perhaps a reference to the pool leaders, or simply King's way of putting him on the defensive. Crerar interpreted the gibe as an attempt by King to force him "to beg for the job, and as far as I was concerned, I was doing no begging." He acknowledged to King that he probably had some political enemies in Manitoba but advised the leader that if he could "find someone from Manitoba to serve your Government more effectively, then I can only say it is your duty to take him." King then calmed the waters by professing that it was Crerar he wanted.

In the discussion of portfolios that followed, Crerar recollected that King mentioned Agriculture and Crerar replied that he considered himself entitled to Railways. It was probably as much a matter of prestige as anything else to Crerar, since Railways was considered a senior portfolio.

King, however, had changes in mind. He was planning to merge Railways into a new Department of Transport, to which C.D. Howe was slated to be appointed. Of more interest to a westerner, he was also contemplating abolishing the old Interior Department, rather an anachronism after the return of natural resources to the prairie provinces in 1930. A much-expanded Department of Mines and Natural Resources (which included forests, surveys, national parks, historic sites, and so on) would have responsibility also for Immigration and

Colonization, as well as Indian Affairs – much the same kind of administrative grab-bag that Interior had been. It meant reorganization of two departments, with four deputy ministers, into a vast and varied department, with several divisions. This change would of course require legislation; but with all this understood, Crerar agreed to become minister of the interior until the new department was created. He then left the meeting.[17]

Such were his interests now that he welcomed this new assignment, and his friend Cameron compared it to the opportunity for national development given Clifford Sifton forty years earlier. But whatever Crerar may have thought, King no longer considered him the senior spokesman for the prairies or the resident expert on western agriculture. These roles would now pass to James G. Gardiner of Saskatchewan, whom King saw as the rising star on the prairie political scene. Clearly King saw Crerar's political effectiveness as being on the wane. It was not a matter simply of age: Crerar was fifty-nine, two years younger than King. Despite the prime minister's tendency to think of Crerar as "over the hill," Crerar would still be in Parliament long after King had gone to his reward.

Even so, Crerar looked ahead eagerly to this new challenge and the new session. He had a touch of regret that his old friend Kirk Cameron would not be with him. Cameron had stood for the Liberals in Mount Royal – a forlorn hope in those days – and lost to the Conservative candidate.[18] The defeat did not sour Cameron, and his close relationship with Crerar went on as before.

Arguably, the cabinet that Crerar joined in late 1935 and served in until the end of the Second World War was the strongest in Canadian history. So entrenched did it become and so convinced of the continuing approval of the Canadian voters, that it well earned Reginald Whitaker's sobriquet of "The Government Party." And govern it did, with a will and a talent that kept the party in power for twenty-two years. Among such colleagues as Dunning, Gardiner, Howe, Ilsley, Lapointe, Macdonald, Power, Ralston, Rogers, and St Laurent, Crerar's performance and influence often went unnoticed. He was the connecting link to the laissez-faire past of the Liberal party and later became its frequently unpopular spokesman in cabinet. He was not especially close to his colleagues, except for Kitchener's W.D. (Bill) Euler at Trade and Commerce, despite his protectionist leanings, and later Angus Macdonald from Nova Scotia. He was fond of "Chubby" Power and continued to admire Lapointe. While he was not a loner, his real confidants remained the Sanhedrin, particularly Dafoe and Cameron.

The first major issue in cabinet in which Crerar was concerned was the wheat surplus, which, despite the general failure of the 1935 crop, demanded immediate action. The dispute went some way to sorting out the players around King. Few in the government had much good to say about Bennett's Wheat Board and its chairman, J.I. McFarland, except for Dunning and Howe, who wished to maintain the board. Almost all the others wished to see a return to the free market. They had little alternative, however, to employing the board in the short term to deal with the accumulated surplus. Changes, however, were sure to come.

Gardiner had hoped that as minister of agriculture he would be given responsibility for wheat policy. King concluded that the matter was too sensitive, both politically and economically. He decided to set up a four-member committee to manage wheat, comprising Gardiner, Dunning (Finance), Euler (Trade and Commerce, and hence responsible for the Wheat Board's administration and selling policy), and Crerar, presumably because of his experience. Both Euler and Crerar wished to get rid of the board as soon as practicable; Gardiner generally agreed, but Dunning wanted to retain it at least until world wheat prices rose.[19]

At Crerar's urging, King and the cabinet agreed that the reconstructed Wheat Board set up by PC 3756 on 3 December 1935 would be temporary, and "the aim should be to get away from unnecessary regulation as much and as soon as possible. [Crerar] said he agreed with this policy, and all in Council were so agreed." Crerar was also successful in pushing the claims of James R. Murray, his former protégé at United Grain Growers who had managed the company from 1917 until Crerar's return at the end of 1922, who now became chairman. According to Grant Dexter, the *Free Press* correspondent in Ottawa, the "anti-McFarland drive in Cabinet was led by Crerar and was supported with great vigour by most of the other ministers – notably Rogers, Ilsley and the Quebeckers."[20]

Crerar was equally pleased with the immediate aftermath. Argentina and Australia had very poor crops that year, and prices began to recover. "I do think there is a good chance of getting rid of our burdensome surplus," he wrote to Dafoe. "We had to bring rather strong pressure to bear on the Pools to turn their wheat over to the Wheat Board but I understand they are doing it now," he continued some days later. He was most excited by the prospect that "if we play fairly with Europe in the next six or eight months – and I am sure that Murray will do this – it will go a long distance indeed in overcoming the prejudices that have been raised there [by the pools] in the last five or six years."[21]

In the event, the board did not disappear with the surplus, as Crerar had hoped. For the next two years, the floor price for wheat set by the cabinet remained below the market price, so there was no pressure on the treasury, thus removing any urgency. So the voluntary board continued, and two years later the battle would begin again in cabinet. The contending views and ambitions of Dunning, Euler, and Gardiner made Crerar's role in the wheat committee critical. So, despite King's opinion, Crerar remained influential in wheat policy and would be closely involved as long as he was in the cabinet.

While he remained concerned about the wheat economy, this was really a regional issue for Crerar at Mines and Resources, a department name that sounded even less comprehensive than Interior. It took almost a year for Crerar and C.D. Howe to give legislative effect to King's consolidation. As a temporary measure, Crerar had been appointed to Mines, to Immigration and Colonization, and to Interior, and Superintendent-General of Indian Affairs. He was also designated, because of his seniority, second in precedence in the government to Senator Raoul Dandurand, which annoyed King not a little.[22]

The administrative revisions involved a slow and ponderous process, requiring over six months of preparations. By early March 1936, King pronounced himself satisfied with the planned reorganization, indicating that Crerar and Howe had "done well in the bills they have prepared and given me to introduce."[23] He did so in the House of Commons in early June, and the bill for Crerar's new department then went to committee. It was justified as an economy measure, but one calculated to increase efficiency. There were, at the time, "four Deputy Ministers, four Assistant Deputy Ministers, four sets of administrative assistants", multiple staffs doing publicity, finance, translation, and so on; and lawyers, architects, doctors, and other professionals spread throughout the four departments. They would all come together under one minister and one deputy minister, supervising four divisions – Mines and Resources, Immigration and Colonization, Indian Affairs (including Inuit and the governments of Yukon and Northwest Territories), and what was left of Interior. Tucked away in these divisions were a bewildering variety of activities, including national parks, the Explosives Act, surveys, maps and charts, the Dominion Observatory, hydro-electric development, and forest management.

In announcing the name of the new department – Mines, Resources and Colonization (this last was dropped almost immediately) – King revealed more than a plan for administrative efficiency.

"It was thought advisable," he said in conclusion, that the new name "should not indicate the functions of the Departments [sic] which are more or less administrative, such as Indian Affairs or Immigration, but rather, that it should express those activities which are more likely to contribute to the future development of the Dominion."[24] Apparently, immigrants and Native peoples had no significant role in such a future. As it turned out, this emphasis seemed just fine for Crerar. Immigration had slowed to a trickle during the Depression and was not to be encouraged. And no one in those days except a dedicated few paid much attention to the difficulties or aspirations of the Native peoples. The new minister responded only to pressing problems in what he considered these minor obligations of his portfolio and left them largely to their administrative overseers.

Like all new ministers after a change of government, Crerar was beset by patronage requests. Understandably, most came from the west, especially Winnipeg. He had no trouble turning aside most of them, but some required deft handling. There were, for example, a surprising number of requests from Dafoe to consider the claims of one or another deserving supplicant. Crerar was not uninterested, but because of the massive reorganization going on in his various divisions and branches he had to pay close attention to the concerns of employees already in the service, especially those at the middle and senior levels who were anticipating or fearing displacement or transfer.

And there was always the pressure to balance French- and English-speaking appointments. Lapointe complained directly to the prime minister that Crerar was ignoring French Canadians in naming senior members of his department. King replied that they lacked the necessary technical training for most positions, but that he and Crerar favoured bilingual employees for "dealing with the public," which seemed to be the routine way of relegating French Canadians to lower-paying positions.[25]

Crerar would and did occasionally push the claims of old friends. In realigning responsibilities in the Indian Affairs Branch, he insisted on bringing in R.A. Hoey of Winnipeg, former minister of education in Bracken's Manitoba government and a long-time friend, as superintendent of Indian education in the west. Despite Hoey's lack of Liberal credentials, "Crerar pressed very hard for the appointment ... [W]e let it pass, but I think there will be much feeling against the Government in not having appointed one of its more immediate supporters to this position. It is true Hoey has quite exceptional qualifications, but I believe these could have been found in another."[26] In this case, Crerar could cloak himself in righteousness;

yet he continually showed concern that an appointee's primary requisite should be merit.

Given this attribute, combined with friendship, he would make great exertions. A vacancy in the Supreme Court of Canada in the spring of 1936 provides a fine example. The death of Mr Justice Lamont, a western member of the court, spurred Crerar (and the Sanhedrin) to action. He wrote immediately to the prime minister on behalf of A.B. Hudson, a charter member of the Winnipeg group. Crerar knew that Saskatchewan Liberals were expecting the opening to go to Judge Martin of their court. He tried to head this off by holding out the possibility that Chief Justice Haultain of Saskatchewan could not be expected to go on much longer and that Martin would then be a candidate for the more senior appointment. He then cited Hudson's long and valuable service to the national Liberal party, his accomplishments as attorney general of Manitoba, and his widely recognized high standing at the bar. Dafoe and Cameron weighed in with pressure on King and Justice Minister Lapointe respectively.

It is really quite remarkable, given King's habit of agonizing for months over the political consequences of senior appointments, that the whole process took only two weeks. Crerar wrote to Dafoe in rather smug satisfaction that he could not "recall an appointment anywhere that has been so well received as Hudson's appointment to the Court here. Lapointe is delighted, the Chief is pleased and the Ottawa bar in full agreement."[27] Hudson's qualifications were better than adequate, if entirely practical, and King had known and admired his abilities – both political and legal – for many years.

So, despite King's occasional resentment towards the Sanhedrin, the elevation of Hudson to the Supreme Court indicates that it was not without influence. Many future meetings of the Sanhedrin – especially after King persuaded Dafoe to accept a position on the Rowell-Sirois Commission the following year – took place in Ottawa, which certainly pleased Cameron, if not Frank Fowler.

Crerar had played an active, behind-the-scenes role in the June 1936 provincial election in Manitoba, working to maintain the Liberal-Progressive alliance that had sustained John Bracken in 1932. But voters, weary of hard times and especially new provincial taxation, had dealt Bracken a stinging setback. The election left his party in a minority position, but he was able to carry on with support from the four Social Credit members, who exacted little in return. At King's request, Crerar had gone to Manitoba shortly after the election to survey the national political situation there.[28] To his satisfaction, Bracken's popularity had begun to rebound, and it later took a sharp jump with Manitoba's presentation to the Rowell-Sirois Commission in 1937.

During the early years of King's new government, Crerar devoted most of his time to prospects and plans for development of the mining industry. He threw himself into this aspect of his portfolio with the zeal of the recently converted, sometimes to the neglect of his other obligations. His deputy minister, C.C. (Charlie) Camsell, was an experienced Ottawa hand, a northerner by birth and affection, who shared his minister's enthusiasm for the mining industry. So the Indian Affairs and Immigration branches received little close scrutiny or direction and were left under the virtually independent control of their directors, which later caused Crerar some difficulties.

Crerar's obvious enthusiasm for the mining industry came from two sources. One was personal. Ever since the 1920s, when Kirk Cameron began to interest him in investing in mining stocks, and especially after his introduction to Noah Timmins and the success of Noranda, he had been convinced that mineral resources would become as important to Canada's development as agriculture had been. Now that he was the minister responsible, he was in a position to do something about it. In those easier days, when conflict of interest was assumed to be negated by personal integrity, he gave too little thought to the dangers involved, to himself and the country.

The second reason was the Depression. There were few bright spots in the economy. The gold industry was exceptional. As long as the price remained fixed at $35 an ounce and most trading nations remained on the gold standard, Canada's revenues from gold mining would continue to increase at such a rate that even new investment was justified. And given enough incentive, other mineral resources could attract development. For Crerar, this area could become the centrepiece of the government's attack on the Depression. Mining development meant jobs, not just in the mines but throughout the economy. Road building, mining equipment, retail and wholesale support, financial services, railway traffic – the spin-off effects were dazzling. As reorganization of the department went forward, Crerar concentrated almost exclusively on the Mining Branch.

His campaign proceeded in two steps. The first was unusual for its day. Crerar took to the radio early in 1936 to show the Canadian public (and most of his cabinet colleagues) the need for a vigorous program of mining development. He was no William Aberhart, but his use of the medium proved effective. He realized the necessity of generating wide public support to persuade the cabinet, and especially Finance Minister Dunning, to entertain his schemes. The second step was to work closely with the leaders of the mining industry to devise the legislative means, including concessions, to encourage investment. Initially, he was unaware of the problems involved.

Only two months after taking over the portfolio, Crerar gave the first of twelve weekly radio broadcasts on Canada's mining industry and its prospects. He emphasized the fact that agriculture occupied only 15 per cent of the nation's land area and that mining would push back the northern frontiers. It would forge new links between east and west, provide traffic for the railways, and further secure Canada's place in international trade. Over and over again, he emphasized the importance of gold, pointing out that, despite the collapse of world trade in the Depression, Canadian gold production had increased every year and that in 1935 it was valued at $116 million. Throughout the broadcasts, he urged that the mining industry be given every encouragement, so it could lead the way to national prosperity. The most pressing need, he argued, was to stabilize and rationalize mining taxation by the dominion and provincial governments.

The public response was gratifying, and newspapers across the country endorsed Crerar's initiatives. In response to "thousands of requests ... from Canada and elsewhere," the texts of the broadcasts were published. The leading figures of the mining industry were delighted and full of advice for the new minister as to the best method of capitalizing on his aggressive policy move.[29] All would be for naught, however, if the cabinet could not be persuaded to cooperate.

Cameron took the point in the assault, prodding Crerar incessantly, organizing the mining men, and exhorting editors to lend their support. He secured an interview with King to try and gain the prime minister's support. Colonel J.L. Ralston, former minister of defence, was retained by the Timmins interests to bring pressure on his fellow Nova Scotian and minister of revenue, J.L. Ilsley, and on Finance Minister Dunning. Behind the scenes, but not very far, were the leaders of the Mining Association of Canada, especially James Murdoch, later president of Noranda Mines, Jack Rankin, who managed the Timmins Corporation, and the Timmins family itself. Cameron was their indefatigable conduit to the minister. So importunate did he become that Dafoe felt it necessary to warn Crerar, remarking sympathetically that he may be "finding Kirk's energy in this matter a trifle troublesome."[30]

The *Free Press* and the *Globe and Mail*, as well as the trade papers such as the *Northern Miner*, gave enthusiastic encouragement to Crerar's public initiatives on behalf of the industry. The critical decision would be made in cabinet as the new government prepared its first budget in the spring of 1936. The debate in council took place on two levels: Crerar made specific recommendations on mining policy, which would entail reductions in revenue, and this latter implication led him to challenge the generally held conviction that a balanced budget was a necessary objective of government fiscal policy. He proposed the novel notion of deliberate stimulation of the economy through short-term deficits and argued that the lost revenue would soon be made up as a result of increased investment in the mining sector. He was now convinced that the mineral industry could be the engine of a reviving national economy. The impediments to expansion, he persisted, were the steady increase in mining taxes since 1926 and Bennett's drastic further increases in 1934. As an example, he pointed to the McIntyre gold mine, which had seen its taxes increase over the period from 14 cents per ton to $1.24.[31]

At council, Crerar urged the government to forgo some half-million dollars in revenue through the following measures: restoration of depletion allowances for mining companies to 40 per cent, a comparable increase in the depletion allowance allowed on income from mining dividends, giving mining companies permission to write off exploration expenses, and an assurance that there would be no increase in mining taxes during the life of the present Parliament. He was rebuffed. Finance Minister Dunning and J.L. Ilsley at National Revenue were adamantly opposed, as was King, who remained wedded to a balanced budget. Only Norman Rogers appears to have agreed with Crerar's argument that increased employment would justify such a move. Most of his colleagues resisted, on the grounds that only the mine owners would benefit. The sole concession that Crerar was able to gain was an exemption from taxes for three years on new mines brought into production.

He expressed his disappointment to King the next day, reminding the prime minister that he had "hoped to see [mining] development increased in a large way. I am the minister responsible for the development of this Department," he went on. "I make recommendations on taxation that in my considered judgement are necessary to stimulate and encourage a development that is readily possible. The Finance Minister rejects all of them... The government is making a very grave mistake." He tried to persuade King to make the desired changes through administrative action but was again unsuccessful.[32] Ironically, and unexpectedly, the one concession he did gain, a three-year exemption from taxation on new mines, prompted of itself a significant increase in mining investment.

Crerar's enthusiasm for mining as the means to alleviate economic depression never slackened, and each year he pressed his colleagues at budget time to encourage investment as much as possible. He was able in 1939 to have the exemption from taxation on new mines extended for a further four years, since the scheme had been so demonstrably successful. But his opinion of the mining magnates themselves became less complacently admiring. The defence minister, Ian Mackenzie, passed on a very disturbing letter from a Vancouver observer of the mining industry. His most serious charge was that mine owners and promoters were also principals in brokerage houses dealing in mining stocks.

Crerar immediately communicated his concern to Cameron. "What we are aiming for," he pointed out, "is the development of the industry in a legitimate way. If our efforts are taken advantage of by those associated with the mining industry to boost share values with the idea of getting the public in and then rigging them, it will not only hurt the industry but will hurt the Government."

Crerar expressly asked Cameron to inquire if members of the Timmins family were in this position. Cameron's reply came back a week later, and it was not reassuring. He had discussed the matter with J.I. Rankin and Leo Timmins, "and we reached the view that under the circumstances nothing can be done at the moment." He conceded that the situation could be dangerous, "but these are risks that will have to be taken if a forward mining policy is to be made effective."[33] From that point onward, Crerar began to distance himself from the mine owners.

His enthusiasm for the industry did not diminish, however, though his tactics certainly changed. For the rest of the decade, he seemed less interested in reducing taxes on mining and mining income than in encouraging development by adapting road construction and railway policy to opening up promising mining districts.[34] As for Cameron, his friendship and correspondence with Crerar continued, but, perhaps sensing that he might have gone too far, he became much less forward in pushing Crerar to support the ambitions of the industry.

Crerar had other ministerial responsibilities, though his interest in them was neither consistent nor very imaginative. He tended rather to react only when they were pressed on his attention. He was drawn into one issue, however, that in its nuances reveals much about the attitudes of political leaders at the time – the suggestion by the BC premier, Duff Pattullo, to relieve the dominion government of its responsibility for the Yukon Territory by incorporating it within that province. It was not a new idea; there had been two previous overtures, and Mackenzie King had toyed with the possibility ten years earlier. It resurfaced as a result of Pattullo's ambitions and Ottawa's constant search for areas in which to cut costs. A casual conversation between Pattullo and Charles Dunning set the proposal in motion once again.[35] Crerar, as minister responsible, soon became involved. With the dominion incurring annual deficits averaging $300,000 for administering the territory in recent years, it seemed at least to Pattullo a convenient manner in which to devolve responsibility.[36]

Pattullo was facing a provincial election in 1937 and wished to use his vision of a prosperous northern future to entice voters. By April 1937, a tentative deal had been struck. Crerar informed Pattullo that Ottawa was prepared to transfer the Yukon Territory to British Columbia subject to certain conditions – continuance of dominion control of Justice, National Revenue, Indian Affairs, and the Post Office in the territory; agreed-on Indian Reserves; a settled boundary with the remaining territories; and an annual subsidy of $125,000 for five years to be paid to the province.[37] Neither party felt any obligation to consult residents of Yukon.

Pattullo, perhaps unwisely, announced the as-yet-unconfirmed agreement a month before the election. He was quickly disabused of the hope that this coup would serve his electoral interest. BC taxpayers feared that additional levies might result from expansion, and public opinion in Yukon was overwhelmingly opposed to the idea.[38] Neither of these objections would determine the issue; two additional factors proved decisive. Crerar's support began to wane when the mining interests of the territory objected to imposition of BC mining regulations and taxes, and British investors made clear their fear of double taxation.

In addition, there was one small Catholic elementary school in Yukon receiving public funds from the territorial administration. By extension, if the two jurisdictions were joined, the educational rights of the Catholic minority in Yukon would have to be either suppressed or extended to all of British Columbia, which had always resolutely opposed any such concession. O.D. Skelton, King's undersecretary at External Affairs, wrote King supporting Crerar's unwillingness to proceed. He feared a repetition of the quarrels of 1905: "The school question is much more difficult and may easily raise a row." For his part, Pattullo was beset by the provincial Orange Lodge and the Vancouver Ministerial Association.[39]

Pressure against any such merger grew rapidly. The Yukon Consolidated Gold Company, the territory's largest producer, lobbied

Crerar extensively and effectively. In September 1937, the *Vancouver News Herald* reported that Crerar's expected visit to announce the union of province and territory had been cancelled because the minister "does not consider the time is ripe."[40] Both sides took refuge in the recently created Rowell-Sirois Commission: Pattullo suggested that the matter be referred to its consideration, and Crerar gratefully and swiftly agreed.[41]

The incident indicates the willingness of governments in the federal system to seek their own interests with little regard for those of others. Only direct pressure and the threat of political repercussions dissuaded them in this case. But there is little evidence that Crerar (or anyone else for that matter) learned much from the fiasco.

Crerar's responsibilities also included Indian Affairs. His private correspondence contains only infrequent references to the Native community and exhibits little more than the usual, stereotyped conception of what was customarily viewed as the "native problem." A letter to J.S. McDiarmid, Manitoba's minister of mines and natural resources, represents his and the government's outlook. He asked his Manitoba counterpart if it would be possible to set aside some small parcels of land adjacent to Manitoba's lakes, where the Indians could fish, since "they are becoming wholly dispirited and useless and a problem for everyone who has anything to do with them."[42] Members of the House showed equal lack of interest, except when the traditional potlatch ceremony was being discussed and usually condemned.[43]

It was not so much that Crerar lacked sympathy for the Native people. In one of the few lengthy debates on Indian Affairs before the Second World War, he acknowledged that government policy was based on an outdated concept of wardship and that it had done little to change that situation, with the result that "we have tended to perpetuate that idea among the Indians themselves." He regretted this situation and hoped to shape policy, especially through education, to remedy "that state of affairs."[44] He never made it clear what policy might replace wardship. He was successful in thwarting Pattullo's scheme of conveying title to Indian lands for reserves to the dominion while retaining water and mineral rights for British Columbia. In 1939, Crerar won cabinet support for a bill to protect wildlife in northern Saskatchewan that provided "fresh opportunities for the Indians to follow their own way of life which will relieve them of the necessity of being on relief."[45]

Promotion of traditional Native pursuit of hunting and gathering was about the limit of Ottawa's imagination at that time. In the House of Commons, occasional discussions of Indian affairs were as remote from the reality of Native life as if they were considering the state of some alien society. Annually, during consideration of departmental estimates, the situation of the Indians of Canada would receive a cursory review; government policy would be questioned, bemoaned, and found wanting; and the whole matter would be turned back to the inadequate bureaucracy for another year. Then it would be forgotten.

Immigration was Crerar's other major responsibility, and he was content to leave it to the branch director, F.C. Blair. But unlike Indian Affairs, matters of immigration policy would force themselves, welcome or not, on the cabinet's agenda. The director's handling of specific problems often forced Crerar to take a direct hand in the branch's affairs.

Most of his interventions concerned isolated events. In December 1936, for example, four representatives of the Republican Government of Spain requested entry to undertake a speaking tour of Canada. All the Quebec members of cabinet were opposed; Crerar and all others present at council supported entry, on grounds of freedom of speech. In a not-untypical Canadian decision, the government allowed the Spanish delegates into the country but directed them to avoid Quebec and threatened them with deportation if trouble should ensue. The following year, during a dramatic strike against General Motors in Oshawa, when Ontario Premier Mitchell Hepburn insisted that any U.S. union organizers from the Auto Workers be deported from Canada, Crerar refused, calmly advising an outraged Hepburn that nothing illegal had taken place.[46]

The issue of Jewish refugees, however, would prove much more intractable. In general, little immigration was expected or encouraged during the Depression, so Blair's inclination to exclusion fit the current mood. Immigration had reached its lowest point of the century in the Depression, averaging just over 12,500 per year from 1933–34 to 1937–38. (By contrast, over 36,000 arrived in Canada in 1915, the smallest annual total in the Great War.[47]) Canada's obligation, it was argued by politicians and civil servants alike, was to protect the jobs of its citizens. In the 1930s only agricultural immigrants with capital over $15,000 to begin farming were encouraged, and then only tepidly. There was little dissent to this policy.

But the shadow of Nazi racial policy creeping over central Europe soon challenged the humanitarian impulse of Canada. Until *Kristallnacht*, on 9 November 1938, Canada ignored the pleas of Jews for safe haven, and afterward, despite the horrors of that savage night and its aftermath, Canada rejected them. It was, for Canadians, a collective failure.

As minister responsible for immigration, Crerar was enforcing government policy in 1936 when he insisted that Jews, like all others, must have sufficient capital to start a successful farm.[48] Jewish applicants for admission were not immigrants, however; they were refugees, whose capital in most cases had been confiscated. Even so, in those years of limited entry to Canada, some Jews did manage to arrive. From April 1930 to March 1938, nearly 68,000 European emigrants entered Canada. Of these, some 49,000 (73 per cent) were from the British Isles, and some 5,700 (8.5 per cent) were Jews ("Hebrews," in the departmental statistics), surpassed in numbers of non-British immigrants only by Germans and Ukrainians.[49] But the Jews of Europe were fleeing not only economic distress but an almost-inconceivable program of calculated genocide. It was only when directly faced with this dreadful reality that Canada's political leaders had to choose between political security and compassion.

There was little disposition in Canada to do more than express sympathy. If Cabinet was representative – and there is no reason to judge otherwise – Canadians were at best insensitive, at worst anti-semitic.[50] The plight of Jewish refugees was pressed on cabinet's attention by outside events, such as Franklin Roosevelt's call for an international response early in 1938 and, more pointedly late in the decade, by Canada's Jewish community, which offered to underwrite all costs of a more understanding and more humane refugee policy.

On four occasions, Crerar, as minister responsible, urged cabinet to admit Jewish refugees, and in other discussions he tried to move his colleagues towards a more generous response. Each time he failed. The ministers from Quebec were invariably opposed, and none of the others, except on one occasion Rogers and Euler, was prepared to act. King told his diary that one must consider the question on humanitarian grounds but told his cabinet that political concerns must prevail: "My own feeling is that nothing is to be gained by creating an internal problem in an effort to meet an international one." Crerar had continually to inform delegations of Canadian Jews that no change in policy could be expected.

Crerar tried hard, despite the opposition; and this was, after all, only one part of his large and busy department. And the evidence against him cited by Abella and Troper in *None Is Too Many* is not always clear, or clearly presented. During the debate in the House in March 1939 on the government's proposal to admit a number of Sudeten Germans, for example, Crerar turned away a critic of this decision by stating that "probably ninety-five per cent of these families are Roman Catholics." Abella and Troper imply that the MP levelled the criticism because he thought that there might be Jews among these refugees. In fact, the questioner feared that there might be communists among their numbers.[51] And Crerar was only responding to that concern.

Abella and Troper, who were critical of Crerar, conceded: "He was not uncaring, only powerless."[52] Despite the validity of their castigation of F.C. Blair, who was demonstrably anti-semitic, and the lack of compassion and courage displayed by the cabinet, it seems somewhat unfair to condemn Crerar on this one issue alone for his "less than distinguished career as minister responsible for immigration."[53] Given all his commitments, Crerar could charge the brick wall of opposition to Jewish immigration only so many times. And he did.

The fate of Europe's Jews was the most reprehensible aspect of Hitler's vision of a Europe dominated by a rearmed and aggressive Reich. After the fall of Austria and Czechoslovakia, the prospect of another continental war could not be dismissed, however much it was deplored in Canada. Throughout most of the 1920s and early 1930s, Crerar had followed Dafoe's lead on collective security, usually voicing support for the League of Nations. After the Liberals returned to power in late 1935, his faith was to be put to the test.

The Italian campaign in 1935 against Abyssinia forced the League of Nations finally to some action. The League's proposal of oil sanctions against Italy divided the Canadian cabinet. King feared that sanctions were imperialistic and risked war. Only Crerar, Gardiner, Ilsey, and Rogers favoured such a response, and the prime minister was convinced that Crerar was representing Dafoe's enthusiastic support of collective action, since the latter now considered war inevitable.[54] But Crerar was slowly coming to the conclusion that the League was part of the problem, rather than a solution. Attendance at the coronation of George VI in May 1937 and the meetings that followed gave him a closer look at Europe's difficulties.

Despite his sturdy Canadianism, Crerar could not but be impressed with the ceremonies in London, attended by representatives from throughout the commonwealth and empire, and from much of the rest of the world as well. "At the time of Edward's abdication last December," he reported to Cameron, "the popular impression in Europe was that Great Britain had suffered a very severe blow. The Coronation ... provided an exhibition of solidity that Europe certainly did not expect to see and thus has unquestionably deepened the impression that Britain is very far indeed from being on the way out."[55] But the aura of pomp and pageantry dissipated quickly amid the conflicting realities of the Commonwealth Conference held after the coronation.

Dafoe had been encouraged by Crerar's inclusion in the Canadian delegation. He wrote to Dexter, dispatched to cover events for the *Free Press*, that Crerar "has the soundest Liberal mind in the Government & I think his influence with King & his colleagues is rising all the time. You will find him useful."[56] But his confidence in the League was ebbing quickly. The sessions on world affairs in London made it quite clear, at least to him, that Britain's perception of national interest differed greatly from that of Canada, and both were at variance with Australia and New Zealand's. "The Conference wisely avoided commitments by any one of the Dominions," he concluded in his letter to Cameron.[57]

One of the highlights of the conference for Crerar had been Anthony Eden's review of the European situation. The Canadians – King, Crerar, Dunning, Lapointe, and Ian Mackenzie, defence minister – listened with increasing apprehension as Eden's pessimistic forecasts unfolded. King was certain of the source of the dangers. "I feel very strongly on the mischief the League has worked," he recorded; and he welcomed the fact that "Crerar, who has always been a pro-League man, said that he felt the sooner we were out of the League, the better." The prime minister feared that membership meant dangerous obligations, while Crerar was now persuaded that the organization was inherently flawed. King insisted that Canada would not agree to any future League commitments, and he was strongly supported by Lapointe and Crerar.[58]

At the close of the conference, Crerar informed Dafoe of his changing views. "I am pretty well convinced now that the League never had a chance ... [Y]ou can't put new wine in old bottles. It got a mortal wound in Manchuria but it had been seriously wounded before that."[59] Dafoe remained unconvinced. King would have been better off "if he had not repudiated all League obligations for in repudiating them he had weakened his defences against the partisans of a common imperial foreign policy."[60] In Dafoe's mind, the League to some extent had served Canada's interest as a counterbalance to imperial centralization; for Crerar, the deteriorating European situation pushed these nationalistic fears into the background. His experience in the cabinet during the Great War made him keenly sensitive to the difficulties and dangers at home, as well as in Europe, that another war would surely provoke.

Just prior to leaving London, Crerar spoke on short notice to the Empire Parliamentary Association, which was miffed that no Canadian official had addressed it. Crerar emphasized Canada's interest in the affairs of an increasingly dangerous world, rather than offering platitudes about the British family of nations. King was moved to congratulate him on "[t]he clear and concise statement you have made about the point of view of [Canada]."[61]

The return to Canada did not mean that European affairs were left behind. At least once, in September 1938, Crerar, as acting prime minister when King was ill, kept all the cabinet in Ottawa, fearing that an emergency in Europe would demand its attention. His correspondence that winter echoed Eden's pessimistic outlook. "It looks as if Eden were right," he wrote to Cameron; "Germany has Austria as completely as if it were an organic part of the Reich. It looks as if another European war is inevitable." In the spring of 1939, "events of the last year ... have demonstrated beyond any shadow of doubt that Eden was right a year ago and Chamberlain was wrong."[62]

His analysis was characteristically blunt. As the European prospect darkened, he complained: "I cannot understand the British ... Chamberlain is again wobbling." He was convinced that "any fool in Britain who thinks that [Germany could be appeased], should be in a lunatic asylum." The evil geniuses, in his view, were British cabinet ministers Sir John Simon and Sir Samuel Hoare, who believed that somehow Germany and Russia would collide and exhaust each other while Britain could safely stand aside. "There has been nothing so stupid and inept in British foreign policy since they lost the American colonies."[63] Crerar was now resigned to another European conflict, and his experience of the earlier war filled him with trepidation.

Whatever cautious optimism about Canada's economy there might have been when Crerar and his colleagues left for London, it dissipated quickly on their return in the light of severe prairie drought. The western provinces were in desperate need of relief, and the financial woes of the national railway were growing ever worse. Hepburn in Ontario and Maurice Duplessis in Quebec charged that dominion expenditures in the west were impoverishing central Canada. But there was no longer any possibility, in an industrialized country racked by depression, of maintaining Mackenzie King's image of a classic federalism in which Ottawa devoted itself to its own exclusive concerns and left all else – in this case, the bitter economic and social results – to the provinces. Whatever King believed or hoped for, the nation was on the verge of an extraordinary departure. Crerar would be the unlikely and somewhat unwitting "point man" in one of its most important aspects.

One response, of which the revolutionary implications were quite unexpected, was the Royal Commission on Dominion-Provincial Relations. Headed by Newton Rowell, it was instructed by cabinet to examine the increasingly complex financial relations of the provinces and the national government and, if nothing else, help postpone some very difficult decisions. The dominion government could not simply sit back and wait. With western provinces facing bankruptcy, Ottawa seemed the last resort ("Once again" muttered Hepburn) for assistance. The dominion budget of 1938 would force Ottawa's hand and, as Blair Neatby has described, set Canada on a new and untried path.[64]

The fiscal woes of the prairie provinces had led Crerar, as early as January 1937, to challenge the conventional wisdom. The separation of dominion and provincial financial responsibilities under normal circumstances "is unquestionably right," he wrote to King, but the danger of Manitoba and Saskatchewan's defaulting was an emergency that threatened the dominion government as well. He advised that their bonds be guaranteed by Ottawa, in order to improve provincial credit and forestall political agitation.[65] He believed that the only way to a general improvement in economic conditions was to ensure that, as much as possible, dominion expenditures "facilitate and encourage the production of new wealth in Canada." To this end, he urged Finance Minister Dunning to avoid passive relief and public works, which saddle the taxpayers (and the government) with continuing maintenance costs. Rather, he tried to persuade Dunning to agree to road-building programs into new mining areas and tourist destinations, both of which would generate revenue for the treasury.[66]

It was not a great step from the notion that increased revenue was the key to alleviating the problems of the Depression to the idea of selective stimulation by government through the budget process. Thus when King wrote to all the ministers in January 1938 exhorting them to reduce their estimates as much as possible in an attempt to achieve a budget surplus, Crerar was distinctly unsympathetic.[67]

In his reply to the prime minister, he was alone among the ministers in rejecting the premises held by King and Dunning. Conceding that a balanced budget was desirable as a general fiscal objective, and sharing King's desire for a tax cut before the next general election, Crerar nevertheless put up a stubborn resistance because of what he termed the "extraordinary circumstances." He argued vigorously that obligations for pensions, relief, defence, and the inevitable railway deficit left government with little discretionary income and less room for manœuvre. Tax increases were out of the question. In Crerar's opinion only three departments of government had any potential for increasing the national wealth. Both Agriculture and Fisheries were stymied by drastic declines in commodity prices around the world. That left Mines and Resources.

Throughout most of the 1930s mining, especially of gold, was one of Canada's few economic bright spots. Crerar's earlier success in winning a three-year tax concession for new mines had paid off handsomely. Tourism, for which he was also responsible, had at least the possibility of generating new revenue. However reluctant Crerar was to abandon traditional Liberal orthodoxy, he now reacted as an experienced businessman attempting to find areas of growth in a depressed world. For the moment he fought alone and unsuccessfully. Dunning and his cabinet committee examining estimates rejected his proposals to stimulate mining further and to promote tourism, and they chopped his departmental estimates, as they did all the others. Discouraged, he repeated to Dunning his conviction that "a very considerable increase in the national income will provide the only way we can finally escape from the financial troubles that beset us in the way of unbalanced budgets and heavy taxation." He had little expectation that Dunning's indiscriminate "repressive influence over expenditures" could be lifted.[68] But assistance was at hand.

Franklin Roosevelt, frustrated and alarmed by the sudden worsening of the Depression in the United States in late 1937, began to use government spending to revive economic activity. Pressure began to mount on the King government to do the same. Though trade talks with Britain and the United States were as yet uncompleted, a budget could no longer be delayed. In an effort led by Norman Rogers and a small number of cabinet colleagues, a decision was finally forced on King and Dunning to consider a stimulative budget. The prime minister appointed a committee of five, including Crerar, to make proposals, which it quickly did, recommending heavy supplementary estimates to increase spending. At this, Dunning finally conceded a limited deficit. The argument was now underpinned by the theories of John Maynard Keynes and his support of cyclical and countercyclical government investment to balance private investment or lack of it. The theory mattered little to Crerar, who now felt vindicated and much less isolated, though he certainly understood the implications of Keynes's proposals.

The economics and politics of the Depression were intertwined. As early as spring 1938, King was ruminating about the most propitious time for an election and was seriously contemplating calling one by the end of the year. As always, there were many considerations. One of them was wheat. Little had improved for the prairie grain grower.

Years of drought and low prices had driven many off the land and left many more dispirited and impoverished. However much the government, including Crerar, might wish to do away with the Wheat Board and restore the open market, it would mean virtual abandonment of the industry, resulting in disastrous political fall-out in the west. Once more, ideology must give way to political necessity.

It was Gardiner who forced the issue in early 1939. He proposed to do away with the Wheat Board, have administration of the Grain Act transferred from Euler to himself, and set a minimum guarantee of sixty cents a bushel for the new crop year, applicable only to pooled grain. Not surprisingly, this overture brought howls and threats to resign from several cabinet members, often for conflicting reasons.[69] The increasingly heated debates continued through March and April until King confessed that "while I had thought I had understood the problem at one time, I had now become so confused as not to be able to say what the consensus of view was or to give any decision." Finally, at Crerar's suggestion, the thorny issue was turned over to the cabinet's wheat committee – Crerar, Dunning, Euler, and Gardiner – for resolution.[70] It somehow managed to find an imaginative compromise, despite the fact that the country, and many of its politicians, were all agog with the first-ever visit by the reigning sovereign, in late spring.

Crerar was detailed to inform the farmers of Manitoba of the new policy, which he did in a radio broadcast in June, immediately after the departure from Canada of the king and queen. The burdensome surplus, he explained, was caused by four factors – fear of war, the desire of European countries to be self-sustaining, the demoralization of international trade, and the good world wheat crop in 1938 – all beyond the control of Canada's farmers and government. To do nothing, however, would probably mean the end of the Canadian wheat industry. So like it or not, Canada, like every other trading country, had to subsidize its producers if the wheat industry were to survive. For the first two crop years of the reborn Wheat Board, the market price had spared the government the need to provide a subsidy; but the 1937–38 crop had cost the dominion treasury some $50 million – an expense that the cabinet was hoping to keep from growing in the future. In addition, the government was obliged to cover emergency relief costs occasioned by drought of an additional $12 million. Therefore the government had decided that, as long as present conditions obtained, the minimum price for wheat would be guaranteed at seventy cents per bushel.

To offset the disappointment of the farmers, who had hoped for an eighty-cent minimum, the government had put in place a quite useful piece of legislation, the Prairie Farm Assistance Act. As Crerar described it in his broadcast, it would not only provide emergency relief to drought-stricken farms but, more important, launch projects for irrigation and prevention of soil erosion across the prairies. (It was also expected that it would solidify the party's hold on prairie seats,[71] the Manitoba portion of which was Crerar's responsibility.)

In any case the timing of a general election would be determined by the deteriorating European situation. Alarms in September 1938 had forced King to abandon any thought of a canvass that autumn, and, while ill at Kingsmere, his retreat in the nearby Gatineau, he had instructed Crerar to prepare the government for possible hostilities.[72] When that crisis dissipated, so also did any plans for a general election that year.

The government did, however, proceed with a series of by-elections in November 1938; one was in Brandon, in western Manitoba, and Crerar took a direct hand. The Liberals were obliged to defend the government's record, which they did vigorously. The CCF proposed old age pensions of $50 per month, and the Conservatives complained that the initial wheat payment should have been set at $1.00 per bushel. Crerar campaigned extensively and raised money for the Liberal candidate, and he took much satisfaction from the fact that loss of the riding in 1935 by 225 votes had been converted to a winning margin of 1,000 votes. He welcomed King's congratulations all the more, since the party had been badly whipped in South Waterloo the same day.[73]

The following spring, with the government in the fourth year of its mandate, election talk began to swirl again. But there were always difficulties. The international situation was certainly no more propitious; the king and queen were to arrive in May for their first visit; and the continuing uncertainty about Dunning's health all combined to feed the prime minister's indecision. There was nothing that could be done about Europe, except to follow events anxiously. The royal visit, it was hoped, would put the Canadian people in a euphoric and contented mood. The stopover in Winnipeg must have occasioned some interesting introductions, as the king and queen arrived escorted by Prime Minister King and greeted by John Queen, the mayor. And it was also hoped that if Dunning had to retire, as seemed more and more likely, J.L. Ralston could be induced to return to political life.

The Tories were using the international uncertainty to float a scheme for a national government, similar presumably to the Union government of the Great War. Even Dafoe was willing to give credence to the scheme, as long as it did not involve amalgamation of the rail-ways.[74] The CNR, always in financial difficulties, was never far from political consideration. The idea of some kind of union of parties persisted. In the spring of 1939, Crerar wrote angrily to Cameron that a drive to save the country with a national government was being mounted by "those brilliant young statesmen, George McCullach and John Bassett" of Toronto. He suspected that Hepburn was probably involved as well.[75] Speculation about a national government at this point seems to have been a tacit admission by the Tories that they had little chance of winning an election.

At King's request the cabinet undertook an electoral survey that summer, looking towards an autumn vote. Except for Ontario, and to a lesser extent British Columbia, where some losses could be expected, the prospects looked good. Crerar reported that of Manitoba's seventeen seats, the Liberals might lose one or two of the fourteen that they held. He felt that in the near future the government would do well across the prairies.

But Crerar was unhappy that the government would not have the Rowell-Sirois Report as a "factor in the election scene." The report, he was convinced (probably through Dafoe), would recommend momentous changes for Canada. He was convinced as well that those changes would be resisted by some provinces. What he would prefer, he told King, was to have the report published and discussed widely, followed by a dominion-provincial conference to consider it. After some provinces had displayed their anticipated reluctance would be the most advantageous time to go to the country, with Rowell-Sirois as a blueprint for the future – to be implemented, of course, by another Liberal government. Such a strategy, he contended, could "settle once and for all time all those contentious questions of jurisdiction now exercising their evil influence upon our public life."[76]

A little more than a month after Crerar wrote this letter, the world was plunged into yet another war, and all thought of an autumn election fell with the autumn leaves.

CHAPTER TWELVE

Men and War,
Federalism and Wheat,
1939–42

Tom Crerar was the only dominion minister to serve in both wartime dominion cabinets. William Lyon Mackenzie King associated him with the Union government of the Great War, and not to Crerar's advantage, but the experience certainly enhanced his stature within the government. When hostilities became inevitable in 1939, King responded by forming an Emergency Council comprising himself, Crerar, Ernest Lapointe, and the ministers of defence and finance ex officio. This was the origin of the Cabinet War Committee, which, with personnel added later, supervised Canada's war effort. Crerar, because of his seniority, was named deputy chairman, and he held this post throughout the conflict.[1]

He had at one time thought of himself as a possible candidate for National Defence when it became clear at the outbreak of war that Ian Mackenzie was to be shifted from that portfolio. King himself had earlier mentioned such a possibility. In reminding the prime minister of the conversation, Crerar commented that Norman Rogers, whom King now favoured for the position after J.L. Ralston had indicated his preference for Finance, might be too inexperienced to deal with the Chiefs of Staff. At the very beginning of the war, it seems, Crerar feared that the army would need to be restrained. He had not forgotten the crises of the Great War over manpower. But King had already made up his mind on Rogers and noted later that Crerar "was very nice about it. Said he was ready to do anything."[2]

The prime minister had a special assignment for Crerar at hand. The British government had requested that each dominion send a minister to London to take part in discussions about the most effective manner of financing and organizing for the war. Much of the negotiating would involve Canada's capacity to provide Britain with money and resources, especially agricultural products, and King recalled that Crerar had clearly remembered that in the Great War "the British were very hard bargainers on everything."[3]

He promised Crerar that he would provide some assistance and cautioned him to observe everything carefully and take copious notes. And in a secret memorandum that Crerar carried with him, the government outlined the limits of Canada's fiscal commitments – about forty per cent of national income could be made available for war purposes. Canada saw the meeting in London not as the beginning of a sort of continuing war cabinet but rather as a single conference, reflecting King's persistent fear of any attempt at imperial centralization. As it turned out, Crerar was in England just short of two months. The assistance that King had promised came in the persons of Brigadier H.D.G. (Harry) Crerar, T.A.'s unrelated namesake, Air Commodore Breadner, Dana Wilgress of Trade and Commerce, and George McIvor, chief commissioner of the Wheat Board. They were joined later by Graham Towers, governor of the Bank of Canada.

Sale of wheat and war financing were the major concerns during Crerar's mission to Britain, but there were other matters to be discussed. Communications between Canada and Britain were confused. Cables were flying back and forth across the Atlantic, not only between cabinets and agencies but between individual bureaucrats as well. Crerar was able to rationalize communications greatly by working with the dominions secretary, Anthony Eden, whom he liked and admired. So he was kept hectically busy in London with a constant round of meetings, conferences, and the inevitable social obligations.

When he had arrived in Britain Crerar had believed that it would be to the advantage of the prairie farmer to maintain the open market and encourage Britain to buy its requirements in the traditional way – that is, through the open market. A decade of drought, foreclosures, and low wheat prices had led Canadian grain growers to see in the increased demand of the war an opportunity to recoup some of their losses. As in all wars, they thought, the price of wheat will advance rapidly. Consequently there was little sympathy in Canada for any long-term contract at fixed prices with Britain and for closure of the futures market, which was already showing some signs of a bullish turn. Crerar had originally shared this view.

A trip to the front in France with the other visiting ministers changed his opinion on wheat sales. In recounting his trip to George McIvor of the Wheat Board, he described his reaction to the Maginot Line: "I am just a farm boy from Manitoba, but I am afraid the Germans will go around that Line." The prospect of a French collapse and Germany in control of western Europe threw the whole question of wheat sales into a different light. A northwestern Europe dominated by Germany would mean a significant loss of Canadian wheat markets on the continent. If Britain became the only substantial purchaser left in Europe, as seemed likely, weakened demand would certainly depress prices.

Crerar began to move around to the idea of a long-term contract. There was some interest in such an arrangement in Britain except for James Rank, who headed the wheat-importing committee of the Cereals Board. He much preferred to take his chances on the open market.[4] After discussions with British officials, Crerar recommended back to Ottawa that the Canadian government enter into a long-term contract for 250 to 300 million bushels at $1 per bushel over two years or, alternatively, 150 to 180 million bushels at 93.5 cents over a shorter period. The cabinet preferred to maintain the open market and rely on a price rise, for obvious political reasons,[5] and this rejection ended Crerar's discussions on wheat. As it turned out, Canadian grain growers would have been much better off if his proposal had been accepted. Just as Crerar and James Rank had surmised, the price of wheat dropped the next spring after the end of the "phoney war" and the German onslaught through the Low Countries and into France.

On other matters such as the British Commonwealth Air Training plan and war financing, Crerar was principally a conduit between cabinets. He did play a useful role in arranging contracts for other foodstuffs, such as bacon, and throughout his stay he was at pains to make clear Canada's attitude towards the war and its reasons for participating. He told Eden that Canada was not in this war simply because of sentiment; "if Britain were in another war like the South African War she would find very little support in Canada." The critical factors were the issues involved and "the fact that if the Totalitarian idea submerged Europe and Asia we, in North America, could not be immune from its effects."[6]

Yet throughout his activities in Britain there seemed a sense of wariness, of trying to establish definite limits to Canada's role in the war. He cabled King, for example: "Anything resembling Argyll House Organization in last war should be wholly avoided," arguing instead that Canadian Military Headquarters should be attached to the Canadian High Commission Office and thus more amenable to Canadian control.[7] At a private meeting of the Empire Parliamentary Committee, with Lord Macmillan, minister of information, in the chair, Crerar stated that Canada planned to raise two army divisions, and beyond that its contribution would be directed towards its share in the cost of the air-training plan and concentration on agricultural and industrial production. He took the same line in a radio address for the British Broadcasting Corporation.[8]

With his mission completed, it took Crerar almost a week to make and receive his round of good-bye visits. He found Winston Churchill "the most interesting personality I have met in London. He has great imagination and apparently a great capacity for work. There is something of the bulldog nature about him. With it all he has an attractive personality."[9]

Crerar arrived back in Ottawa on Christmas Eve. King was more than pleased with his performance. After Crerar reported at length to the cabinet, King wrote in his diary: "He really has done exceedingly well, and was quite obviously the best man to have go abroad for the purpose" – an opinion fully seconded by Anthony Eden in a letter to the prime minister.[10] While tired but generally satisfied with it all, Crerar confided to Dexter that he was somewhat disappointed that his proposal for a wheat contract had been turned down, feeling that his colleagues had been short-sighted, whatever the pressures upon them. And he was not alone in this view. Charlie Dunning informed Dexter that he "knew all about Mr. Crerar's deal and he thinks it was a good deal and should have been accepted." It could have been done without closing the market.[11] Crerar gained little satisfaction from being proved right the following summer.

After a brief Christmas holiday, Crerar quickly plunged back into the daily grind. King had reorganized the government once again.[12] Crerar remained deputy chairman of an expanded Cabinet War Committee (CWC) and now chaired the committee on fuel and power, in addition to sitting on the food production and marketing committee and the everlasting wheat committee. His heavy and varied departmental responsibilities continued, but more and more he left daily operations in the hands of his officials, intervening only on political matters. CWC met almost daily. The full cabinet had its regular weekly meeting, as did caucus when the session was on. With his other committee obligations to be met, and they were often onerous, Crerar had little time left but for his war duties. Only the most senior patronage issues seemed to intrude during the war. King had held up appointment of a new lieutenant-governor for Manitoba until Crerar had returned from Britain and supported R.F. McWilliams, who was eventually named to the post by the prime minister; and appointments to the bench always received careful consideration.[13]

But the most important political preoccupation for the government was the election that had to come in 1940. The only question was, "when?" The answer fortuitously came from Ontario. Mitchell Hepburn, still the stormy petrel of Canadian Liberalism, had lifted his feud with Ottawa to an astonishing level. On 18 January 1940, the premier had moved a resolution in the provincial house condemning the dominion government for its alleged lackadaisical prosecution of the war effort. He was of course cheerfully seconded by George Drew, leader of the Conservative opposition.[14]

Prime Minister King was at first somewhat disconsolate but quickly began to see the opportunity he had been handed by the intemperate Hepburn. He had been planning on a short session of Parliament and then an election, but now he decided on immediate dissolution. He canvassed the cwc on 22 January 1940, with only Crerar, Lapointe, Power, and Ralston present; and only the finance minister showed any reluctance. The subsequent cabinet meeting later that day was not informed. At a full cabinet meeting the following day, King hinted at a quick election, and Crerar "concluded I would be wise to have a dissolution at once and all seemed to be heading in that way." Crerar may have served as a stalking horse for King on this occasion. The prime minister announced the dissolution to a stunned House when the new session opened three days later. The issue was clear, at least in King's mind – confidence in the government's ability to prosecute the war vigorously and effectively.[15]

Crerar's role in the campaign was equally clear. He was responsible for Manitoba in particular and expected to hold it solidly in the government column. So he left for the west almost immediately. First, however, he wrote to King, urging him to accept a speaking date in Winnipeg and to bring Lapointe with him to emphasize the theme of unity: "Your appearance would be symbolic of that unity."[16] On arrival in Winnipeg he brought together the Liberal executive and representatives from all provincial constituencies. He reported to King that the common opinion in western Canada was that "the bluff of Hepburn and Drew had been called" and that that had been the right thing to do. He repeated his invitation, claiming that "if you and Lapointe can come to Winnipeg it will mean tens of thousands of votes over Canada. That may seem an exaggeration but it is not."[17]

At the outset of the campaign, Crerar summarized Liberal prospects in the west by explaining that there was a good deal of resentment against Hepburn and Drew and that Robert Manion, Tory leader of the Opposition in Ottawa, was "not considered to be a safe man to trust with the business of government in the present critical times." There were scattered references to conscription on the prairies, but Crerar did not consider them significant. He did mention that "among the population of foreign extraction there is some fear that someone may bring in conscription. They are practically one hundred per cent against it." He advised Liberal candidates to "avoid making appeals for foreign-born support on the grounds that the Liberal party would not introduce conscription. This result will come without making it an issue for discussion publicly."[18] King would no doubt agree.

On a more general level, the Toronto *Globe* noted that Crerar had declared that Germany was using the censure motion of the Ontario legislature as propaganda to demonstrate "the supposed divisions that existed in Canada." This could have a great effect on neutrals in Canada, according to Crerar. Canadians must be made aware that the "issues involved are everything that is best in Christian civilization. If they win in Europe the whole continent will revert to paganism."[19] The duty of Canadians was therefore obvious. There is no reason to think this approach insincere, despite the hyperbole. For Crerar and his colleagues, the conflict had become, as Jack Granatstein has effectively demonstrated, "Canada's War."

King accommodated Crerar by appearing at a major rally in Winnipeg. Ernest Lapointe, fresh from the Liberals' victory over Maurice Duplessis's Union Nationale in the Quebec provincial election, was a great hit and seemed to embody a united commitment to the Liberal war effort. The only sour note was the absence of Premier Bracken. According to Dafoe, he had pledged his support for Crerar but declined an invitation to introduce the prime minister at the meeting.[20] Bracken's reluctance proved to be only a minor disappointment in an otherwise-successful western campaign. Crerar spoke at meetings throughout Manitoba and lent a hand on occasion in Alberta and Ontario. He also tended his own riding of Churchill carefully.

In Winnipeg the Sanhedrin swung into action in support of its comrade. John Dafoe, after some nostalgic flirtation with the idea of a national government, lent steady editorial support to the Liberal cause. Frank Fowler was Crerar's campaign manager and fundraiser. Cameron was the contact with the mining companies, which appreciated Crerar's staunch advocacy with the government. Jack Rankin forwarded campaign contributions from the Hollinger and Timmins corporations. Fowler, in acknowledging the help, told Cameron that he was "always afraid of an election that looks as easy as this one."[21]

He need not have worried. Polling day was 26 March 1940, and the Liberals won handily, dealing the Tories the worst election hammering they had ever suffered. The Liberal government received

181 seats; the Tories were reduced to forty. The Sanhedrin was well satisfied as its members gathered for lunch to send Crerar back to Ottawa and, as Fowler put it, "gave him plenty of advice." They had reason to be pleased. Of Manitoba's seventeen seats, the Liberals won fifteen and narrowly missed in Souris. The CCF held its Manitoba citadel in Winnipeg North. Crerar had taken a direct hand throughout the province, both on the stump and in organization. Norman Lambert, national secretary of the party, thought Manitoba's a splendid result. Under Crerar's leadership and Fowler's management, the Liberals raised $59,155 and spent $56,338, leaving, as Reginald Whitaker put it, "a prudent surplus."[22]

Crerar's confidence going into the election had not been misplaced. In a letter to Cameron summing up he wrote: "Well might the shades of Sir John A. Macdonald say, 'Varus, oh Varus, where are my legions?' His prediction to King and Lapointe at the Winnipeg meeting that they "might well be watching the destruction of the Conservative Party" was not far off the mark, at least in the short term. But he worried that the "overwhelming majority the Government received and its result to the Conservative Party will likely produce effects for the future that may be far-reaching and unfortunate."[23] Politicians, it seems, are difficult to satisfy. There was time for a brief holiday; and Crerar, along with Norman Lambert, spent a few days with King near Norfolk, Virginia.[24] It would be his last respite for many months.

When the phoney war ended and Germany slashed through the Low Countries and into France in May and June 1940, Canada suddenly was Britain's major overseas ally. It had indeed become Canada's war. Of the many aspects of this new situation that faced the government in Ottawa, one in which Crerar was deeply involved, as usual, was the issue of wheat. His worst fears of the preceding autumn had been realized. With continental European markets closed, futures prices began to slip, and the surplus began to mount. The cabinet's wheat committee came under steady pressure to deal with the problem.

There was no indication of how long this restriction of markets would last. Whatever the committee recommended, the prairies must not be left in a situation where they were unable to respond quickly and effectively to changed circumstances. Throughout much of the next crop year, the committee wrangled over the alternatives, and it finally produced a majority proposal, which had not persuaded Crerar, in March 1941. The plan was based on the conviction that wheat acreage must be reduced by one-third. To achieve this, it recommended payments of four dollars per acre for land not seeded but summer fallowed; two dollars per acre for that portion of reduced wheat acreage planted to oats or barley; and two dollars per acre for reduced wheat acreage sown to grass, with a further payment of two dollars made on 1 July 1942.

In a long memorandum to cabinet, Crerar set forth his objections to this scheme. He was convinced that it would create more problems than it solved. While he agreed that six or seven million acres of wheat acreage should be eliminated, he objected to paying four dollars per acre to summer fallow the land, since, as a result, yield per acre would be increased in 1942, thus defeating the purpose of reducing wheat acreage. He objected as well to the bonus of two dollars per acre to switch from wheat to coarse grains. This would lead to greatly increased production of oats and barley, for which only a domestic market existed. This glut in turn would drive their prices down and lead to substantial increase in hog production and probably a bacon surplus. As well, there would be heavy inspection costs to ensure that there was no cheating, and a system of individual quotas would have to be established. The overall result would be a heavy drain on the treasury, and more surpluses.

Crerar suggested that seven million acres be taken out of cereal production entirely. He proposed that farmers be paid twenty-five cents per bushel on one-third of the wheat acreage they planted the preceding year, based on average yield and conditional on their not planting those acres to any cereal grain. This would cost the treasury much less and avoid other surplus effects, and the land could be brought back into production quickly when circumstances changed, as in fact they did in 1943.[25]

Cabinet settled on a mix of the two proposals, conscious of the political necessity of maintaining farm income. The result was an extraordinary intervention – for Liberals – into the grain economy. It involved introduction of delivery quotas, maximum quotas, and payments for reducing wheat acreage. The government's politically directed concern seemed divided equally between controlling surpluses and supporting farm incomes.[26] The next round of changes would come in mid-1943.

Another post-election issue with which Crerar became closely involved was the report of the Rowell-Sirois Commission, appointed in 1937 to examine and make recommendations about dominion-provincial relations, especially in finance. It had grown out of the inability of the provinces, especially in the west, to cope with the economic and human costs of the Depression and Ottawa's unwillingness to assume new responsibilities. The commission included

Crerar's confidant John Dafoe of the *Free Press* as a member. Though received by the government just prior to the election of 1940, the report was not made public until after the ballots were cast.

The implications of the report for Canadian federalism were enormous. With the objective of creating roughly equal levels of services across the nation, it asked the provinces to forgo income, corporation, and succession taxes. Ottawa would redistribute income by a system of national adjustment grants. Alberta, British Columbia, and Ontario would not be eligible for such grants and thus could be expected to balk. And they did, claiming that wartime was no occasion for such constitutional radicalism. Ottawa bureaucrats, rather disingenuously, argued quite the opposite – that such broad taxing power was necessary to prosecute the war. They failed to acknowledge that it would be even more useful for managing the postwar reconstruction of the nation.[27]

Unlike many of his colleagues, Crerar strongly supported full implementation of the report. He did so as a result of his respect for Dafoe's opinion; the persuasive leadership of Premier Bracken of Manitoba, who had urged the commission to endorse equalization of opportunities and responsibilities; and, most important, his own conviction that the experience of the Depression demanded an effective and compassionate rearrangement of the fiscal relations of the dominion. He was in a position to advance his ideas when he was included in a cabinet committee, led by Finance Minister Ilsley, mandated to consider the report.[28]

The commission's report had been made public during the summer and had obtained a generally favourable reception. The cabinet committee recommended that a dominion-provincial conference be called to sound out the provinces on implementation of the recommendations. The cabinet, it turned out, was rather doubtful. Only Ilsley and Crerar were strongly in favour of a conference; many of the others felt it pointless. The finance minister's position, urged on him by his department and the Bank of Canada, was utterly pragmatic – either implement the report fully and permanently or, failing agreement with the provinces, implement the financial provisions for the balance of the war. The money had to be found somehow.[29] Ilsley surveyed the provinces and received a mixed message, ranging from Manitoba's vociferous support to Ontario's flat rejection of what it felt was a species of constitutional robbery. When he reported this gloomy news to his colleagues late in October there was little enthusiasm for pushing ahead.

Crerar remained determined, however, and wrote a long letter to King reiterating the views he had put forth in cabinet. When the commission had been appointed in 1937, he began, there was broad agreement "that a new allocation of powers and responsibilities between the Provinces and the Federal Government had become necessary." The commission had done its work well, and its report had received "widespread approval." The war was taxing Canada's resources to the limit, and the government needed the fiscal flexibility to act vigorously.

But beyond that, Crerar, veteran of a previous war cabinet, sought to avoid the problems that he recalled had followed the last war because of a "hodge-podge of taxing methods and of governmental responsibilities" that had resulted in confusion. It was, he argued, the government's "plain duty to put our house in order to meet these difficulties and dangers when they come as they assuredly will." He acknowledged that Hepburn was opposed to any consideration of the report until after the war. But that made it even more important for Ottawa to assert its leadership. "There are not many people, even in Ontario," he claimed, "who think that Ontario is a sort of independent sovereignty of almost as much importance as the Dominion."

Politically, he felt the government held the high ground and risked missing an opportunity to confront Hepburn successfully. Not to call a conference would incur public criticism, he warned King, and there was little danger involved. If the conference failed because of provincial obstruction, "the responsibility for blocking action which public opinion in Canada I believe supports, would be clearly fixed."[30] There was no need for Crerar to keep urging King to action. The day he wrote his now-redundant letter cabinet finally concurred, and the invitations to the provinces were sent out on 2 November, the following day.

Yet there was little optimism. King noted in his diary, "All members of Cabinet excepting Crerar expressed themselves as believing that the conference will amount to nothing."[31] Dexter reported to Dafoe that Alex Skelton, who had been named secretary of the commission, is "almost without hope of real achievement at the coming conference. T.A. has been trying to get King to screw his courage up to the fighting point. He would go as far as to have a general election on the issue." Hyperbole aside, Dexter was right in predicting that King would speak bravely and then avoid any direct fight with Hepburn – and, as it turned out, Alberta's Aberhart and Pattullo of British Columbia as well, who also proved recalcitrant. Hepburn demolished the government's argument of wartime expediency by pointing out quite correctly that the dominion government had only to invoke its emergency powers to extend its taxing authority to any length it chose.[32]

204 Ministry of Talents, 1935–45

Despite the apparent failure of the conference in mid-January 1941, King was not at all displeased; he felt "relieved and happy." As Crerar had predicted, the government had avoided attack for not calling the conference, and King had received the "pledge of the provinces to let us take their revenues if we need them – a tremendous achievement." The rejection by Ontario, Alberta, and British Columbia of the principle of equalization did not seem important to King at the time.[33]

Crerar hastened to write a full report of the conference to Dafoe, who had an obvious interest in the outcome. It had been the most momentous gathering since the Charlottetown Conference in 1864, in Crerar's opinion, and had been surrounded by due ceremony. King and the premiers gathered around the clerk's table in the House of Commons surrounded by the provincial delegations, members of the Commons, officials, and full public galleries. The prime minister delivered his carefully prepared opening address, which had been approved by cabinet beforehand, after many revisions. King acknowledged the desire of the national government to see the report implemented but was as conciliatory as possible.

As far as Hepburn was concerned, King might have saved his breath. According to Crerar, Hepburn paid no attention and rose immediately after King finished to make Ontario's "opposition unmistakably clear." He was supported by Pattullo, who was "a compound of inordinate vanity and ... thick-headedness." The third opponent was Aberhart who "possesses all the arts of the successful demagogue." Crerar had to fall back on an image of Rider Haggard's in describing him as a "political medicine man."

At King's suggestion, the prime minister, Lapointe, and Crerar met the nine premiers the following morning to see if any progress was possible. The initial agenda had scheduled a series of committees, but when King broached the idea "Hepburn soon made it clear, and Pattullo also, that they would not go to committees. They accused the Federal Government ... of trying to push through the recommendations of the Commission in a war atmosphere." Hepburn went on to imply that the entire scheme "was designed wholly and solely to help Quebec." Though the other six premiers were willing to go to committees, two hours of wrangling made it clear that they were going nowhere, with Hepburn sneering at the commission as "being composed of three university professors and a newspaper man in Winnipeg who had always had his knife into Ontario" – which may have made Dafoe wince.

The conference broke up that afternoon, with King putting the best face on things, which allowed Crerar to hope, rather forlornly, that it might be resumed at a later date. Ilsley, however, left no doubt that the dominion government would move into the provincial taxing sphere as soon as necessary to finance the war. In summing up his long account to Dafoe, Crerar reflected, rather Whiggishly: "It seems a strange phenomenon that men like Hepburn and Pattullo and Aberhart can be placed in high positions of responsibility and maintained there by our democratic system. Are people losing their capacity to reflect and think and can any demagogue win and hold the ear of the people against any appeal to reason and common sense?"[34] Since no one else in Ottawa had expected any better result, Crerar could share his disappointment only with his old friend.

But there was genuine reluctance in Canada to undertake any radical changes during the war. The deepening conflict fully occupied the time and attention especially of members of the Cabinet War Committee (cwc). At the outset, King had emphasized that Canada's commitment would be limited; its primary effort would be in supplying food and materials of war. An infantry division had been raised and sent overseas, commanded by General A.G.L. McNaughton, and a second division had been authorized for duty in Canada. On 17 December 1939, while Crerar had been preparing to leave Britain, the prime minister had announced the safe arrival there of the First Division and signing of the agreement setting up the British Commonwealth Air Training Plan (BCATP), which included a carefully worded acknowledgment by the United Kingdom that this was to be Canada's major contribution to the war effort. When Crerar had returned to Canada there seemed little sense of urgency during that winter of the phoney war.

The awakening had come in the spring of 1940. First Denmark and Norway fell, and then the Wehrmacht swept through the Low Countries and into France. Britain barely escaped with its army from the shores of Dunkirk. Canada was now Britain's major ally, and King's hope for a limited land war was ended. Two further divisions and a tank brigade were sent to Britain, and Parliament in June 1940 passed the National Resources Mobilization Act (NRMA), which conscripted Canadians for home defence – the third section of the act explicitly stating they were not to be sent overseas.

But these actions did not satisfy those who were demanding an even greater effort and sought a "national" government to prosecute the war. The attack was not unexpected. As Crerar informed Dafoe, the railing at King "had its origins in Toronto and then spread to Montreal. I strongly suspect that those two wonder-boys, McCullagh [Globe and Mail] and Bassett [Telegram] had the main hand in it. They honestly think it is sort of a sacrilege that, when Canada is at war, the disloyal Liberals should be in charge and they, themselves, have no part in it."[35]

To some extent, however, the government was losing control of the situation. Canada's carefully limited initial role in the war had gone by the boards, and no new limits had yet been established. It meant that CWC was put in the position of reacting to events rather than planning for eventualities. In that alarming summer of 1940 the Canadian forces began to expand rapidly. A Canadian Corps of three divisions was authorized, and the elements of a fourth were being gathered. General H.D.G. (Harry) Crerar became chief of the General Staff (CGS).

In June 1940, as France fell to the Nazi invaders, Norman Rogers was killed in a plane crash, and his death necessitated a cabinet reorganization. Colonel J.L. Ralston went to National Defence and was later joined by two associates – Chubby Power, as minister for air and in charge of the BCATP, and Angus L. Macdonald, who left the premiership of Nova Scotia to become minister of naval services. James Ilsley succeeded Ralston at Finance. All were members of the CWC. In the radically changed circumstances, the government was now forced to abandon its narrowly conceived design for Canada's war. Unfortunately, as it turned out, since no new limits were agreed on, there would later be a heavy political cost.

After the fall of France, the CWC became more than an emergency committee that met infrequently. From that point on, it met regularly, often daily, and took on the effective control of Canada's prosecution of the war. While Crerar and his colleagues retained their departmental duties, more and more they found themselves wrestling with the difficult problems of wartime manpower and finance. It was the former that engaged much of Crerar's attention. He shared King's fear that an expanded military effort could lead to a demand for conscription and beginning in 1941 fought determinedly against the army's plans for increased manpower.

And those plans were ambitious indeed – so much so that in May 1941 CWC discussed the possibility of conscription and Ralston said that he hoped that it would not be ruled out in all circumstances, at which point Ernest Lapointe immediately said that he would in that case have to resign.[36] Compulsory service was already being promoted in some sectors of the press and had been advocated in the House by one or two Conservatives. Crerar was concerned enough to sound out opinion at home. He knew Dafoe's mind on the issue, and they did not always agree, so he wrote to Ewan McPherson, chief justice of the Court of King's Bench in Manitoba and an old friend, "I would be grateful if you would write me confidentially what you think of the possibility of the conscription issue's coming up and what, in your judgement, would be the popular reaction to it. There is little doubt that it would create cleavages almost as bad, if not as bad, as those created in the last war."[37]

Part of his concern arose from the talk constantly swirling around Ottawa about the plans of the military. Dexter informed Dafoe in a memorandum that Victor Sifton (of the Winnipeg Siftons), who was serving under Ralston as master general of ordnance, had told him that Generals McNaughton and Crerar were scheming to double the size of the army. "These people want 2 Corps of 3 divisions each plus 1 armoured division and 1 tank brigade, each. ... [T]he voluntary end would be nearly 9 divisions instead of nearly 8 [sic] as at present."[38] The reality was more modest, but daunting enough for a nation of Canada's size. The mature proposal came forward in the autumn of 1941. It called for creation overseas of a two-corps Canadian Army composed of three infantry divisions, two armoured divisions, two tank brigades, and ancillary troops.

But the debate in cwc over what became known as the "Big Army" took place in radically altered circumstances. In November the Conservatives chose Arthur Meighen, author of the Military Service Bill in the Great War and still a vigorous advocate of conscription, as their new leader. And Japan's attack on Pearl Harbor on 7 December extended the war to the Pacific, exposing Canada's western flank.

Meighen's anticipated return to the Commons threatened to exacerbate the situation. As Crerar wrote to Dafoe, "The Conservative party are out for conscription of men for Overseas service and it appears reasonable to assume that Meighen will drive for this with all his force." He will "throw the country into a turmoil of dissension in order to raise at the outside a few more divisions [which] is very shortsighted and lacking in a clear understanding of what is essential to the defeat of Germany." It was not a question of men for the army, he went on, "Germany's successes have been due entirely to her superiority in equipment." Mechanized warfare was the key to victory. "When Stalin makes a speech, it is equipment he pleads for, not men; when Churchill speaks it is the same thing." Crerar concluded this long and dispirited letter with a clear statement of his own view of the situation: "[I]f I were convinced that conscription of men for service Overseas was the most effective contribution which Canada could make to the defeat of Hitler, I would be for it, but I am convinced that ... it would not produce this result – indeed, a result vastly different." Simultaneously, C.D. Howe, who had taken on the tasks of minister of munitions, was arguing strongly for continuation of the voluntary system until war industries became fully operational.[39]

It was not sufficient for Crerar to complain privately. In a speech to the Toronto Board of Trade in October 1941, he confronted the conscription campaign directly. He reminded his audience that he had supported compulsory service in the Great War and had joined Borden's cabinet, which gave effect to it. "But now many thoughtful Canadians doubt that Canada gained much for its part in that war. We do know that it set forces in motion that were detrimental to our unity and that lasted for 20 years until Quebec overwhelmingly supported the war effort in 1939." Even so, he went on, "The issues in this war are so great, the outcome so fraught with good or ill, that I believe most Canadians would support overseas conscription if it meant the defeat of Hitler. Yet I am equally convinced this assumption has no basis in common sense."

After defending the willingness of French Canadians and "foreigners" to enlist, he turned to the Canadian Legion, which was advocating immediate conscription and had suggested matching Germany's army of forty divisions. He dismissed the proposal as absurd, arguing that "talk of conscription may lead Canadians to put emphasis in the wrong place. Germany had victories because they had more tanks, planes and guns than all the countries opposed to her. 100,000 men cannot fight 10,000 tanks." He concluded with a warning: "If we had conscription of men it is bound to raise the question of conscription of capital and labour. The turmoil and dissension this would create would cause our effectiveness to suffer and suffer greatly."[40]

The Big Army program was presented to CWC at the beginning of December, and Ralston was firmly behind the plan for a two-corps Canadian Army, even if conscription became necessary to achieve it. Ilsley and Macdonald were silent, Power was absent, and Howe was away in Washington, DC. According to Dexter, it "became a tussle between T.A. [Crerar] and Ralston," with Crerar asserting that the major emphasis should be placed on production and development of air and sea power – a position with which King readily agreed.[41] The next day, the new CGS, General Kenneth Stuart (General Harry Crerar had been transferred overseas) assured the CWC that the 1942 program could be accomplished with voluntary enlistments, but his claim changed few opinions. Crerar was more affected by Victor Sifton's comment that he was "troubled by Ralston's subservience to the general staff." Clearly, neither of them trusted the generals.[42]

Entry of Japan into the war provoked demands for deployment of troops to Canada's west coast. The army planners were not to be deflected, however, as they maintained that there was no need for transfer of any considerable body of troops. The Pacific coast could be garrisoned by NRMA men. The general staff, not surprisingly, seemed unconcerned with the political forces at work in the country, but it was really the duty of the government to exercise overall control.

Ralston's credibility was shaken when the debate resumed on 16 December. The manpower projections indicating availability of plenty of men turned out to be seriously flawed. While apologetic, the defence minister considered "that this was purely academic" and the program must be pushed along. This simply revived the debate over men versus material, with King and others pointing out that "the general staff itself had said that the most important effect of Japan's attack would be the diversion of equipment by the United States from Britain and Russia to its own needs." Ralston continued to maintain that the voluntary system could produce the men required. When Crerar intervened to say that this position was based on inaccurate projections and that the voluntary system might fail, Ralston replied that the government "must then use whatever means were necessary including conscription."[43] The impasse was critical. Even though Ralston's arguments were based on suspect figures, opponents of the Big Army had no better information and thus were increasingly under pressure to accept the advice of the military.

By accepting the Big Army program, the government would be taking the risk that the plan could not be fulfilled without conscription. It would then have to escape the commitment in clause three of the NRMA not to send conscripts overseas. Hence the CWC began to discuss the feasibility of a plebiscite to seek release from the limitation. Opponents of the Big Army were not thrilled by the prospect. As Crerar pointed out, even if it were successful, a plebiscite would simply delay the issue, not resolve it.[44]

Early in the new year the debate reached its climax. At the meeting of 5 January 1942 Crerar tried unsuccessfully to block addition of a second armoured division in order to concentrate on production, but the Big Army proposal was approved. Ralston would still not concede that this would be the final shape of the overseas army. Dexter wrote to the *Winnipeg Free Press*: "King has bowed to Ralston and told T.A. prior to yesterday's meeting that he thought there was no alternative but to accept Ralston's programme and take a chance on the experts being right. T.A. is deeply disappointed and relationships apparently are badly strained all round. Ralston is scarcely speaking to him."[45]

The debate left an unhappy cabinet and divided war committee. Ralston's role as advocate for the army left Crerar, and C.D. Howe as well, "very suspicious of [the defence minister] – believing that he mistrusts his colleagues, has small use for the government [and] is a tool of the generals who will never be satisfied however large the army is."[46] But the cabinet, particularly the CWC, was equally to blame. It never faced the issues of just how large the Canadian army overseas should be, the priority of Canada's various wartime obligations, and the country's capacity to meet them.

Crerar was conscious that a corner had been turned. He attempted to take up the issue with King without delay. Arguing that approval of the Big Army, in addition to the needs of the air force and navy, would create an alarming drain on available manpower, he tried to persuade King that a cap must be placed on the growth of the army. He repeated his arguments to Dafoe, but the latter was of the opinion that one could not foresee events and therefore any arbitrary limit on the army would be unwise. Crerar reluctantly accepted this view, but, as they all knew, leaving the issue open-ended increased the likelihood that conscription would sooner or later become necessary.[47]

Ralston did little to allay such fears. He continued to insist during meetings of CWC that the top priority rested with getting more men for the army. To many observers, in and out of government, he seemed more and more inflexible, and his reputation for always being immersed in detail was exasperating his colleagues. Crerar considered that he was a "national disaster as minister of national defence and ought to be moved. But while criticizing Ralston's incapacity as an executive." Dexter went on in a report to Dafoe, "T.A. is very just. He appreciates Ralston's integrity and patriotism. There is, he conceded, nothing finer in the way of character than Ralston." C.D. Howe exploded in the House of Commons, protesting at the large numbers of men being called to the army, claiming that production would surely suffer and Canada's contribution to ultimate victory would be weakened.[48]

But the attention of the ministry had shifted to a possible plebiscite early in 1942. Its public position was that the government was seeking to be released from the obligation not to conscript for overseas service so as to obtain freedom of action to meet any eventualities. This was not, it insisted, a request to impose full conscription. The distinction, however, was illusory. Those who favoured compulsory service would have no choice but to vote "yes," and those strongly opposed would not risk giving the government freedom to take such action.

Crerar, however, feared that the very decision to hold a plebiscite would isolate French Canadian supporters of the government, who would have great difficulty defending the action in Quebec. So he arranged a private meeting with P.J.A. Cardin, his colleague in cwc and now, since Lapointe's death at the end of 1941, senior minister from Quebec. He told Cardin that in his opinion the campaign in favour of conscription was designed as much to force King from office as to provide more men for the army. And King was the best hope of avoiding conscription. If the government were given freedom of action, then English Canada would be mollified and "conscription could be threshed out later." New manpower priorities would have to be established, favouring production, not military service. "I reiterated that in my judgement the army was too large." Apparently he persuaded Cardin that it was essential for the government to stay united and not to divide on the decision to hold the plebiscite.[49]

Crerar's status within the Liberal party changed during these months. With the deaths of Ernest Lapointe and Raoul Dandurand, he became the senior privy councillor in the government. He also became the prime minister's seat mate and his representative when King was out of the House. While this distinction gave him somewhat greater political visibility, it had little effect on his views on public issues.[50] But it did mean much more frequent contact with the prime minister. Indeed, the death of Lapointe and the earlier passing of O.D. Skelton had depreived King of his two closest political confidants. No one ever really replaced them, despite King's sense of isolation; but he did turn more frequently to the older members of cabinet such as Crerar for consultation.

The run-up to the plebiscite taken on 27 April 1942 was marked by the expected emotional appeals for and against conscription. Just like the other ministers, Crerar went home to campaign in its support. They all expected at least a national majority in favour of giving the government freedom of action. The critical question was what King would wish to do as a consequence. It does not appear that he had any preconceptions.

The expected majority materialized, but the massive rejection by Quebec certainly shook King's confidence. Most of the cabinet, however, felt that the government was obliged to respond to the result of the plebiscite by making its intentions known. Some statement about implementation would clearly be expected. The prime minister was warily feeling his way, and on 28 April he sought out Crerar, who advised him that the restriction in the NRMA should be removed without delay and "that we could then decide how far we could go." Later in the day he recalled Crerar and urged on him "the need for caution and steadiness in the Cabinet until we saw how matters were shaping themselves."[51]

Two days later, Crerar set forth his ideas in a memorandum for King. First, Parliament must "remove the legal limitation on the Government's action which the plebiscite vote removed in a moral sense." Second, this amendment to the NRMA must be "accompanied by a declaration on the part of the Government that it will continue to use every means possible to get men for overseas service by voluntary enlistment." No conscripted men would be sent overseas "unless and until in the judgement of the Government it is necessary to do so to maintain effectively Canada's war effort."[52]

King was prepared to accept Crerar's advice, but he still had one major reservation. He seemed adamant that his past commitments obliged him to go back to Parliament before conscription was actually imposed. In the bitter dispute that followed, leading up to Ralston's offer of resignation in August, this was the crux of the matter. Would Parliament be consulted first, and then conscription follow by order-in-council? Or would the order-in-council come first, and then a vote of confidence be sought from Parliament?[53]

The battle lines were clear. Ralston and Angus Macdonald were privately talking about resignation, if King meant to have a second debate in the House over conscription. Ilsley supported them, but was not quite as vigorous. The three Nova Scotians were opposed by most of the cabinet, led by Louis St Laurent, who had succeeded Lapointe as King's primary Quebec adviser.[54] Crerar, whom King consulted often during these anxious weeks, was trying to find some method of bridging the differences. He worked on Macdonald, both in the Centre Block and on the golf course, trying to persuade him to hold off. He even brought Dafoe's considerable influence to bear. The latter scolded "Angus L.," telling him that it was his duty to try and keep the government together. The alternatives, he pointed out, were much worse.[55]

As for the prime minister, Crerar attempted to have him accept the position that, if conscription should become necessary, it would be implemented by order-in-council and then a test of confidence could be taken in the House.[56] The issue remained unresolved, even after introduction in June 1942 of Bill 80, which amended the NRMA by repealing the limiting third clause. King seemed to indicate to his colleagues that there would be a return to Parliament before compulsory service was put in place, and so Ralston, in July, submitted his resignation. Crerar felt that King should have accepted it, since Ralston was not willing to consider the effect of a rupture between French and English.[57] It might have saved some hard times later on, if Ralston had left the government at that point.

To some extent, King was forced to back down. He smoothed over
the dispute with the defence minister by conceding that conscription,
if necessary, would be imposed by order-in-council before any return
to Parliament.[58] Ralston agreed not to press his resignation but
reserved his freedom of action. His letter of resignation, however,
was not returned by the prime minister. The immediate crisis passed,
but the issue did not; it smouldered on, to break out anew frequently.
The members of the Cabinet War Committee especially were conscious that the key word in King's concession was "necessary." For
Ralston, badgered by his military advisers, this meant essential to
maintaining the army at authorized strength. For the prime minister,
it meant required to win the war. This was not merely a procedural
dispute but ultimately an unbridgeable difference.

T.A. Crerar was dead right, as Granatstein has reminded us; the
plebiscite solved nothing – it simply postponed the confrontation
over conscription. But for the moment that was sufficient for the
weary Cabinet War Committee. Two of its members exchanged notes
in the House:

As one can see, the two men maintained their friendship, as well as
some sense of humour.[59]

ANGUS L.
The House is dull, the day is cool
The links are pleasant to behold.
Let Ilsley grind his taxing mill
While we good golf scores do unfold.
T.A.C.

TO T.A.C.
From the grim coldness of the Commons Chamber,
Fain would I fly to vistas more serene
Hong Kong is past, there's no immediate danger,
So let us hie to fairway and to green.
A.L.M.

CHAPTER THIRTEEN

War and Reconstruction,
1942–45

Like many of his colleagues, Crerar wished at least a brief escape from the supercharged atmosphere of Ottawa. Members of the Cabinet War Committee (CWC) especially were showing the strain of three years of war and the constant burden of difficult and emotional decisions. They were always tired, often irritable, and seemed to live in each other's pockets much of the time. Even when Crerar was able to slip off for an occasional round of golf – if time and weather permitted – it was invariably with a colleague, and they could hardly avoid discussing current topics. So in August 1942, with Bill 80 behind them, Crerar invited Malcolm MacDonald, the British high commissioner, to accompany him on a ministerial tour (by light plane!) of mining properties in the North West Territories. The trip ended in Winnipeg with a luncheon with the Sanhedrin. Dafoe reported to Dexter that Crerar arrived "eight days late, owing to being repeatedly grounded owing to the smoke from vast forest fires and says for nearly two weeks he didn't see a newspaper, get a telegram or have a telephone call: thus an enjoyable time was had."[1]

When Crerar flew back to Ottawa he plunged once again into the endless round of meetings and departmental affairs. Politics, however, could never be entirely set aside, and the affairs of the Tory Opposition were followed closely. The stunning defeat of Arthur Meighen in the York South byelection in February by the CCF candidate, abetted by the Liberals' decision not to field a candidate, had removed the spectre of the country's most articulate proponent of conscription and national government. His return to the House would have set everyone on edge, especially the prime minister. The pending question of a successor to Meighen kept the Liberals alert, and Crerar in particular maintained a watching brief, since speculation seemed to point to Premier John Bracken of Manitoba as the party's likely choice.

As early as the summer of 1942, Crerar had learned that Meighen had gone to Winnipeg some months earlier on a scouting trip. Meighen himself had consulted Bracken before his own abortive return to active politics. The rumour seemed reasonable enough, according to Crerar's information. Bracken had been premier for twenty years while maintaining a non-partisan reputation and was well regarded by the farmers.[2] He was sought out not by the more forward-looking Tories who had met at Port Hope that summer to try and give the party a new direction, but by the "old guard," led by Meighen and Graydon. According to Dafoe, Bracken's insistence that the party's name be changed to "Progressive Conservative" did not sit well with other potential candidates such as Murdo MacPherson of Regina, who refused Meighen's request to step aside for precisely that reason.[3]

At the convention in December 1942, even though the motion to change the party's name was tabled until after the new leader was chosen, Bracken was an "eleventh hour" candidate and won the leadership on the second ballot. Crerar remarked that if Bracken had not come forward, President Sidney Smith of the University of Manitoba would surely have been drafted and won.[4] In any case, Bracken's "act in associating himself with those whose policies he had criticized for twenty years created at first a very painful impression which ripened into more or less open hostility. Most of those who knew him have completely lost faith in him."[5]

Crerar's rather dispassionate recollection, written two years after the event, belies his outrage at the time. In his view, Bracken had betrayed the Liberal party and the people of Manitoba – to say nothing of political friends such as he – who had given the premier their support over the years. A day after the selection, King noted in his diary, Crerar had heard Bracken referred to in the Rideau Club as "the Laval of Canada." And Crerar urged King to get Bracken into the House as quickly as possible. "He would be deflated in six months."[6]

Cameron received a long account of the proceedings at Winnipeg and Crerar's emphatic observation that "Meighen and the Old Guard wanted Bracken for one, and only one, reason and that was that they thought he could make a strong appeal to the rural vote." Crearar predicted that "before another election rolls around, both Bracken and the Conservative Party will be heartily sick of one another."[7]

His bitterness was more evident in a letter to Donald McKenzie, chief commissioner of the Grain Commission in Winnipeg. If

Bracken was unhappy with the performance of the dominion government, it would have been more admirable to have said so publicly. At least he would have been given credit for sincerity. "And would it not have been more frank and honest to have gone to his old friends in the Legislature who had stood by him loyally for twenty years and told them his convictions could no longer let him support the Government in Ottawa?"[8]

Grant Dexter informed Dafoe that there was as yet "no intelligent reaction to Bracken's leadership. T.A. is too angry to think about it in any objective sense. And he is bound that the Tories must be hurled out of the Manitoba gov't and will be keenly disappointed if this does not come to pass." The disappointment had to be borne, however, since Stuart Garson, the new Liberal premier of Manitoba, declined to follow Crerar's advice that he end the coalition. Garson's view was thoroughly pragmatic. Continuance of the coalition favoured incumbents, and since the Liberals were the majority of the incumbents, he saw no good reason to take the risk. In sending his congratulations to Garson, Crerar readily accepted the new premier's decision on the coalition, but his dislike of Manitoba Tories was not at all assuaged.[9] Crerar's judgment was otherwise on the mark. Neither Bracken nor the Conservatives found much profit in their marriage of convenience.

Crerar was also involved, albeit reluctantly, in Ottawa's curious about-face on wheat policy. As a member of the cabinet's wheat committee, he participated in a series of compromises and accommodations that led to creation of a compulsory, monopoly wheat board – exactly the reverse of the Liberals' intentions when they had returned to office in 1935. As noted above, in 1941 the government had intervened sharply in the wheat economy by imposing delivery quotas and acreage payments in order to reduce production in the face of mounting surpluses resulting from continental European markets being closed to Canada. Crerar had helped achieve a cabinet consensus on that occasion. But the circumstances changed radically and unexpectedly in 1943.

The winter of 1942–43 had been particularly severe. Heavy yields in 1942 and transportation problems had led to a choked elevator system and subsequent demand on the government for cash advances on farm-stored grain. This unwelcome raid on the treasury, which Crerar actively opposed, was fortuitously avoided by an unexpected surge in American "buy orders" for Canadian wheat. The weather had also dealt a serious blow to the American winter-wheat and coarse-grain crops, just as u.s. demand for feed grains was increasing as a result of rising emphasis on meat production. In a letter to Cameron in early May 1943, Crerar noted the sudden American purchase of over eight million bushels of wheat in a two-week period. He estimated that this demand could reach fifty million. His guess fell far short of the reality;[10] it actually rose to 150 million bushels over the next year.

By early autumn concern for surpluses had given way to a scramble to meet rising demand. The American appetite for feed grains was such that oats and barley supplies were quickly exhausted and wheat of all grades was being sought for feed. The Wheat Board was already committed to bulk sales to Britain, required additional supplies for Russia, and also needed wheat for relief purposes, for all of which it would have to compete on the open, rising market. This excessive demand was tempting more and more farmers to sell on the open market, rather than to the board, and was also driving up futures prices. So the wheat committee of cabinet and the government faced a nasty choice; every increase of one cent in wheat prices was costing the treasury dearly. In addition, any inflationary rise in wheat prices was threatening the government's overall wage and price policy.

There now seemed only two options – close the open market and give the Wheat Board monopoly control, or impose arbitrary price ceilings. Either course would create resentment. Almost-daily meetings of the wheat committee took place in September, with the cabinet anxiously looking on. After insistent demands by Finance Minister Ilsley, the decision was taken by the committee to close the open market and create a monopoly wheat board, which also covered coarse grains. Crerar felt to the end that the market should be kept open. It was his position, as it had always been, that the market was the most reliable determinant of wheat prices. Arbitrary controls would inevitably lead to higher costs to the treasury. The fact that he was right did not answer the present crisis.

The crunch came on 27 September at cabinet. "Crerar," King recorded later, "was the only one to hold out for a different course. He gave good reasons for his views. ... [W]ith seventeen against him I thought he should be prepared gracefully to yield, which he did."[11] In summing up the long and difficult struggle, C.F. Wilson, who himself played such a lengthy and key administrative role in wheat policy decisions, commented that Crerar's "contributions to policy formation were highly effective when the Cabinet was split upon the issues and Crerar quietly pointed the way toward acceptable compromise. Crerar was an effective antidote to Gardiner when the latter's political judgement tended to err."[12]

The cabinet's continuous concern about wartime manpower, as well as the need for careful political monitoring of any major decisions, meant that Crerar gave little attention to his departmental obligations, other than the Mining Branch. He relied on his directors to assume most of the administrative load, and, as we saw in the case of Blair at Immigration, this could and did cause problems. In the event, he did not ignore these other branches of his department entirely. The fall of Hong Kong at Christmas 1941 and the subsequent further incursion of the Japanese into China made him conscious of Canada's interest in China both in the present and especially in the future. Britain's loss of prestige in China and the enthusiastic welcome that the Chinese gave to American military aid prompted Crerar to address his concerns to the prime minister.

He was convinced that Canada's standing in China had also suffered and proposed that something be done about it. The most obvious problem, he advised King, lay with the Chinese Exclusion Act – not so much in Canada's refusal to accept Chinese as residents as in the legislated "badge of inferiority" that the act proclaimed. As well, China resented the failure of Canada to appoint a minister to China. Crerar expected great development in China after the war and expanded opportunities for trade. "We should put ourselves in at least as good a position as the United States to share in that trade and development." To this end, he said, "As far as the repeal of the Exclusion Act is concerned, I see no reason why that should not be done at the next session of Parliament." He hinted that his Sanhedrin friend, Edgar Tarr, president of Monarch Life in Winnipeg, knew China well. And he proposed, as a public and dramatic signal of change, that Canada send a fighter squadron to China's aid – a sort of Canadian Flying Tigers![13]

King, rather surprisingly, replied immediately, indicating that he was quite willing to repeal the Exclusion Act at the next session, urging Crerar to persuade Tarr to accept the post of minister to China, and evading the suggestion of sending a fighter squadron. The Exclusion Act was not repealed at the next session, and neither Crerar nor King succeeded in convincing Tarr to take the Chinese post.[14] While the exchange came to little at the time, it did indicate that Crerar was not set against change in immigration matters (and quite audacious and imaginative in foreign policy).

That certainly could not be said for his colleagues in Cabinet War Committee (CWC). They were faced with an overture from the government of the United Kingdom, which was concerned about surplus labour in the West Indies. The Canadian minister of labour proposed sending a delegation to the Caribbean to investigate the possibility of recruiting workers there for Ontario's hard-pressed sugar-beet harvest. Despite the labour shortage in Canadian primary

industries, CWC turned the idea down flat, stating: "[T]he government was not prepared, on the grounds of general policy, to permit
the entry into Canada of colored labor." It preferred to seek additional workers from Newfoundland.[15]

The government continued to exhibit little compassion for the
plight of Jewish refugees, even orphaned children whose support the
Canadian Jewish community would have eagerly guaranteed. In his
last annual report before retirement, the consistently anti-semitic
director of immigration, F.C. Blair, informed the House that Canada
had agreed to accept one thousand refugee Jewish children, who had
been orphaned, from unoccupied France, but "unfortunately ... the
occupation of the part of France in which they were living, by
German forces, has so far prevented their being removed." It was
never Canada's fault; but they never came. There was little that
Crerar could do to influence his cabinet colleagues on Jewish refugees, despite his attempts, but he could and ought to have restrained
Blair. He was the minister.

Blair's replacement by A.L. Jolliffe brought greater flexibility, but
not much more in the way of effective humanity.[16] Jolliffe did little
better, whatever his sympathies. The government was unmovable.
When U.S. President Franklin Roosevelt called on all free nations to
accept "Jews and other races ... and undertake the provision of
refuge and support pending the return of these victims to their own
countries," there was no compassion in Canada. A Cabinet Conclusion marked "Most Secret" stated: "*It was agreed* that, at this time, no
similar statement should be made in Cabinet, nor any concurrence
announced."[17]

After mid-1943 the government was unlikely to take any political
risks. Pressure from the left would force new domestic initiatives, but
usually without Crerar's support. The relentless pressure had begun
to take its toll on him, as on many of his colleagues. In March 1943,
he was temporarily out of commission. Both Cameron and Euler
(now in the Senate) commented that he was "looking very tired and
a bit ragged."[18] The concern of the Sanhedrin was sharpened when
Crerar was admitted to hospital for surgery on 9 March.[19] Dafoe
wrote to Dexter that he had realized "for the past year that Tom was
over the summit and going down hill but I charged it to the war. I
think if I had to take the responsibility of joining in decisions such
as the govt has to make it would put me out of business in no time."
But his fears for his old friend were patent.[20]

Crerar was suffering a recurrence of a problem that had plagued
him since the 1920s. At times of great stress, small growths appeared

in his bladder, causing him to urinate blood. They were burned off physically by instruments placed directly in the bladder – a most painful intervention. According to Dexter, this procedure had been necessary once a month during the 1942 session. But a larger growth prompted Crerar's physician to hospitalize him in March 1943 because he judged that surgical removal was now essential. "He has come through it splendidly," Dexter reported to Dafoe, though "I am worried about him. He seems to be aging rapidly and his color is changing in some odd way – a transparency of the skin and flesh. But his spirit is splendid and he has guts to burn." Dafoe replied with much relief that "the news about Crerar was very acceptable."[21] Crerar bounced back well: he quite astonished Dexter by diving head first into the St Lawrence River a few months later.[22]

Crerar's difficulties were not unique in that sorely tried inner Cabinet. King's diary often reflected anxiety about ageing and over-tired colleagues. In his opinion, Howe, Ralston, and Ilsley were all showing the strain of the war. As for Crerar, he "has lost his grip. Is too old. Talks too much and is wholly inactive in organization, though most loyal and, on policy, sounder than some others." In other words, he agreed with the prime minister – most important, on the manpower issue. The ministers in turn worried about their leader. Angus L. Macdonald noted in his diary a visit from Crerar during which they discussed King's health. Crerar wondered if King's "hardening of the arteries did not produce fits of depression."[23]

The growing unease among the country's leaders in 1943 may have resulted in part from the political unrest that seemed to be rising all about them. The bad news began in Ontario in August, when the Tories swept the Liberals from office and established a dynasty that would last for decades. Given the erratic performance of Mitchell Hepburn, who had stepped down as premier in 1942, the loss could hardly have been unexpected. But the more disturbing threat came from the Co-operative Commonwealth Federation (CCF). To some extent, its appeal came from fear of a return to depressed conditions after the war; but more excitingly, if a country could be centrally directed to organize for war as effectively as the Liberals had mobilized Canada, then similar planning and control should be able to ensure a more prosperous and secure future. The CCF had finished a strong second in Ontario (it would win Saskatchewan in 1944) and in September 1943 startled perhaps even itself when the Gallup poll indicated a near–dead heat in the nation, with the CCF at 29 per cent and the Tories and Liberals tied at 28 per cent. For King, the only effective response would be to demonstrate that the

Liberals could be best trusted to lead the country after the war was over. This meant of course a determined move to the left to usurp the field.

There was another possibility that appealed to some Liberals, including Crerar. The government should not risk its credibility any further and should call an election immediately; and he so advised the prime minister. "The results in Ontario [and recent by-election losses] will be regarded generally without doubt as a loss of confidence in the government," he wrote to King, "and we may expect our political enemies to exploit this situation in every way they can." He saw only two courses open to the government. His preferred option was "to dissolve Parliament immediately and tell the country bluntly and flatly that we wish to know whether or not they have confidence in us to finish the job of the war and make the peace. It is a bold stroke but, I believe, it would tell." The alternative, he pointed out, "is to carry along with continuous sniping from the two wings of our opponents ... a steady loss of prestige – and, in the end, a heavy defeat, if not disaster."[24]

Crerar's attitude was provoked partly by the strain of the war and his disappointment that the country seemed unmindful of the government's accomplishments. And he was not alone in his frustration. Others in the cabinet, Ilsley in particular, strongly favoured immediate dissolution. King as usual temporized, seeking a safer way ahead.[25] In trying to account for the government's nose dive in popularity, Dexter suggested to Dafoe that wartime controls, especially the wage ceiling, were probably major factors, though he noted as well that "the one certain casualty of a war is the government that conducts it." The members of the inner cabinet who favoured an immediate election were proud men, he went on, who could look forward only "to months of hard, weary work while the CCF and the other oppositionists taunt them with being afraid to go to the country."[26]

As the political clouds darkened during that mid-year of the war, the prime minister persuaded himself that the difficulty lay with his cabinet colleagues who would not follow him in new departures. King was always a good deal more liberal in his diary than at the council table where the decisions were made. Throughout the year, he bemoaned the reluctance of his ministers to help him create a benign and caring future for the country under his leadership. Ever since he had published *Industry and Humanity* in 1918, he had seen his destiny in serving the needs of working Canadians. But in reality he would never seize a new idea or an innovative policy until its political time had come – not for him the chancy business of being in the vanguard. However, while his inner cabinet remained immersed in the problems of war, he at least was trying to chart a postwar course for the party, though he never took any of the blame for missteps or wasted opportunities.

During 1943 King sought on several occasions to put social welfare matters before the cwc. Health insurance and family allowances were considered, as well as a labour code, arising out of strikes in the coal and steel industries especially. Crerar drew steady criticism from the prime minister for his reluctance to support such measures.[27] These were complex issues, he belived, not simply matters of social justice, as their supporters insisted. Reacting to the information that the wage-control policy was causing severe hardship in the textile industry, Crerar would not accept the argument that urban workers were entitled to higher wages while farmers suffered tight controls on production and prices. He objected, as did Finance Minister Ilsley even more vigorously, that if exceptions were made wartime wage controls would go by the board. As well, it was not good policy, he maintained, to supplement inadequate incomes by use of the public purse for social welfare.

He summed up his position in October, just before he left for Winnipeg to attend a testimonial to Dafoe's sixty years in journalism. On family allowances, he told King, he was opposed for two reasons: first, if the principle were adopted, family allowances should fall under the heading of social security and not be justified as a means of redressing poor industrial wages; and second, they would draw accusations, especially in the west, that the government was pandering to Quebec, where large families were normal. "I have neither sympathy nor patience with this sort of miserable criticism ... but this anti-French feeling may well develop into an anti-Catholic feeling." He fully agreed, he continued, that substandard wages should be remedied, but by some other means than family allowances. About a labour code, he was equally explicit: "The collective bargaining principle should be embodied in the Code ... but if a Labor Union makes a contract with an employer covering their relationships, neither side should be free to violate its terms without penalties."[28] Dexter got it mostly right, however, in his Christmas summary to Dafoe: "The Cabinet is most unhappy. T.A. is more discouraged and fed up than ever before and wishes that he could get out. He says that whether or not he goes into the Senate he does not think he will run again. He is out of sympathy with the current talk of social security. He is a hard bitten individualist."[29]

Crerar was not at cabinet when the final decision to implement family allowances was taken. He had returned to Winnipeg once again, in January 1944, this time to attend the funeral of John Dafoe: the pivot of the Sanhedrin had been removed. Only C.D. Howe was openly opposed in cabinet to the new family support scheme, though Ilsley had never been keen on the idea. Angus Macdonald noted in his diary after Crerar's return: "He is opposed to [family allowances]. Generally he thinks our social program is too ambitious." Crerar also told Macdonald apparently that "he did not wish to run again and would like to be appointed to the Senate." King had already informed Crerar that he was holding a seat there available for him.[30]

There is no doubt that Crerar was opposed to initiating family allowances at that time and that he felt that the government was not directly responsible for the welfare of every Canadian. This stance has marked him as the reactionary soul of the cabinet. But his opposition was in reality the core of his liberalism. King was well aware of his views on these matters because Crerar had set them down in detail before he left for Winnipeg. Second only to organization and direction of the war effort, he began, "nothing is more important than the matters we have been discussing in council during the past few days." Various committees and subcommittees had been studying postwar options, and it was up to the government to reduce these ideas to something practical and capable of being accomplished. "It is not the responsibility of the government to provide everyone with jobs," but it should create opportunities for employment. The amount of money the government spends is less important than how usefully and wisely it spends the funds. Much of the cabinet discussion was based on the presumption that the war would be followed by economic difficulties.

From these precepts, Crerar turned to Ilsley's proposals for the future, prepared by the ambitious and interventionist leaders of Ottawa's mandarins. He was in full agreement that the taxation proposals of the Rowell-Sirois Commission were highly desirable. But he now argued that there was no prospect of ever persuading the larger provinces to forgo their taxing roles within their jurisdictions. "In these circumstances [that is, without dominion control of income and corporation taxes, as well as succession duties], we should be very careful about assuming financial commitments ... for services ... which are, under normal conditions, the responsibilities of the Provinces." His other criticism was that Ilsley's proposals did not target dominion spending effectively so as to increase national assets.

In other words, he was not against dominion expenditures per se but contended that they should be, as much as possible, of the self-liquidating variety. He specifically advocated slum clearance, housing, rural electrification, and creation of community centres in rural areas. Crerar urged as well that the government undertake water conservation and protection of the forest cover. He reminded King that wartime rates of taxation would have to come down. Therefore social programs could be accomplished only through agreements with the provinces. All the foregoing, he concluded, was in accord with the principles of liberalism, the most fundamental of which was the "freedom of the individual as against the State. The Socialist magnifies the State as against the individual. If we attempt to mix these too much we may well fall between two stools." There is no evidence that any of this had the slightest effect on King or his charge that Crerar was unprogressive.[31]

Nevertheless Crerar was made chairman of a committee to prepare for a dominion-provincial conference (really a second attempt to deal with the implications of Rowell-Sirois) planned for early 1945, which, with its various subcommittees organized by Brooke Claxton, an ambitious and talented Montreal MP, took a great deal of time, as evidenced by the records, now in the Bank of Canada's files.[32]

All these concerns, important as they were and would surely become, were for the CWC secondary to the daily anxieties of running the war and dealing with the problems of manpower. The pressure on the CWC was relentless, and its members' obligations were elastic, as we have seen in Crerar's case. King obviously preferred to exercise control through this inner cabinet, and to it he delegated the most crucial tasks.

With the somewhat ambiguous resolution of the conscription issue in passage of Bill 80 in the summer of 1942, that immediate crisis had been averted. But that did not mean an end to the disputes. Ralston, responding to the pressure of his military advisers, continued to demand more and more men. At the same time, C.D. Howe insisted that manpower in such critical industries as steel, mining, and lumbering be frozen. In October 1942, for example, Howe demanded that forestry troops be brought back from England to help alleviate a desperate shortage of BC spruce. Ralston responded weakly that this might impair morale overseas. Employment in this sector was frozen, over the defence minister's objections. Dexter reported: "Howe hit Ralston like a tank ... T.A. did not even have to open his mouth."[33] They all seemed caught up in the battle. At the end of the year, King complained that the need to ration butter was the fault of "too large an army. They have been buying up most of the butter."[34]

Maintaining an overseas army of five divisions and ancillary units required five thousand additional men every month. The manpower situation slowly deteriorated, and even the air force and navy began to experience shortages. Ralston and Howe became increasingly adamant that their requirements were the more crucial. At one point, Howe said that he could not go on, as lack of miners was affecting coal and steel production. Ralston, increasingly isolated in the CWC, stubbornly repeated his demands for more men.[35] The constant bickering went on until the Normandy invasion in June 1944 changed the mood, if only briefly.

The subsequent breakout from Normandy brought the end of the war in Europe tantalizingly near. And when the CGS, General Kenneth Stuart, reported that the reinforcement situation was satisfactory, even the manpower disputes subsided, despite the record of unreliability of military forecasts in the past.[36] Crerar and his colleagues could now dare to hope that the poisoned chalice of conscription might be avoided.

The summer of 1944 was a time of some reflection for Tom Crerar. When King had gone to London in April for the Commonwealth prime ministers' meeting, he had named Ralston to act in his absence, despite Crerar's seniority. It was all handled very delicately – the ostensible reason being that Crerar's failing hearing would limit his effectiveness in the House – and he had remained president of the council and acting chairman of the CWC. But clearly he had been disappointed as his stock with King so obviously fell.[37] The two did go on to discuss Crerar's reluctance to run again, and King reiterated his promise of a Senate seat before the next election. As if to confirm their new relationship, Crerar chaired the dinner given to King on the twenty-fifth anniversary of his prime ministership.[38] And later in the summer he wrote a long, rather detached letter, advising King to capitalize on the successful prosecution of the war and the government's legislative record by basing the next campaign on the issue of Canadian unity.[39]

In September, leading members of the government (and their wives) trooped off to Quebec City in almost a holiday mood to attend the events surrounding a meeting between Churchill and Roosevelt. In an ill-advised speech to the Quebec Reform Club, King boasted that he had kept Lapointe's pledge to Quebec – despite plebiscites and Bill 80, there had been no conscription for overseas service, and under his government there never would be. In a biting account of the affair, Dexter reported: "The conscriptionists – Ralston, Angus and the rest, were sitting right at the head table. You can imagine their feelings. Even T.A. who was always the Colonel's opponent on the army, found it too much."[40] If the prime minister was unwise in his comments, he was not being inconsistent. It had always been King's position that conscription would be justified only if it were necessary to win the war. In that euphoric summer, with allied armies racing across eastern France, a few thousand Canadian conscripts would add little in the balance. Unhappily the euphoria vanished with the season.

Disquieting reports were received that the reinforcement situation was not at all as satisfactory as General Stuart had forecast. Ralston quickly hurried to Europe to see for himself and was anything but reassured. The Canadian army had been assigned the dangerous and costly task of clearing the Schelde estuary in Holland, fighting over very difficult terrain against seasoned troops. The General Staff's casualty projections were wildly inaccurate. It had simply accepted badly flawed British military estimates without question and passed them on to Ralston and, ultimately, the CWC. This was little comfort for those cabinet members such as Crerar who distrusted all the generals. In any case, when Ralston returned to the CWC on 18 October 1944, he announced that it was now necessary to send the NRMA men overseas to meet the infantry crisis and keep the overseas army at strength.

Crerar had just returned, gloomy and dispirited, from the west. Opinion there seemed to demand that the so-called Zombies (the NRMA men) be sent to the battlefield immediately. After consulting with the prime minister, King noted that Crerar "had opposed increases in the army at every stage, but now he felt that the Zombies ought to be sent overseas. He thought all the defence departments were no good and said so right along."[41] Rumours that King was considering McNaughton as a replacement for Ralston prompted Louis St Laurent to observe that "everyone had great confidence in the General and would accept his view of what was, or was not, necessary."[42] Ralston clearly no longer had the same credibility.

The first three weeks of November 1944 brought dramatic changes to the ministry and war policy, framed by two cabinet meetings – an official one on the first, and an informal one on the twenty-second. At the famous cabinet meeting of Wednesday, 1 November, King acted on Ralston's two-year-old letter of resignation, which had neither been withdrawn nor accepted, and announced that he would be replaced by General McNaughton. With great dignity, Ralston rose, said good-bye to his colleagues, and left the room. Alone. Most accounts of this dramatic event suggest or imply that Ralston's colleagues had failed him – that those who supported conscription should have faced up to King and gone with him. In fact, Ralston retained the respect and affection of his former colleagues, but he no longer had their support. They felt that he had been badly served by his military advisers and that he had fatally compromised himself by too often staking his position on their aggressive and frequently inaccurate advice. He had been less a cabinet colleague than a spokesman for the army. The ministers were adamant that a final decision be taken but realized that the issue could be resolved only after Ralston's departure, given his relationship with King. For any large number of them to resign would have wrecked the government, with the war so nearly won, and denied McNaughton one last chance to make the voluntary system work.[43] On 22 November, when it was clear that McNaughton had failed, Crerar called Howe, Macdonald, Ilsley, and two others to a meeting in his office at which they all agreed to resign if overseas conscription were not imposed that day. King finally conceded that evening.[44] What happened in the three weeks between these two events?

On the night of the critical council meeting of 1 November, Angus Macdonald had noted in his diary before retiring: "Crerar took a certain glee in Ralston's sacking. [He] thinks that Ralston has been very badly treated, but on the other hand, seems to believe that this will be somewhat of a lesson to the General Staff, for which Crerar has little use."[45] The next day, Crerar wrote to Ralston to express his continuing friendship and regard, despite the fact that "over the past three years none of your colleagues has differed with you more than I have done." But there is no doubting his position, surely shared by some of the others, when he continued, "The incident in last evening's Council meeting, in which you were relieved of your portfolio, shocked me greatly. This was occasioned, *not by your leaving the Administration*, but by the manner in which it was done." In Crerar's view, the Liberal party owed much to Ralston, and he deserved better from its leader.[46]

Among the many legacies of this affair was that Crerar's reputation for loyalty was, in King's mind, no more. As one of the prime minister's literary executors had put it, "Until the crisis of 1944, [King] found a certain comfort and sympathy in his relations with T.A. Crerar who after Lapointe's death, was his only contemporary in the Cabinet."[47] King, however, seldom forgave those who disagreed with him on important issues.

Crerar had fought for three years against a large overseas army precisely to avoid the situation in which the government now found itself. Circumstances now dictated that he change his course; and characteristically, that decision having been taken, there were no regrets and no looking back. Two days after Ralston's departure, Crerar wrote to the prime minister, reminding him that the reinforcement issue had not been settled and asking explicitly if use of the NRMA men was "definitely 'out'" as a matter of government policy"? King replied a week later, noting in his diary as he did so that it was taking up much of his time: "It is a crime that a colleague like Crerar should be thus embarrassing me at a time when every colleague should be helpful." In his reply to Crerar, the prime minister referred to his statements in the House during the debate on Bill 80 in 1942, which had caused much of the confusion. It was not a very illuminating response, but not untypical.[48]

Crerar was in no mood to let matters lie. After a further week – it was now 17 November – he wrote again to King, stating frankly that he had been disappointed in the prime minister's answer. There was no disputing the urgency of obtaining reinforcements, he began, and there was only one place to get them – from among the trained men of the NRMA. If they do not come forward voluntarily, then the terms of Bill 80 must be applied. The men in Europe could not be left unsupported, he continued, and the people of Canada expected the government to comply with its own policy as announced in Bill 80. At least in the first particular, this was rather a new argument for Crerar. In any case, he insisted that King make it very clear where he now stood. He concluded by saying that if the men did not come forward in the required numbers by the end of November, "I shall be unable longer to support the present policy."[49]

That same evening Crerar had a long talk with Angus Macdonald, who passed the former's views on to Ralston. He reported that Crerar was "ready to take the final plunge." If by the following Wednesday, 22 November, the decision had not been taken, then he was prepared to resign. As Macdonald pointed out, however, those who opposed King's policy would be in honour bound to remain in the House and, if necessary, fight an election on the issue. Ralston and Macdonald had hoped to retire from politics, and "Crerar, himself, as you know, had hoped to leave and be translated to the Senate. He sees that appointment fading away and despite his sixty-eight years he is prepared to don the armour once more."[50]

Crerar was aware that his determination to force King to a decision might cost him the promised Senate seat. Yet he still felt obliged to act with honour, and his loyalty to country and party did not lessen – it seemed as strong as ever. The following Monday, 20 November, he wrote again to King, this time in a more contemplative vein. He asserted at the outset that the issue of dispatching the NRMA men overseas must now be faced. If the government did so, "it would receive overwhelming support in every province outside of Quebec." There it would encounter stiff opposition, but "it would not proceed to anything like the lengths you feel it would." At the worst, Crerar forecast, it might result in a solid bloc of French Canadian members opposed to the Liberals after the next election.

If, however, the government refused to act or delayed in acting on the question, "the effect upon the future of the Liberal Party may well be disastrous." The resentment of English Canadians against Quebec would be intensified, however unjustified, and the scars would remain. Canada's greatest danger, he argued, was in provoking a "solid Quebec, whether in the Liberal Party or in any other." If the province aligned completely with the Liberals, the party would come to be regarded as being dominated by Quebec. "Nothing could be more fatal, or more injurious to the country's future, than that this feeling should persist. You have done much for Canada and much for the Liberal Party, but ... the Liberal Party has also done much for you." The members of the caucus were in great distress, Crerar concluded, but if the cabinet refused to act it would not be carrying out its honourable intentions. "The moral issue involved, of keeping our word, transcends everything else."

Thus staking out the high ground, he insisted again that King must act. If the French Canadians left the government, "we would say to the rest of Canada that we understood Quebec and urge all Canadians to try and understand as well." Only in this way could the country (and the party) be saved. "None could do this as effectively as Liberals, who have sensed and understood the value of unity and have recognized that, for good or ill, our two peoples have to live together in the future."[51] Like most Liberals, Crerar believed that the fate of the party and that of the nation were inextricably interwoven.

Two days later, on the twenty-second, Crerar wrote his letter of resignation. McNaughton's appeal for volunteers would not succeed, he told King, and the need for reinforcements grew more critical. It "seems equally clear that the Government refuses to face this, and will delay, on one pretext or another, dealing decisively with this pressing matter. I see no honourable alternative to resigning from the Government."[52] On Monday, 20 November, King had agreed that the question of sending the NRMA men overseas would be discussed at caucus on Wednesday after the newly recalled House rose. Crerar told the prime minister "that I would feel obliged to make my position clear at caucus and Ilsley and Macdonald took the same position."[53] At a meeting of the CWC on the twenty-first, King still seemed reluctant to address the issue directly; the next morning Crerar dictated his resignation letter, "and this I had decided to sign and hand it to him at the conclusion of caucus."[54] When King informed caucus on the twenty-second that he wished to discuss the matter further in council and would recall caucus for the next day, Crerar could wait no longer.

C.D. Howe had informed Crerar at lunch that he was ready to break with King, and so, as the inconclusive caucus disbanded, Crerar called an immediate meeting in his office, attended by Howe, Gibson, Ilsley, Macdonald, and Mulock. Crerar suggested that "whatever action was taken should be taken to-gether; not necessarily that we should send a joint resignation but that our several resignations should go in at the same time."[55] He then read the resignation letter that he had dictated that morning. Angus Macdonald noted that night in his diary that "all present were firm in their resolution".[56] Thus agreed, they adjourned till the cabinet meeting that evening.

General McNaughton had informed him, King began, that the required men were not coming forward, so he had reluctantly decided that it was now time to compel the necessary number of NRMA soldiers to proceed overseas. Gardiner suggested that this about-face had been forced by threatened resignations, which King denied, though he could hardly have been unaware of what was coming if he had not acted. The prime minister informed caucus of the decision the next day.[57] Crerar was never again admitted to King's confidence.

For the next five months, until he resigned from cabinet, Crerar was more observer than player. King had made their new relationship clear when, after informing the House of the change in policy, he turned to Crerar and said that "he and others who were supporting conscription should never have put me in the position I was now in unless they were prepared to take over the government themselves."[58] Many of his diary entries are in the same vein; the real issues to King were loyalty and political value, rather than policy. Thus there would no longer be any room for Crerar or his opinions among the prime minister's advisers. He would simply be ignored.

It was hardly a principled decision on King's part. The prime minister considered Angus Macdonald, who was now determined to return to Nova Scotia, beyond the pale as well. Ilsley and Howe, however, who were equally if less publicly among the defectors, were reappointed to cabinet after the 1945 election, presumably because they were still politically useful.

Crerar was coolly correct with King, but he was not at all intimidated. He even had some small victories. He proposed that Indians remain liable for compulsory service under the NRMA but be exempted from posting overseas under the new policy, and his proposed was accepted. He also succeeded in having Chinese women who married Canadian servicemen exempted from the provisions of the Oriental-exclusion regulations and allowed to return to Canada with their husbands.[59]

The debate on the founding of the United Nations drew his close attention. King seemed rather bemused when Crerar insisted that Parliament be kept in session during the founding conference in San Francisco in April 1945.[60] The reason, as Crerar informed Dexter who was now back in Winnipeg, was his fear "that participation by Canada in meeting any international crisis which might arise may be restricted by conditions that Parliament would have to be consulted" before Canada could take any action. In other words, he simply did not trust King. He urged Dexter to have the *Free Press* take the line that agreement should be secured in Parliament as to the position that the Canadian delegation would take and that Canada "should throw its weight in the Conference in creation of machinery which could move swiftly and effectively to curb the law-breaker." This could not be done if Canada's representative were bound by prior conditions.[61]

Partisan politics receded quickly for Crerar, though he did meet his obligation to attend the gathering of the Manitoba party association in mid-January 1945. He reported to King that Liberal prospects in the province seemed favourable but advised him to take the position that the Canadian voters would be much better off if the country were represented at the peace conference and in other postwar settlements and opportunities by the experienced statesmen who had guided Canada through the war years. He also noted (wrongly, as it soon proved) that the turmoil over conscription had abated.[62]

In writing to Dexter about McNaughton's crushing defeat in the North Grey (Ontario) by-election the following month, Crerar was now of the opinion that the reinforcement question was the overriding issue and that people feared that the government was lukewarm or indifferent. He became convinced that if King called an election before Germany was decisively beaten "nothing under heaven can keep the conscription issue out." Everything else would be pushed aside.[63]

So also would Crerar, though he had little interest in remaining in the House. His relations with King during their final months as colleagues revealed a great deal about each of them. On the occasion of King's seventieth birthday in mid-December 1944, Crerar led the cabinet delegation to offer congratulations and, according to King, made "a nice little speech." In writing his thank-you letters to his colleagues, the prime minister "could not express myself quite in the same terms to either Crerar or Macdonald as I did to the others. Altered their letters accordingly."[64] When discussing nominations with visiting Winnipeggers, King "let them know quite frankly that I thought Crerar's day was past; also that he had been anything but helpful to myself in the recent crisis."[65]

King's undisguised animosity led some of Crerar's friends to fear that he would be denied the promised Senate seat. Dexter, Victor Sifton, and others sought to hold King to his earlier promises.[66] And there was reason for their concern, for King's pettiness and vindictiveness were well known. When he made a brief visit to Washington in early March, King refused to allow Crerar to act in his place for the few days – a courtesy to which his seniority entitled him. King chose Ilsley instead, noting in his diary that "Crerar deserves nothing from me, because of his behaviour in the recent crisis though I know he won't like it."[67] The prime minister apparently had convinced himself that Crerar had been the leader of cabinet dissent. So he left Crerar hanging until nearly the last minute.

Crerar's letter of resignation, dated 17 April 1945, was brief, mentioning only his gratification at having shared in the conduct of the war. The order-in-council calling him to the Senate was passed the following day.[68] When it was over, Cameron informed Euler that Crerar "was tremendously relieved. ... He was very uneasy that there might be a slip up. He is of opinion the P.M. would have passed him over but for fear of the reaction in Winnipeg."[69] The sixty-nine-year-old Crerar, whose "time was past," would go on to serve for over two decades in the upper house. And they were to be happy and effective years, in which his experience made him a very useful, if sometimes cantankerous, member.

PART FIVE

The Senate and After, 1945–75

Crerar in 1950, when he was named chairman of the Senate Committee on Banking. Courtesy Archives and Special Collections, Dafoe Library, University of Manitoba

CHAPTER FOURTEEN

Guarding the Treasury, 1945–57

His translation to the Senate opened an unconsidered world for Tom Crerar. There is no documentary evidence that he ever gave the upper chamber a serious, second thought prior to his summons, other than on those occasions when he served on ad hoc joint committees to resolve infrequent disputes between the two legislative bodies. Once a member, however, he suddenly discovered the Senate's undeveloped potential and denounced the government's refusal to give it a useful role. Sir George Foster's diary entry on being appointed to the Senate was well known: "I have today signed my warrant of political death … How colourless the Senate … the entering gate to coming extinction."[1] Crerar's early years in the upper chamber indicated his determination that it need not be necessarily so.

Foster's resigned observation was, however, an accurate reflection of the reputation of the red chamber. It was largely ignored by prime ministers, except for party purposes; by the House of Commons, armed with the righteousness of popular election; by journalists, preoccupied with the immediacy of the daily cut and thrust of the House; and by scholars, who have been drawn to the exercise of power. And to some extent, as Crerar himself remarked soon after his own appointment, the Senate's woeful reputation was not undeserved. Over the years he would contribute significantly to an attempt to refurbish that image.

The political ambience of the Senate was already changing, and Crerar arrived at an opportune time. As becomes the Senate, the change was gradual and had begun some years before Crerar's entry. One of the few recent scholarly examinations of the modern Senate dates this event precisely to the session of 1940, and the Senate's defeat of the Farmers' Creditors Arrangement Bill. The attack was led by recent Liberal appointee and former cabinet member W.D. (Bill) Euler, a close friend and colleague of Crerar's. Such willingness to challenge the government eventually led the Senate to a significant "degree of independence and quasi-impartiality after the end of World War 11."

From 1945 until its defeat in 1957, the Liberal party had majorities in both chambers. No bills were defeated in the upper house, but dozens were amended, many of them in their most important provisions. Effective opposition in the Senate had passed from the declining Tories to what King referred to as a "wilful little group" of Liberals.[2] Among the leading critics of the government during these years were the prime minister's former cabinet mates Crerar, Euler, and Chubby Power (when he arrived in 1955); Norman Lambert, former secretary and chairman of the party; and Liberal Senators Farris, Paterson, Roebuck, and (sometimes) Haydon. By October 1946, during the battle over the Foreign Exchange Bill (of which more below), King was complaining to Grant Dexter that he had "no confidence in the Senate in general and T.A. in particular."[3] Senator Crerar, had he known, would probably have been pleased.

There was some irony, however, in Crerar's letter to Angus Macdonald shortly after the opening of his first Senate session in the autumn of 1945. "There are really some quite able men in the Upper Chamber but they are pretty well stalled." This was King's fault, according to Crerar, since he "has treated the Senate with scant courtesy, particularly in the last five years." Courtesy, however, was in rather short supply during the war, and Crerar had been an influential member of King's government. After a further month's observation, he wrote again to the Nova Scotia premier, suggesting that "the Senate has largely got itself to blame for the situation it has drifted into." The problem, as Crerar saw it, was the Senate's unwillingness to exercise its proper constitutional functions. If it remained content with "merely crossing the t's and dotting the i's of what the House of Commons does then it will become merely a useless piece of machinery that could well be discarded."[4]

Crerar's first major test of this belief came in his second session, with arrival in the upper chamber of the Foreign Exchange Control Bill. This legislation gave statutory sanction to orders-in-council, approved under the authority of the War Measures Act, granting sweeping powers to a Foreign Exchange Control Board to regulate movement of money and goods moving across Canadian borders. The board, composed of civil servants, could, among other things, remake acts of Parliament to suit its purposes and discriminate in favour of (or against) groups or individuals, and it gave customs officers at borders the right to search people, even if they objected, without the need to secure a warrant. It was compared by one senator to the power exercised in pre-war Nazi Germany.[5]

According to Kunz, the Speaker of the Senate reluctantly agreed to the rare procedural action of referring the bill to committee *before* second reading was complete because many senators considered it so crucial that they wished to seek expert advice before debating the *principle* of the legislation.[6] This is incorrect, according to Crerar. He spoke against the bill on second reading, objecting in particular to the granting of "very extraordinary powers to a group of Civil Servants." He claimed in a letter to Bruce Hutchison of the *Winnipeg Free Press* that the bill would have been defeated if allowed to come to a vote on second reading. The action of Senator Wishart Robertson, Government Leader in the Senate, in diverting the bill to the Banking and Commerce Committee, was a manoeuvre "to try and whip recalcitrant senators into line." To Victor Sifton, Crerar explained that this tactic would "enable Rasminsky [later governor of the Bank of Canada] or someone else to come before the Committee and mesmerize it as the Committee in the House of Commons was mesmerized."[7] The danger, to Crerar and the other senators opposed to the bill, was the attempt to institutionalize the habit of command acquired by senior civil servants during the war. In the interests of maintaining a liberal state, this thrust must be limited.

While the *Free Press* declined to attack the bill editorially, since it considered some of the provisions "a necessary evil," it did run an extensive account of Crerar's speech to the Senate on its editorial page, noting approvingly that his objections to the measure were cast in a vigorous defence of liberalism, which, the senator argued, must always be concerned with encroachments by the state.[8] The battle in committee resulted in some sixty-seven amendments, the most important limiting the Export Control Board's power to a period of three years. The government reluctantly accepted the changes.

It was a significant victory, Crerar told Angus Macdonald, since "the legislation gives a good illustration of the approach in official circles here .... [G]et all the powers from parliament that you can think of, whether it will be necessary to use them or not. What I had to say was as much a protest against this sort of thing as it was against the Bill itself." As a general and fundamental proposition, he concluded, "No democratic government should ask for more than the minimum of powers it may require to achieve a certain objective."[9]

Vigilance against extension of unaccountable power seemed to have become Crerar's senatorial watchword. And it applied equally to his life-long preoccupation with marketing of western grain. He had been remarkably consistent on this issue over his long public career. He had concurred in the need for government control of wheat marketing during the emergency conditions of the Great War. But after the war, in 1920, he was opposed to any permanent government involvement in the area. During the debate in 1923 over the pool movement, which favoured a government Wheat Board, he had advised western farmers that their system of cooperation could accomplish more than any government board. His United Grain Growers (UGG) had consistently supported the open market as the farmers' best option. He had never opposed a voluntary Wheat Board, as we saw above; but he utterly rejected any monopoly board. In 1943, as a member of the cabinet, he had once again accepted a wartime monopoly board, though he fully expected that it would soon lapse after the war ended.

The wheat pools of western Canada, conditioned by the recession that followed the Great War, shared the general fear of a postwar slump after 1945, and when Britain indicated interest in a long-term contract to purchase wheat at a fixed price they enthusiastically supported Agriculture Minister Gardiner's willingness to negotiate. The result was the British Wheat Agreement, concluded in the summer of 1946, under which Canada agreed to provide the United Kingdom with a minimum of 600 million bushels of wheat over the next four crop years. Prices were set at $1.55 per bushel for the first two years and were to be negotiated for the final two years later but were not to fall below $1.25 per bushel in the third year and $1.00 in the fourth – for an average price of at least $1.35 per bushel over the life of the agreement. Another clause, which provoked bitter controversy later, declared that the British would "have regard to" any difference between the fixed price and the world price prevailing during the contract. This was to ensure that Canadian farmers would not have to bear any loss if the world price went above $1.55 per bushel. At the time of the agreement the world price was $2.00, but it was widely expected to fall (in fact, it remained at slightly above $2.00).

The wheat pools applauded the deal, urging complacently that long-term price stability and a guaranteed market were more important than any short-term gains that might be forgone. The magnitude of the sale persuaded the government that it would have to extend the monopoly of the Wheat Board to cover the contract period so as to ensure adequate supplies to meet the commitment to Britain. Crerar did not share the optimism of the agreement's supporters and flatly opposed extension of the board's monopoly power. In the Senate he described the agreement as the greatest short sale in history.

"Gardiner got his way," he told Angus Macdonald, "and I fear it will turn out to be a most unwise agreement."[10]

In the autumn of 1946, for the editorial page of the *Free Press*, he wrote a series of articles on the marketing of wheat, which was later published as a pamphlet. He pointed out that under a government monopoly of wheat marketing there would be continuous criticism that the government was doing either too much or too little for prairie farmers, which might lead to divisive sectional grievances. If the government were going to guarantee a return to the grain growers through monopoly marketing, why not do the same for fishermen, or pulp and paper, or minerals, or any other commodity of international trade? As one might expect, good politics was not always good economics, and consistency was an unnecessary distraction.

Crerar's prescription for the future derived from his long experience and firm convictions. Monopoly in marketing, except in emergency conditions, was always bad. The futures market should be reopened, despite the uninformed prejudices of some of the farmers. Three royal commissions had studied the free market in grain and in every case had found the futures market the best means of avoiding risks and narrowing the margin of costs between producers and millers anywhere in the world. He also recommended that the three prairie wheat pools and UGG cooperate and establish a central export agency. With their combined strength they could have a salutary effect on the market. He even reverted to his old insistence on lowering production costs and on cooperative purchasing, and he urged diversification of crops and rural electrification. These policies had always guided the farm movement, he concluded; "cut the cost wherever possible in marketing and production."[11]

He became bitterly disappointed during the next two years. In the spring of 1947 the government secured amendments to the Wheat Board Act that would create a five-year compulsory pool to ensure supplies for the British agreement and an enabling clause to extend the monopoly to cover coarse grains (oats and barley). And it put forward further amendments to the act in early 1948. Crerar noted their significance to Dexter: first, their assumption that the Wheat Board would be a permanent marketing institution, since it would now be providing a pension plan for its employees; second, then confirmation of its monopoly control of coarse grains (it was no longer simply permissive); and third, their granting to it of power to make additional payments on wheat marketed from 1945 to 1948.

The amendments of 1948 reached the Senate on 22 March, two days before the scheduled spring adjournment. Crerar and Lambert led the charge against the bill on second reading, denouncing it as a violation of the Liberal tradition of free enterprise. The next day it went to the Banking and Commerce Committee, where their attack was supported ably by Senator Norman Paterson. They persuaded enough colleagues to join them to delete the provision for including coarse grains. In Senate that afternoon, Senator Robertson, the government leader, was able to have the clause restored and the bill passed, by twenty-five to seventeen, but nine of the opposing votes were cast by Liberals.[12]

Crerar was also concerned about other aspects of the continuing intervention in wheat marketing. The government had used the Emergency Powers Transition Act to give these extraordinary powers to the Wheat Board. This was a complete misuse of the Transition Act, Crerar wrote to Angus Macdonald, since no "emergency" existed in the marketing of western grain. He was even more exercised when the Justice Department claimed that the power existed anyway in the federal government's right to control export and inter-provincial trade. If this reasoning were sound, he protested, the government could slap rigid controls on any article of export trade.

To ensure greater control of the movement of wheat, the bill declared all grist mills in the prairies "works for the general advantage of Canada." "If this theory holds water," Crerar predicted, "it opens up almost unmeasurable fields of controversy." Such "power in the hands of the Federal Government could completely transform the property and civil rights provisions of the B.N.A. Act." Crerar blamed this power grab, as he saw it, on the "the Higher Civil Servants and some members of the government" who wish to centralize more and more power in Ottawa.[13]

But of all the faults in the amendments of 1948, the most dangerous for the long term, in Crerar's opinion, was the government's argument that it needed the additional powers to ensure that it could meet its commitment to the farmers of an average price of $1.35 per bushel over the life of the British agreement. Since the whole scheme was an invasion of provincial rights (the bill required provincial legislation to make it constitutional), to what extent was the government laying itself open to demands from the farmers for compensation if the world price remained above $1.35, as now seemed likely?[14] It turned out to be a prescient concern.

Meanwhile, after difficult and lengthy negotiations, Canada became a participant in an International Wheat Agreement in 1949. It comprised thirty-seven wheat-importing countries and five producers, among which Canada was the largest player, committing itself to supplying 203 million bushels annually over the life of that agreement. Minimum and maximum prices were established (averaging about $1.55 per bushel), which tended to be significantly below the world price. Little noticed at that point and potentially costly to the dominion government, however, was the "have regard to" clause of the British Wheat Agreement of 1946, whereby Britain had implied that it would compensate Canadian farmers if the world price of wheat rose above the contract price. It had become clear by 1948 that Britain intended to do nothing of the sort.[15] Thus began the argument that the Canadian government was somehow responsible for this "lost revenue." Crerar was appalled.

The *Winnipeg Free Press*, with Crerar's active support, had been criticizing bulk contracts at fixed prices since 1946. It had predicted that wheat producers in western Canada would inevitably be the losers. When the world price of wheat hit $3.10 per bushel in early 1947, there was a complacent "I told you so" from Grant Dexter, now the editor.[16] But there was as much ideology as economics in the positions of Dexter and Crerar. There is simply no way of calculating what the so-called world price of wheat would have been for 1946–50 if the millions of bushels of Canadian wheat sold to Britain under the agreement had been sold on the international market.

Crerar's position was of course conditioned by his life-long commitment to free cooperation, free trade, and the rough justice of the free market. Once the Wheat Board became compulsory, and thus an agent of the government rather than of the producers, he invariably took a dead set against the government's wheat policies. As he wrote to Dexter in the summer of 1950, when Howe yet again introduced amendments to the Wheat Board Act, "My own judgement is that it is not necessary to perpetuate the compulsory features of the Wheat Board to carry out the International Wheat Agreement. Canada could operate just as they are operating in the United States" – that is, meet commitments by buying in the open market.[17]

Crerar was not content to fire his fusillades from the safe obscurity of the Senate chamber. In August 1950 he trekked out to his old hometown of Russell to speak to the Farmers' Protective Association and sharply opposed, among other things, compulsory marketing of coarse grains, which he said should be withdrawn from the Wheat Board.[18] This position embroiled him in an exchange with the *Manitoba Co-operator*, voice of the Manitoba Wheat Pool, which took exception to his remarks.

In his rejoinder, he pointed out that the *Co-operator*'s editorial had agreed that "'everybody has a perfect right to decide for himself what to do with his property'. In this statement the Co-operator evidently agrees with me." In Parliament and at the Russell meeting he had stated that he "was opposed to the compulsory features in the legislation. No farmer in Manitoba can market wheat, oats or barley without a permit from a government agency since the Wheat Board, under the law, is the agent of the government.... This is simply naked compulsion against farmers in the doing of things they have a natural right to do." He repeated what he had often maintained – that he had no objection to the Wheat Board as such; any farmer (Crerar included) who so wished should be free to use its services. "What I objected to was that it compelled me to use it against my will. This is a form of cooperation that I cannot understand." The Wheat Board should be an agent of the producers who wish to use it, he concluded, not an agent of the Crown.[19]

Crerar feared that the government's wrong-headed wheat policies would lead to a raid on the federal treasury. In a letter to his old friend and wheat trader in Britain James Rank, he claimed that the British Wheat Agreement had been entered into despite the opposition of the Wheat Board itself and "of everyone who knew anything about wheat marketing in this country." This had been done simply to satisfy the leaders of the Wheat Pools. "I have the satisfaction of having said it was unsound at the time it was made." It would have been quite proper, he went on, to have given Britain wheat at the price negotiated, "but the Wheat Board should have bought the wheat to fill the agreement at the market price," and the people of Canada as a whole should have made up any difference. "Now we are recreating the same thing in this miserable International Agreement. In this the theorists in Washington are as much to blame as our theorists in Ottawa." The current price of wheat being sold outside the agreement was twenty-five cents per bushel above the contract price. Further demand on the government could thus be expected – "the inevitable result of having Governments messing around in matters of this kind."[20]

As Crerar had predicted, in early 1951 the government of King's successor, Louis St Laurent, bent to pressure from the farmers, who demanded "compensation" for "losses" suffered under the British Wheat Agreement and proposed a settlement of $65 million. There was heavy criticism from the Montreal newspapers and from the *Winnipeg Free Press* (with its "I told you so!"). Crerar urged Dexter to flay the government for its decision and to place the blame exactly where it belonged – with the wheat pools and the Canadian Federation of Agriculture, which had supported the deal with Britain in the interests of price stability. They should be obliged to live with the consequences, he argued, or other agricultural producers would soon be lining up, cap in hand, at the treasury door.

The fundamental mistake, he repeated to many of his correspondents, had been making the Wheat Board an agent of the government, rather than of the grain growers. "My own view is," he pontificated, "that the Government would have been wiser to have refused to pay anything on the ground that the farmers' organizations asked for this, but that now they had to accept the consequences." By accepting the argument that something should be paid, "there is no valid reason why they should not make good the whole loss."[21]

When the compensation bill came to the Senate, Crerar and Norman Lambert attacked it bitterly and tried unsuccessfully to amend it, arguing that it would open the floodgates to raids on the treasury, and all because of a bad principle.[22] It would be little consolation to Crerar to learn that he has been proven right: political pressure has ensured that agricultural subsidies have become a way of life.

As in the House of Commons, much of the important and interesting work of the Senate takes place in committees. Crerar's scope for effective contribution broadened greatly when he was appointed chairman of the Senate Standing Committee on Finance in 1950. His first major assignment, appropriately enough, had been to head the Senate's Natural Resources Committee. But moving to the top job on the potentially more prominent Finance Committee would allow him to monitor government actions and air his own, increasingly critical views. His long political experience and wide acquaintanceships were the key to his effectiveness.

His influence on the Finance Committee was personal rather than partisan. Most Senate committees seemed content merely to lay out the information that they were able to collect. But Crerar was able to carry the Finance Committee with him most of the time, and he did not hesitate to express his opinion about government spending policies. His first departure as chairman was procedural, but extremely significant. Prior to 1950 the Senate had not examined the government's spending estimates but rather waited for legislation passed by the House as a result of those estimates. Crerar was concerned with government spending per se, its trends, and its implications, so he insisted that the estimates be sent to his committee for examination immediately after their passage by the Commons. This was done by specific reference.

The success of this innovation depended very much on Crerar's connections. In a letter to Edgar Tarr in Winnipeg, he explained his procedure. He had asked Clifford Clark, deputy minister of finance, if he had any objection "to my getting an analysis of the main estimates from young [R.B.] Bryce, who is acting secretary of the Treasury Board. I knew from my experience on Treasury Board that he had all the data." Clark was agreeable, and Crerar consulted Bryce. "What I wanted was a comparison of the expenditures for the current fiscal year, the last fiscal year and the comparative figures for 1939."[23]

Crerar was pleased with the result and, in particular, the non-partisan way in which his request had been met. Essentially, his was an information-gathering exercise and an attempt to discern patterns in government spending, using 1939 as a baseline. His actions inspired the nearly moribund Public Accounts Committee of the Commons to come to life, using leads coming from him to try and bedevil the government.[24] He conceived of his role in a manner somewhat akin to what the modern auditor general does – seeking out and exposing extravagance.

After presenting his first committee report in January 1951, he wrote, enclosing a copy, to Charlie Dunning, a former finance minister. He described an "appalling and reckless growth in public expenditures. There are more Federal civil servants on the payroll today than at the peak of the war." He pointed especially to the rapid growth of External Affairs and its expenditures abroad on residences and furnishings. "They appear to be based on the theory that we must keep up with the Joneses. ... This smacks too much of a Rotary Club." The government's building boom in the Ottawa area, including a new printing plant in Hull, a new veterans' building, and a complete gutting of the East Block of the Parliament Building for External, seemed to point the way to the future of the budget.[25]

The report ended with the first of the many annual warnings that Crerar derived from the committee's labours: "The steady growth of dependence upon the state, can lead to only one of two results: Either a steady increase in the power of the state over the rights of the citizen, or the breakdown of democratic government. The lessons of history are clear for all to read."[26] Jeremiah had indeed found his pulpit.

His committee followed a slightly different approach the following year. Rather than try to examine the estimates in toto, it decided to concentrate on a few departments, intending to do others in future. This method would allow for more intensive analysis. The result certainly pleased Crerar's old friend Arthur Meighen, who wrote to him to express his appreciation of the committe's work "in the way of exposing public extravagance." He went on to urge that "nothing stand in the way of the continued functioning of this Committee ... which will bring credit to the Senate, to the Committee and to the man who fathers it."[27]

Crerar made it clear in his reply, however, that he was concerned about more than just specific instances of extravagance. The estimates revealed to him abdication of political leadership – "the easy conception which prevailed following the war (and partially arising out of the war) that a few bright minds [in the civil service] could manage our economy and keep it upon an even keel." This had led Liberals, Tories, and the CCF alike to abandon their traditional principles for political expediency and opportunism. The result had been ever-growing appropriations, especially for social welfare, driven by "Paul Martin and a few of the other Liberal do-gooders." Sooner or later "this vast edifice of expenditures will have to be drastically revised. When I suggest this to some of my friends, however, they say I am out of date, and it may be that I am lingering on the stage too long."[28]

The work of the Senate committee changed government practice. Crerar's method of examining projected departmental spending in terms of standard objects of expenditure shook up the Finance Department, which began to add such itemized breakdowns to its estimates, "thus giving a truer picture of the how and wherefore of our expenditures than milling through the data." Crerar was gratified that his reports were given wide circulation by the press and read by members of many legislatures.[29] Because of his friendship with many of Ottawa's mandarins, they continued to cooperate with his committee, despite his often-critical attitude. According to Senator Haig, leader of the Conservatice Opposition in the upper house, it was Crerar's ability to gain the cooperation of civil servants and ministers that made the revivified Finance Committee so effective.[30]

Arthur Meighen seconded the plaudits that were coming his way, commenting that Crerar's committee "has done more to maintain public regard for the Senate than anything else that has happened for many a day."[31] He probably would have endorsed as well Crerar's obiter dictum on presenting the 1952 report: "The increasing tendency of people to demand that the government do something about all sorts of problems which the community or individual should solve for itself or himself is, we believe, accountable for much mounting public expenditure [which will ultimately] undermine our system of government."[32] Not all the senators shared Crerar's apprehensions about interventionist government, but the Finance Committee's members never seriously objected to his annual reports. Part of the reason may have been simple inertia. As Crerar remarked to

Meighen, "[T]he difficulty is to get the members of the Committee to do their homework – that is to study the data provided and form intelligent judgements upon it."[33]

There was little enthusiasm within the ministry, however, for the Senate committee's new-found investigative zeal. When it was reported to Crerar that Finance Minister Walter Harris wished to talk to him, he sought him out going into caucus one day, but Harris politely turned him aside. "I think the Government looks upon me with suspicion," he told Dexter, who had passed on the information, "which does not worry me a bit."[34] Nor did he have any intention of muting the annual criticism emerging from his committee's hearings.

But he could be obstructed. In 1955, his committee was not authorized to begin its examination of the estimates until three weeks before the budget. Perforce it could look into only a few departments. Crerar chose the Civil Service Commission as one of his targets. The results received wide circulation in the *Free Press* chain. Crerar pointed out that the civil service had grown from 46,000 employees in 1939 (his base year) to 1955's figure of 175,000, to which must be added the 138,000 people working for crown corporations. Civil service salaries had grown from $40 million to $554 million in the same period, exclusive of the crown corporations. He hoped that his probing would make the government more conscious of rising expenditures, but, as he told his old crony Cameron, "no political party to-day wishes to take the slightest risk of giving offence to any section of voters."[35]

In presenting what turned out to be his final report as chairman of the Finance Committee, in June 1955, Crerar proffered a warning: "People may clamour for security – many are doing that to-day – but it should never be forgotten that if personal freedom is sacrificed for personal security provided by Governments, the individual can have no guarantee that in the end he will have neither freedom nor security."[36] But it was now time, he concluded, for him to move aside.

In the next session, as he told the government leader, now Senator Ross Macdonald, he did not wish to be reappointed. He disapproved of the u.s. Senate's principle of seniority for committee chairmanships and advocated that the Canadian Senate follow a rotation system. It was as much a break with tradition as had been his vigorous examination of government estimates. Despite attempts by Macdonald to have him reconsider his decision, he resigned in early 1956, about the time of his and Jessie's golden wedding anniversary.[37]

Crerar reached his eightieth birthday that year, long past the age when most people seek retirement. Yet aside from perfunctory references to his advancing age and occasional bouts of infirmity, he seemed unwilling to let go. Clearly he drew strength from his surroundings, and the habits and interests of a lifetime would not be cast aside easily. He liked "being at the centre of things." But there was now a drawing back – a desire to play a less forward role. He enjoyed his assignments, especially the Banking and Commerce Committee, and some issues could still galvanize him. Crerar, however, was becoming more familiar and content with the role of self-styled veteran observer and commentator.

His network of correspondents had changed. The Sanhedrin, his support for so many years, was no more. Only Cameron still lived, and their friendship of almost fifty years was maintained by visits and letters. He also revived old acquaintanceships. Arthur Meighen, Eugene Forsey, and Grattan O'Leary exchanged letters with him frequently. And he wrote often to Bruce Hutchison. They all kept up a lively interest in public affairs, and 1956 provided much to talk about. Events were dominated by the pipeline debate and the crisis in Suez.

The fiasco over the pipeline did not come as a complete surprise to Crerar. Early in the year he had complained to Symington: "Whatever be the merits of Trans-Canada Pipe Lines, Clarence Howe got out on a limb over a year ago when he assured the promoters that the Government would guarantee their bonds, without first having cleared it with the Cabinet."[38] The opposition parties would be more than delighted to cut off the limb.

In writing about the increasingly raucous scenes in the House to his daughter, Dorothy, and her husband, Bernard Naylor, in Victoria, Crerar seemed to accept the opposition's simplified version of the issue. The Tories and the CCF argued that since the government was putting up the money to build a pipeline, the profits from which would go to American capitalists, the dominion government ought to own and run it. The ministry claimed that the emergency (a potential shortage of energy in central Canada) was such that "further delay must be avoided and that in any case the Government had protected itself against any capital loss." If the Liberals tried to force the bill through by closure, he predicted, it "would be politically dangerous."

His fears were well grounded. Howe did get his way, but amid some of the wildest scenes ever witnessed in the Commons. "Nothing but an election," Crerar concluded when it was over, "will clear up the aftermath of the pipeline controversy." In his view Parliament itself had suffered most, and the cherished claim of the Liberals to be the party of confidence and competence was badly undermined.

"If the government attempts to placate Quebec Liberals by protecting Speaker Beaudoin, whom they had just humiliated," he told Dorothy, "they will have many unhappy moments."[39] Even so, he did not see the pipeline débâcle as a fatal check to Liberal hegemony.

Even less did he see domestic political danger in the Suez crisis, which followed on the heels of the pipeline issue. His long antipathy to imperial/Commonwealth centralization would condition his response. He was, however, very impressed by Pearson's performance in defusing the confrontation through the United Nations. The criticism that Pearson drew from Canadian Anglophiles provoked only scorn from Crerar. He wrote to Chubby Power that "there will be those who will wring their hands over the Commonwealth and the effect this will have on it. I shed no tears." The Second World War "had weakened the props under it and they are slipping away one by one." The sooner Britain joins Europe the better, he went on presciently, and Britain should "not be deterred by any views from Canada or the others."[40]

The ending of the Liberals' long run in office by John Diefenbaker's Conservatives in June 1957 had no single cause, though the pipeline debate and Suez were major contributors. It was probably because of public boredom with Liberal governments as much as anything else. But on the prairies resentment against the government was open and sometimes noisy; and the problem, not surprisingly, was wheat marketing. In describing for Power a rowdy campaign meeting at Morris, Manitoba, at which C.D. Howe patronized and infuriated local farmers, Crerar forecast a shock for the government.[41] Three weeks later, prairie voters reduced the Liberal complement in the House from seventeen to six. The security of the Senate now found him less partisan, if not less Liberal, and Crerar thought that a term in opposition might be good for a party grown fat and complacent.

As for himself, he was now over eighty, but, sustained by Jessie, his friends inside and outside the Senate (and perhaps by his undiminished ego), he felt no inclination to step outside. He and his wife did, however, finally escape from Winnipeg's winters, taking up seasonal residence in Victoria. From there and his seat in the Senate, he continued an active observer of political life.

CHAPTER FIFTEEN

The Last Gladstonian Liberal, 1957–66

Lester Pearson carried Crerar's (and many others') hopes for a reinvigorated Liberal party. Because of his long and distinguished diplomatic career and despite his nearly ten years in St Laurent's cabinet, Crerar saw him as personifying the Liberal future. Quite idealistically (if not naïvely), he also saw Pearson as a moral rather than a political force in the party and somehow expected that he would recommit it to a purer, more traditional brand of liberalism, uncorrupted by the materialism of recent electoral bartering. These hopes, however, would be dashed; there would be no going back. The political world would keep changing, drawing further away from Crerar's constant verities.

St Laurent's resignation after the election of 1957 necessitated a convention, which was called for mid-January 1958 in Ottawa. Pearson's stock, already high, was enhanced by his winning the Nobel Prize in the autumn. Paul Martin mounted a serious challenge but was not expected to prevail. The more important question for Crerar thus became the direction in which Pearson would lead the Liberals. He was not encouraged by the preparations for the convention.

His old friend Kirk Cameron had hoped and fully expected to be invited. Quite impossible, decided George Marler, his MP, who preferred to invite more active members from his riding. Crerar was incensed, pointing out sharply to Marler that Cameron was perhaps the only Liberal alive who had attended every party convention since 1893 and had been friend and informal adviser to Laurier, Fielding, King, Lapointe, and many other leading Liberals. He complained as well to John Connolly and Chubby Power, both convention officials, who assured him that provision would be made for former prominent members. He remained bitter, however, asserting "that if I did not have the status of a Senator I would be on the outside looking in. The powers-that-be in the Party today do not look kindly upon those of us who stray far enough to offer some criticism."

Crerar had little confidence that the conclave would produce much of a program. The party's rejection at the polls in 1957 had not been an accident, as some Liberals had so blithely concluded. It lost because "the Liberal Party had become spineless and because it had committed blunders enough to warrant its defeat."[1] Ironically, Crerar came down with the flu the day before the convention and was kept abreast of the detailed happenings by Cameron, who did attend after all.

However, since much of the activity occurred in the Chateau Laurier hotel, where he and Jessie now stayed while in Ottawa, Crerar missed little of moment. Paul Martin he thought a credible candidate, but his convention tactics were rather too aggressive and American for Crerar's taste. Pearson was much more to his liking, but he confided later to his daughter, "Between ourselves, he could improve his method of speaking. It is definitely better than it was a year ago," he added hopefully, "and I have no doubt it will improve more."

The resolutions, as he feared, were simply a pastiche of planks for special interests, "and then, of course, there was more social security. Indeed, almost more of everything. This is a fatal flaw." The country's most imminent danger, according to Crerar, was inflation, and it was never mentioned. "The wisest thing Pearson can do is to largely ignore this programme."

The new leader was starting out with a great fund of goodwill and public acceptance, he judged, and if "he has the necessary political acumen to build upon this and develop it he may well rank in the tradition of Laurier and Macdonald"![2] To Cameron he predicted: "I am not so pessimistic about the future of the Liberal Party as you are. I believe it can become a great revitalizing force in our public life and I have confidence that Pearson can do this."[3]

On taking his position as Leader of the Opposition in the House, Pearson was faced with a motion to go into Committee of Supply – normally an occasion for moving want of confidence. Following advice from Jack Pickersgill, Pearson instead denounced the Diefenbaker government's economic policies and suggested that it resign and return direction of affairs to the Liberals, as if it were the natural governing party. "The amendment Pearson moved a week ago Monday was a thoroughly stupid performance," Crerar railed to Cameron, and Pearson had known so immediately. Crerar tried to absolve the new leader somewhat by complaining that "some of the front benchers in the opposition had not yet realized that the Party was definitely rejected by the Canadian people last June." A good term in opposition is what the Liberals deserved and needed, he concluded, and Pearson must immediately start searching out new colleagues.[4] He certainly got his wish in the spring of 1958, when the Conservatives scored the most overwhelming electoral victory in Canadian political history till then.

Crerar was neither surprised nor dismayed by the "cyclone [that] swept Canada." The Liberals would govern the country again if they learned the lessons of the elections of 1957 and 1958, he told Chubby Power. The rot had begun to set in twenty years earlier. King's concern for himself and his place in history allowed the party organization to fall into disrepair. The worst mistake, however, had been to abandon traditional Liberal philosophy and follow the chimaera of the welfare state and centralization of power in Ottawa. The consequent complacency and arrogance of the St Laurent years brought the inevitable retribution. Diefenbaker, "shallow and superficial as he is," spotted the flaw and made the Liberals pay the price. But the new prime minister "will be in a good deal of trouble before 2 years are gone, and I don't think he has the qualities to deal with them." Crerar still had confidence in Pearson, "but he needs to ditch some of the intellectuals who have been advising him."[5]

Later in the year he was surprised (and probably flattered) to learn that he himself might play a role in the party's revival. With no representation in the House from the prairies, Pearson called on Crerar to chair a committee to advise him on western agricultural policy.[6] The senator was seldom reluctant to give advice, and not just on agricultural matters. He wrote to the leader occasionally, urging him to carve out a clear identity for the party. "The basic difficulty in our political system today," he argued on more than one occasion, is that "there are no sharp distinctions between our main political parties. This is not healthy … and has a corrosive influence on public opinion. No free system of government can endure with a public that becomes politically lethargic or indifferent." Pearson would always send politely soothing replies. At bottom, however, Crerar was concerned much more with the fate of Canadian liberalism, as he interpreted and tried to perpetuate it, than with that of the Liberal party.[7]

A test of the party's liberalism soon appeared in what became known as the "Coyne affair." James E. Coyne had been appointed in 1954 to a seven-year term as governor of the Bank of Canada. During 1960, concerned about the effect of the government's management of the economy, Coyne made a series of speeches critical of Ottawa's fiscal policies. Crerar had noted approvingly and told Kirk Cameron that "a majority of the Cabinet are in varying degrees critical of Coyne, although I doubt if [Finance Minister Donald] Fleming in his inmost thoughts shares this." In the senator's opinion, the Conservatives had wandered far astray in their pursuit of power from their conventional economic thinking of the past.[8] That they should also prompt Coyne to stray from his normal bailiwick of monetary policy simply indicated the serious deterioration of the country's economy.

Matters between Coyne and the government worsened in the ensuing year, to the point where Diefenbaker had concluded that the governor must be removed, despite his having only a few months remaining in his term of office. An opportunity arose with the approval, after long study, of a new pension plan for the governor and deputy governor by the bank's board of directors. The government let it be known that it considered the change improper, implying that Coyne was feathering his own nest at taxpayers' expense. Accordingly, when Coyne refused to resign at Fleming's request, the government introduced a bill declaring the position of governor vacant. And then, in a stunningly stupid bit of politics, the government would not permit the bill to go to committee, where Coyne could defend himself, even though the Tories had an overwhelming majority there. The bill was pushed through the Commons and sent on to the Liberal-dominated Senate.

Crerar's interest in the Coyne affair was personal, partisan, and public. James Coyne (or "Jimmy," as Crerar referred to him) was the son of J.B. ("Bogus") Coyne, a Winnipeg lawyer, sometime associate of the Sanhedrin, and a life-long friend of Crerar's. Coyne's reputation and that of his son, the governor, were a matter of some concern to the senator. The attempt to dismiss Coyne by the government was, in his opinion, "a perfectly stupid performance."[9] At the insistence of the Liberal majority in the Senate, the bill was sent to the Senate Standing Committee on Banking and Finance, on which Crerar served. Coyne was accorded an opportunity to appear and defend himself, thus allowing Liberals and their supporters across the country to stake out their commitment to fair play. When the Tories proposed to report out of committee, without amendment, the bill declaring Coyne's office vacant, the Liberals resisted, thus effectively killing it.

"Coyne made a moving statement in his summation of the whole matter, and indicated clearly that if his integrity were vindicated in the Senate he intended to retire from the Bank immediately," Crerar reported to Cameron. This was the key to the actions of the Senate Liberals. It is unlikely that they would have rejected the bill if Coyne had intended to stay on at the Bank until the end of his term.[10] That would have posed a challenge that the government could not have refused; and the senators had no desire to see an election fought on a trumped-up issue of Senate reform.

Assured by Coyne that he would resign, the Senate Liberals had the best of all possible results. Coyne, vindicated by the committee, which concluded (by majority) that he had not misbehaved in office, could leave with his dignity and integrity intact; the Senate's Liberal majority could cast itself as defender of the individual against the awesome power of the state; and the Tory Government was exposed as inept, petty, and vindictive.

All in all, it was a good piece of work, Crerar concluded afterward. "The Diefenbaker Government had no right to ask for Jimmy Coyne's resignation. He was responsible to Parliament and not to the Cabinet." So the Senate "vindicated a very sound principle," since the "most serious problem today is the tendency of the Cabinet to gather power unto itself."[11] Liberal senators went home elated by the session. Their actions on the Coyne issue, their revision of a tariff bill, and "our killing of the dictatorship of the Revenue Department" seemed to gain wide approval. The Senate should do "more of this when the occasion requires it," was Crerar's satisfied conclusion to his colleague Arthur Roebuck.[12]

The saga of James Coyne had been clear-cut, politically fruitful, and readily grasped by the public, but the most complex and potentially explosive public question of the 1960s was none of these. The aggressive vigour and nationalist rhetoric of Jean Lesage's new Liberal government in Quebec awakened perplexed anxiety in English Canada about that province's place in Confederation. Even Tom Crerar's five decades in public life made him no better prepared than his fellow citizens to deal with it, though he immediately sensed the danger of ignoring the awakening of Quebec.

He conceded in 1963 that there was some substance to Quebec's complaints about Confederation, without being at all specific, but found himself "at a loss to understand what our French friends mean." Quebec's premier, Jean Lesage, was not being at all helpful, he felt, by claiming that the British North America Act, 1867, "must be re-written but he does not say what changes he desires to make in it." Crerar recognized the ferment in Quebec but considered it another recurrence of French-Canadian nationalism, of which there had been several in the past. What he feared was that this resurgence might "arouse opposition among impulsive and unthinking people in the English community."

Yet he was not prepared to accept the argument that French Canadians had been relegated to being "hewers of wood and drawers of water" by the English. It was their own fault, he claimed, since the

254 The Senate and After, 1945-75

French-Canadian elite had clung to an educational system that "did not give an opportunity to young French Canadians to equip themselves for commercial and managerial operations." But there was blame enough for all. He would prefer that "everyone in Canada, whether English or French, Catholic or Protestant, be able to speak the French language as well as the English language. I think we English have failed a good deal in this respect."[13] He remarked quite enviously several times on the facility, even eloquence, of his French-Canadian colleagues in English and the breadth of their humanist learning. However, in the modern age, he was certain, that was not enough.

Crerar gave much thought to the problem, and he was not hopeful when Lester Pearson (who led the Liberals to minority governments in 1963 and 1965) appointed the Royal Commission on Bilingualism and Biculturalism in 1963. To Eugene Forsey he wrote that the growing tension might not be culturally based at all. He was puzzled by "the Quebec attitude." The declining influence of the Catholic church meant to him that "the anchor was drifting." However stereotyped his view of Quebec may have been, the current difficulties of the federation could be determined. His former faith in the principles of Rowell-Sirois had been badly shaken; and he now saw the federal government more as a problem than a solution. "Thirty years ago it seemed to me it was important to enhance the power of the central authority if we were ever to become a nation. Now I am not so sure." The tendency to "centralize authority in Ottawa ... has been an important factor in producing the present unrest in Quebec, and at times it appears to me this difficulty is as much one of prestige and money as it is of culture."[14]

The senator took his concerns directly to Jean Lesage, with whom he had served in Parliament. He was "greatly puzzled over the present Quebec situation," he confessed, though he was wholly in sympathy with that province's objection to the accelerating concentration of power in Ottawa. (Crerar now seemed persuaded that this was the root of all current political evils.) At the same time he explained that English Canadians found it difficult to accept the charge that French Canadians "have been relegated to a secondary place in our Canadian development." After all, the governor general (Georges Vanier) and the chief justice of the Supreme Court of Canada (Robert Taschereau) were both French Canadians; two of the nation's most notable prime ministers (Laurier and St Laurent) had come from Quebec; and "some of the most distinguished Cabinet Ministers were of French Canadian origin." He repeated to Lesage his belief that it was Quebec's educational system that had left young

French Canadians unprepared for modern society. In a deft compliment to the Quiet Revolution's educational reforms, he predicted (presciently, as it turned out) that within thirty years "the big jobs in our banks and insurance companies and in industrial concerns will be occupied by French Canadians." He concluded with what was becoming his favourite solution to the country's many dilemmas – return income and corporation taxes to the provinces and, along with them, responsibility for social services, thus reversing the concentration of power in Ottawa.[15] He expected Lesage to welcome such a suggestion.

In his reply, Lesage conceded that the mood of Quebec might be difficult for other Canadians to understand as it "lives its quiet revolution. It is the sum of past frustrations, present ambitions and hopes." But he was not at all prepared to allow Crerar his stereotypical opinions about Quebec. The governor general and chief justice might be French Canadians for the moment, but young Québécois were asking pointedly, "How many key posts do we hold in the federal civil service and Crown corporations?" And he rejected the notion that Quebec's traditional, non-technical education must bear the blame for lack of advancement. Had not the English magnates who built the economic empire been products "of the classical education of Oxford and Cambridge"? The short history of Hydro Québec, he claimed proudly, demonstrates that French Canadians can equal their English-speaking counterparts.

The current ferment was a good thing, he told the senator, since "French Canada has to live its crisis, clean its body in order to make better and great things. Our aim is to give our community a sense of dignity, achievement and self-confidence." To do so – and here the two agreed – "we need to repatriate our own constitutional powers and some measure of fiscal independence. I am very happy to have your support in this matter," he concluded.[16] Despite the civility, Crerar's opinions did not change, and the two concurred only on the need for greater decentralization, for quite different reasons.

A year later, while applauding Quebec's creation of a Department of Education, with its own minister, he still blamed the former system for the province's economic domination by outsiders. French Canada's complaints offered further evidence of the need to overhaul the federal fiscal system – a complete reversal of the process launched at the time of the Rowell-Sirois recommendations, and which he had strongly approved.[17]

During his last few years in Parliament, Senator Crerar attracted a rather unusual amount of attention for a member of the upper house.

This was partly because of his great age; though in his late eighties, he was still vigorous, attentive to public issues, and always ready with an opinion. He was often seen as a gauge of how much Canada had changed over his public career, allowing people to define and measure their concept of progress against his long life. His own beliefs and values remained constant, though his ideas about the role of the national government had come full circle. As a result of some of the newspaper articles about him, he now took to calling himself a "Manchester School liberal" or a "Gladstonian liberal." He rejected the contemporary notion that government could be all things to all people, still convinced that people, individually or cooperatively, were better able to do things for themselves than any government could. The role of the federal government should be to facilitate, not to manage and, especially, not to control. Whether marketing boards or pensions, tariffs or Indian treaty money were the agent, dependence, once created, would ultimately result in loss of freedom. This had long been a fixed conviction with Crerar; but now he also concluded that the greatest evil of activist government was the overwhelming tide of debt. In his last public years he attempted to stem it, though not at any price. Not surprisingly, he was often misunderstood.

The Tories' federal budget of 1962 had begun to lay the groundwork for an election that had to be called shortly. It contained, among other things, a proposal to increase the old age pension by ten dollars per month. Crerar's contribution to the debate that followed did not go unnoticed. His reluctance to vote for an increase in expenditure led the Regina *Leader-Post* to scold him for being unconcerned with the lot of pensioners and to suggest that a better way of saving money would be to "reform" the Senate. The paper regretted that his former Progressive sympathies had been forgotten now that "senators enjoy many privileges and financial rewards."[18]

The *Globe and Mail*, in contrast, in a lead editorial, commented that the eighty-five-year-old Manitoba senator "provided a powerful argument against those who want an age limit in the Senate." It nodded approvingly at Crerar's objection to "putting the pensioner on the auction block every time an election rolls around." It saved its fullest praise, however, for Crerar's attack on the principle of universality. During the debate on the matter in the upper house, he had said: "I am not opposed to old age pensions for those who need them. If it is the pensioner's only means of support, then $65 or even $75 is not enough. I am opposed to paying pensions to those who do not need them. The millionaire and the pauper can and do get them equally today."[19] For the *Globe*, Crerar had put his finger on the basic weakness of Canada's welfare programs. Until there was a system of contributory pensions in place (which Crerar favoured as well), pensions should be paid only to those in actual need, and they should be adequate to those needs.[20]

But the *Globe* was an exception. Crerar complained to Bruce Hutchison that most headline writers spread in black letters – "'Crerar opposed to Old Age Pensions' – so I got properly belted in about a dozen letters."[21] Yet he was well aware that those were the risks of the game. Taking the popular position had never been his style.

His preferred scheme for pensions was intended to free the government completely from obligation. He advocated a national plan under which all who worked would be compelled by law to contribute a portion of their annual earnings to a pension fund, managed as a non-profit operation by the insurance companies (presumably under a fee arrangement). If the funds were wisely invested (again, through the insurance industry), this plan should provide an adequate pension at retirement "and gradually make the switch over from the present method of paying pensions, which are now the charge of the Treasury." The government would thus be relieved eventually of any monetary support of pensions. He saw nothing wrong with thus ensuring the continued viability of insurance companies such as Great-West Life, on whose board he had sat for decades. Hence he readily favoured such a scheme over yet another government bureaucracy.[22]

The Canada Pension Plan, devised by the Liberal government in the mid-1960s, brought a mixed response from the senator. He approved of the contributory features, even the obligation of employers to contribute, but with its management left to the government, he feared for its cost and its stability.

Ottawa's track record on such programs did not encourage confidence. The calculations on which the existing Old Age Pensions were based had proved faulty; both the Superannuation Fund for civil servants and the Government Annuities Fund (which had been touted as actuarially sound) had had to be bailed out by the treasury; the costs of Family Allowances, introduced when Crerar was in cabinet, had exceeded expectations; and the Unemployment Insurance Fund (which was, in theory, soundly based) was beginning its long run in deficit. All this, the senator confessed, "has raised a doubt in the minds of many Members." He was convinced that the various programs must be put on a means test. "There is no sense in expanding a bureaucracy … to pay welfare to people who do not need it and who could well get along without it."[23]

Once again he took his case to the prime minister. The heart of the problem, he argued to Pearson, was Ottawa's willingness to abandon the division of responsibilities, which was the essence of the federal system. "What an absurdity it is! Over the last twenty years Ottawa has relieved the Provinces of their obligations in the whole broad field of social welfare." Though this undertaking was now costing the federal government more than it took in from personal and corporate income taxes, "the Provinces claim they must have a greater share of these taxes. A journey down that road will lead straight to ruin." Would it not be much more satisfactory to strike at the root, he asked Pearson? Say to the provinces, "you take back all your responsibilities and we will give you back your corporation and personal income taxes." Crerar conceded that this would bring about the end of equalization payments; but he now described as a fallacy the notion that all Canadians, anywhere in the country, should be treated equally. He did not explain why this was now so.[24]

Either Pearson's reply was an attempt at misdirection, or the two men were on different wavelengths. He expressed his pleasure at receiving Crerar's views on relations with the provinces, "with which I have much sympathy. I am willing to show an infinity of patience," he went on to say, "to meet every legitimate proposal from Quebec or any other Province but the time is rapidly approaching when we will have to put forward the federal position in no uncertain terms."[25] The prime minister was preoccupied with political relations, while Crerar was "blowing the whistle" on financial arrangements. The senator may have been out of step, but he was not out of touch. "Canadians," he told Eugene Forsey, "appear to have become bemused with the notion that you can have permanent prosperity built upon a foundation of public and private debt."[26]

To most Canadians who thought about matters political, and certainly to most other politicians, Tom Crerar had become a sort of Cassandra, wailing his predictions of fiscal doom from the comfortable security of an unaccountable Senate. But his strictures were more than the rantings of a grumpy old man. His primary target was hypocrisy – the blatant disingenuousness of those who professed to have espoused the modern economics of Keynes, who argued for an activist government to manage the economy, but who shrank from the application of theory to practice. Politicians of all stripes were quick to spend in order to stimulate a slow economy, as Keynes had prescribed, but reluctant to lower the temperature of an economy in heat.

It had been Crerar, after all, who had been one of the first in the late 1930s to challenge the old orthodoxy of balanced budgets and argue for a stimulative deficit. When the economy revived under the stress of war and then began to expand rapidly, he was equally ready to apply the other side of Keynes's cycle, proposing that the government continue very heavy, wartime-level taxation in order to retain fiscal control. Indeed, in his letter to Pearson cited above he recommended a return to such tax levels to deal with the debt.

So it was no surprise to those who knew him at all well when he wrote to the *Ottawa Journal* at the close of 1964 to express publicly his disappointment with the Liberal government. The publisher of the *Journal*, Norman Smith, decided to "give it the real good play such a letter from such a person deserves." He gave it pride of place on the editorial page – "the most-featured letter we have ever run in the Journal," Grattan O'Leary informed Crerar. In his letter, Crerar reflected on the steady growth of indebtedness in Canada (then at $40 billion for the three levels of government) and rejected the claim that it did not matter as long as gross national product (GNP) was increasing. "What happens if adverse winds begin to blow and the GNP ceases to grow or recedes?," he asked. However, his major point was that politicians of all parties refused to apply the economic doctrine in which they professed to believe: "For four years we have had a buoyant economy and the Budget has been in deficit hundreds of millions each year. If we cannot pay our way when times are good, what happens when they turn bad? The besetting sin of the present Government, as it certainly was of the last one, is the desire to please everyone."[27] It was a refrain he continued to repeat.

In the spring of 1966 he was not anxious to retire, though his ninetieth birthday was coming in June. His and Jessie's sixtieth wedding anniversary had occurred in January, but her health was giving him pause. She had suffered a fall and broken her hip, but a simultaneous concussion had not been diagnosed. Mental confusion followed, and, as her strength declined, it became apparent that she would no longer be able to accompany the senator to Ottawa, as she had done, when he was in Parliament, during almost fifty years. As he put it to several friends, "I do not want to be spending the greater part of my time in Ottawa while my wife is in Winnipeg."[28]

Crerar informed his Senate colleagues at the beginning of April 1966 that he would be stepping down at the end of May, though he hoped to make "'one more speech before I walk out of those doors for the last time.' It is something to look forward to. This man is one of the great Canadians," the *Montreal Gazette* editorialized.[29] It became something of an occasion in the usually sheltered life of the upper chamber. Senators rose from their sick beds to attend. The press gallery was, for a change, well populated. Editorial writers all across the country were poised to comment. And Crerar did his best not to disappoint anyone.

Tall, erect, and still slender, he spoke for an hour, with few notes, to an attentive and affectionate Senate. To most Canadian liberals of the day he was a throwback, an anachronism, a man badly out of touch and lacking sympathy for the concept of a caring and active government. But Crerar's sturdy liberalism, if now no longer fashionable, was fully intact and sustained in him by the values of his early manhood – honesty, hard work, self-reliance, and the cooperative spirit. He gave his colleagues a full dose of his "common sense," as one newspaper described the speech. The Canadian people were sound, he thought, but they could be misled. That had been the great problem of the recent past – a result of the failure of political institutions and, especially, of leadership.

He began his "swan song," as he called it, with a brief reference to the beginning of his long parliamentary career and paid tribute to some of his early and more recent colleagues. But he was not there that day to praise. It disturbed him greatly, he lamented, to take his departure with the reputation of Parliament at such a low ebb, as a result of "the failure of Parliament to maintain its standards. It is a great misfortune for a democratic country when its people commence to lose faith in their governing institutions." There will always be differences of policy and in the manner in which public persons discharge their duties; but "there should always be a respect for the public men ... who are members of Parliament ... but that respect must be earned." Much of the blame he laid at the doors of Lester Pearson and John Diefenbaker. He hoped "to live long enough to see the prestige of Parliament restored." But that would not happen, he asserted "with all frankness and with all candor," since "we shall never get right in our parliamentary institution here until we have had a change in leadership in both the two major parties." In the present circumstances, both leaders and both parties were incapable of winning the confidence of the Canadian people.

Crerar turned to some problems that needed to be solved. The first was the "dangerous degree" to which federal affairs and provincial affairs had been mixed. Canadians had been foolish to abandon the division of powers laid down by the Fathers of Confederation as the essence of the federal system. His solution, as he had been preaching for some years now, was to turn the clock back – to return personal and corporate income taxes, as well as succession duties, to the provinces and let them meet the responsibilities assigned to them in the British North America Act. "It is clearly absurd that the federal Government should through the provinces or any other agency, contribute money to build a skating rink in Saskatoon or pave a street in Antigonish." Such intervention was never intended by the Fathers, and the result was that we "will have differences in opinion and squabbling over money as to who shall do this or that or the other. That is no way to build unity and harmony in this country."

He conceded that if Ottawa surrendered some of its authority, "it could not organize and plan our fiscal and tax matters to prevent depressions and stimulate booms." Just so, he agreed; but "I am bound to say that I have no great faith in that kind of planning. We are working today, and have been for years, under the theories of John Maynard Keynes. How has that worked out?" One of Keynes's essential postulates, Crerar argued, was that during good times the government should budget for a surplus, increasing taxes if necessary. Despite a blip in 1961, he pointed out, the preceding decade had on the whole been prosperous: "Nevertheless, there has not been one year in the last ten in which we have balanced our budget." The result had been "the degree of inflation we have in our economy today. I say quite soberly that at the moment there is no more insidious danger facing us than inflation." The great move to the left – the building of the welfare state – had been accomplished at the price of the erosion of purchasing power. "I say it is just folly, supreme folly, to think we can go on spending here, spending there, never balancing our budgets, and at the same time imagine that we can avoid trouble in the future. It just cannot be done."

There was more. Crerar had suggestions on industrial relations, government spending, the Canadian Broadcasting Corporation, and much else. "We are the most over-governed country in the world," he concluded. The reason was that "we must have everything at once, and governments feel they must give the people everything at once. The result has been a mounting debt, a mounting expenditure, a mounting inflation, and a mounting discontent among the people."[30] It was rather an accurate summary and forecast for the next several years.

He sat down amid the plaudits of his colleagues. A week later, with his office cleaned out, he boarded the train from Ottawa for the last time.

CHAPTER SIXTEEN

Retirement and Reflection, 1966–75

Jessie Crerar died in February 1967, a few months after "T.A." returned to Winnipeg.[1] So he was now alone and without the busy political world of Ottawa to divert him. He made no concession to the sad irony. Though active politics was behind him, there was no retreat into depression or self-pity. Canada's Centennial summer and autumn he spent in Manitoba, but he had no desire to endure another winter there. Early in 1968 he purchased a house on Lansdowne Road in Victoria, where he lived with Dorothy and her husband, Bernard Naylor. There was genuine warmth between the generations, and it turned out a happy and convenient arrangement.

He stayed in contact with Canada beyond Vancouver Island through his correspondence and his remaining directorships in which he still took an active interest – Canada Steamship Lines and Algoma Steel. He even managed to attend their annual meetings in Montreal and Sault Ste Marie, respectively, in late 1969, but he carefully avoided Ottawa. His letters during this period are rather less interesting. All the other members of the Sanhedrin were dead. Cameron – the last, save for Crerar himself, and his correspondent for almost fifty years – had died in the early 1960s. It was only in his letters to Chubby Power, Bruce Hutchison and, to a lesser extent, Senator John Connolly that he displayed his wonted frankness, intimacy, and often-opinionated concern.

Crerar's commitment to the old liberal faith never wavered; one of his great satisfactions, as he saw it, was his life-long attendance at the Gladstonian altar. His devotion, however, could also make him vulnerable, as we see below. He realized that he had been out of step with Liberal party policies for at least three decades, but the degree of alienation was now startling. In a letter of encouragement to Wallace McCutcheon, who was seeking the Conservative leadership in

1967, he condemned both traditional parties for "policies that inch by inch add to the authority of the State and the bureaucracy." The danger "lies mainly with well-intentioned people," he continued, "honest but stupid, who think every social ill can be cured by passing laws or spending money. Too many people forget that free demo-cratic government was intended to keep people in order so every honest citizen could work in security."[2]

The Tory party, even its right wing, would now find Crerar a curi-ous throwback. Electoral politics had no place for traditional princi-ples. Who else in Canadian politics in the 1970s would acknowledge his credo to be Laurier's famous definition of Canadian Liberalism, announced one hundred years earlier, as Crerar did in a letter to Senator Donald Cameron?[3] The essence of his Liberalism remained the freedom of the individual, including freedom from government.

In the late 1960s, however, his devotion to nineteenth-century lib-eralism could attract some odd acolytes. A new journal of political news and comment entitled *Canada Month* began publishing. To achieve some credibility, it sought out public figures whose ideas and stature might enhance its appeal. There is little doubt that Crerar's head was turned by this sudden attention. That a journal of current opinion published in Toronto should seek him out on far-off Vancouver Island seemed to give a continuing relevance to his con-victions. His correspondence with Jack Doupe, editor and publisher of the new magazine, quickly became familiar, if not intimate. The neo-conservative bent of *Canada Month* drew Crerar's immediate approbation, especially its attacks on public spending and the growth of the bureaucracy. In response to Doupe's invitations, he was happy to offer advice.[4]

He was not so naïve, however, as to be taken advantage of by the enterprising Mr. Doupe. When it was suggested that Crerar be appointed "Senior Consulting Editor," he sought refuge in modesty. "I am not at all certain," he replied, "that my name appearing on your masthead might be more of a loss than a gain to you." He preferred to remain an anonymous, if willing sympathizer.[5] It was an interesting juxtaposition nevertheless – the conjunction of views of nineteenth-century liberalism and what passed for the "new right" in Canada.

Crerar's brief engagement with the rather short-lived *Canada Month* was indicative of his continuing interest in contemporary political issues. A proposal in the Liberal government's White Paper on taxa-tion in 1969 to eliminate the three-year exemption from corporate taxes on new mines coming into production brought a long response from the former mines minister that appeared in the *Northern Miner*. He recounted his struggle in 1937 to persuade Finance Minister Charlie Dunning that such a policy would have a fertilizing effect throughout much of the Canadian economy. It had been a successful innovation, and Crerar vigorously protested any attempt to rescind it.[6]

His opinion on the current problems of the wheat farmers, particularly Canada's expensive and apparently unsaleable surplus, similarly reflected his past attitudes. He had never really abandoned his conviction that controlling production costs was a better route to competitive success in the grain business than reliance on supply management, with or without a Wheat Board. The large surplus of wheat in Canada in 1970 sparked considerable concern and wide debate.

In response to an editorial in the *Winnipeg Free Press* on the matter, Crerar did not hesitate to add to the clamour. The root of the current surplus, he maintained, dated back to the late 1940s and the beginning of international wheat agreements (which he had opposed). Advancing inflation had provoked exporting countries to shelter their high-cost producers by negotiating long-term pricing arrangements with often-reluctant importers. Eventually this system had encouraged production of inferior, cheaper wheat (which could still sustain life), thereby undercutting the internationally managed price. Canada's Wheat Board loyally stuck to the agreement, even when countries such as Argentina and the United States began to lower prices to protect markets – hence the unsold Canadian surplus. The latest international agreement on wheat prices – part of the so-called Kennedy Round of the General Agreement on Tariffs and Trade (GATT) – had collapsed and Crerar wished it good riddance. His prescription was for the Wheat Board to cut prices until the surplus was sold. Markets thus regained could be held only through lowering of production costs. Crerar was not specific on how this reduction was to be achieved.[7] His analysis differed little from his ideas on marketing in the 1920s, but the dynamics of the international wheat market had not changed much either. It was still a buyer and a seller sitting across a table.

The volume (if not the quality) of his correspondence during his nineties is impressive, and much of it was retrospective. Perhaps it was therapeutic for him to rethink his long career. At least one senior Canadian historian who interviewed the ageing Crerar recalled for me that the old man was rather resentful that his contributions over so many years had not been better acknowledged. But there is little ill-temper in the surviving letters. He took pains with young students who sent questions, gave considerable time to university students who inquired about his career, and revealed few inconsistencies when writing to old friends. There were some surprises, however.

In responding to one student's inquiry, Crerar explained his version of the 1935 cabinet-selection process. His desire to regain the Railways portfolio was a result entirely of his fear that the Canadian National Railways would be gobbled up by the rival Canadian Pacific in a government attempt to rid itself of obligations during the Depression. This was certainly the attitude of the Sanhedrin in Winnipeg, as was its suspicion of Finance Minister Dunning's empathy with the private railway. But this account appears rather facile.[8] The traditional prestige of the portfolio could not have been far from his considerations.

More interesting and perhaps more believable were Crerar's recollections of the origins of and justification for the Family Allowances introduced in 1944. In a long letter to his old Ottawa friend Louis Rasminsky, James Coyne's successor as Governor of the Bank of Canada, he traced the story. The starting point, Crerar explained, was the creation of the Wartime Prices and Trade Board, set up by King's government early in the war to head off the inevitable inflationary effects of the conflict. The freezing of wages caused severe hardship to the families of some workers in the shoe and textile factories of eastern Ontario and Quebec. An investigation of these cases by Judge Charles McTague, head of the Labour Relations Board, confirmed that the advance of the cost of living by some 19 per cent had left these workers and their families in great difficulty. Rather than endanger the price and wage policies by allowing exemptions, McTague recommended "instituting some form of family allowances for these particular cases." According to Crerar, this was the first time the "phrase was introduced into our economic thinking."

The government had considered and rejected this specific recommendation. It did, however, go on to create a universal plan covering all families, regardless of income. According to Crerar, almost thirty years later, there were two reasons for this – a desire to earn some political favour and (the major reason) "that it would bring about, to some degree, a redistribution of income which would cushion the deflation that was expected to follow after the war." As we see below, Crerar thought that this counsel from the government's financial advisers was quite wrong and did not justify such a radical innovation.[9] Crerar's dislike of the scheme was well known in 1944 and augmented his reputation as an opponent of social welfare programs funded by government, though his primary concern was with the principle of universality.

In a letter to Senator John Connolly (written shortly after the letter to Rasminsky), Crerar stated that he had considered resignation on the issue but had concluded that "the importance of the war was paramount to everything else." He had, however, urged "King not to introduce this measure but to wait and see what kind of a world we would live in after the war was over."[10] He had not been persuaded by the fiscal arguments and dismissed as mere pandering for votes any political advantage that might be gained.

The final step in Crerar's reconstruction of these events occurs in a story that he told in 1969 to, among others, K.R. MacGregor, president of Mutual Life. In the summer of 1945, Crerar had been lunching with Clifford Clark, deputy minister of finance. He found Clark very worried that the end of the war with Japan would bring rapid demobilization of several hundred thousand military, termination of war-related contracts, sharp deflation, and political agitation. All this had seemed to Crerar reminiscent of the justification advanced for Family Allowances eighteen months earlier. Crerar scoffed at the deputy minister's fears, and Clark asked him how he could see it any other way. Crerar proffered two reasons. First, people had been denied goods for four years by the war – not simply items of immediate consumption, but durable goods, such as washers, refrigerators, automobiles, and farm equipment. Houses had not been built. Manufacturers had been unable to expand. Second, the government had sold billions of dollars' worth of bonds to finance the war effort. The immediate future would bring inflation, not deflation.

Clark conceded that Crerar might have a point but added that we "must get the economy up to a higher plateau." Does that mean a measure of inflation, Crerar asked? After a moment's hesitation, Clark replied, "I think perhaps it would not hurt." After pondering this conversation over the weekend, Crerar called a broker and sold the $15,000 in government bonds that he had accumulated during the war; he invested the proceeds in equities "and started from there to build up an estate."[11]

In other words, the Family Allowance scheme had been introduced partly to help deal with a projected economic difficulty, which never occurred. The Canadian economy began a fifteen-year boom, which Crerar had predicted in his conversation with Clark.

Things may have happened that way, though Crerar's account suffers from some misplaced emphasis. What he had described as a minor attraction – the political gain to be achieved – was not at all inconsequential to W.L. Mackenzie King and younger, reform-minded colleagues, watching with alarm the growing appeal of the CCF in 1943. But his account does provide an economic rationalization that agrees with what we know of the ideas of Clifford Clark and the Department of Finance at the end of the war.

He harked back to the years of the Second World War frequently in his correspondence. These had offered him the most intense, exciting, and rewarding political experience of his life, whatever his public reputation. And like most old men, Crerar was little impressed with those who came afterward. He was particularly incensed by the complaints of politicians about their demanding schedules. In a typical outburst, he recalled for journalist Michael Barkway that he had been simultaneously minister of mines and resources, deputy chairman of the Cabinet War Committee, and a member of Treasury Board and of two or three other active committees. After Lapointe's death, he filled in for King as chairman of cabinet during the prime minister's absence. "It was a twelve to fourteen hour-a-day job and colleagues like Howe, Ralston, and Ilsley were working harder than I was ... When I see Trudeau today with an official family of around thirty, costing in salaries alone several hundreds of thousands a year, and Ministers with their Parliamentary Secretaries and Executive Assistants, complaining of the load they are carrying – well it makes me laugh ... and then it makes me angry."[12] It was all an inevitable consequence, he grumbled, of the government's trying to be all things to all citizens.

His last three years were spent quietly. He sent few letters, and his daughter, Dorothy, replied to some inquiries from old friends asking how "T.A." was getting along. Even so, he had not been completely forgotten. In 1974, he was appointed a companion of the Order of Canada, the first politician to be so honoured. He died peacefully on 11 April 1975, in his ninety-ninth year. Editorial comment and obituaries emphasized his early years with the agrarian movement, the creation of United Grain Growers, and his lengthy service in federal cabinets. T.A. Crerar would have been most pleased that many of the commentators seemed bemused that in a century of such rapid change a man in public life for sixty years never felt compelled or tempted to change his principles.

Notes

CHAPTER ONE

1 Information on Crerar's early life came from several sources: Queen's University Archives (hereafter QUA), Kingston, Ontario; Crerar Papers (hereafter CP), (Boxes) 6 and 11; CP 41, Crerar to Sgt. Wm. Crerar, 29 Jan. 1918; *Russell Banner*; and CP 172, "The Story of Tom Crerar," a personal interview by Hopkins Moorhouse, Feb. 1916.

2 CP 11.

3 *Russell Banner*, 8 Sept. 1906.

4 CP 172, Moorhouse, "Story."

5 In all the massive Crerar Papers there is only one letter to his wife, written shortly after their marriage. Crerar guarded his privacy, and it is only in his letters to close friends that one finds references to Jessie Crerar, but they were always full of affection and concern.

6 United Grain Growers (hereafter UGG) Library, Winnipeg, Board of Directors Minutes, vol. 1.

7 CP 11, circular dated 15 June 1907 and printed on the stationery of the Russell Farmers' Elevator Company.

8 Ibid., Partridge to Crerar, 15 May 1907, also 4 July 1907.

9 Ibid., 27 June 1907.

10 UGG, Board Minutes, 16 July 1907; Colquette, *The First Fifty Years* (Winnipeg, 1957), 58–62.

11 Grain Growers' Grain Company (hereafter GGGC), Annual Report, 1908.

12 UGG, Board Minutes, vol. 1; CP 11, Crerar to E.P. St. John, 21 Aug. 1909.

13 GGGC, Annual Report, 1908.

14 Ibid., 1909.

15 Ibid.

16 CP 11, Kennedy to Crerar, 26 Aug. 1909.

17 GGGC, Annual Report, 1910.

18 CP 11, Crerar to St. John, 21 Aug. 1909.

19 CP 3, Crerar to George Armstrong, 19 June 1912.

20 Ibid.

21 Colquette, *First*, chap. 15, recounts the details of these events.

22 *Grain Growers' Guide*, letter from William Moffat, 26 June 1912.

23 CP 12, Crerar to Sidney Graham, 28 June 1912.

24 GGGC, Annual Report, 1912.

25 *Grain Growers' Guide*, 24 July 1912.

26 GGGC, UGG, Minutes of Board of Directors, passim. See also CP 29, Crerar to Partridge, 15 Sept. 1916, and reply.

27 CP 12, Crerar to Graham, 28 June 1912.

28 CP 11. This file contains Crerar's early ideas on elevators.

29 For details, see Colquette, *First*, chap. 13.

30 Public Archives of Manitoba (hereafter PAM), Winnipeg, Roblin Papers, Crerar to Roblin, 13 May 1912; CP 12, Roblin to Crerar, 8 June 1912.

31 Roblin Papers, Crerar to Roblin, 2 July 1912.

32 CP 12, Crerar to R.J. Henderson, Manager of the Terminal Elevator, 25 Nov. 1912.

33 CP 15, Crerar to George Finch, Lunham & Moore, 27 Aug. 1913; CP 16, Crerar to Charles A. Robinson, Produce Exchange, N.Y., 19 Nov. 1913.

34 GGGC, Annual Report, 1913.

35 CP 16, John Appleton to Crerar, 28 Nov. 1913.

36 CP 12, Shipton, Anderson and Company to Crerar, 1 July 1911; Crerar to Springman, 31 July 1914.

37 CP 16, Crerar to Springman, 19 Nov. 1913; CP 18, passim.

38 CP 18, Crerar to Springman, 28 April 1914.

39 Ibid., Aide Memoire.

40 CP 105, Crerar to Dunning, 24 Sept. 1914; QUA, Dunning Papers, file 1, Dunning to Chipman, 19 Dec. 1914; CP 28, Crerar to Springman, 30 May 1916; CP 17, Crerar to Murdo Cameron, 4 Feb. 1914.

41 See, for example, CP 18, Crerar to John Evans, 21 April 1914.

42 CP 24, Crerar to Springman, 12 July 1915.

43 Ibid.

44 CP 24, Springman to Crerar, 11 Aug. 1915.

45 Ibid.

46 CP 25, Crerar to Springman, 2 Sept. 1915.

47 CP 14, W.C. Clark to Crerar, 15 Nov. 1915.

48 Ibid., Crerar to Clark, 16 Nov. 1915.

49 Colquette, *First*, gives a fair account of the negotiations.

50 CP 29, Crerar to Rice-Jones, 16 Dec. 1916; CP 31, Crerar to Wood, 27 Dec. 1916.

51 CP 33, O'Donohoe to Crerar, 8 March 1917.

52 CP 20, Crerar to W.C. Good, 20 Sept. 1914.

271 Notes to pages 24–34

53 CP 13, Crerar to W.C. Good, 20 Sept. 1914.
54 Crerar to Manitoba Grain Growers' Association, in *Grain Growers' Guide*, 3 June 1914.
55 UGG, Board Minutes, 17 July 1916.
56 Ibid., 18 July 1911, 24 Sept. 1915, 13 Dec. 1916.
57 A comprehensive and detailed account of the creation and work of the board may be found in C.F. Wilson, *A Century of Canadian Grain* (Saskatoon, 1978), chap. 5.

CHAPTER TWO

1 CP 11, Crerar to H.P. Hamilton, 18 Nov. 1909.
2 CP 13, Crerar to Louis Post, 30 Jan. 1913.
3 CP 17, Crerar to Cowan, 17 Jan. 1914; CP 32, Crerar to Grose, 7 Feb. 1917.
4 CP 15, Crerar to F.J Dixon, 20 Aug. 1913; CP 19, passim; CP 20, Crerar to J.W. Scallion, 3 Oct. 1914.
5 CP 4, Notice, 20 Oct. 1912; CP 20, 6 Oct. 1914; *Round Table*, 3 (1912–13), 482, 489.
6 CP 93, Crerar to Tregillus, 4 Nov. 1912.
7 CP 11, Crerar to Vivian, 21 Oct. 1910.
8 Ibid., Crerar to J.M. Murray MacDonald, London, 19 Dec. 1910.
9 CP 28, Crerar to Editor, *Winnipeg Tribune*, 7 April 1916.
10 The fullest account remains W.L. Morton, *The Progressive Movement in Canada* (Toronto, 1950); but see also G.A. Friesen, *A History of the Canadian Prairies* (Toronto, 1984), for a shorter account.
11 CP 12, Crerar to Green, 7 Feb. 1912.
12 CP 17, Crerar to Duncan Stewart, 20 Feb. 1914; CP 21, Crerar to H.B. Cowan, 18 Dec. 1914.
13 *Canadian Annual Review* (hereafter *CAR*), 1917, 40, reporting on the convention of the Manitoba Grain Growers' Association, 10–12 Jan. 1917.
14 CP 14, Crerar to Meighen, 7 May 1913; see, for example, CP 25, Rogers to Crerar, telegram, 14 Oct. 1915; Crerar to Rogers, 19 Oct. 1915.
15 CP 12, Crerar to A. Garnet, 3 July 1912; CP 17, Crerar to Cowan, 6 Jan. 1914.
16 CP 33, Kennedy to Crerar, 22 March 1917.
17 Copy in CP 32.
18 CP 30, Crerar to Cowan, 25 Oct. 1916; CP 33, Cameron to Crerar, 16 March 1917.
19 CP 34, Laurier to Crerar, 10 April 1917; Crerar to Laurier, 18 April 1917.
20 CP 32, Crerar to Rice-Jones, telegram, 19 Feb. 1917.
21 CP 34, Crerar to MacMaster, 18 May 1917.

CHAPTER THREE

1 CP 34, Crerar to Murray, 30 May 1917; Kennedy to Crerar, 31 May 1917; CP 35, Collyer to Crerar, 17 June 1917. Collyer was a director of the GGGC.

2 CP 35, Crerar to Bain, 20 June 1917.

3 University of Manitoba Archives (hereafter UMA), Dafoe Papers, Box 4, Dafoe to Sifton, 27 June 1917.

4 CP 35, Crerar to Doig, 13 July 1917.

5 Ibid., Morrison to Crerar, 27 July 1917; Waldron to Crerar, 28 July 1917.

6 CP 36, Crerar to Waldron, 3 Aug. 1917.

7 Ibid., Wood to Crerar, 4 Aug. 1917.

8 Ibid., 36, Crerar to Wood, 2 Aug. 1917; and on conscription, Crerar to Bain, 3 Aug. 1917.

9 Dafoe Papers, Dafoe to Graham, 30 July 1917.

10 *CAR*, 1917, 575–7; *Manitoba Free Press*, 10, 17 Aug. 1917; David J. Hall, *Clifford Sifton*, II (Vancouver, 1981), 286.

11 CP 36, Crerar to Glen, 17 Aug 1917; Borden to Crerar, telegram, 15 Aug. 1917.

12 For full accounts see Henry Borden, ed., *Robert Laird Borden: His Memoirs*, II (Toronto, 1938); Roger Graham, *Arthur Meighen*, I (Toronto, 1960); Hall, *Sifton*, II; English, *The Decline of Politics* (Toronto, 1977); and *CAR*, 1917.

13 Saskatchewan Archives Board (hereafter SAB), Calder Reminiscences, 121.

14 H. Borden, ed., *Borden: Memoirs*, II, 742; and R. Craig Brown, *Robert Laind Borden*, II (Toronto, 1980).

15 CP 36, Crerar to Glen, 27 Aug. 1917.

16 Ibid., Crerar to Cowan, 27 Aug. 1917.

17 Ibid., Crerar to Glen, 6 Sept. 1917.

18 NA, Meighen Papers, vol. 2, Pitblado to Meighen, 1 Oct. 1917.

19 CP 99, Crerar to Cameron, 8 Nov. 1957; SAB, Calder Reminiscences, 123–6.

20 H. Borden, ed., *Borden: Memoirs*, II, 759; SAB, Calder Reminiscences, 131–3.

21 King, *Diary* (Toronto, 1973), 9 Oct. 1917.

22 CAR, 1917, citing *Manitoba Free Press*; Dafoe Papers, Box 1, Dafoe to Chisholm, 14 Oct. 1917.

23 CP 37, Crerar to Chipman, telegram, 14 Oct. 1917; Crerar to W.J. Short, 25 Oct. 1917; Crerar to Deachman, 15 Oct. 1917.

24 Cited in J.H. Thompson, *Harvests of War* (Toronto, 1978), 129; see also CP 37, Robert Dol, Marquette, to Crerar, 27 Oct. 1917.

25 CP 140, Crerar to Magill, n.d.; CP 37, Crerar to Springmann, 26 Oct. 1917.

CHAPTER FOUR

1 *Manitoba Free Press*, 23 Oct. 1917; Roger Graham, *Arthur Meighen*, I (Toronto, 1960), 185; *CAR*, 1917, 185.
2 CP 37, R.F. Chapman, Souris, to Crerar, 15 Oct. 1917.
3 Ibid., Crerar to C.B. Piper, 26 Oct. 1917.
4 Ibid., Crerar to W.J. Short, 25 Oct. 1917; Crerar to J.G. Rutherford, 26 Oct. 1917.
5 CP 38, To the Electors of Marquette, 26 Nov. 1917.
6 CP 36, Crerar to Rutherford, 26 Oct. 1917.
7 CP 161, Memorandum to Council, 10 Nov. 1917. Administrative tribunals were set up across the country to hear and decide on requests for exemption from conscription. Many of the tribunals themselves drew criticism.
8 QUA, Dexter Papers, vol. 13, Memorandum re: Conscription; CP 38, Crerar to Valentine Winkler, Minister of Agriculture, Manitoba, 26 Nov. 1917; CP 39, Crerar to Reynolds, 26 Nov. 1917.
9 CP 38, Crerar to O'Donohoe, 9 and 19 Nov. 1917.
10 Ibid., Crerar to Capt. C.E. Flett, 26 Nov. 1917; Crerar to Reynolds, 26 Nov. 1917; J.L. Granatstein and Hitsman, *Broken Promises* (Toronto, 1977), 86 and passim.
11 *Labor News*, 4 Dec. 1917; CP 39, Weir to Crerar, 1 Dec. 1917; Rice-Jones to Crerar, 3 Dec. 1917; and *Calgary Herald*, 6 Dec. 1917.
12 CP 39, Crerar to Wood, 10 Dec. 1917; Crerar to Rice-Jones, 14 Dec. 1917.
13 Ibid., Letters of thanks; Crerar to Lockhart, 24 Dec 1917; Crerar to Glen, 31 Dec 1917; J.H. Thompson, *Harvests of War* (Toronto, 1978), 141.
14 Henry Borden, ed., *Robert Laird Borden: His Memoirs*. II (Toronto, 1938), 753; Roger Graham, *Arthur Meighen*, I (Toronto, 1960), 176.
15 CP 39, Tarr to Crerar, 18 Dec. 1917; H.L. Montgomery to Crerar, 20 Dec. 1917; Lambert to Crerar,? Dec. 1917.
16 CP 40, King to Crerar, 18 Dec. 1917.
17 Ibid., Burnell to Crerar, 5 Jan. 1918; CP 43, Crerar to Burnell, 20 Feb. 1918.
18 CP 42, Crerar to W.W. Wilson, 8 Jan. 1918.
19 CP 47, Crerar to Hudson, 29 April 1918.
20 QUA, Chipman Papers, Box 1, Chipman to Crerar, 30 Jan. 1918; CP 41, Crerar to Thornton, 28 Jan. 1918; CP 43, Crerar to Fowler, 18 Feb. 1918.
21 CP 40, Rice-Jones to Crerar, 4 Jan. 1918; CP 43, Crerar to Chipman, 11 Feb. 1918; CP 148, passim; Chipman Papers, Box 1, Crerar to Chipman, 21 Feb. 1918.
22 CP 44, Crerar to Wood, 15 March 1918.
23 Chipman Papers, Box 1, Crerar to Chipman, 21 Feb. 1918.
24 Ibid.

25 H. Borden, ed., *Borden: Memoirs*, II, 801–3.

26 CP 47, Crerar to Chipman, 18 April 1918; CP 49, Crerar to Kennedy,
   30 May 1918; CP 161, Memorandum to Cabinet, 16 May 1918.

27 CP 49, Crerar to Kennedy, 30 May 1918; CP 50, Crerar to Cowan,
   29 May 1918.

28 CP 50, Chipman to Crerar, 3 June 1918; Lambert to Crerar, 11 June 1918.

29 CP 54, Crerar to Chipman, 25 Sept. 1918; CP 148, Crerar to C.J. Doherty,
   2 Oct. 1918; CP 55, Crerar to D.W. Buchan, 17 Oct. 1918; Margaret
   Prang, *Newton Rowell* (Toronto, 1975), 268.

30 CP 55, Crerar to Chipman, 17 Oct. 1918; CP 56, Crerar to Murray,
   4 Nov. 1918.

31 CP 37, Springmann to Crerar, 30 Oct. 1917; CP 40, Crerar to Springmann, 5 Jan. 1918.

32 CP 55, Crerar to Rice-Jones, 30 Sept. 1918; Rice-Jones to Crerar, 12 Oct.
   1918.

33 CP 5, Crerar to Lambert, 19 Oct. 1918; Crerar to Wood, 25 Oct. 1918.

34 CP 46, Crerar to Wood, 3 April 1918; QUA, Lambert Papers, Box 1,
   Crerar to Lambert, 19 Oct. 1918; ibid., Lambert to Wood, Oct. 1918.

35 H. Borden, ed., *Borden: Memoirs*, II, 860, 862.

36 Prang, *Rowell*, 286; CP 56, Crerar to White, 22 Nov. 1918; CP 60, Crerar
   to Burford, 11 March 1919.

37 *The Farmers' Platform: A New National Policy for Canada*, Winnipeg,
   29 Nov. 1918.

38 Chipman Papers, Box 1, Crerar to Chipman, 8 March 1919; CP 67,
   Crerar to Wood, 28 March 1919.

39 Lambert Papers, Box 1, Lambert to Crerar, 5 April 1919; Crerar to Lambert, 10 April 1919.

40 CP 58, Crerar to Frank Fowler, 9 Jan. 1919; Chipman Papers, Box 1,
   Crerar to Chipman, 16 Jan. 1919; Crerar to Chipman, 17 Feb. 1919;
   Crerar to Chipman, 10 April 1919.

41 Chipman Papers, Box 1, Crerar to Chipman, 28 March 1919; Chipman
   to Crerar, 5 April 1919.

42 CP 60, Crerar to Rice-Jones, 28 March 1919; CP 61, Crerar to Murray,
   24 April 1919.

43 H. Borden, ed., *Borden: Memoirs*, II, 966.

44 CP 13, Crerar to Borden, 4 June 1919; Borden to Crerar, 4 June 1919.

45 Cited approvingly by the *Victoria Times*, 6 June 1919.

CHAPTER FIVE

1 CP 63, Crerar to F.S. Jacobs, 28 June 1919; Dafoe Papers, Box 4, Dafoe
  to Sifton, 21 July 1919; for a fuller account see Box 1, Dafoe to Augus-
  tus Bridle, 14 June 1921.

2 Dafoe Papers, Box 4, Dafoe to Bridle, 14 June 1921; copy of a Lapointe speech in CP 66, dated 18 Oct. 1919.

3 CP 67, Crerar to Bureau, 19 Jan. 1920.

4 CP 66, Crerar to Bowman, 5 Dec. 1919; CP 69, Crerar to C.T. Watkins, 22 April 1920.

5 CP 74, Crerar to David Douglas, 4 Jan. 1921; Canada, House of Commons, *Debates*, 1919, 1165–6; CP 66, Crerar to J.W. Scallion, 3 Nov. 1919.

6 CP 66, Crerar to A.D Cartwright (son of Sir Richard, the doctrinaire free trader), 31 Dec. 1919; *Grain Growers' Guide*, 17 Sept. 1919; 11 June 1919.

7 cp 63, Crerar to Dr T.A. Patrick, 20 June 1919; Crerar to John Kennedy, 23 June 1919; CP 67, copy of interview with the *Post*.

8 CP 134, Crerar to A.G. Sinclair, 17 June 1919; CP 63, Crerar to F.S. Jacobs, 28 June 1919.

9 CP 63, Crerar to Hudson, 21 June 1919; Lambert to Crerar, 25 June 1919; Crerar to Jacobs, 28 June 1919; CP 64, Crerar to Michael Clark, 18 July 1919; Dafoe Papers, Box 4, Dafoe to Sifton, 21 July 1919.

10 CP 64, Murphy to Crerar, 18 July 1919; CP 65, Roebuck to Crerar, 25 July 1919; CP 64, Crerar to Haydon, 22 July 1919.

11 Dafoe Papers, Box 4, Dafoe to Sifton, 24 July 1919.

12 UGG, Board of Directors Minutes, vol. 4; Executive Committee Minutes, 21 Dec. 1920.

13 CP 64, Crerar to Allison Glen, 30 Aug. 1919.

14 A good survey is included in CP 65, Lambert to Crerar, 22 Sept. 1919.

15 Lambert Papers, Box 1, Crerar to Lambert, 7 Oct. 1919; CP 66, Crerar to Charles Stewart, 15 Nov. 1919.

16 CP 71, Crerar to T.W. Caldwell, 28 Sept. 1919.

17 17 CP 66, Chipman to Crerar, 17 Dec. 19, provides the details.

18 CP 65, Crerar to Morrison, 4 Sept. 1919.

19 Ibid., Crerar to W.F. MacLean (of the *Toronto World*), 31 Oct. 1919; Crerar to J.L. Brown, 31 Oct. 1919.

20 CP 66, Morrison to Crerar, 2 Nov. 1919.

21 *CAR*, 1919, 610.

22 Ibid., 390.

23 There is a good account of the meeting in L.A. Wood, *Farmers in Politics* (Toronto, 1924), 352ff.

24 See W.K. Rolph, *Henry Wise Wood of Alberta* (Toronto, 1950), 89–90.

25 A copy of Crerar's speech is in CP 67.

26 CP 68, Crerar to Chipman, 20 March 1920.

27 Ibid., Crerar to Johnson, 8 March 1920; Crerar to Chipman, 10 March 1920; CP 69, Crerar to Johnson, 6 May 1920.

28 CP 153, Crerar to Wood, 30 Jan. 1920; Wood to Crerar, 9 Feb. 1920; Crerar to Wood, 13 Feb. 1920.

276 Notes to pages 74–80

29 See, for example, CP 69, Crerar to Morrison, 7, 28 May 1920; Crerar to Drury, 12 May 1920.

30 Ibid., Lambert to Crerar, 3 May 1920; CP 70, Lambert to Crerar, 3 June 1920; Crerar to Thomson, 17 July 1920.

31 CP 70, Crerar to Meighen, 10 July 1920; Meighen to Crerar, 14 July 1920.

32 CP 71, Crerar to Morrison, 4 Oct. 1920; Crerar to Drury, 4 Oct. 1920.

33 Ibid., Murphy to Crerar, 25 Oct. 1920; Crerar to Drury, 27 Oct. 1920; CP 72, Crerar to Murphy, 13 Nov. 1920.

34 *CAR*, 1920, 500.

35 See, for example, NA, Sifton Papers, Dafoe to Sifton, 19 Nov. 1920.

36 CP 153, "Memorandum re. H.W. Wood," private, 4; CP 73, Chipman to Crerar, 20 Dec. 1920 (enclosing letter from King).

37 *Maclean's Magazine*, 1 Feb. 1921; CP 97, Crerar to Cameron, 24 Jan. 1921.

38 CP 77, Crerar to Cowan, 16 May 1921.

39 The issue is discussed in CP 76, Crerar to Lambert, 3 March 1921; CP 110, Murray to Crerar, 14 April 1921; Dafoe Papers, Box 4, Dafoe to Sifton, 2 May 1921; CP 77, Crerar to J.B. Livesay (General Manager of the Canadian Press), 9, 19 May 1921, Livesay to Crerar, 20 May 1921; and, especially, CP 78, Crerar to J.K. Munro (*Toronto Telegram* and political columnist for *Maclean's Magazine*, 8 July 1921.

40 Dafoe Papers, Box 4, Dafoe to Sifton, 30 June 1921.

41 *CAR*, 1921, 367; CP 97, Crerar to Cameron, 2 July 1921; CP 78, Crerar to Gardiner, 4 July 1921; CP 77, Crerar to Morrison, 30 June 1921.

42 Rolph, *Henry Wise Wood*, 105.

43 NA, Cameron Papers, vol. 33, Crerar to Cameron, 19 July 1921.

44 CP 78, Crerar to Brownlee, 20 July 1921; *Free Press*, 20 July 1921.

45 Cameron Papers, vol. 33, Crerar to Cameron, 20 Sept. 1921.

46 CP 107, Crerar to Stewart Lyon (editor of the *Toronto Globe*), 9 Dec. 1921; CP 79, Crerar to Musselman, 5 Jan. 1922; CP 125, Crerar to Morrison, 29 Nov. 1921. Many sources state that the Progressives won sixty-four seats in the 1921 election. I count A.B. Hudson (officially described as an Independent Liberal) as a Progressive; he was Crerar's closest adviser in the House, always voted with the Progressives, and was recognized by all as a colleague of Crerar's.

47 CP 110, Crerar to Good, 23 Jan. 1954.

48 CP 105, Memorandum for Dexter, 25 March 1955.

CHAPTER SIX

1 See F.W. Gibson, *Cabinet Formation* (Ottawa, 1970), chap. 2; *King Diary* (Toronto, 1973), 13 Sept. 1921.

2 CP 137, Crerar to John Stevenson, n.d.

3 CP 107, Crerar to Lyon, 9 Dec. 1921; Dafoe Papers, Box 4, Dafoe to Sifton, 7 Dec. 1921; CP 97, Cameron to Crerar, 10 Dec. 1921.

4 Dafoe Papers, Box 4, Dafoe to Sifton, 31 Dec. 1921.

5 Ibid., Sifton to Dafoe, 8 Dec. 1921; CP 78, Dafoe to Crerar, same date.

6 CP 152, Wayling to Crerar, 8 Dec. 1921.

7 CP 97, Cameron to Crerar, 10 Dec. 1921; *King Diary*, 8, 13 Dec. 1921.

8 CP 113, Crerar to Haydon, 9 Dec. 1921; see also Gibson, *Cabinet Formation*, 77.

9 CP 97, Cameron to Crerar, coded telegram, 10 Dec. 1921.

10 Cameron Papers, vol. 33, Crerar to Cameron, 10 Dec. 1921.

11 Ibid., Cameron to Crerar, 12 Dec. 1921.

12 Ibid., Cameron to Crerar, 13 Dec. 1921; CP 78, Morrison to Crerar, 13 Dec. 1921; Crerar to Morrison, 14 Dec. 1921; CP 110, Harvey Anderson (Toronto *Globe*) to Crerar, 15 Dec. 1921.

13 *King Diary*, 14 Dec. 1921.

14 Ibid., 14, 15 Dec. 1921.

15 Dafoe Papers, Box 4, Dafoe to Sifton, 19 Dec. 1921.

16 Lambert Papers, Box 1, Lambert to John Stevenson, 20 Dec. 1921.

17 Copy in CP 78.

18 Cited in Anthony Mardiros, *William Irvine* (Toronto, 1979), 116.

19 CP 78, Crerar to Hudson, telegram, 20 Dec. 1921; see also *King Diary*, 20 Dec. 1921.

20 *King Diary*, 21 Dec. 1921; see also NA, A.B. Hudson Papers, which contain a memoir of events.

21 CP 97, Cameron to Crerar, 23 Dec. 1921. The letter was awaiting Crerar when he arrived in Ottawa from Toronto.

22 *King Diary*, 23 Dec. 1921.

23 *Farmers Sun*, 21 Dec. 1921; CP 78, Crerar to Drury, 21 Dec. 1921; CP 96, Crerar to Caldwell, 6 Jan. 1922.

24 Lambert Papers, Box 1, Lambert to Atkinson, 31 Dec. 1921.

25 CP 96, Crerar to Caldwell, 6 Jan. 1922.

26 *King Diary*, 24, 28 Dec. 1921.

27 Cameron Papers, vol. 33, Cameron to Crerar, 28 Dec. 1921; Lambert Papers, Box 1, Lambert to Atkinson, 31 Dec. 1921; *Maclean's Magazine*, 1 Feb. 1922; Cameron Papers, vol 33, Crerar to Cameron, 19 Jan. 1922.

28 W.C. Good, *Farmer Citizen* (Toronto, 1958), 126.

29 Cited in Mardiros, *William Irvine*, 117–18; *Grain Growers' Guide*, 17 Jan. 1922; *Canadian Forum* (Nov. 1923); Paul Sharp, *Agrarian Revolt in Western Canada* (New York, 1971), 155.

30 See *CAR*, 1922, 216; CP 107, Fielding to Crerar, 11 Jan. 1922.

31 CP 104, Crerar to Fred Davis, 19 Jan. 1922.

32 CP 105, memorandum for Dexter.

33 CP 104, Crerar to Davis, 19 Jan. 1922.

34 *CAR*, 1922, 227.

35 *Maclean's Magazine*, 1 April 1922.

36 The issue is treated fully in T.D. Regehr, *The Canadian Northern Railway* (Toronto, 1976); and more succinctly in G.A. Friesen, *The Canadian Prairies* (Toronto, 1984); CP 139, Crerar to Arthur Doig, 29 March 1922.

37 Dafoe Papers, Box 4, Dafoe to Sifton, 30 March, 8 June 1922; CP 120, Crerar to Lambert, 9 May 1922.

38 CP 79, Crerar to Dafoe, 26 June 1922; Chipman Papers, Box 1, Crerar to Chipman, 27 June 1922.

39 *CAR*, 1922, 217; W.K. Rolph, *Henry Wise Wood* (Toronto, 1950), 132.

40 Lambert Papers, Box 1, Crerar to Lambert, 23 March 1922; CP 125, Crerar to Murray, 1 April 1922.

41 Chipman Papers, Box 1, Crerar to Chipman, 11 April 1922.

42 CP 125, Crerar to Murray, 31 March 1922.

43 See G. Ramsay Cook, *The Politics of John W. Dafoe and the Free Press* (Toronto, 1963), 121.

44 Dunning to Motherwell, 22 May 1922, in David Smith, *Prairie Liberalism* (Toronto, 1975), 180; McPhail to Violet McNaughton, 8 Aug. 1922, in H.A. Innis, *The Diary of A.J. McPhail* (Toronto, 1947), 37; Dafoe Papers, Box 3, Dafoe to Maclean, 9 Sept. 1922.

45 Cited in Smith, *Prairie Liberalism*, 100.

46 Chipman Papers, Box 1, Chipman to Crerar, 23 March 1922; Crerar to Chipman, 5 May 1922; Dafoe Papers, Box 4, Dafoe to Sifton, 5 July 1922; John Kendle, *John Bracken: A Political Biography* (Toronto, 1929).

47 *Maclean's Magazine*, 1 June 1922; CP 133, Roebuck to Crerar, 19 June 1922.

48 *King Diary*, 22, 23 Sept. 1922; Cameron Papers, vol. 7, Hudson to Cameron, 17 Oct. 1922.

49 Cameron Papers, vol. 33, Crerar to Cameron, 11 Aug. 1922.

50 Ibid., Crerar to Cameron, 21 Oct. 1922.

51 Sifton Papers, 163251, Dafoe to Sifton, 9 Nov. 1922. Chapter 7, below, ends with an analysis of Crerar's letter of resignation.

CHAPTER SEVEN

1 *King Diary* (Toronto, 1923), 11 Nov. 1922; *Maclean's Magazine*, 1 Dec. 1922; Cameron Papers, Crerar to Cameron, 30 Nov. 1922.

2 UGG, Board Minutes, 12 Oct. 1922.

3 CP 4, Crerar to Cameron, 6 Nov. 1922; Dafoe Papers, Box 4, Dafoe to Sifton, 2 Nov. 1922; CP 105, Crerar to Drury, 9 Dec. 1922.

4 UGG, Board Minutes, 4 Jan, 24 Sept. 1923.

5 CP 101, Crerar to W.G. Gates, 26 Feb. 1923; Dafoe Papers, Box 4, Dafoe to Sifton, 12 March 1923.

6 Cameron Papers, vol. 33, Crerar to Cameron, 12 Oct. 1923; CP 79, Crerar to Cameron, 28 Nov. 1923.

7 CP 79, Massey to Crerar, 10 Sept. 1924, Crerar to Massey, 13 Oct. 1924; CP 93, Aide-Memoire, 11 Oct. 1924.

8 CP 94, Crerar to Borden, 16 Sept. 1925; CP 79, Crerar to L.H. Jelliff (a Progressive candidate), 2 Oct. 1925; UGG, Board Minutes, 7 Oct. 1925.

9 *King Diary,* 1 Nov. 1922.

10 The *Grain Growers' Guide* covered his tour throughout 1923.

11 UGG, Board Minutes, 4 July 1923; see also *Grain Growers' Guide* for July and August 1923.

12 C.A. Wilson, *A Century of Canadian Grain* (Saskatoon, 1978), chap. 4.

13 PAM, R.A.C. Manning Papers, f. 146, contains a prospectus.

14 See the introduction to Arthur Johnson, *Breaking the Banks* (Toronto, 1986).

15 CP 97, Cameron to Crerar, 29 May 1923.

16 CP 152, Crerar to Wayling, 11 Sept. 1923.

17 CP 134, Crerar to Robb, 30 Jan. 1924.

18 I am greatly indebted to Mr James Daschuk, a graduate student at the University of Manitoba, who scoured the newspapers for accounts of the Home Bank affair.

19 *Grain Growers' Guide* and the *Toronto Globe* gave considerable space to the bank story throughout October 1923 and May 1924, during the hearings of the McKeown Commission in Winnipeg. See also an important letter of Crerar to William Southam (CP 134, 18 Feb. 1925), in which Crerar complains of attacks on him in the *Winnipeg Tribune* and recapitulates his testimony.

20 CP 134, Crerar to Santhom, 18 Feb. 1925.

21 Ibid., Crerar to Symington, 19 Feb. 1925; Symington to Crerar, 24 Feb. 1925.

22 CP 79, Crerar to Caldwell, 9. Nov 1922; Lambert Papers, Box 1, Lambert to Morrison, 14 Nov. 1922; Sifton Papers, 163251 – 96 to 100, Dafoe to Sifton, 9 Nov. 1922.

23 All intervening citations are from CP 79, Crerar to Caldwell, 9 Nov. 1922.

24 Lambert Papers, Box 1, Lambert to Morrison, 14 Nov. 1922.

CHAPTER EIGHT

1 See, for example, *Round Table,* 13 (1922–23), 622.

2 Sifton Papers, 163251, 108–12, Dafoe to Sifton, 10 Dec. 1922.

3 CP 136, Crerar to Sifton, 8 Feb. 1923.

4 Dafoe Papers, Box 4, Dafoe to Sifton, 12 Feb. 1923; CP 136, Dafoe to Sifton, 1 March 1923.

5 Cameron Papers, vol. 33, Crerar to Cameron, 6 Nov. 1923.

6 CP 94, Crerar to H.W. Baldwin, 29 May 1923; and see especially a long letter to Sir Robert Borden setting out his views in late 1923 in CP 95, Crerar to Borden, n.d.

7 CP 123, Crerar to McMaster, 24 Jan. 1923.

8 CP 120, Crerar to Lapointe, 28 Feb. 1923.

9 CP 79, Crerar to Cameron, 29 Dec. 1924.

10 Cameron Papers, vol. 33, Crerar to Cameron, 20 Feb. 1923; ibid., vol. 7, Cameron to Fielding, 26 Feb. 1923; Fielding to Cameron, 1 March 1923; NA, Murphy Papers, vol. 6, Crerar to Murphy, 26 July 1923; CP 96, Crerar to Cahill, 17 March 1923; CP 123, Crerar to McMaster, 24 Jan. 1923.

11 CP 152, Wayling to Crerar, 10 Jan. 1923; NA, Loring Christie Papers, file 6–8, Dafoe to Christie, 17 Jan. 1923; Crerar to Christie, 10 Feb. 1923; Christie to Crerar, 13 Feb. 1923.

12 CP 79, Crerar to Barnes, private and confidential, 4 March 1925.

13 Cameron Papers, vol. 33, Crerar to Cameron, 30 Nov. 1922.

14 QUA, Dunning Papers, file 2, Crerar to Dunning, 28 Dec. 1922; CP 110, Crerar to Good, 24 Feb. 1923.

15 CP 107, Crerar to Forke, 3, 12 March 1923.

16 King Diary (Toronto, 1973), 10 March 1923; Dafoe Papers, Box 4, Dafoe to Sifton, 12 March 1923; CP 79, Crerar to Hudson, 14 March 1923.

17 Maclean's Magazine, 1 Feb 1924.

18 CP 4, Crerar to Morrison, 20 July 1923; CP 125, same to same, 30 Oct. 1923.

19 H. Blair Neatby, William Lyon Mackenzie King, II, The Lonely Heights (Toronto, 1963), 12–14.

20 King Diary, 5 Dec. 1923.

21 CP 97, Cameron to Crerar, 11 Dec. 1923; Cameron Papers, vol. 7, Cameron to Lapointe, 17 Dec. 1923; vol. 33, Crerar to Cameron, 21 Dec. 1923. It never seemed to occur to Crerar that adding two Winnipeggers to the cabinet at one time might cause difficulties.

22 King Diary, 26, 27 Dec. 1923; 6 Jan. 1924.

23 CP 97, Lyon to Cameron, 9 Jan. 1924.

24 King Diary, 11 Jan. 1924. It seems difficult to comprehend King's remark that Crerar was not a good administrator, given his track record.

25 Ibid.

26 CP 154 contains a copy of Crerar's press statement.

27 Cameron Papers, vol. 33, Crerar to Cameron, 2 Jan. 1928.

28 CP 138, Thornton to Crerar, 10 March 1924; Crerar to Thornton, 17 March 1924; CP 135, Crerar to Senator J.G. Turriff, 6 June 1924.

29 CP 110, Crerar to Allison Glen, 17 April 1924.

30 *Maclean's Magazine*, 1 April 1924.

31 *Russell Banner*, 22 May 1924.

32 *Maclean's*, 15 May 1924.

33 Cameron Papers, vol. 33, Crerar to Cameron, 1 Aug. 1924. Crerar's criticism of Forke was somewhat unfair. It was hardly the fault of the new Progressive leader that the party was fundamentally and irreconcilably divided.

34 CP 79, Crerar to Forke, 27 Jan. 1925.

35 Ibid., Crerar to Glen, 7 March 1925; Chipman Papers, vol. 1, Crerar to Chipman, 15 May 1925 and 23 June 1925.

36 CP 79, Crerar to Cameron, 5 Aug. 1925.

37 Ibid., Crerar to Fred Johnston, 4 Sept. 1925.

38 *King Diary,* 8 July, 28 Aug. 1925.

39 UGG, Board Minutes, vol. 4, 7 Oct. 1925.

40 CP 97, Crerar to Cameron, 4 Sept. 1925.

41 CP 79, Crerar to Gordon Waldron, 29 Sept. 1925; CP 97, Crerar to Cameron, 26 Sept., 14 Oct. 1925.

42 CP 79, Crerar to Livesay, 31 Oct. 1925.

43 CP 97, Crerar to Cameron, 3 Nov. 1925. This long letter also includes the following analysis by Crerar.

44 Ibid.

CHAPTER NINE

1 CP 97, Crerar to Cameron, 7 Nov. 1925; Dafoe Papers, Box 2, Dafoe to Forke, 16 Nov. 1925.

2 CP 97, Crerar to Cameron, 28 Nov. 1925.

3 Dafoe Papers, Box 4, Dafoe to Sifton, 5 Dec. 1925.

4 Cited in H. Blain Neatby, *William Lyon Mackenzie King*, II, *The Lonely Heights* (Toronto, 1963), 99.

5 CP 119, Crerar to King, 5 June 1926; CP 137, Crerar to Stewart, 5 Jan. 1926.

6 CP 80, Crerar to Fred Johnston M.P., 11 Jan. 1926; Crerar to Forke, 18 Jan. 1926.

7 *King Diary* (Toronto, 1973), 29 Jan. 1926; Hudson Papers, vol. 2, 30 Jan. 1926; CP 97, Crerar to Cameron, 1 Feb. 1926.

8 *King Diary,* 6 Feb. 1926; Hudson Papers, vol. 2, telegram King to Hudson, 10 Feb. 1926; Dafoe Papers, Box 2, Dafoe to Forke, 15 Feb. 1926.

9 G.R. Cook, ed., *The Dafoe-Sifton Correspondence* (Ottawa, 1966), Dafoe to Sifton, 16 Feb. 1926; Hudson Papers, vol. 2, King to Hudson, 15 Feb. 1926.

10 CP 80, Crerar to Forke, 20 Feb. 1926.

11 See Neatby, *King*, II, 122–5, for details.

12 CP 119, Crerar to King, 16 April 1926; King to Crerar, 3 May 1926.

13 CP 80, Crerar to Allison Glen, 12 June 1926.

14 NA, Stevenson Papers, Box 1, file 1, Meighen to Stevenson, 8 June 1951.

15 CP 97, Crerar to Cameron, 29 June 1926.

16 PAM, Maybank Papers, Box 5, file 88.

17 CP 80, Crerar to Glen, 21 July 1926; Glen to Crerar, 23 July 1926; Crerar to Wm. Grayson (chairman in Marquette), 27 July 1926; Crerar to Brownlee, 24 July 1926; Crerar to Cameron, 28 July 1926.

18 CP 109, Crerar to Andrew Doig (an old friend in Marquette), 28 July 1926.

19 CP 80, Crerar to Cameron, 28 July 1926; NA, King Papers, vol. 130, King to Crerar, 19 Aug. 1926; CP 119, 14 Sept. 1926.

20 CP 104, Crerar to Andrew Doig, 28 July 1926.

21 CP 80, Crerar to Cameron, 15 Sept. 1926.

22 CP 107, Crerar to Forke, 17 Sept. 1926.

23 CP 121, Crerar to Morrison, n.d.

24 CP 97, Crerar to Cameron, 2 Oct. 1926.

25 H.A. Innis, ed., *The Diary of Andrew McPhail* (Toronto, 1940), 2 Feb. 1925, 75.

26 Chipman Papers, I, Crerar to Chipman, 17 Feb. 1925.

27 See, for example, CP 79, Crerar to Brownlee, 14 April 1925; CP 131, Crerar to C.W. Peterson of the *Farm and Ranch Review*, 14 Jan. 1926; and published addresses by Crerar on "Relations between UGG and the Pools," 25 Nov. 1926; Annual General Meeting of UGG in 1926 and "Grain Marketing, Buying and Selling," to the Winnipeg Banking Lecture Club, 31 March 1927.

28 See UGG, Board Minutes, 23 Nov. 1925; 4 Jan. 1926; 15 June 1926; 27 Sept. 1926; 26 Nov. 1926; 7 April 1927.

29 CP 154 contains his Notes on European Trip.

30 Ibid.

31 CP 84, Crerar to R.A. Love (a British importer), 8 April 1930.

32 CP 93, Crerar to Wood, 4 Dec. 1929; Wood to Crerar, 6 Dec. 1929.

33 CP 82, Crerar's notes on a telephone call from Premier John Bracken, 20 Feb. 1930.

34 Ibid., Memorandum for Prime Minister, 14 Feb. 1930; Crerar to Chipman, 21 Feb. 1930.

35 Ibid., Notes on Crerar's telephone call to Bracken, 21 Feb. 1930.

36 CP 93, Crerar to Love, 24 Feb. 1930.

37 CP 83, J.R. Murray to Crerar, 5 March 1930; CP 87, Crerar to King, 25 Nov. 1930; Cameron Papers, Box 15, Crerar to Cameron, 21 Sept. 1930.

38 CP 84, Crerar to Charlie ?, 7 April 1930.

39 Ibid., Crerar to F.J. Collier, 1 April 1930.

40 CP 100, Crerar to J.W. Ward, Secretary, C.C.A., 26 March 1928.

41 UGG, Board Minutes, 6 Jan. 1927; 7 April 1927.

42 CP contains one box labelled "financial papers," from which this information is taken; most of the material deals with the 1920s. See also CP 97, Crerar to Cameron, 25 May 1927; 27 June 1927.

43 CP, "financial papers"; CP 98, Cameron to Crerar, 7 Nov. 1927; 9 Dec. 1927; 12 Dec. 1927; Crerar to Cameron, 2 March 1928; Cameron Papers, vol. 14, Cameron to Timmins, 10 April 1928.

44 CP 136, G.W. Allen (of Great West) to Crerar, 10 May 1928; *Russell Banner*, 17 May 1928.

45 CP 97, Crerar to Cameron, 21 Dec. 1926; CP 99, Crerar to Cameron, 17 Feb. 1927; CP 137, Crerar to Symington, 15 March 1927.

46 CP 97, Cameron to Crerar, 22 May 1927; Crerar to Cameron, 1 April 1927.

47 Ibid., Crerar to Cameron, 1 April 1927.

48 CP 80, Crerar to Cameron, 21 Oct. 1927.

49 *King Diary*, 27 Feb. 1928; CP 133, King to Crerar, 11 July 1928; PAM, Bracken Papers, Box 20, King to Bracken, 7 July 1928.

50 *King Diary*, 1 May 1929.

51 PC 1272, 1928.

52 *King Diary*, 1 Nov. 1929.

53 Ibid.

54 Ibid., 2 Nov. 1929; 21 Nov. 1929; 22 Nov. 1929.

55 *King Diary*, 28, 29, 30 Nov. 1929; King Papers, vol. 160, Crerar to Dunning, 29 Nov. 1929; *King Diary*, 2, 3 Dec. 1929; *Toronto Globe*, 11 Dec. 1929.

56 *King Diary*, 30, 31 Dec. 1929.

57 CP 80, Cobb to Crerar, 7 Dec. 1929; Crerar to J.B. Mathews, 9 Dec. 1929.

CHAPTER TEN

1 *Toronto Globe*, 11 Dec. 1929.

2 CP 83, Crerar to Thornton, 27 March 1930.

3 Canada, House of Commons, *Debates*, 31 March 1930.

4 Details are in CP 83.

5 CP 81, Crerar to F.C. Mears, 21 Jan. 1930; King Papers, Crerar to King, 12 March 1930; CP 86, Crerar to Senator A.B. Copp, 5 June 1930.

6 *King Diary* (Toronto, 1973), 24, 25 April 1930; Dafoe Papers, Box 3, Dafoe to King, 22 April 1930.

7 For details, see H. Blain Neatby, *William Lyon Mackenzie King*, III, *Prism of Unity* (Toronto, 1976), chap. 16.

8 Cameron Papers, vol. 15, Crerar to Cameron, 3 April 1930.

9 *King Diary,* 23 April 1930; *Debates,* 10 March 1930.

10 *Debates,* 13, 15 May 1930; CP 86, Chipman to Crerar, 21 May 1930.

11 *King Diary,* 2 May 1930.

12 *Debates,* 12 May 1930.

13 *King Diary,* 30 June, 1 July 1930.

14 CP 86, Crerar to Cobb, 5 June 1930; Cobb's letter is in CP 85; CP 86, 23, 29 June 1930.

15 King Papers, vol. 72, King to Crerar, 29 July 1930.

16 *King Diary,* 1 Aug., 29 July 1930.

17 Dafoe Papers, Box 6, Dafoe to B.C. Nicholson (*Victoria Times*), 6 Aug. 1930.

18 Cameron Papers, vol. 33, Crerar to Cameron, 1 April 1927.

19 King Papers, vol. 184, Crerar to King, 5 Jan. 1931.

20 See, as a good example of this thinking, CP 98, Crerar to Cameron, 2 Nov. 1931.

21 King Papers, vol. 184, Crerar to King, 2 Sept. 1931.

22 See ibid., Crerar to King, 4 May 1931; King to Crerar, 23 May 1931; Crerar to King, 29 Jan. 1931; Crerar to King, 7 Oct. 1931; CP 119, King to Crerar, 9 Nov. 1931.

23 For details of the Beauharnois affair, see H. Blain Neatby, *William Lyon Mackenzie King,* II, *The Lonely Heights* (Toronto, 1963), and T.D. Regehr, *The Beauharnois Scandal* (Toronto, 1990), passim.

24 CP 98, Crerar to Cameron, 31 Aug. 1931.

25 King Papers, vol. 184, Crerar to King, 2 Sept. 1931.

26 Ibid., King to Crerar, 9 Nov. 1931.

27 CP 98, Crerar to Cameron, 31 Aug. 1931; CP 153, re Crerar's local activities; CP 88, Lapointe to Crerar, 31 Oct. 1931.

28 Cameron Papers, vol. 7, Cameron to Dafoe, 21 Dec. 1931; Dafoe to Cameron, 2 Jan. 1932.

29 Ibid., Dafoe to Cameron, 18 Jan. 1932.

30 There is a good account of the incident in the King Papers, vol. 190, Crerar to King, 23 Dec. 1932.

31 Cameron Papers, vol. 34, Crerar to Cameron, 4 July 1933, has many of the details.

32 King Papers, vol. 190, Crerar to King, 4 Jan. 1932.

33 Cameron Papers, vol. 34, Crerar to Cameron, 31 May 1932.

34 CP 98, Crerar to Cameron, 8 Aug. 1932.

35 Ibid., Crerar to Cameron, 19 Sept. 1932; CP 119, King to Crerar, 22 Aug. 1932; King Papers, vol. 190, Crerar to King, 22 Aug. 1932; Crerar to King, 23 Oct. 1932.

36 King Papers, vol. 190, Crerar to King, 4 Jan. 1932; Cameron Papers, vol. 34, Crerar to Cameron, 8 March 1932; CP 98, Crerar to Cameron, 8 Aug. 1932; Dafoe Papers, Box 2, Dafoe to Dexter, 16 Sept. 1932.

37 Enclosed in CP 124, Crerar to Massey, 23 Jan. 1932.

38 CP 119, King to Crerar, 30 Jan. 1933.

39 CP 121, Lambert to Crerar, 7 Feb. 1933.

40 See *Debates* for early months 1933; Neatby, King, *iii*, 42–4.

41 CP 121, Lambert to Crerar, 7 Feb. 1933.

42 CP 119, King to Crerar, 16 Jan. 1932; Lambert Papers, Box 9, Diary (hereafter Lambert Diary), 19 Jan., 23 March, 24 March, 1 April 1933. See also John Kendle, *John Bracken* (Toronto, 1979), and, especially, Robert Wardhaugh, "Mackenzie King and the Prairie West," PhD dissertation, University of Manitoba, 1995.

43 King Papers, Crerar to King, 8 March 1932.

44 Cameron Papers, vol. 34, Crerar to Cameron, 31 May 1932.

45 King Papers, vol. 190, Crerar to King, 6 June 1932. The results of the elections were: government 40, Conservatives 11, and Labor 4; CP 98, Crerar to Cameron, 8 Aug. 1932.

46 CP 119, King to Crerar, 22 Aug. 1932; Wardhaugh, "Mackenzie King," passim.

47 Lambert Diary, 14, 20, 21 June 1933, 21 July 1933.

48 Ibid., 25 Sept. 1933; CP 121, Lambert to Crerar, 11 Dec. 1933.

49 This long story can be followed in CP 121, Crerar to Lambert, 17 Feb. 1933; Cameron Papers, vol. 34, Crerar to Cameron, 4 July 1933; CP 121, Lambert to Crerar, 21 Oct. 1933; King Papers, vol. 199, Crerar to King, 16 Feb., 6 April 1934; CP 121, Crerar to Lambert, 12 Sept. 1934.

50 CP 121, Crerar to Lambert, 7 Nov. 1932.

51 Ibid., King to Crerar, 7 Feb. 1933.

52 Ibid., Crerar to Lambert, 17 Feb. 1933.

53 CP 98, Crerar to Cameron, 9 March 1933.

54 King Papers, vol. 195, Crerar to King, 30 June 1933; Cameron Papers, vol. 34, Crerar to Cameron, 23 Aug. 1933.

55 Cameron Papers, vol. 35, Crerar to Cameron, 22 June 1934.

56 King Papers, vol. 190, Crerar to King, 22 Aug. 1932.

57 Ibid., Crerar to King, 23 Nov. 1932; vol. 195, Crerar to King, 21 March 1933; Dafoe Papers, Box 3, Dafoe to Massey, 29 Dec. 1932.

58 King Papers, vol. 199, Crerar to King, 8 Jan. 1934; CP 119, Crerar to King, 25 June 1934; Dafoe Papers, Box 2, Dafoe to Dexter, n.d.

59 See Cameron Papers, vol. 35, Crerar to King, 8 Jan. 1934; CP 98, Crerar to Cameron, 4 April 1934; Lambert, Diary, 18 May 1934. See also a quite discouraged letter from Crerar to Cameron in Cameron Papers, vol. 35, 29 March 1934.

CHAPTER ELEVEN

1 King Papers, vol. 205, Crerar to King, 26 Jan. 1935; Cameron Papers, vol. 35, Crerar to Cameron, 12 March 1935.

2 King Papers, vol. 205, Crerar to King, 26 Jan. 1935.

3 Cameron Papers, vol. 35, Crerar to Cameron, 1 May 1935.

4 Copy in ibid., Crerar to King, 19 June 1935.

5 CP 121, Crerar to Lambert, 26 June 1935; H. Blair Neatby, *William Lyon Mackenzie King*, III, *Prism of Unity* (Toronto, 1976), 104–9.

6 CP 119, King to Crerar, 17 April 1935; Crerar to King, 21 June 1935.

7 CP 121, R.H. MacNeill, The Pas Liberal Association, to Crerar, 27 March 1935.

8 Cameron Papers, vol. 35, Crerar to Cameron, 18 May 1935.

9 Ibid., Crerar to Cameron, 20 June 1935; CP 119, King to Crerar, 22 June 1935; King Papers, vol. 205, Crerar to King, 5 Aug. 1935; Lambert diary, 24 Aug. 1935.

10 CP 119, "Extract from Mr. King's Diary," 8 July 1963.

11 CP 119, "Extract"; Dafoe Papers, Box 2, Dafoe to Wallace Dafoe, 26 Nov. 1935.

12 *King Diary* (Toronto, 1973), 21 Dec. 1935.

13 Cited in Reginald Whitaker, *The Government Party: Organizing and Financing the Liberal Party, 1939–1958* (Toronto, 1977), dated 11 Jan. 1944.

14 CP 119, "Extract."

15 Cameron Papers, vol. 20, Dafoe to Cameron, 22 Oct. 1935.

16 Neatby, *King*, III, 130; Robert Bothwell and William Kilbourn, *C.D. Howe* (Toronto, 1979), 70.

17 CP 119, "Extract"; NA, RG 32, Copy of PC 3373, 23 Oct. 1935, which appointed Crerar minister of mines, minister of immigration, and superintendent general of Indian affairs.

18 Cameron Papers, vol. 20, Dafoe to Cameron, 22 Oct. 1935; vol. 35, Crerar to Cameron, 17 Oct. 1935.

19 Lambert Diary, 24 Oct. 1935, citing an interview with James Richardson of Winnipeg; *King Diary*, 28 Oct 1935; C.F. Wilson, *A Century of Canadian Grain* (Saskatoon, 1978), 498, says that Dunning agreed with his three colleagues; PC 3455, 31 Oct. 1935, set up the cabinet wheat committee.

20 *King Diary*, 31 Oct. 1935; Wilson, *Century*, 511; Dexter Papers, Box 1, "Memo on Wheat," 31 Oct. 1935.

21 CP 104, Crerar to Dafoe, 7 Dec. 1935; CP 119, Crerar to Dafoe, 17 Dec. 1935.

22 NA, RG 32, PC 3373, 23 Oct. 1935.

23 *King Diary*, 6, 21 March 1936.

24 Canada, House of Commons, *Debates*, 2 June 1936, 3200ff; copy of the speech in King Papers, vol. 215.

25 *King Diary*, 3 Nov. 1936.

26 Ibid., 3 Nov. 1936.

27 The story can be followed in King Papers, vol. 216, Crerar to King, 12 March 1936; Dafoe Papers, Box 1, Dafoe to Crerar, 27 March 1936; CP 104, Crerar to Dafoe, 17 March 1936, 31 March 1936.

28 Lambert Diary, 28 July 1936.
29 Copies of the broadcasts are in the Crerar Papers. For reaction see, for example, *Annual Report of the Department of Mines for the Fiscal Year ending March 31, 1936;* CP 98, Cameron to Crerar, 1 Feb. 1936; Cameron Papers, vol. 35, Crerar to Cameron; Toronto *Globe,* 17 Feb. 1936.
30 Dafoe Papers, Box 1, Dafoe to Crerar, 2 Dec. 1935.
31 CP 104, Crerar to Dafoe, 7 Dec. 1935; see also Neatby, King, *iii,* 163ff, for a full discussion by cabinet of the use of budget deficits to stimulate recovery.
32 King Papers, vol. 215, Crerar to King, 30 April 1936.
33 Cameron Papers, vol. 35, Crerar to Cameron, 20 April 1936; Cameron to Crerar, 29 April 1936.
34 See, for example, a long speech by Crerar when introducing his estimates to the House in *Debates,* 29 May 1936; and Department of Mines and Resources, *Annual Reports,* 1937–39, passim.
35 Provincial Archives of British Columbia (PABC), Pattullo Papers, 76/17, Pattullo to Dunning, 24 Jan. 1936; Dunning to Pattullo, 31 Jan. 1936; Pattullo to King, 5 Feb. 1936; and for full background see Richard Stuart, "Duff Patullo and the Yukon Schools Question of 1937," *Canadian Historical Review,* 64 (March 1983), 125–44.
36 Pattullo Papers, 71/12, Crerar to Pattullo, 9 Jan. 1937.
37 Ibid., Crerar to Pattullo, 5 March 1937; Pattullo to Crerar, 8 March 1937; Crerar to Pattullo, 17 April 1937.
38 Robin Fisher, *Duff Pattullo of British Columbia* (Toronto, 1991), 295ff.
39 NA, RG 25, D1, vol. 719, file 32, Crerar to King, 27 Aug. 1937; Skelton to King, 4 Oct. 1937; Stuart, "Duff Pattullo."
40 King Papers, vol. 233, Crerar to King, 4 Oct. 1937; *Vancouver News Herald,* 18 Sept. 1937.
41 Pattullo Papers, 71/12, Pattullo to Crerar, 6 Oct. 1937; Crerar to Pattullo, 8 Oct. 1937.
42 Bracken Papers, Box 101, file 1093, Crerar to McDiarmid, 17 July 1937.
43 House of Commons, *Debates,* 30 March 1936, 1217; 23 Aug. 1936, 2121, for examples.
44 Ibid., 13 June 1938, 3793.
45 Pattullo Papers, 97/1, Crerar to Patullo, 9 May 1938; NA, RG 1222, vol. 97, Pattullo to Crerar, 23 July 1938; *King Diary,* 20 Jan, 3 Feb. 1938.
46 *King Diary,* 18 Dec. 1936; Neatby, *King,* III, 208.
47 Canada, Department of Mines and Resources, *Report, 1937–38;* Urquhart and Buckley, *Historical Statistics* (Ottawa, 1983), Series A350.
48 Irving Abella and Harold Troper, *None Is Too Many* (Toronto, 1982), 15.
49 Mines, *Report, 1937–38.*
50 Abella and Troper, *None, passim.*
51 Ibid., 61; House of Commons, *Debates,* 9 March 1939.

52 *King Diary,* 29 March, 26 April, 7 June, 13, 22, 23, 24 Nov., 1, 8, 21 Dec. 1938; 8, 9 March 1939; Lambert Diary, 15 April 1938; Abella and Troper, *None,* 25, 34–5, 47, 111, 150, 157.

53 Abella and Troper, *None,* 229.

54 *King Diary,* 26 Feb., 11 June 1936; 10 Feb. 1937.

55 Cameron Papers, vol. 35, Crerar to Cameron, 15 June 1937.

56 Dexter Papers, Box 1, Dafoe to Dexter, 20 April 1937.

57 Cameron Papers, vol. 35, Crerar to Cameron, 15 June 1937.

58 *King Diary,* 21 May, 8 June 1937.

59 CP 119, Crerar to Dafoe, 15 June 1937.

60 Dexter Papers, Box 1, Dafoe to Dexter, 20 June 1937.

61 King Papers, vol. 233, Crerar to King, 19 Aug. 1937; King to Crerar, 21 Aug. 1937.

62 Cameron Papers, vol. 35, Crerar to Cameron, 12 March 1938; 27 March 1939; CP 119, King to Crerar, 8 Sept. 1938.

63 Cameron Papers, vol. 35, Crerar to Cameron, 27 March 1939.

64 Neatby, *King,* III, chap. 4, passim.

65 King Papers, vol. 233, Crerar to King, 25 Jan. 1937.

66 Ibid., Crerar to Dunning, 27 Jan. 1937.

67 CP 119, King to Crerar, 18 Jan. 1938.

68 Lambert Diary, 27 March 1938.

69 *King Diary,* 21 March 1939.

70 Ibid., 21 March 1939, 25 April 1939.

71 CP 154, Radio Address, 16 June 1939.

72 CP 119, King to Crerar, 12 Sept. 1938.

73 *King Diary,* 14 Nov. 1938; Cameron Papers, vol. 35, Crerar to Cameron, 22 Nov. 1938.

74 Lambert Diary, 29 May 1938.

75 CP 98, Crerar to Cameron, 5 April 1939.

76 King Papers, vol. 266, Crerar to King, 25 July 1939.

CHAPTER TWELVE

1 C.P. Stacey, *Arms, Men and Governments* (Ottawa, 1970), 113; J.W. Pickersgill, ed., *The Mackenzie King Record,* I (Toronto, 1960), 26.

2 *King Diary,* 28 Sept. 1939.

3 Ibid., 21, 27 Sept. 1939.

4 For corroboration see the memoir of George McIvor in C.F. Wilson, *A Century of Canadian Grain* (Saskatoon, 1978), app. 7.

5 Crerar to King, cable, 2 Dec. 1939, and Euler to Crerar, cable, 5 Dec. 1939, cited in Wilson, *Century,* 644–5. For cabinet's opinion, see *King Diary,* 7 Dec. 1939.

6 CP 155, Diary of Crerar's trip to London, 1939.

7 Cited in Stacey, *Arms,* 206.

8 Copy of speech in Pattullo Papers, vol. 98, file 3. It was given 6 December 1939.
9 CP 155, memorandum, 14 Dec 19.
10 *King Diary*, 3 Jan. 1940; King Papers, vol. 825, file 716, Eden to King, 2 April 1940.
11 Dexter Papers, Box 2, Interview with Dunning, 11 Jan. 1940.
12 NA, RG 2/18, PC 4017.5, 5 Dec. 1939.
13 See, for example, *King Diary*, 6 Dec. 1939.
14 For details, see J.L. Granatstein, *Canada's War: The Politics of the Mackenzie King Government, 1939–1945* (Toronto, 1975), 76.
15 *King Diary*, 22, 23 Jan. 1940; Dexter Papers, Box 2, memorandum, 31 Jan. 1940; Granatstein, *Canada's War*, 76–80.
16 King Papers, vol. 286, Crerar to King, 1 Feb. 1940.
17 Ibid., Crerar to King, 3 Feb. 1940.
18 Ibid.
19 Toronto *Globe*, 3 Feb. 1940.
20 Dafoe Papers, vol. 2, file 3, Dafoe to Dexter, 22 Feb. 1940; King Papers, vol. 286, King to Crerar, 28 Feb. 1940.
21 Cameron Papers, vol. 27, Cameron to Fowler, 11 March 1940; Fowler to Cameron, 13 March 1940; see also Reginald Whitaker, *The Government Party: Organizing and Financing the Liberal Party, 1930–1958* (Toronto, 1977), 125.
22 Cameron Papers, vol. 27, Fowler to Cameron, 29 March 1940; vol. 35, Crerar to Cameron, 3 April 1940; Whitaker, *The Government Party*, 127; J.M. Beck, *Pendulum of Power* (Scarborough, 1968), 238–9.
23 Cameron Papers, vol. 35, Crerar to Cameron, 3 April 1940.
24 *King Diary*, mid-April 1940; Dexter Papers, Box 1, Dexter to Dafoe, 10 April 1940.
25 CP 152, Memorandum on the Canadian Wheat Situation, 11 March 1941.
26 For details see Wilson, *Century*, 786ff.
27 A cogent summary of the report and its implications may be found in Granatstein, *Canada's War*, 160–3.
28 NA, RG 2/18, vol. 1, fc-10.
29 There are several good accounts of the conference and its background, written from different perspectives. See, among others, Granatstein, *Canada's War*; Robin Fisher, *Duff Pattullo* (Toronto, 1991); John Saywell, *Mitchell Hepburn* (Toronto, 1991); and John Kendle, *John Bracken* (Toronto, 1979).
30 CP 119, Crerar to King, 1 Nov. 1941. Crerar noted in the margin that the letter had not been sent.
31 *King Diary*, 6 Dec. 1940.
32 Dexter Papers, Box 2, Memorandum, 30 Dec. 1940; Granatstein, *Canada's War*, 166–8.

33 *King Diary,* 15 Jan. 1941.
34 The foregoing paragraphs are based on a copy in the Dexter Papers, Box 1, of Crerar to Dafoe, 16 Jan. 1941.
35 CP 104, Crerar to Dafoe, 10 June 1940.
36 *King Diary,* 9 May 1941.
37 CP 88, Crerar to McPherson, 23 May 1941.
38 Dexter Papers, Box 2, Memo, 12 June 1941.
39 CP 104, Crerar to Dafoe, 13 Nov. 1941; NA, CWC, 19 Nov. 1941.
40 The speech was reprinted in the *Winnipeg Free Press,* 15 Oct. 1941. It did not note the reaction of Toronto's businessmen.
41 Dexter Papers, Box 2, Memo, 5 Dec. 1941; Stacey, *Arms,* 401; *King Diary,* 3 Dec. 1941.
42 Dexter Papers, Box 2, Memo, 5 Dec. 1941; Pickersgill, ed., *Mackenzie King Record,* 303–4.
43 Dexter Papers, Box 2, Dexter to George Ferguson, 15 Dec. 1941.
44 *King Diary,* 18 Dec. 1941.
45 Dexter Papers, Box 3, 6 Jan. 1942.
46 Ibid., 20 Jan. 1942.
47 King Papers, vol. 322, Crerar to King, 8, 16 Jan. 1942; Dafoe Papers, Box 1, Dafoe to Crerar, 12 Jan. 1942.
48 Dexter Papers, Box 3, 13 March 1942; House of Commons, *Debates,* 16 June 1942.
49 CP 88, Memorandum of interview with Cardin, 16 Jan. 1942.
50 See, for example, *King Diary,* 15 Jan. 1942.
51 Ibid., 28 April 1942.
52 CP 119, Memorandum, 1 May 1942.
53 *King Diary,* 5 May 42.
54 See Dexter Papers, Box 3, memoranda, 6 May, 16 June 1942.
55 Ibid., memorandum, 6 May 1942. Crerar kept King informed of the exchanges, which were carried out through Dexter.
56 King Papers, vol. 322, Crerar to King, 30 May 1942.
57 *King Diary,* 9 July 1942.
58 There is a day-by-day account of the crisis in QUA, Power Papers, Box 1, file 2, Memorandum for the Record; and an excellent summary in Granatstein, *Canada's War,* chap. 6.
59 CP 88 for copies of the notes. Macdonald's reference is to the Hong Kong inquiry, which was just ending.

CHAPTER THIRTEEN

1 Dexter Papers, Box 1, Dafoe to Dexter, 23 Aug 1942.
2 Before his resignation from cabinet became effective on 25 May 1945, Crerar wrote an extensive memorandum about Bracken (Bracken

Memo). There is a copy in CP 119 and an additional copy in the King Papers, 0340283–90. This reference is to page 3.

3 Ibid., 3.

4 Ibid., 5.

5 Ibid., 7.

6 *King Diary* (Toronto, 1973), 18 Nov., 11 Dec. 1942; King Papers, vol. 322, Crerar to King, 15 Dec. 1942.

7 CP 98, Crerar to Cameron, 14 Dec. 1942.

8 Ibid., Crerar to McKenzie, 18 Dec. 1942.

9 Dexter Papers, Box 3, Memo, 17 Dec. 1942; CP 98, Crerar to Garson, 12 Dec. 1942; PAM, Garson Papers, Crerar to Garson, 12 Dec. 1942, 5 Jan. 1943; a full analysis of the exchanges between Garson and Crerar may be found in Mark Vacjner, "The Public Career of Stuart Garson: The Manitoba Years," MA thesis, University of Manitoba, 1993.

10 Cameron Papers, vol. 35, Crerar to Cameron, 3 May 1943.

11 *King Diary,* 27 Sept. 1943.

12 C.F. Wilson, *A Century of Canadian Grain* (Saskatoon, 1978), 788.

13 King Papers, vol. 322, Crerar to King, 17 Sept. 1942.

14 Ibid., King to Crerar, 18 Sept. 1942, Crerar to King, 2 Oct. 1942.

15 CWC, vol. 46, 4, 6 Feb. 1943; 5, 23 March 1943.

16 See CWC, vol. 46, 8, 10 Sept. 1943; Department of Mines and Natural Resources, *Annual Report*, 1942–43, 173.

17 NA, RG 2, 16, vol. 1, Cabinet Conclusions, 24 March 1944.

18 Cameron Papers, vol. 32, Cameron to Euler, 25 Feb. 1943; Euler to Cameron, 2 March 1943.

19 *King Diary,* 9 March 1943.

20 Dexter Papers, Box 1, Dafoe to Dexter, 14 March 1943.

21 Ibid., Box 3, memo, 14 March 1943; Dafoe Papers, Box 2, Dafoe to Dexter, 19 March 1943.

22 Ibid., memo, 3 Sept. 1943.

23 Public Archives of Nova Scotia (hereafter PANS), A.L. Macdonald Papers, file 391, 2 Sept. 1943.

24 King Papers, vol. 339, Crerar to King, 14 Aug. 1943.

25 Dexter Papers, Box 3, memo, 3 Sept. 1943.

26 Ibid., memo, 1 Sept. 1943.

27 See *King Diary,* 12, 14, 22 Jan. 1943; 5 Nov. 1943, for examples.

28 King Papers, vol. 339, Crerar to King, 13 Oct. 1943.

29 Dexter Papers, Box 3, memo, 23 Dec. 1943.

30 *King Diary,* 13 Jan. 1944; Macdonald Papers, Diary, 13, 20 Jan. 1944; see also J.L. Granatstein, *Canada's War: The Politics of the Mackenzie King Government, 1939–1945* (Toronto, 1975), 283, for a fuller account. Crerar's grief at the loss of his lifelong friend remained private. Only in letters to Cameron does he indicate how much it had affected him.

31 CP 119, Crerar to King, 8 Jan. 1944.
32 NA, Bank of Canada Papers, DPC/RS3, Cabinet Committee on Dom-Prov Conference, 17/2/44–29/9/44.
33 Dexter Papers, Box 3, 24 Oct. 1942; see also CWC, 23 Sept. 1942.
34 J.W. Pickersgill, *The Mackenzie King Record*, I (Toronto, 1960), 464.
35 See, for example, CWC, 14 April 1943.
36 Ibid., 3 Aug. 1944.
37 *King Diary*, 20, 21 April 1944; Pickersgill, ed., *Mackenzie King Record*, I, 659–60.
38 *King Diary*, 15 July 1944.
39 CP 119, Crerar to King, 9 Aug. 1944.
40 Dexter Papers, Box 3, 22 Sept. 1944.
41 CWC, 18 Oct. 1944; *King Diary*, 18 Oct. 1944.
42 D.C. Thomson, *Louis St. Laurent* (Toronto, 1968), 148ff.
43 A full exposition of this argument may be found in my article, "The Conscription Crisis: What Really Happened?" *The Beaver* (April–May 1994), 10–19.
44 NA, Ralston Papers, vol. 84, Crerar, "Notes for the Record …," 26 Dec. 1944.
45 Macdonald Papers, Diary, 1 Nov. 1944.
46 Ralston Papers, vol. 84, Crerar to Ralston, 2 Nov. 1944.
47 Pickersgill, ed., *Mackenzie King Record*, I, 8.
48 King Papers, vol. 385, Crerar to King, 3 Nov. 1944; King to Crerar, 10 Nov. 1944; King Diary, 10 Nov. 1944.
49 CP 119, Crerar to King, 17 Nov. 1944.
50 Macdonald Papers, file 385/15, Macdonald to Ralston, 18 Nov. 1944.
51 A copy of this letter was found in the Macdonald Papers, file 385/29, Crerar to King, 20 Nov. 1944.
52 CP 119, Crerar to King, 22 Nov. 1944. A marginal note, initialled by Crerar, observes that the decision taken at that evening's council meeting made his resignation unnecessary.
53 Crerar, "Notes for the Record," in Ralston Papers, cited in Stacey, *Arms, Men, and Governments* (Ottawa, 1970), 470.
54 H. Blair Neatby, ed., *Mackenzie King Record*, II (Toronto, 1963), 226; Crerar, "Notes for the Record."
55 Crerar, "Notes for the Record."
56 Macdonald Papers, file 392, 22 Nov. 1944.
57 Crerar, "Notes for the Record."
58 *King Diary*, 28 Nov. 1944.
59 CWC, 22 Dec. 1944; NA, RG 2/18, Heeney to Crerar, 26 Dec. 1944; CWC, 24 Jan. 1945.
60 *King Diary*, 2 March 1945.
61 Dexter Papers, Box 4, Crerar to Dexter, 7 March 1945.

62 King Papers, vol. 380, Crerar to King, 31 Jan. 1945.
63 Dexter Papers, Box 4, Crerar to Dexter, 2, 7 Feb. 1945.
64 *King Diary,* 16, 20 Dec. 1944.
65 Ibid., 8 Jan. 1945.
66 See, for example, ibid., 9, 28 Jan. 1945.
67 Ibid., 8 Mar. 1945.
68 King Papers, vol. 380, Crerar to King, 17 April 1945; King Diary, 18 April 1945.
69 Cameron Papers, vol. 32, Cameron to Euler, 28 April 1945.

CHAPTER FOURTEEN

1 Foster Diary, 28 Aug. 1920, cited in Power Papers, vol. 5, Power to Crerar, 24 Feb. 1954.
2 Kunz, *The Modern Senate of Canada* (Toronto, 1965), 130–1.
3 Dexter Papers, Box 4, memo of interview with King, 17 Oct. 1946.
4 CP 122, Crerar to Macdonald, 13 Sept., 22 Oct. 1945.
5 Canada, Senate, *Debates,* 1946, 601 (cited in Kunz, *The Modern Senate,* 153).
6 Kunz, *The Modern Senate,* 155.
7 CP 117, Crerar to Hutchison, 16 Aug. 1946; Crerar to Victor Sifton, 19 Aug. 1946. See also *Halifax Chronicle,* 7 Sept. 1946.
8 CP 117, Hutchison to Crerar, 29 Aug. 1946; *Winnipeg Free Press,* 29 Aug. 1946.
9 CP 122, Crerar to Macdonald, 2 Sept. 1946.
10 Ibid., Crerar to Macdonald, 4 Sept. 1946.
11 T.A. Crerar, "Canada's Wheat Problem," Winnipeg Free Press Pamphlet No. 10, 1946.
12 A full account may be found in C.F. Wilson, *A Century of Canadian Grain* (Saskatoon, 1978), 960–77.
13 Dexter Papers, Box 4, Crerar to Dexter, 26 April 1947; CP 122, Crerar to Macdonald, 30 April 1947; Dexter Papers, Box 4, Crerar to Dexter, 3 May 1947; CP 105, Crerar to Dexter, 13 May 1947.
14 Dexter Papers, Box 4, Crerar to Dexter, 3 May 1947; CP 105, Crerar to Dexter, 1 March 1948.
15 For a detailed account of the wheat agreements see Wilson, *Century,* passim.
16 For an interesting, if somewhat controversial, examination of the *Free Press* and the wheat trade, see Patrick Brennan, "Stuck in Playing the Old Tunes: The *Winnipeg Free Press* and the Canada–United Kingdom Wheat Agreement," *Prairie Forum* (spring 1994).
17 CP 105, Crerar to Dexter, 5 June 1950.
18 *Russell Banner,* 10 Aug. 1950.

19 CP 88, Crerar to Editor, *Manitoba Co-operator*, 4 Sept. 1950.
20 Ibid., Crerar to Rank, 26 Feb. 51.
21 CP 152, Crerar to D.L. Campbell (Premier of Manitoba), 27 Feb. 1951;
   CP 106, Crerar to Dexter, 3 March 1951; CP 152, Crerar to Stanley Jones
   (Winnipeg Grain Exchange), 5 March 1951; Crerar to Dexter, 7 March
   1951; CP 117, Crerar to Hutchison, 14 March 1951.
22 For a favourable comment on Crerar's speech, see CP 88, Senator
   Arthur Hardy to Crerar, 30 March 1951. Hardy was unable to attend
   the debate.
23 CP 135, Crerar to Tarr, 6 May 1950.
24 Ibid., Crerar to Tarr, 23 June 1950.
25 CP 88, Crerar to Dunning, 16 May 1950; CP 135, Crerar to Tarr, 23 June
   1950.
26 Senate, *Debates*, 1951, 288.
27 CP 125, Meighen to Crerar, 29 May 1952.
28 NA, Meighen Papers, vol. 219, Crerar to Meighen, 31 May 1952.
29 Ibid.
30 Senate, *Debates*, 27 June 1952.
31 CP 88, Meighen to Crerar, 14 July 1952.
32 Senate, *Debates*, 26 June 1952.
33 Meighen Papers, vol. 219, Crerar to Meighen, 31 May 1952.
34 CP 105, Crerar to Dexter, 21 Feb. 1953.
35 CP 99, Crerar to Cameron, 12 Aug. 1955; see, for example, *Lethbridge
   Herald*, 10 Aug. 1955.
36 Senate, *Debates*, 16 June 1955, 628.
37 CP 89, Crerar to Macdonald, 8 Dec. 1955; Senate, *Debates*, 15 Feb. 1956.
38 CP 89, Crerar to Symington, 24 Feb. 1956.
39 Ibid., Crerar to D[orothy] & B[ernard], 11 May, 3 Aug. 1956.
40 Power Papers, vol. 5, Crerar to Power, 16 Nov. 1956.
41 Ibid., Crerar to Power, 21 May 1957.

CHAPTER FIFTEEN

1 CP 99, Crerar to Marler, 6 Jan. 1958.
2 CP 89, Crerar to [Dorothy and Bernard], 17 Jan. 1958.
3 CP 99, Crerar to Cameron, 22 Jan. 1958.
4 Ibid., Crerar to Cameron, 30 Jan. 1958; for a full account of the incident, see John English, *The Worldly Years: The Life of Lester Pearson, 1949–
   1972* (Toronto, 1992), 199–201.
5 Power Papers, Box 5, Crerar to Power, 7 April 1958. The final reference
   was to Tom Kent and Jack Pickersgill.
6 CP 131, Pearson to Crerar, 22 Oct. 1958.
7 See, for example, ibid., Crerar to Pearson, 10 July 1958.
8 CP 99, Crerar to Cameron, 25 March 1960.

9 Power Papers, Box 5, Crerar to Power, 2 Sept. 1961.
10 CP 99, Crerar to Cameron, 13 July 1961.
11 Power Papers, Box 5, Crerar to Power, 2 Sept. 1961; CP 136, Crerar to McCaskill, 31 May 1966.
12 CP 90, Roebuck to Crerar, 8 Aug. 1961.
13 Ibid., Crerar to Weir, 29 May, 6 June 1963.
14 Ibid., Crerar to Forsey, 8 Oct. 1963.
15 Ibid., Crerar to Lesage, 29 Oct. 1963.
16 Ibid., Lesage to Crerar, 6 Dec. 1963.
17 CP 91, Crerar to Grant, 15 May 1964; Crerar to Rice-Jones, 12 June 1964.
18 *Leader-Post*, 9 Feb. 1962.
19 Senate, *Debates*, 6 Feb. 1962.
20 *Globe and Mail*, 7 Feb. 1962.
21 CP 117, Crerar to Hutchison, 9 Feb. 1962.
22 CP 112, Crerar to David Kilgour, President of Great-West Life, 10 June 1963.
23 Ibid., Crerar to Kilgour, 2 July 1964.
24 CP 131, Crerar to Pearson, 3 July 1963.
25 Ibid., Pearson to Crerar, 9 July 1963.
26 CP 91, Crerar to Forsey, 2 July 1964.
27 *Ottawa Journal*, 7 Dec. 1964; CP 91, O'Leary to Crerar, 8 Dec. 1964.
28 Crerar to Turgeon, 31 March 1966.
29 *Montreal Gazette*, 2 April 1966.
30 Senate, *Debates*, 25 May 1966.

CHAPTER SIXTEEN

1 Jessie Crerar died on 25 February 1967. See CP 92, Crerar to Agnes Macdonald, 8 Dec. 1969.
2 CP 92, Crerar to McCutcheon, 22 Aug. 1967.
3 CP 98, Crerar to Cameron, 8 Feb. 1970.
4 CP 92, Crerar to Doupe, 2 Feb. 1968.
5 Ibid., Crerar to Doupe, 24 Feb. 1968.
6 *Northern Miner*, 4 Dec. 1969.
7 CP 199, Crerar to Editor, *Winnipeg Free Press*, 6 Feb. 1970. See also CP 198, Crerar to Arthur Beaubien, 7 March 1970.
8 CP 198, Crerar to Foster Griezic, 15 July 1969.
9 CP 199, Crerar to Rasminsky, 9 Dec. 1968. While Crerar is not specific as to the source of the advice, it could have come only from senior officials at Finance.
10 CP 92, Crerar to Connolly, 29 Feb. 1968.
11 CP 92B, Crerar to MacGregor, 24 March 1969.
12 CP 198, Crerar to Barkway, 2 Feb. 1970.

A Note on Sources

Since this study so closely follows the ideas and activities of T.A. Crerar, I have relied heavily on primary sources. The two hundred boxes of Crerar Papers at the Queen's University Archives formed the core of my research material. They contain all of Crerar's public correspondence for both his business and his political careers. There is as well one letter to his future wife, Jessie Hamilton, probably included by mistake, since there are no other family papers, except a very few exchanges with their daughter, Dorothy Naylor, during his later years. Though the Crerar papers contain many letters on the stationery of departments that he led, his ministerial papers have remained with the departments.

The hundreds of letters that Crerar exchanged with influential Liberal A. Kirk Cameron of Montreal during a friendship of nearly fifty years are broad, frank, and rich, comprising an extraordinary record of Canadian political affairs from the Great War to the early 1960s. Almost all are in the Crerar Papers, and many are reproduced in the Cameron Papers.

Several other manuscript collections were enlightening, especially the papers of J.W. Dafoe, Norman Lambert, Kirk Cameron, and, in particular, Grant Dexter. Contemporary newspapers often provided me with information about, and were a vehicle for, Crerar's political ideas and intentions. Secondary sources provided context, corroboration, and conflicting opinions; those that I used most frequently are cited in the Notes, above. Following are the primary sources:

NATIONAL ARCHIVES OF CANADA (NA), OTTAWA

Manuscript Division
  A.K. Cameron Papers
  Loring Christie Papers
  A.B. Hudson Papers

W.L.M. King Papers
Arthur Meighen Papers
Charles Murphy Papers
J.L. Ralston Papers
Clifford Sifton Papers
John Stevenson Papers

Public Records Division
  RG 2   Privy Council Office
  RG 10   Indian Affairs
  RG 15   Interior
  RG 21   Energy, Mines and Resources
  RG 22   Indian Affairs and Northern Development
  RG 25   External Affairs
  RG 32   Public Service Commission
  RG 76   Immigration

PROVINCIAL ARCHIVES OF BRITISH COLUMBIA (PABC),
VICTORIA

Bank of Canada Papers
T. Dufferin Pattullo Papers

PROVINCIAL ARCHIVES OF MANITOBA (PAM), WINNIPEG

John Bracken Papers
Stuart Garson Papers
R.A.C. Manning Papers
Ralph Maybank Papers

PUBLIC ARCHIVES OF NOVA SCOTIA (PANS), HALIFAX

Angus L. Macdonald Papers

QUEEN'S UNIVERSITY ARCHIVES (QUA), KINGSTON,
ONTARIO

G.F. Chipman Papers
T.A. Crerar Papers
Grant Dexter Papers
C.A. Dunning Papers
Norman Lambert Papers
C.G. (Chubby) Power Papers

SASKATCHEWAN ARCHIVES BOARD (SAB), REGINA

James A. Calder, Reminiscences

UNIVERSITY OF MANITOBA ARCHIVES (UMA), WINNIPEG

J.W. Dafoe Papers
W.L.M. King Diary
United Grain Growers Papers

Index

Aberhart, William, 203, 204, 205
Agrarian Revolt, 86
Alberta Co-operative Elevator Company, 21, 24
anti-semitism in Canada. *See* Jewish refugees
appeasement policy, British: Crerar's views on, 187–8
armed forces, Canadian: Big Army, 207; Crerar opposes Siberian involvement of (1918), 59; size of, 206, 207, 208–10, 224
autonomy, Canadian, 112–14; and Chanak affair, 92, 110; Crerar's views on, 28–9, 65, 72, 108, 110–14; and free trade with the United States, 112–14; Sanhedrin's views on, 111

Baldwin, Daniel, 169
Bank of British North America, 15
Bank of Montreal, 20–1
Barnes, Julius, 113–14
Bassett, John, 193
Beauharnois scandal (1931), 151
Beck, Adam, 41
Bennett, R.B., 140, 163

Bennett New Deal, 167
Big Army, 207, 208–10
Blackburn, A.M., 17
Blair, F.C., 184, 219
Blake, Edward, 6–7
Board of Grain Supervisors, 25
Boivin, Georges, 130
Borden, Robert, 35, 42, 58, 62; resigns, 75; western hostility to, 41
Bourassa, Henri, 36
Bowman, C.A., 141
Bracken, John, 92, 136, 139, 150, 158–9, 199, 202; wins Conservative leadership, 214–15
Brandon by-election (1938), 192
British Commonwealth Air Training Plan (BCATP), 196, 206
British Wheat Agreement, 238
Brownlee, J.E., 78
Buck, Tim, 169
Bureau, Jacques, 130
Burrell, Martin, 51–2
Byng, J.H.G., 1st Viscount Byng: and constitutional crisis of 1926, 130

Cabinet War Committee (CWC), 50, 194, 205–7; approves "Big Army"

plan, 208–10; refuses to recruit West Indian workers, 218–19; responsibilities of, 197, 206
Calder, J.A., 40, 42–3
Caldwell, T.W., 71–2
Cameron, A. Kirk, 32, 33, 80, 85, 138, 179, 199; and Liberal-Progressive alliance, 80
Camsell, Charles C., 178
Canada Month: Crerar's involvement with, 263
Canada Pension Plan: Crerar's views on, 257
Canadian Council of Agriculture (CCA), 31, 59, 72; attempts to create new Wheat Board, 102; collapse of, 137–8; and Liberal-Progressive alliance, 83–4; proposes new Wheat Board, 90–1
Canadian Forum, 86
Canadian Manufacturers' Association, 58
Canadian Military Headquarters: Canadian control of (1939), 196
Canadian National Railway Amalgamation Act, 1930, 145
Canadian National Railways: and Duff Commission, 155–8

Canadian Northern Railway, 65–6; and Crow Rate, 88–9
Canadian Pacific Railway, 66
Cardin, P.J.A., 211
Central Manitoba Mines, 139
Central Selling Agency, 102–4, 134–5
Cereals Board, 196
Chanak affair: and Canadian autonomy, 92, 110
China: Crerar's views on Canada's relations with, 218
Chinese Exclusion Act, 218; Crerar's views on, 218, 230–1
Chipman, George, 44, 60, 71
Christie, Loring, 113
Churchill, Winston, 197, 225
Churchill constituency: Crerar as incumbent, 169–70
Citizens' Committee (Winnipeg), 153
civil service: Crerar opposes growing power of, 236, 237, 244
Civil Service Commission: Crerar's investigation of, 246
Clark, Michael, 30, 73–4, 78
Clark, W. Clifford, 22, 266
Claxton, Brooke, 224
Cobden Club, 30
collective bargaining: Crerar's views on, 222
Commonwealth Conference (1937), 187
conscientious objectors: Crerar's views on, 56–7
conscription, 47, 198–9, 206–7, 224, 226–30; administrative tribunals on, 273n7; advocated by Conservatives, 207; Crerar's views on,

48–9, 50, 65, 73, 207–8, 226, 227, 228–9; plebiscite on, 210–11; UFA's views on, 37–8; Wood's views on, 37–8. See also National Resources Mobilization Act
constitutional crisis of 1926, 129–30
Coolidge, Calvin, 129
Co-operative Commonwealth Federation (CCF), 120, 160–1; Crerar's views on, 161–2; rising popularity of (1940s), 220–1
cooperative ideal: among western farmers, 29–30; Crerar's views on, 4, 29
coronation (1937): and Commonwealth solidarity, 186–7
Coyne, J.B., 32, 252
Coyne, James E.: and the "Coyne affair," 251–3
Crerar, Audrey, 25; death of, 93
Crerar, Dorothy (Naylor), 25, 149, 247, 262
Crerar, H.D.G. (Harry), 142, 195, 206, 208
Crerar, Jessie Hamilton, 13, 25, 153, 259; death of, 262
CRERAR, THOMAS A.:
– school and early career of, 12–13
– business career: and Grain Growers' Grain Company, 14–26; and United Grain Growers, 68–9, 93, 97–9, 142
– friendships of, 32–3. See also Sanhedrin
– political career: canvasses European grain merchants (1928), 134–5; represents cabinet in Britain (1939), 194; resigns from Unionist government (1919), 62–3; resigns Progressive

leadership (1922), 93, 107–9; retires, 259–61; serves on Turgeon Commission (1927), 141; in Senate, 235–48
– portfolios of: Agriculture, 4, 26, 43, 55–6; Mines and Resources, 178–86; Railways and Canals, 142, 144–5. See also Immigration Branch; Indian Affairs Branch
– political philosophy of, 27–8, 31–2, 246, 256, 263; on centralization of powers, 254–5; on civil service, 237, 244–6 passim, 254–5; on cooperative ideal, 4, 29; on government expansion, 237, 240, 243–6 passim, 261; on government fiscal responsibility, 258–9; on grain marketing, 237–43; pro-western bias of, 28, 36, 37, 40; on universality of social programs, 6, 256–8, 265–6
– private life of: family, 25, 149, 152, 153; health, 219–20; personal finances, 25, 69, 132, 138–9
– school and early career of, 12–13
Crerar, William, 12, 13
Crerar family, 11–12
Crow's Nest Pass rates, 4, 88–9; Crerar's views on, 89

Dafoe, John Wesley (Jack), 4, 32, 36, 64, 68, 80, 199; death of, 223; and Liberal-Progressive alliance, 80; on Rowell-Sirois Commission, 201–2; views on: Canadian autonomy, 110, 111, minority language

rights, 38, Union government, 43
Dandurand, Raoul, 211
Department of Mines and Resources: creation of, 175–6; Crerar's handling of, 178–81. *See also* Immigration Branch; Indian Affairs Branch; mines and mining
Depression: efforts to alleviate, 189–90; in the United States, 190; in western provinces, 188, 190–2
Dexter, Grant, 174, 207, 216
Direct Legislation League, 28
Dominion-Provincial Conference: 1927, 140; 1941, 202–5
Drayton, Henry, 71
Drew, George, 198
Drury, E.C., 71, 74, 76–7
Duff, Lyman, 156
Duff Commission on Railways, 155–8; Sanhedrin's views on report of, 156–7
Dunning, Charles A., 21, 39, 91, 126, 127, 128, 136, 174
Duplessis, Maurice, 188

East Elgin by-election (1920), 75–6
Eccles, William, 128
Eden, Anthony, 187, 195
elections, federal: 1917, 47–8, 49–50; 1919, 71–2; 1921, 4, 78–9, 276n46; 1925, 122, 123; 1926, 130–1; 1930, 147–9; 1935, 5, 167–8, 170; 1940, 197–200; by-elections: Brandon (1938), 192; East Elgin (1920), 75–6; Medicine Hat (1921), 77; North Grey (1945), 231; York

South (1942), 214; Sanhedrin's views on, 125, 199
elections, provincial: Alberta: 1921, 77–8; Manitoba: 1922, 91–2; 1927, 150; 1932, 151, 159; 1936, 177–8; Ontario: 1919, 71
elevators, grain: ownership of, 19–20
Emergency Powers Transition Act: and Wheat Board, 240
equalization payments: Crerar's views on, 5
Euler, W.D. (Bill), 173, 174

Family Allowance: Crerar's views on, 222, 223, 265–6; origins of, 265–7
Farmers' Creditors Arrangement Bill: defeated in Senate, 235–6
Farmers' Elevator Company, 12
Farmers' Platform, 4, 31, 34, 36, 37, 64; revised (1916), 59–60
Farmers' Sun, 71; on Liberal-Progressive alliance, 84–5
Farmers' Union of Canada, 102; opposes UGG and Crerar, 133
federal-provincial relations: Crerar's views on, 254–5, 257, 260–1. *See also* Rowell-Sirois Commission
Fielding, W.S., 6–7, 64–5, 67, 116; and Liberal-Progressive alliance, 80, 82
Finance, Senate Standing Committee on: and Crerar, 243
Foreign Exchange Control Bill: Senate amendments to, 236–7
Forke, Robert, 114, 132, 140

Foster, George, 41, 76
Fowler, Frank, 32, 199; views on transportation policy, 53
free trade: and Canadian autonomy, 112; Crerar's views on, 30, 53–4, 60–1, 73, 102, 108, 119; and western farmers, 29–31
Free Press. See Manitoba Free Press; Winnipeg Free Press

Gardiner, James G., 6–7, 173, 174, 230
Gardiner, Robert, 77
Garland, E.J., 84
Garson, Stuart, 216
General Agreement on Tariffs and Trade: Crerar's views on, 264
George, Henry: and Single Tax movement, 28
Ginger Group, 119–20, 121
Glen, J. Allison, 40, 50, 131
Globe, Toronto, 118
Globe and Mail, 179, 256
Good, W.C., 86
Gouin, Lomer, 80, 89, 116; and Liberal-Progressive alliance, 80
Gould, O.R., 71–2, 74
Graham, George, 33
grain, marketing of, 20–6, 135–7, 237–43; Board of Supervisors, 25–6; Crerar canvasses merchants in Europe (1928), 134–5; Crerar's views on, 89–90; by Grain Growers' Grain Company, 20–3; wartime restrictions on, 200–1. *See also* Wheat Board
Grain Growers' Associations: endorse New National Policy of CCA, 60

Grain Growers' Export Company Incorporated (New York), 23

Grain Growers' Export Company Limited (Winnipeg), 20, 23, 24

Grain Growers' Grain Company, 4, 11, 13, 14, 15–26

Grain Growers' Guide, 17, 18, 24, 57, 71

Grand Trunk Pacific, 65–6

Graves & Reilly, 12

Green, F.W., 31

Guaranty Trust (New York), 21

Hawkes, Arthur, 34

Haydon, Andrew, 68, 76, 81; and Beauharnois scandal, 151; and Liberal-Progressive alliance, 81, 82

Henders, R.C., 76

Hepburn, Mitchell, 184, 188, 198, 202–5, 220

Hoey, R.A., 176

Home Bank, 15, 21, 104–6; Crerar's views on, 105–7

Hoover, Herbert, 113–14, 129

Howe, C.D., 6–7, 207–8, 209–10, 224, 230

Hudson, A.B. (Bert), 32, 36, 39, 52, 276n46; appointed to Supreme Court, 177; and Turgeon Commission, 141

Hudson Bay Railway, 140

Ilsley, James, 202, 205, 206, 217, 221, 230

immigrants: numbers of, 184

Immigration Branch, 178, 184, 218, 219. *See also* Chinese Exclusion Act; Jewish refugees

Imperial Conference: 1921, 76; 1924, 111–12

Imperial Economic Conference (1932), 154–5

imperialism. *See* autonomy, Canadian

Indian Affairs Branch, 176, 178, 183–4

Industrial and Reconstruction Association, 58

International Wheat Agreement, 240

J. Rosebaum Grain Co. (Chicago), 20

J.I. Case company, 12

Jacobs, Sam, 132

Japan attacks Pearl Harbor, 207

Jewish refugees, 132, 184–6, 219; Crerar's efforts on behalf of, 185–6; Crerar's views on, 132

Johnson, R.M., 74

Jolliffe, A.L., 219

judicial appointments: Crerar's views on, 52

Kennedy, John, 13–14, 106

Keynes, John Maynard, 5; Crerar's views on theories of, 258, 261

King, Tom, 51, 76

King, William, 88

King, William Lyon Mackenzie, 67, 71, 159–60; and freer trade with the United States, 113–14; and Liberal-Progressive alliance (1920–21), 80–1; seeks western support, 126–8

Ku Klux Klan, 145

Lambert, Norman, 51, 56, 75, 77, 85–6

Langley, George, 21

language rights, minority: Dafoe's views on, 38; in Manitoba, 36; in Ontario, 36

Lapointe, Ernest, 6–7, 65, 71, 117, 199; death of, 211; and Liberal-

Progressive alliance, 82; opposes conscription, 206

Lash, Zebulon, 106

Laurier, Wilfrid, 33–4, 35

League of Nations: Crerar's views on, 65, 108, 186, 187

Lesage, Jean, 253

Liberal party (federal): Crerar disillusioned with, 249–50, 251, 252, 259; leadership convention (1958), 250; Quebec control of, 36, 38, 81–2; reform of, 152; western convention of (1917), 39

Liberal party (Manitoba): reconstruction of, 158–9

Liberal-Conservative party, 73

Liberal-Progressive alliance (federal), 80–5; Sanhedrin's views on, 83

Liberal-Progressive coalition (Manitoba), 158–9, 160

Liberal-Progressive Executive Commitee, 160

Lockhart, Hugh, 50

Lyon, T.S., 117

McCullach, George, 193

Macdonald, Angus L., 173, 206, 212, 230

Macdonald, E.N., 33

MacDonald, Malcolm, 214

McFarland, John L., 168

McGibbon, Peter, 147

MacHaffie, W.M., 106

McIvor, George, 195

Maclean's Magazine, 76, 86, 88, 97, 119

McMaster, Andrew, 34, 62

McMurray, E.T., 140

McNaughton, A.G.L., 205, 226; defeated (1945), 231

MacPhail, Agnes, 161

McPhail, Andrew J., 91, 102, 103, 133
MacPherson, Murdo, 215
McWilliams, R.F., 197
Maloney, J.J., 145
Manion, Robert, 198
Manitoba Cattle Company, 138
Manitoba Free Press, 4, 32, 34, 38, 43, 51, 85, 112, 127, 146, 153. *See also* Dafoe, John Wesley; *Winnipeg Free Press*
Manitoba Grain Growers' Association, 13, 19; 1917 convention, 33
Manitoba Liberal Association: response to emergence of CCF, 161
Mann, Donald, 43, 88
Martin, Paul, 249
Mason, James, 105
Massey, Vincent, 99, 127, 128
Maybank, Ralph, 131
Medicine Hat by-election (1921), 77
Meighen, Arthur, 32, 42, 76, 207; becomes prime minister, 75; defeated by CCF, 214; and transportation policy, 52; and Union government, 73
Military Service Act, 35, 47, 51; exemptions, 48–9, 55–6. *See also* conscription
mines and mining: Crerar's enthusiasm for, 178–9; Crerar's radio broadcasts on, 179; depletion allowances, 180; gold, 178; tax exemptions for, 180, 181
Mining Association of Canada, 179
Montreal Gazette, 259
Morrison, J.J., 37, 71, 74–7 passim, 79, 116; and Liberal-Progressive alliance, 82

Mulock, William, 41
Munro, J.K.: on Crerar, 97, 115–16
Murdoch, James, 179
Murphy, Charlie, 68, 76
Murray, James R., 17, 174

National Liberal Federation, 152
National Policy, 3–4
National Resources Mobilization Act, 205; Bill 80 amendments to, 212–13. *See also* conscription
Natural Products Marketing Act, 163
Naylor, Bernard, 247, 262
New National Policy, 59, 72. *See also* Farmers' Platform
Noranda Mines, 179
Norris, T.C., 36, 50
North Grey by-election (1945), 231

O'Donohue, Jimmy, 24, 49
Old Age Pensions, 256–7; Crerar's views on, 256–7
Ottawa Journal, 259

parties, political, 116; breakdown of two-party system, 66–7; Crerar opposes occupational or class, 73–5, 77, 108, 109, 116; Crerar's views on party system, 73–5, 86. *See also names of individual parties*
Partridge, E.A., 11, 13–14, 15, 19; conflict with Crerar, 16–18
Partridge Plan, 19
Paterson, Norman, 240
Pattullo, Duff, 181–3, 203, 204, 205
Pearl Harbor, attack on, 207
Pearson, Lester: Crerar's opinion of, 249, 250
Pellatt, Henry, 106

Persse, John, 106
Pickersgill, Jack, 250
Pitblado, Isaac, 42, 50
politics, non-partisan: Crerar's views on, 27, 28, 33, 40, 52
pools, commodity, 101–2. *See also* wheat pools
Power, "Chubby," 173, 206
Prairie Farm Assistance Act, 191–2
Progressive Conservative party, 215
Progressive party, 76; beginnings of, 66–7, 73–4; Crerar resigns leadership, 93, 107–9; defection of Ginger Group, 119–20; election of 1921, 4, 276n46; role in Parliament, 1921–22, 86–8
"prosperity Budget" (1926), 128–9
protectionism. *See* free trade; tariffs, protective
Public Press Limited, The, 18, 24

Quebec: control of Liberal party by, 36, 38, 81–2; Crerar's views on, 254; Quiet Revolution in, 253–5; western attitudes to, over Military Service Act, 51

railways: Duff Commission on, 155–8
Ralston, J.L., 168, 179, 194, 206, 208, 212–13, 224; Crerar's views on, 210; ousted from cabinet, 226–7; supports Big Army plan, 208–10
Rank, James, 196
Rankin, Jack, 179, 199
Reconstruction and Development Committee (1917), 50
Regina *Leader-Post*, 256

regionalism, western, 114
Reynolds, J.B., 49
Rice-Jones, Cecil, 34, 53, 68–9, 133
Robb, James, 106, 141; and "prosperity Budget" (1926), 128–9
Robertson, Gideon, 76
Robertson, Wishart, 237
Roblin, Rodmond: and government-owned elevators, 19
Roebuck, Arthur, 68
Rogers, Norman, 180, 194, 206
Rogers, Robert, 41, 42
Roosevelt, Franklin, 225; and economic depression, 190; statement on Jewish refugees, 219
Round Table, 110
Round Table Society, 28
Rowell, Newton W., 36, 56–7
Rowell-Sirois Commission, 183, 189, 201–3; Crerar supports tax proposals of, 223; effect on Canadian politics, 5; report of, 193
Royal Commission on Bilingualism and Biculturalism, 254
Royal Commission on Dominion-Provincial Relations. See Rowell-Sirois Commission
Royal Commission on Wheat Supplies, 25
royal visit (1939), 192
Russell Farmers' Elevator Company, 11
Russell Liberal Association, 13

St Laurent, Louis, 212
Sanhedrin (Winnipeg), 5, 35–6, 41, 139–40, 149
Sapiro, Aaron, 100
Saskatchewan Co-operative Elevator Company (SCEC), 20,

21, 23, 57–8; merges with Saskatchewan Pool, 134; opposes Wheat Board, 102
Saskatchewan Grain Growers' Association: resolutions of 1919, 60
Savings and Loan Bank, 105
schools, Manitoba Catholic, 153
Senate, Canadian: Crerar's views on, 236–7; growing power of, 235–6
Shipton, Anderson & Co., 20–1; dissolution of, 57
Sifton, Arthur L., 40, 42–3
Sifton, Clifford, 34, 37, 40, 41, 81; and Liberal-Progressive alliance, 81; supports Canadian autonomy, 110–11
Sifton, Victor, 207
Single Tax movement, 28, 108
Sinnot, Archbishop, 153
Skelton, Alex, 203
Skelton, O.D., 111–12, 182
Smith, Sidney, 215
Smoot-Hawley Tariff (U.S.), 145
Social Democratic party: government ban on, 56–7
social programs: Crerar opposes universality of, 6, 256–8, 265–6
Social Service Council of Manitoba, 28
social services programs, 222–4; Crerar's views on, 222–4
Soviet Union: Crerar's views on, 150
Spencer, Henry, 86
Spencer, Nelson, 77
Square Deal Grain Company, 18
Standing Committee on Finance (Senate): Crerar as chairman, 243

Stemper, Henry, 20, 22, 24
Stevens, H.H., 6–7, 130
Stevenson, John, 76
Stewart, Charles, 127, 140
Stuart, Kenneth, 208, 225
Suez crisis: Crerar's views on, 248
Symington, H.J., 32

tariffs, protective: and Commonwealth preference, 145–6, 147, 154–5; Crerar's views on, 53–4, 66, 76, 134, 154–5, 264; Sanhedrin's views on, 154; and western farmers, 29–31. See also free trade
tariffs for revenue: Crerar's views on, 76
Tarr, Edgar J., 51, 218
Taylor, E.L., 52
Territorial Grain Growers' Association, 11
Thompson, Levi, 73–4
Thornton, Henry, 118, 144, 156
Thornton, R.S., 50
Thorson, Joseph, 158, 160, 170
Timmins, Noah, 138–9
Toronto Star, 85, 118
Toronto World, 51, 76
Towers, Graham, 195
Trans-Canada Pipe Lines: Crerar's views on, 247–8
transportation policy: Crerar's views on, 52–3, 65–6, 72
Tregillus, W.J., 29
Turgeon, Mr Justice, 141
Turgeon Commission, 140–1

Union Bank, 106
Union government: cabinet of, 50; Crerar's views on, 41–2; King's views on, 43; under Meighen, 73; negotiations for, 40–3; reactions

to, 43; Reconstruction and Development Committee, 50; War Committee, 50; western support for, 47

United Church of Canada, 119

United Farmers of Alberta (UFA), 23–4, 72; views on conscription, 37–8

United Farmers of Manitoba (UFM), and election of 1922, 91–2

United Farmers of Ontario (UFO), 31, 70–1; on Liberal-Progressive alliance, 81, 84–5

United Grain Growers (UGG), 4, 7; Crerar's leadership of, 97–9; expansion of, 68–9; founding of, 24

utilities ownership: Crerar's views on, 65–6

Victory Loans: interest on, not taxed, 56

Vivian, Henry, 30

Waldron, Gordon, 37

war. See World War I; World War II

War Committee. See Cabinet War Committee

War Measures Act, 5–6, 23

Wartime Elections Act, 35; Sanhedrin's views on, 42–3

Wayling, Tommy, 69, 81; on UFO and Liberal-Progressive alliance, 81

Webb, Ralph, 169

Weir, James, 49

Wheat Board, 89–91, 163, 168–9; Crerar's views on, 89–91; gets monopoly, 216–17; reconstruction of (1935), 174–5; revived by Bennett government, 137

Wheat Board Act: Senate debate on 1947 amendments to, 239–40

wheat industry: crisis (1939), 190–2; government policy on, 216–17, 237–43

wheat pools, 100–1, 102–4; Crerar's views on, 102, 133–4; and stock market collapse (1929), 135. See also Wheat Board

White, Thomas, 62, 105, 106

Wilgress, Dana, 195

Willison, John, 58

Winnipeg Electric Railway, 153–4

Winnipeg Free Press, 156, 171, 173, 174, 179, 202, 237, 239, 241, 242, 264. See also Dafoe, John Wesley; Dexter, Grant; Manitoba Free Press

Winnipeg General Strike, 67

Winnipeg Grain Exchange, 13, 14, 16

Winnipeg Tribune, 106; views on free trade, 30

women: at western Liberals' convention (1917), 39

Wood, Henry Wise, 23, 25, 34, 40–1, 49, 56, 70, 72, 74, 108; and Liberal-Progressive alliance, 83–4; opposes Crerar, 77; views on conscription, 37–8

Woodsworth, J.S., 119, 161

World War I: effect on grain markets, 21, 23, 25; effects of, on grain marketing, 24; War Committee, 50

World War II: "Big Army," 208–10; Canadian autonomy of action in, 196; Canadian contributions to, 196–7; Crerar represents cabinet in Britain, 194; Crerar's views on, 196, 199; defence of Canada's west coast, 208–9; fall of France (1940), 205; War Measures Act, 5–6, 23. See also armed forces, Canadian; British Commonwealth Air Training Plan

York South by-election (1942), 214

Yukon Consolidated Gold Company: opposes union of Yukon and British Columbia, 182–3

Yukon Territory: proposed transfer to British Columbia, 181–3

Zombies, 226